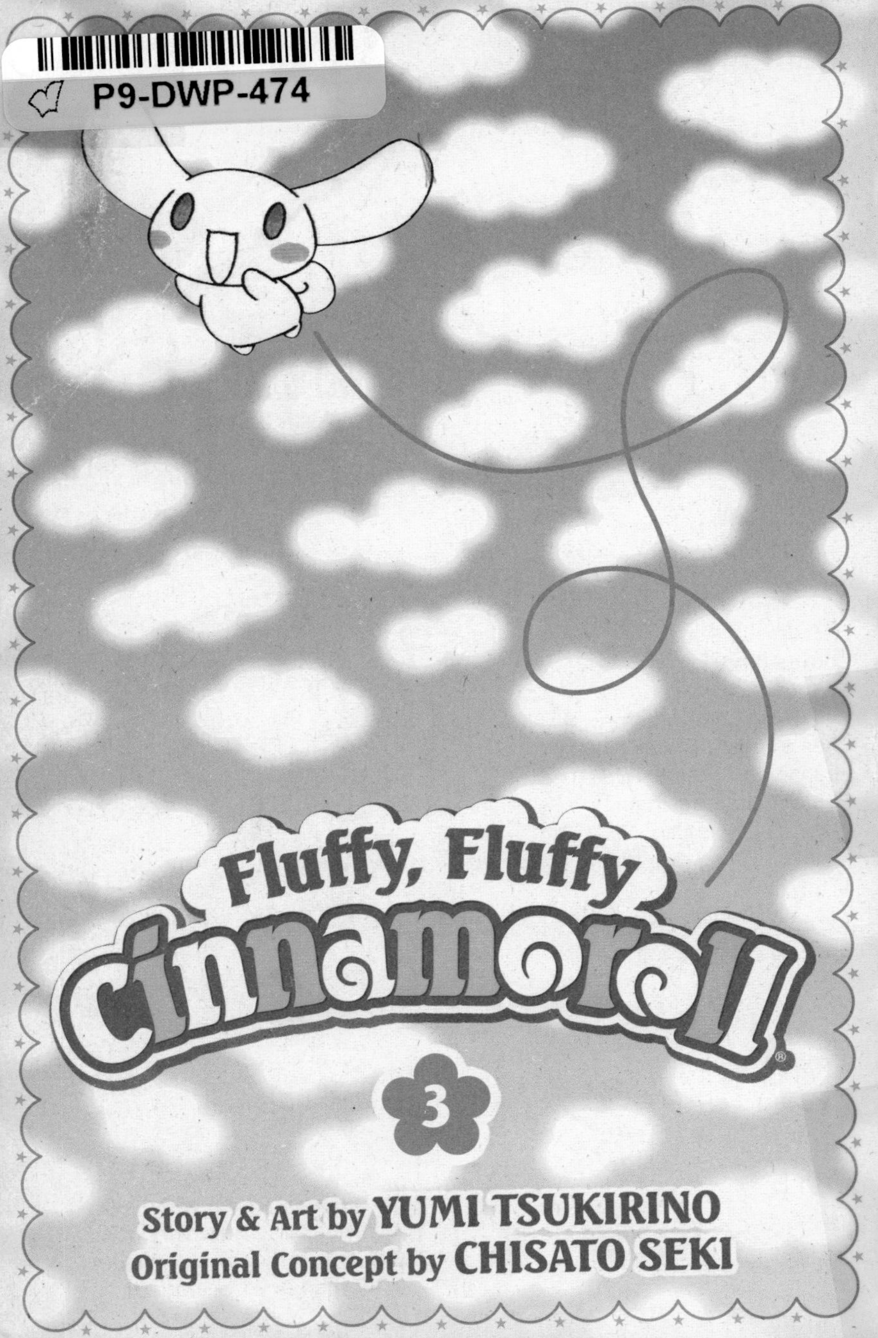
Fluffy, Fluffy
Cinnamoroll®
3
Story & Art by YUMI TSUKIRINO
Original Concept by CHISATO SEKI

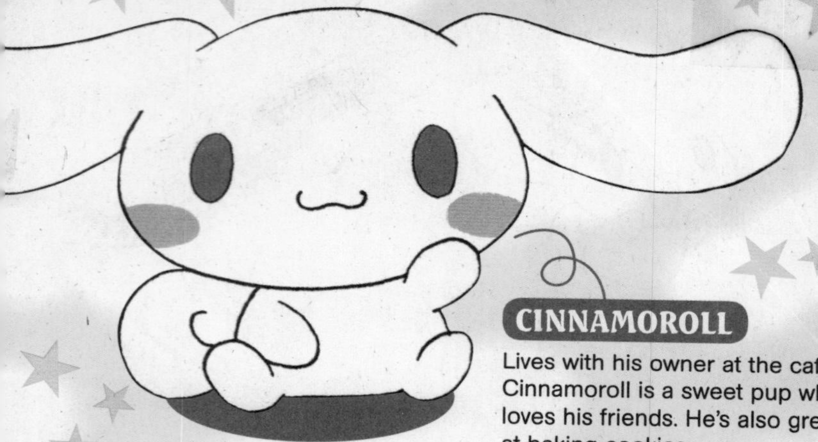

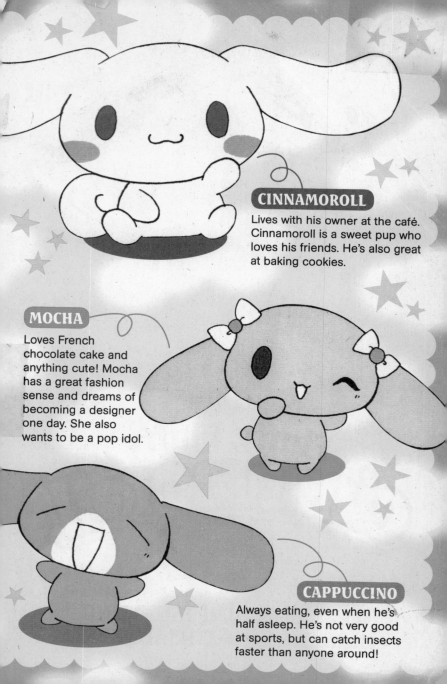

## CINNAMOROLL

Lives with his owner at the café. Cinnamoroll is a sweet pup who loves his friends. He's also great at baking cookies.

## MOCHA

Loves French chocolate cake and anything cute! Mocha has a great fashion sense and dreams of becoming a designer one day. She also wants to be a pop idol.

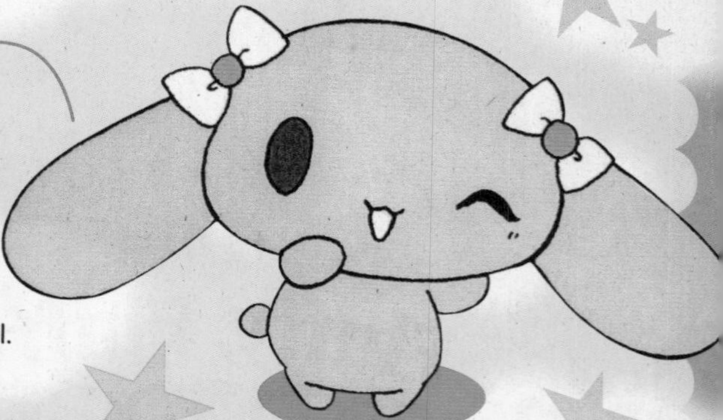

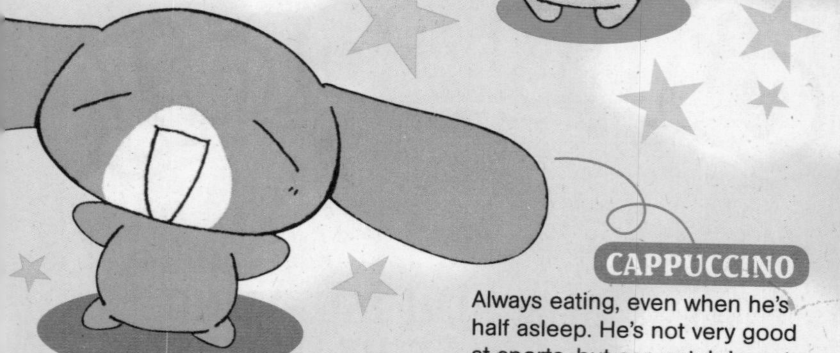

## CAPPUCCINO

Always eating, even when he's half asleep. He's not very good at sports, but can catch insects faster than anyone around!

# The Cinnamon Friends' SPECIAL SKILLS!

### CHIFFON

Better at sports than any boy. Chiffon can often be found in the forest or park building forts or collecting stones and fruits.

### ESPRESSO

Has a wealth of knowledge that comes from being a hard worker. He enjoys driving around town in his beloved car.

### MILK

Skilled at gulping down large quantities of milk! Little Milk wants to be like Cinnamoroll and works hard at practicing flying. He also works hard at eating his vegetables.

# Fluffy, Fluffy Cinnamoroll

3

## Contents

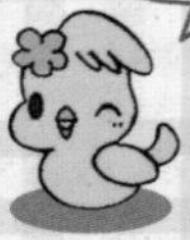



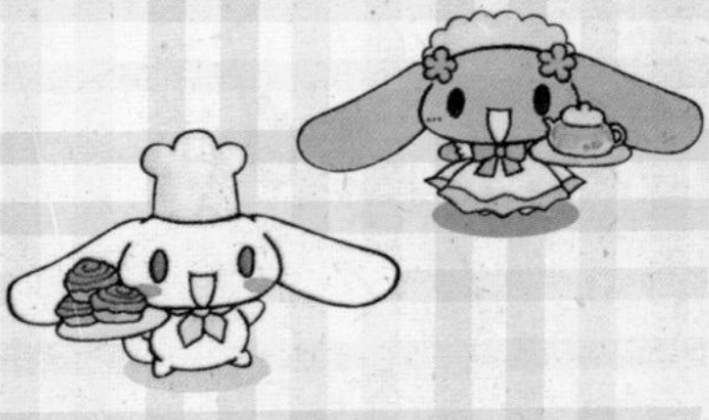

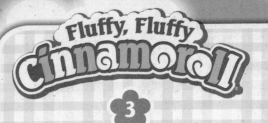

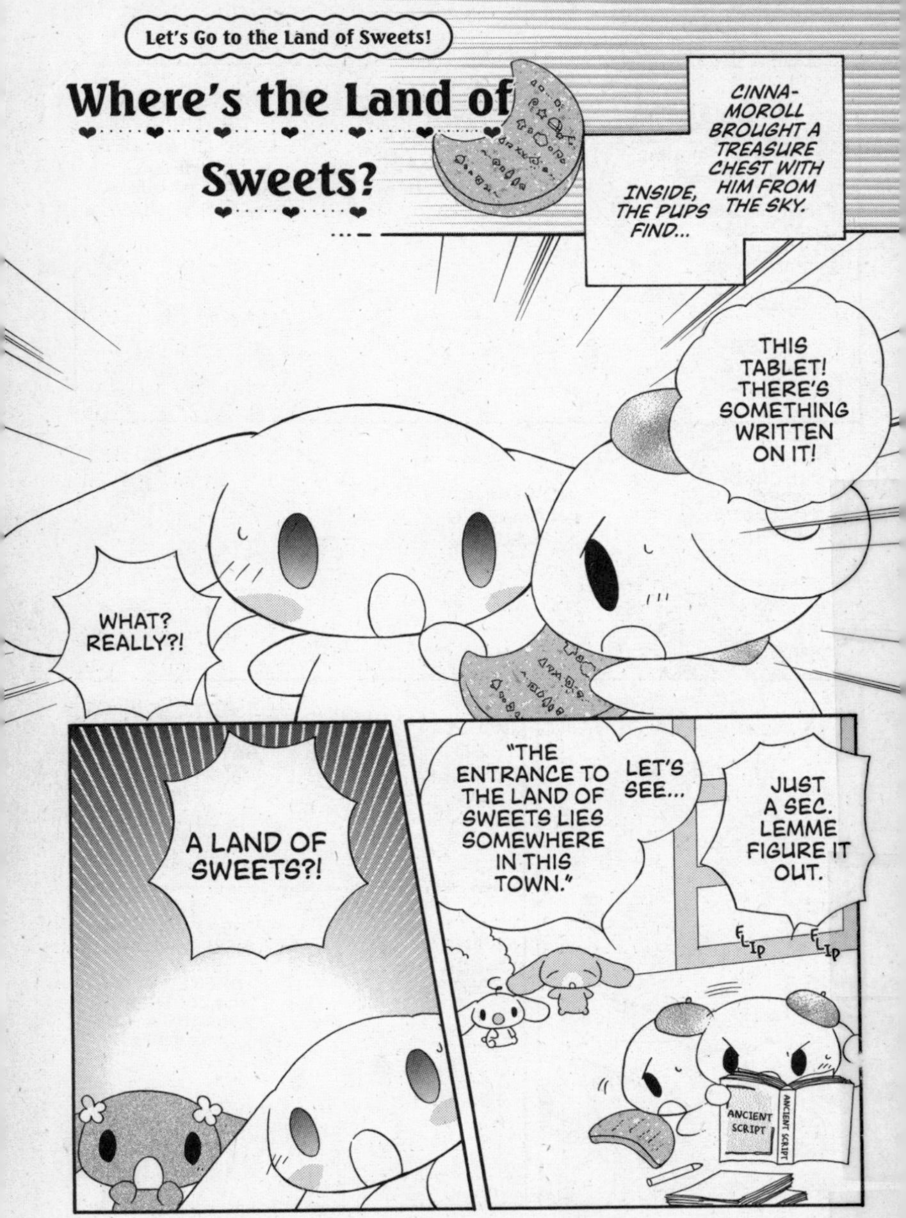
Let's Go to the Land of Sweets!
Where's the Land of Sweets?
CINNA-MOROLL BROUGHT A TREASURE CHEST WITH HIM FROM THE SKY.
INSIDE, THE PUPS FIND...
THIS TABLET! THERE'S SOMETHING WRITTEN ON IT!
WHAT? REALLY?!
JUST A SEC. LEMME FIGURE IT OUT.
FLIP
FLIP
ANCIENT SCRIPT
LET'S SEE...
"THE ENTRANCE TO THE LAND OF SWEETS LIES SOMEWHERE IN THIS TOWN."
A LAND OF SWEETS?!

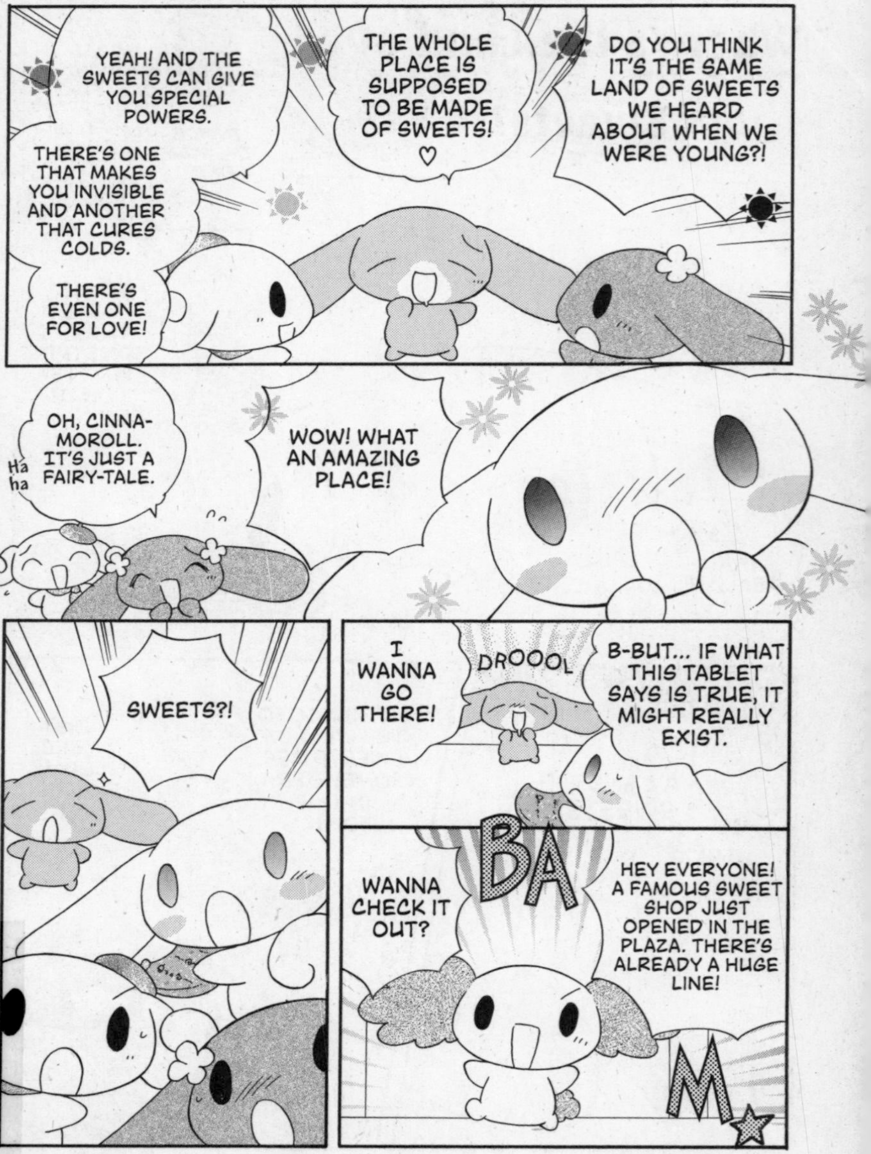
DO YOU THINK IT'S THE SAME LAND OF SWEETS WE HEARD ABOUT WHEN WE WERE YOUNG?!
THE WHOLE PLACE IS SUPPOSED TO BE MADE OF SWEETS! ♡
YEAH! AND THE SWEETS CAN GIVE YOU SPECIAL POWERS.
THERE'S ONE THAT MAKES YOU INVISIBLE AND ANOTHER THAT CURES COLDS.
THERE'S EVEN ONE FOR LOVE!
WOW! WHAT AN AMAZING PLACE!
OH, CINNA-MOROLL. IT'S JUST A FAIRY-TALE.
Ha ha
B-BUT... IF WHAT THIS TABLET SAYS IS TRUE, IT MIGHT REALLY EXIST.
DROOOL
I WANNA GO THERE!
BAM
HEY EVERYONE! A FAMOUS SWEET SHOP JUST OPENED IN THE PLAZA. THERE'S ALREADY A HUGE LINE!
WANNA CHECK IT OUT?
SWEETS?!

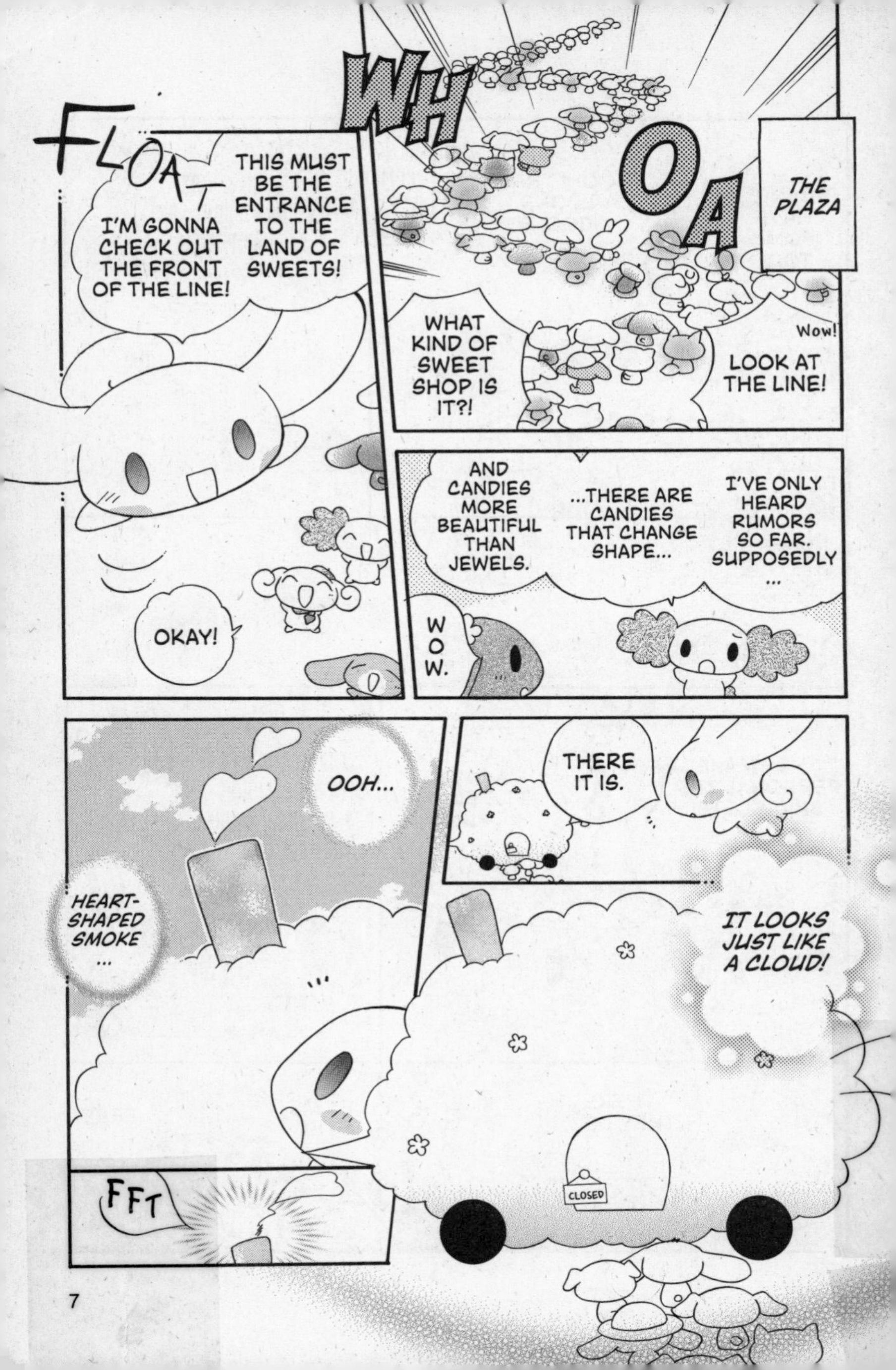
THE PLAZA
WHOA
Wow!
LOOK AT THE LINE!
WHAT KIND OF SWEET SHOP IS IT?!
I'VE ONLY HEARD RUMORS SO FAR. SUPPOSEDLY...
...THERE ARE CANDIES THAT CHANGE SHAPE...
AND CANDIES MORE BEAUTIFUL THAN JEWELS.
WOW.
THIS MUST BE THE ENTRANCE TO THE LAND OF SWEETS!
I'M GONNA CHECK OUT THE FRONT OF THE LINE!
FLOAT...
OKAY!
THERE IT IS.
OOH...
HEART-SHAPED SMOKE...
IT LOOKS JUST LIKE A CLOUD!
CLOSED
FFT

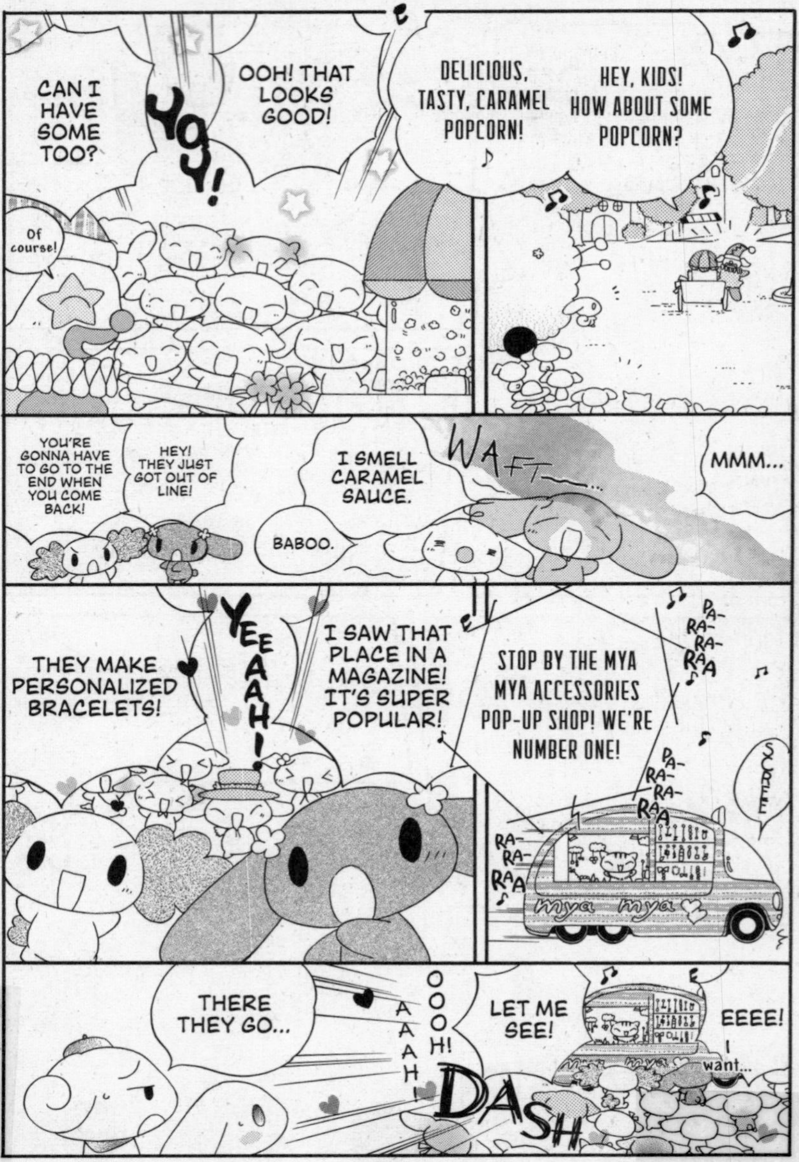
HEY, KIDS! HOW ABOUT SOME POPCORN?
DELICIOUS, TASTY, CARAMEL POPCORN! ♪
OOH! THAT LOOKS GOOD!
YAY!
CAN I HAVE SOME TOO?
Of course!
MMM...
WAFT...
I SMELL CARAMEL SAUCE.
BABOO.
HEY! THEY JUST GOT OUT OF LINE!
YOU'RE GONNA HAVE TO GO TO THE END WHEN YOU COME BACK!
PA-RA-RA-RAA
STOP BY THE MYA MYA ACCESSORIES POP-UP SHOP! WE'RE NUMBER ONE!
PA-RA-RA-RAA
SKREEE
RA-RA-RAA
mya mya
I SAW THAT PLACE IN A MAGAZINE! IT'S SUPER POPULAR!
YEEAAH!
THEY MAKE PERSONALIZED BRACELETS!
EEEE! I want...
LET ME SEE!
OOOOH!
AAAAH!
DASH
THERE THEY GO...

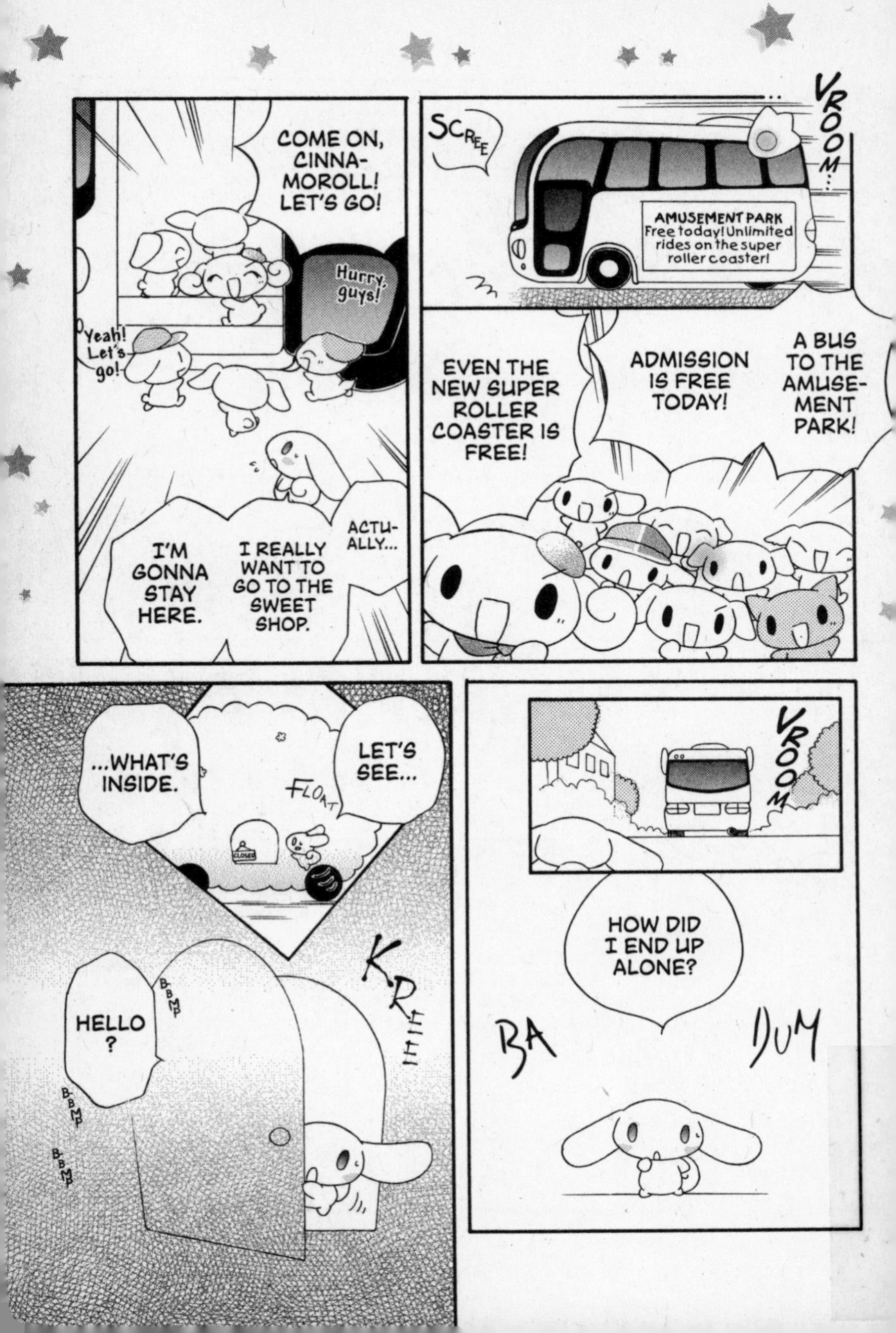
VROOM...
SCREE
AMUSEMENT PARK
Free today! Unlimited rides on the super roller coaster!
A BUS TO THE AMUSEMENT PARK!
ADMISSION IS FREE TODAY!
EVEN THE NEW SUPER ROLLER COASTER IS FREE!
COME ON, CINNAMOROLL! LET'S GO!
Hurry, guys!
Yeah! Let's go!
ACTUALLY...
I REALLY WANT TO GO TO THE SWEET SHOP.
I'M GONNA STAY HERE.
VROOOM
HOW DID I END UP ALONE?
BA
DUM
LET'S SEE...
...WHAT'S INSIDE.
FLOAT
CLOSED
KREEE
HELLO?
B-BMP
B-BMP
B-BMP

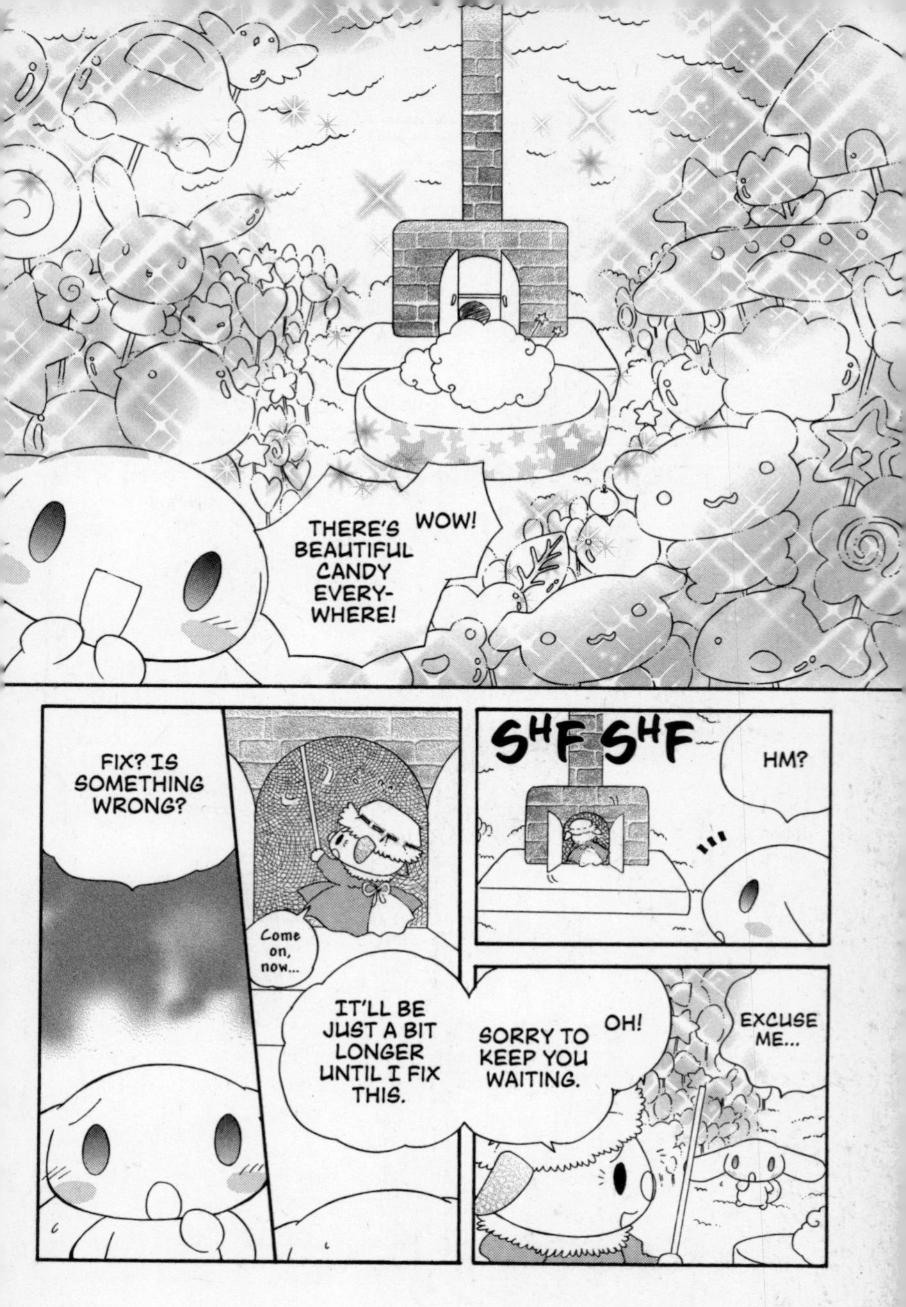
WOW!
THERE'S BEAUTIFUL CANDY EVERY-WHERE!
SHF SHF
HM?
EXCUSE ME...
OH!
SORRY TO KEEP YOU WAITING.
Come on, now...
IT'LL BE JUST A BIT LONGER UNTIL I FIX THIS.
FIX? IS SOMETHING WRONG?

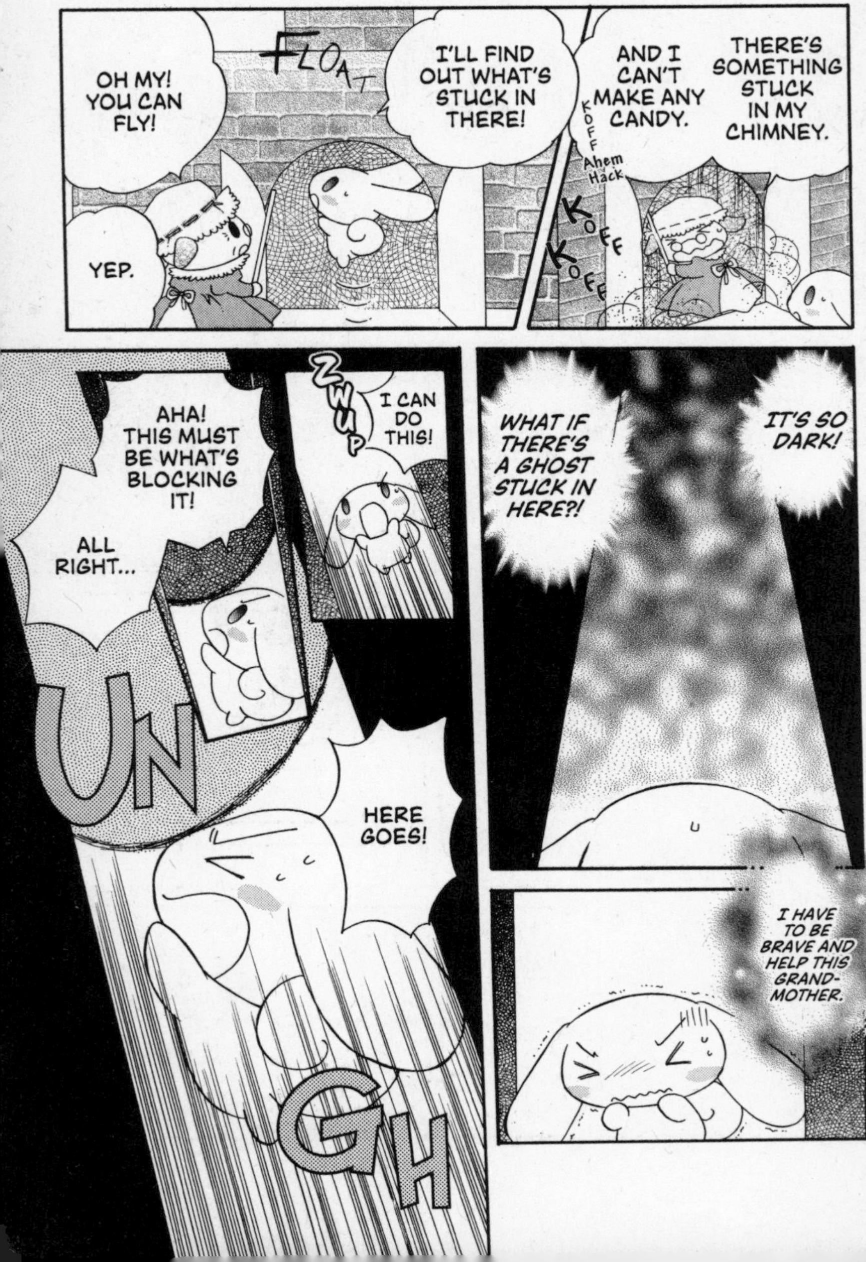
THERE'S SOMETHING STUCK IN MY CHIMNEY.
AND I CAN'T MAKE ANY CANDY.
KOFF
Ahem Hack
KOFF
KOFF
I'LL FIND OUT WHAT'S STUCK IN THERE!
FLOAT
OH MY! YOU CAN FLY!
YEP.
IT'S SO DARK!
WHAT IF THERE'S A GHOST STUCK IN HERE?!
I HAVE TO BE BRAVE AND HELP THIS GRAND-MOTHER.
ZWUP
I CAN DO THIS!
AHA! THIS MUST BE WHAT'S BLOCKING IT!
ALL RIGHT...
UN
HERE GOES!
GH

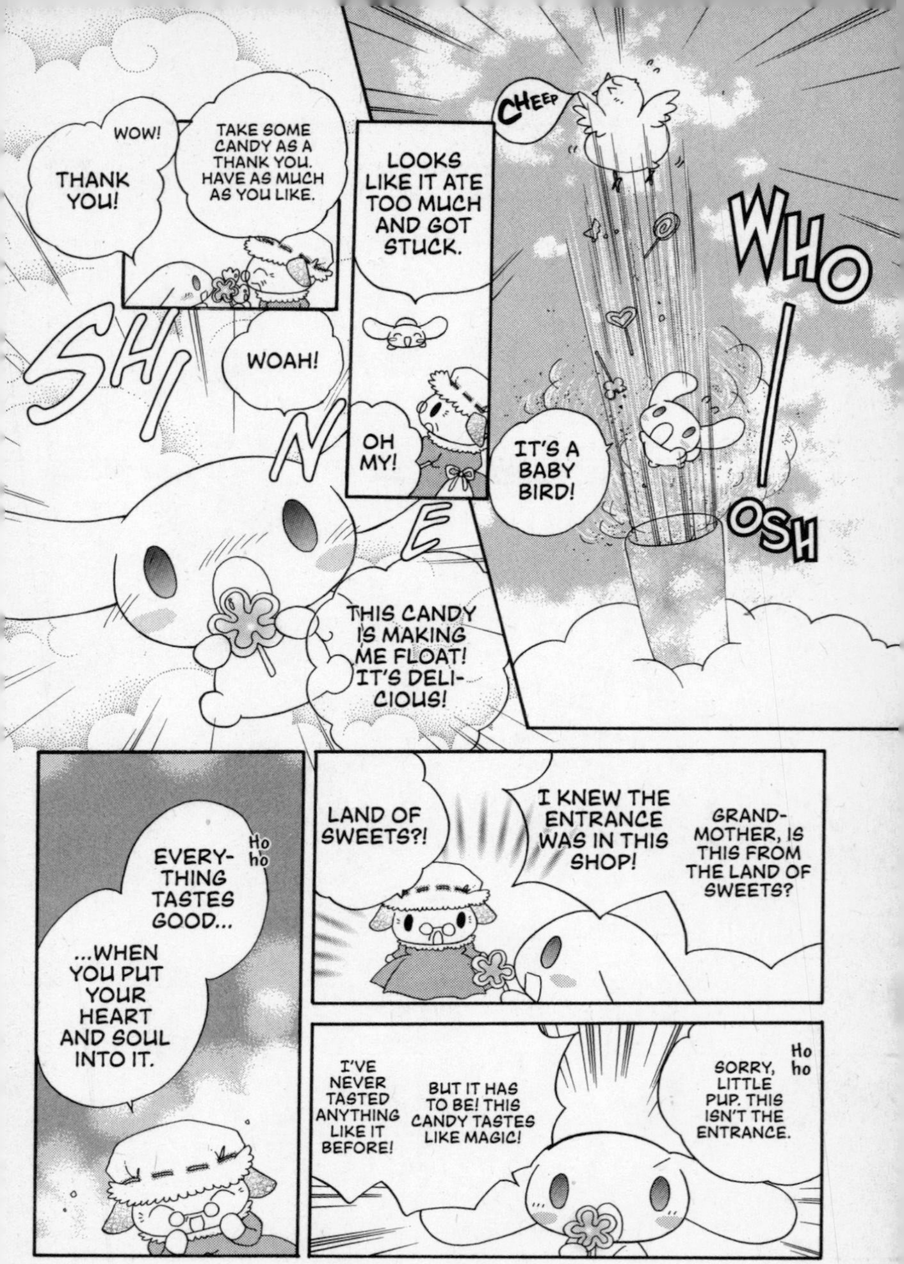
CHEEP
WHOOSH
IT'S A BABY BIRD!
LOOKS LIKE IT ATE TOO MUCH AND GOT STUCK.
OH MY!
TAKE SOME CANDY AS A THANK YOU. HAVE AS MUCH AS YOU LIKE.
WOW!
THANK YOU!
SHINE
WOAH!
THIS CANDY IS MAKING ME FLOAT! IT'S DELICIOUS!
GRANDMOTHER, IS THIS FROM THE LAND OF SWEETS?
I KNEW THE ENTRANCE WAS IN THIS SHOP!
LAND OF SWEETS?!
Ho ho
SORRY, LITTLE PUP. THIS ISN'T THE ENTRANCE.
BUT IT HAS TO BE! THIS CANDY TASTES LIKE MAGIC!
I'VE NEVER TASTED ANYTHING LIKE IT BEFORE!
Ho ho
EVERYTHING TASTES GOOD...
...WHEN YOU PUT YOUR HEART AND SOUL INTO IT.

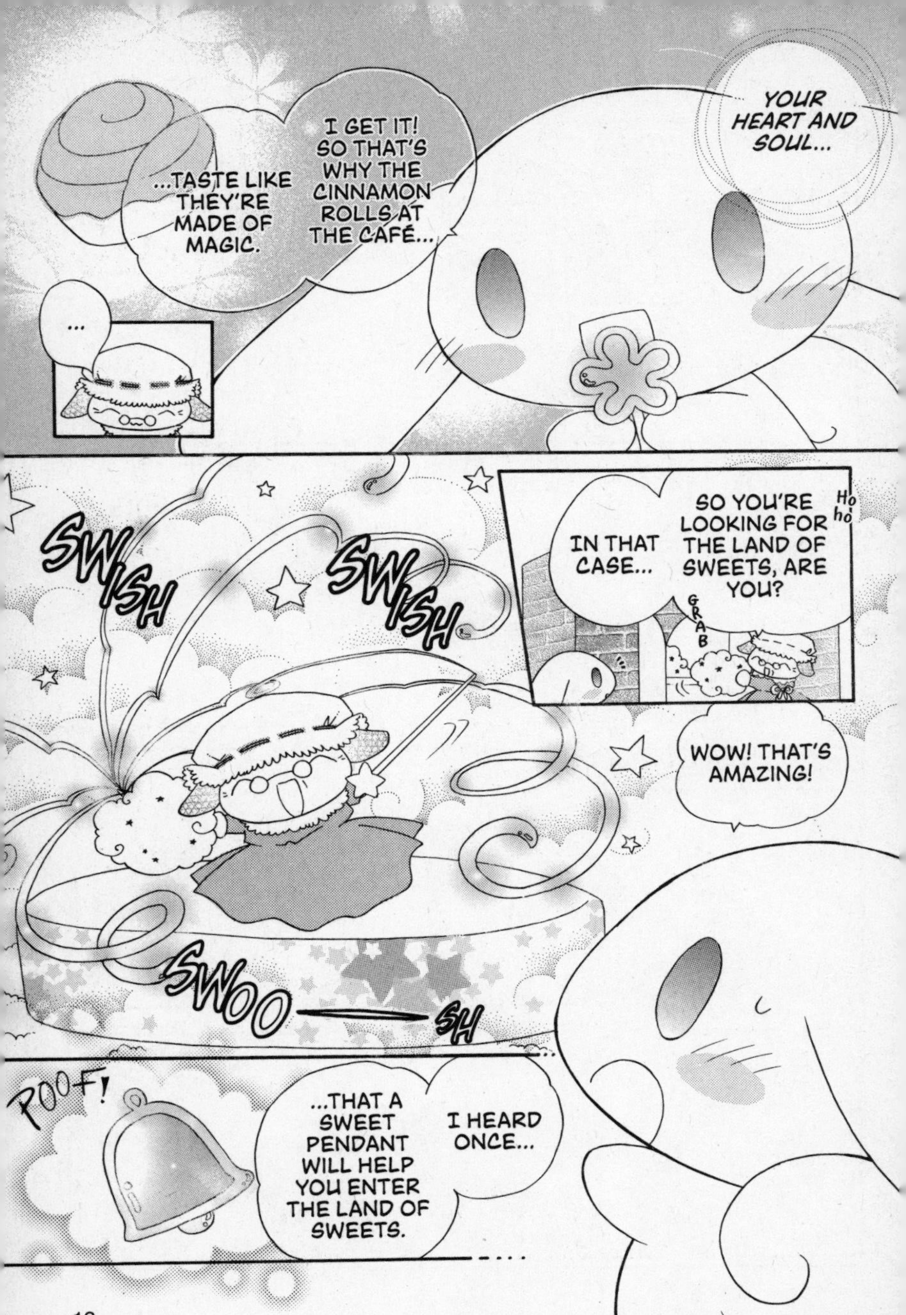
YOUR HEART AND SOUL...
I GET IT! SO THAT'S WHY THE CINNAMON ROLLS AT THE CAFÉ...
...TASTE LIKE THEY'RE MADE OF MAGIC.
...
SO YOU'RE LOOKING FOR THE LAND OF SWEETS, ARE YOU?
Ho ho
IN THAT CASE...
GRAB
WOW! THAT'S AMAZING!
SWISH
SWISH
SWOO—SH
I HEARD ONCE...
...THAT A SWEET PENDANT WILL HELP YOU ENTER THE LAND OF SWEETS.
POOF!

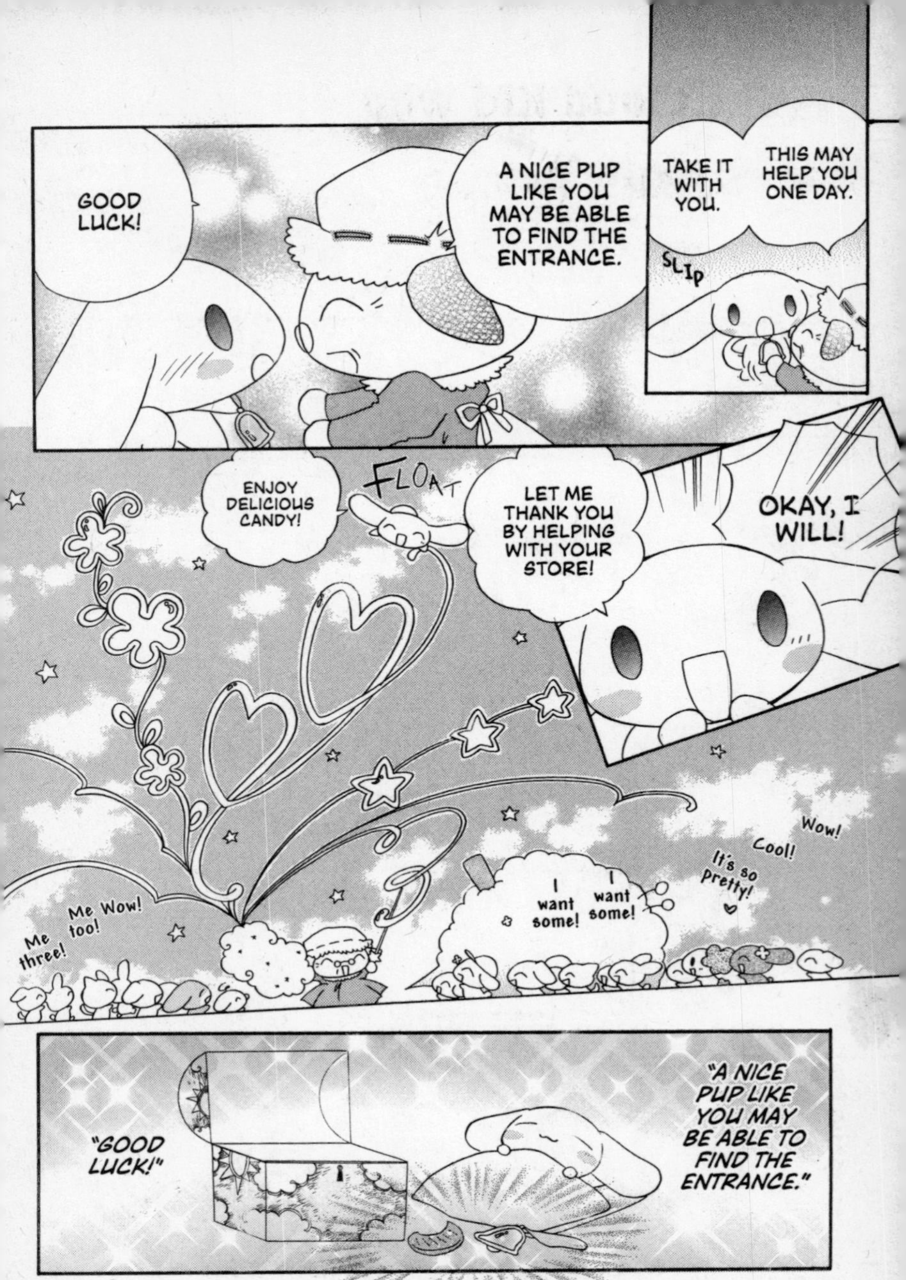
THIS MAY HELP YOU ONE DAY.
TAKE IT WITH YOU.
SLIP
A NICE PUP LIKE YOU MAY BE ABLE TO FIND THE ENTRANCE.
GOOD LUCK!
OKAY, I WILL!
LET ME THANK YOU BY HELPING WITH YOUR STORE!
FLOAT
ENJOY DELICIOUS CANDY!
Wow!
Cool!
It's so pretty!
I want some!
I want some!
Wow!
Me too!
Me three!
"A NICE PUP LIKE YOU MAY BE ABLE TO FIND THE ENTRANCE."
"GOOD LUCK!"

# The Cloud Kid Who Didn't Belong

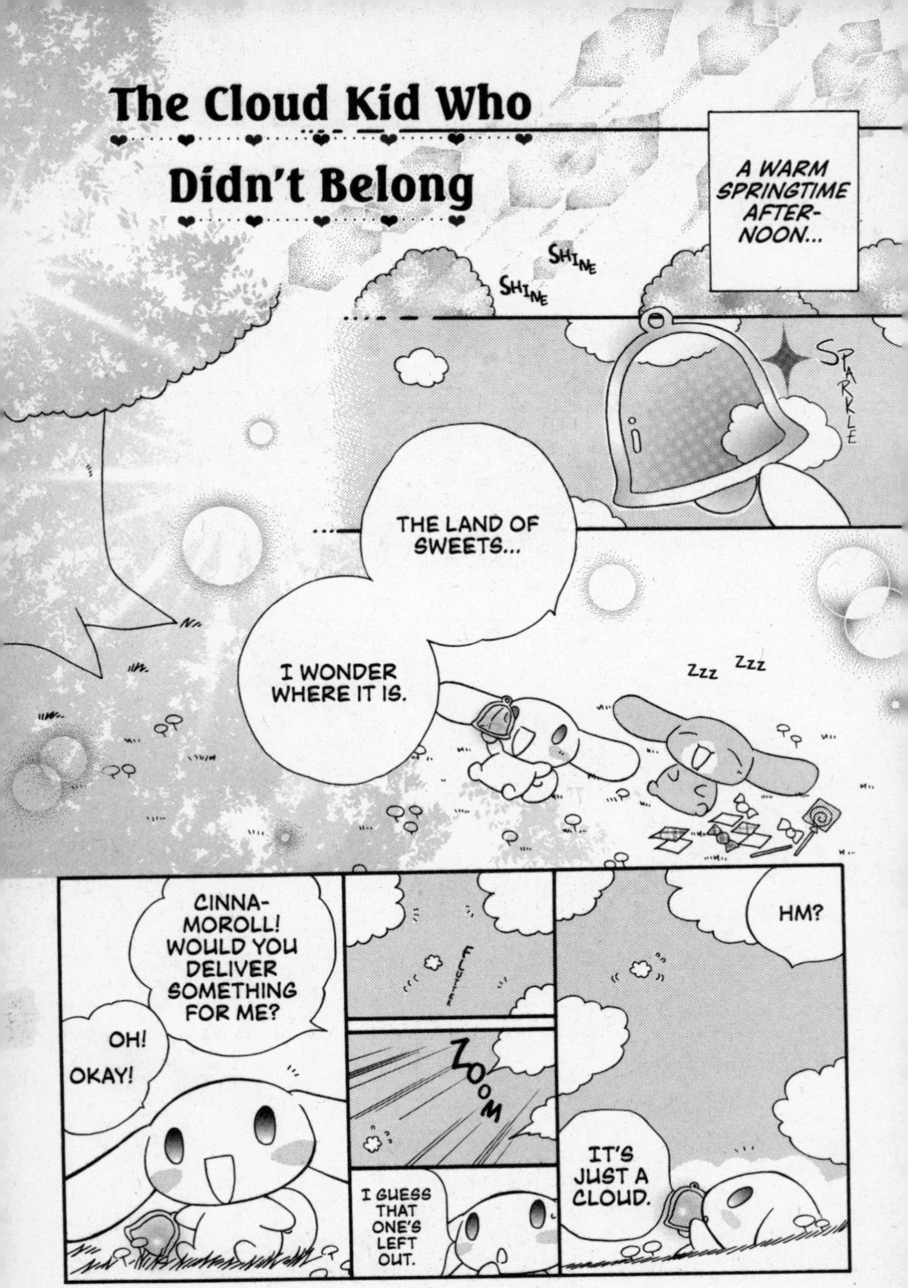

A WARM SPRINGTIME AFTER-NOON...
SHINE
SHINE
SPARKLE
THE LAND OF SWEETS...
I WONDER WHERE IT IS.
Zzz Zzz
HM?
IT'S JUST A CLOUD.
FLUTTER
ZOOM
I GUESS THAT ONE'S LEFT OUT.
CINNA-MOROLL! WOULD YOU DELIVER SOMETHING FOR ME?
OH!
OKAY!

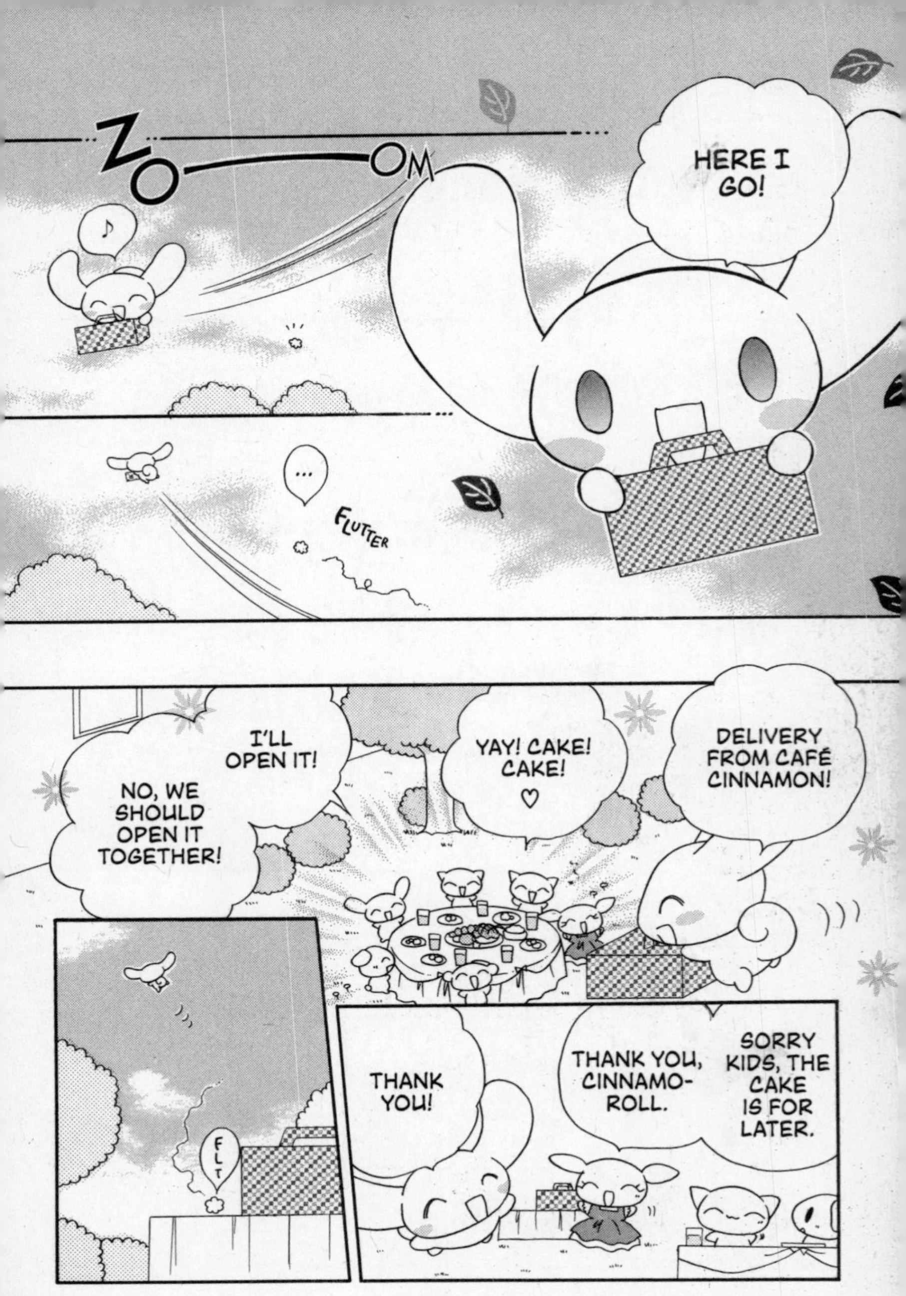
HERE I GO!
ZO—OM
♪
...
FLUTTER
DELIVERY FROM CAFÉ CINNAMON!
YAY! CAKE! CAKE! ♡
I'LL OPEN IT!
NO, WE SHOULD OPEN IT TOGETHER!
SORRY KIDS, THE CAKE IS FOR LATER.
THANK YOU, CINNAMO-ROLL.
THANK YOU!
FLT

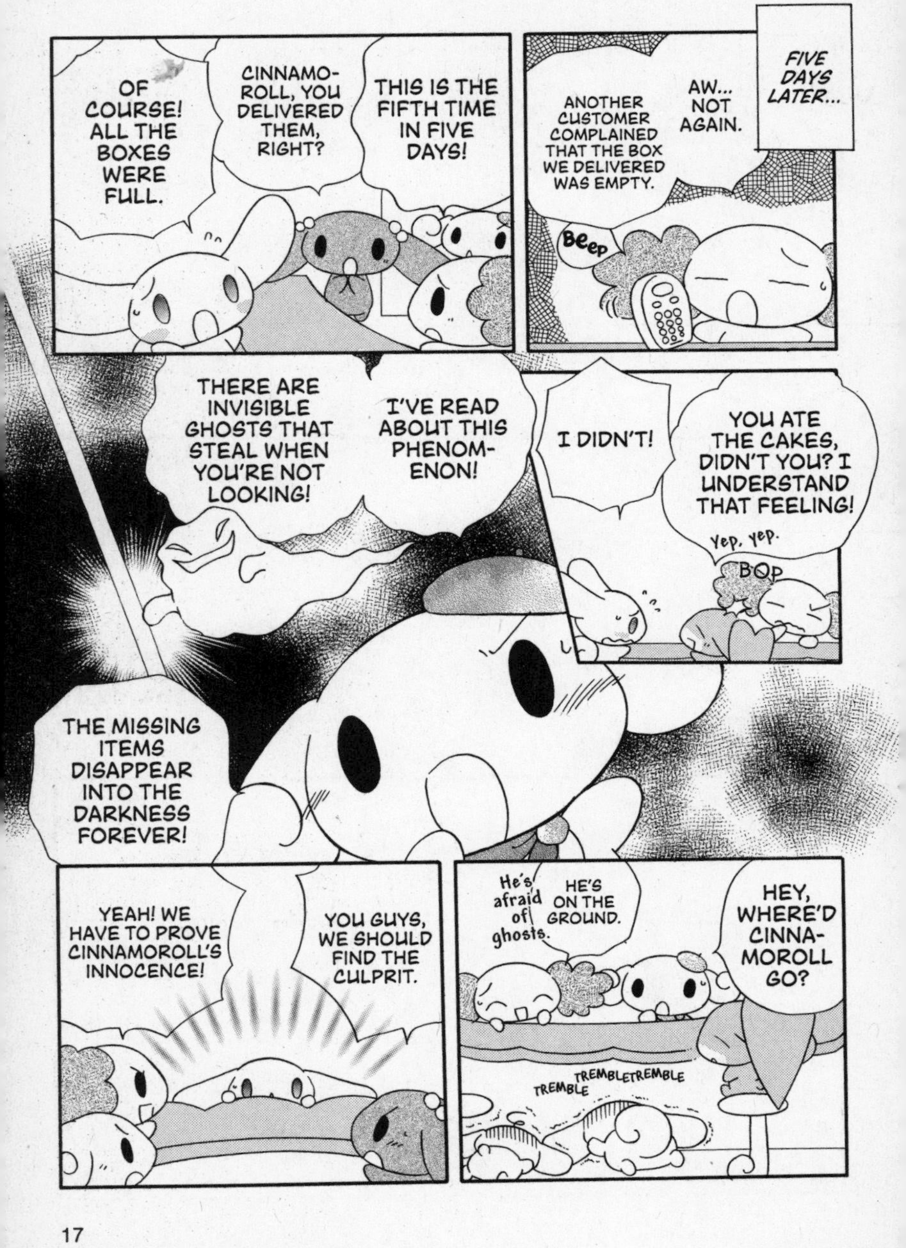
FIVE DAYS LATER...
AW... NOT AGAIN.
ANOTHER CUSTOMER COMPLAINED THAT THE BOX WE DELIVERED WAS EMPTY.
Beep
THIS IS THE FIFTH TIME IN FIVE DAYS!
CINNAMO-ROLL, YOU DELIVERED THEM, RIGHT?
OF COURSE! ALL THE BOXES WERE FULL.
YOU ATE THE CAKES, DIDN'T YOU? I UNDERSTAND THAT FEELING!
I DIDN'T!
Yep, yep.
BOP
I'VE READ ABOUT THIS PHENOM-ENON!
THERE ARE INVISIBLE GHOSTS THAT STEAL WHEN YOU'RE NOT LOOKING!
THE MISSING ITEMS DISAPPEAR INTO THE DARKNESS FOREVER!
HEY, WHERE'D CINNA-MOROLL GO?
HE'S ON THE GROUND.
He's afraid of ghosts.
TREMBLETREMBLE TREMBLE
YOU GUYS, WE SHOULD FIND THE CULPRIT.
YEAH! WE HAVE TO PROVE CINNAMOROLL'S INNOCENCE!

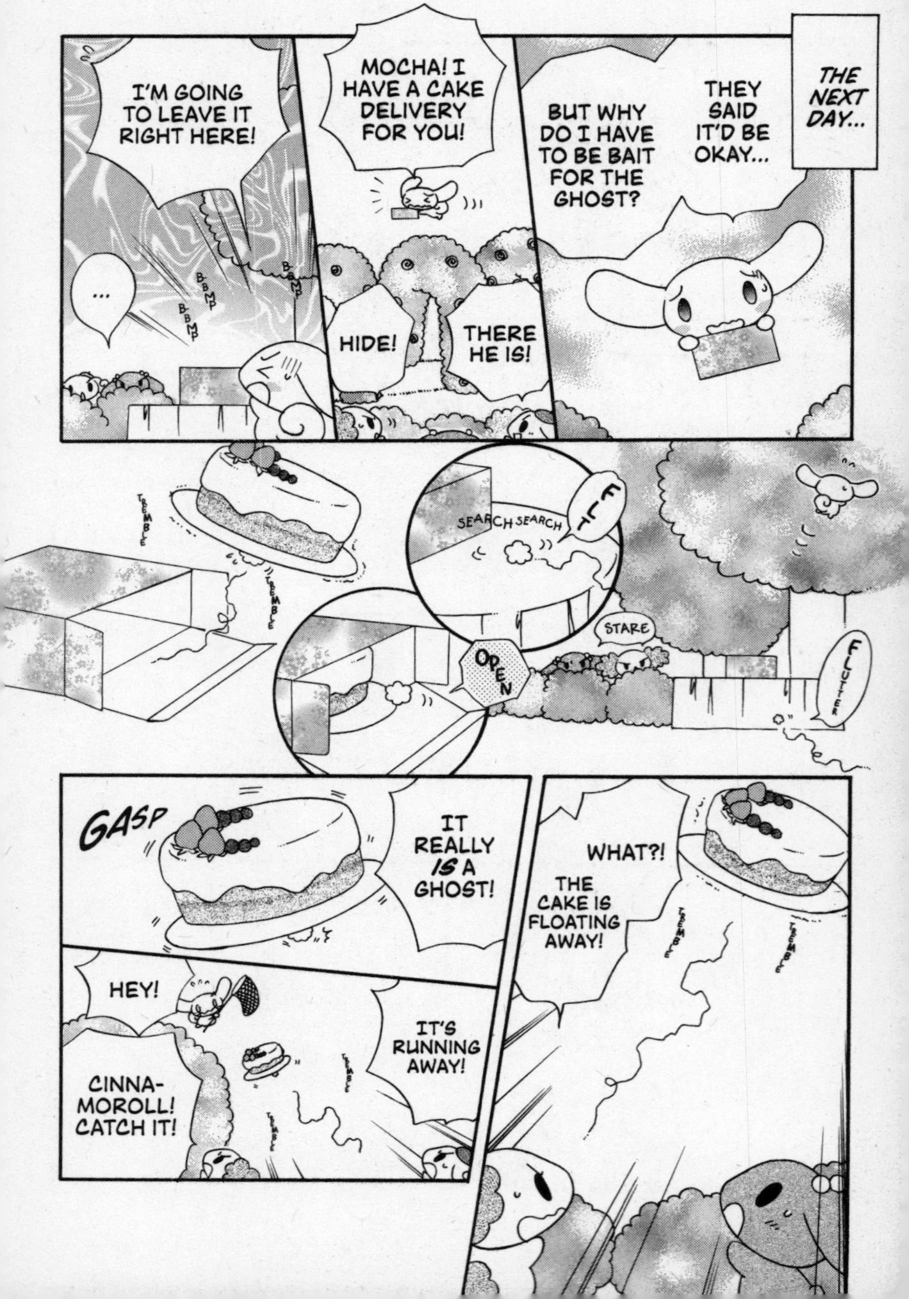
THE NEXT DAY...
THEY SAID IT'D BE OKAY...
BUT WHY DO I HAVE TO BE BAIT FOR THE GHOST?
MOCHA! I HAVE A CAKE DELIVERY FOR YOU!
THERE HE IS!
HIDE!
I'M GOING TO LEAVE IT RIGHT HERE!
BBMP
BBMP
...
FLUTTER
STARE
FLIT
SEARCH SEARCH
OPEN
TREMBLE
TREMBLE
WHAT?!
THE CAKE IS FLOATING AWAY!
TREMBLE
TREMBLE
IT REALLY *IS* A GHOST!
GASP
IT'S RUNNING AWAY!
HEY!
CINNA-MOROLL! CATCH IT!

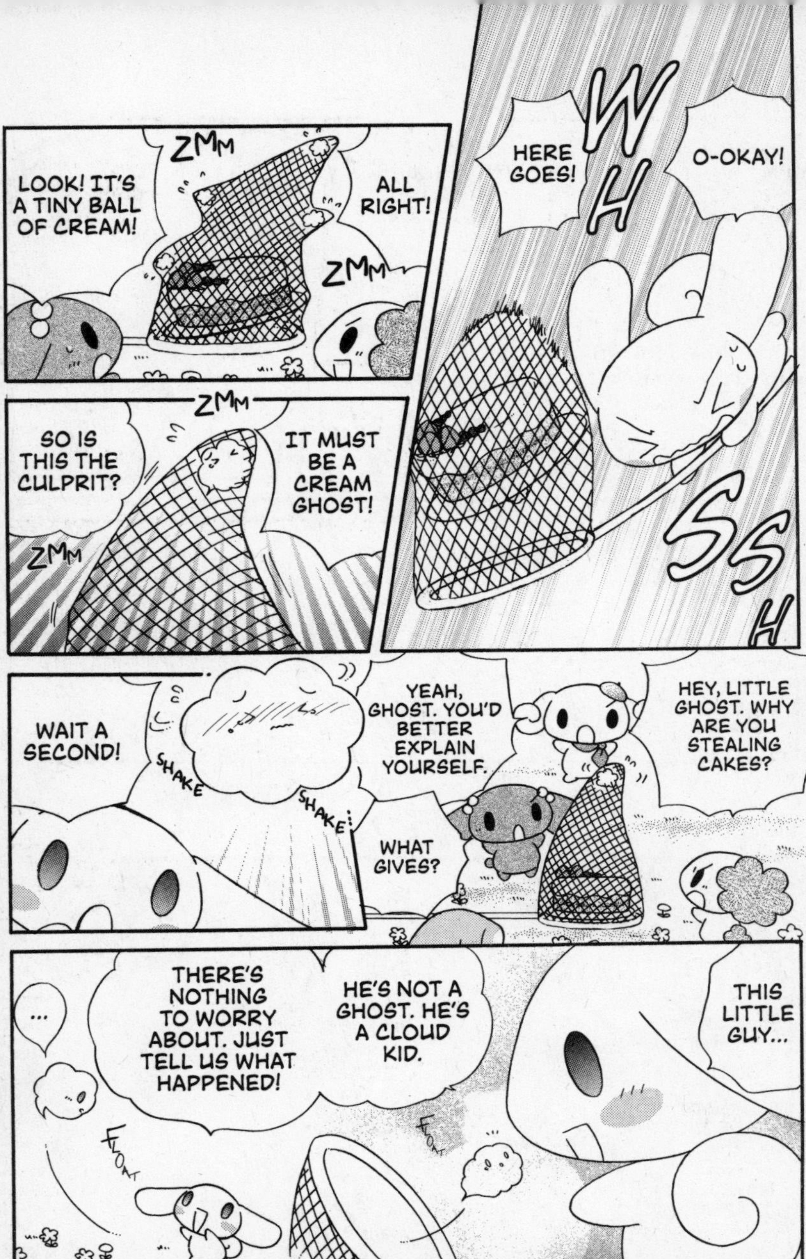
O-OKAY!
WH
HERE GOES!
SSH
ALL RIGHT!
ZMM
LOOK! IT'S A TINY BALL OF CREAM!
ZMM
ZMM
IT MUST BE A CREAM GHOST!
SO IS THIS THE CULPRIT?
ZMM
HEY, LITTLE GHOST. WHY ARE YOU STEALING CAKES?
YEAH, GHOST. YOU'D BETTER EXPLAIN YOURSELF.
WHAT GIVES?
SHAKE
SHAKE
WAIT A SECOND!
THIS LITTLE GUY...
HE'S NOT A GHOST. HE'S A CLOUD KID.
THERE'S NOTHING TO WORRY ABOUT. JUST TELL US WHAT HAPPENED!
FLOAT
...
FLOAT

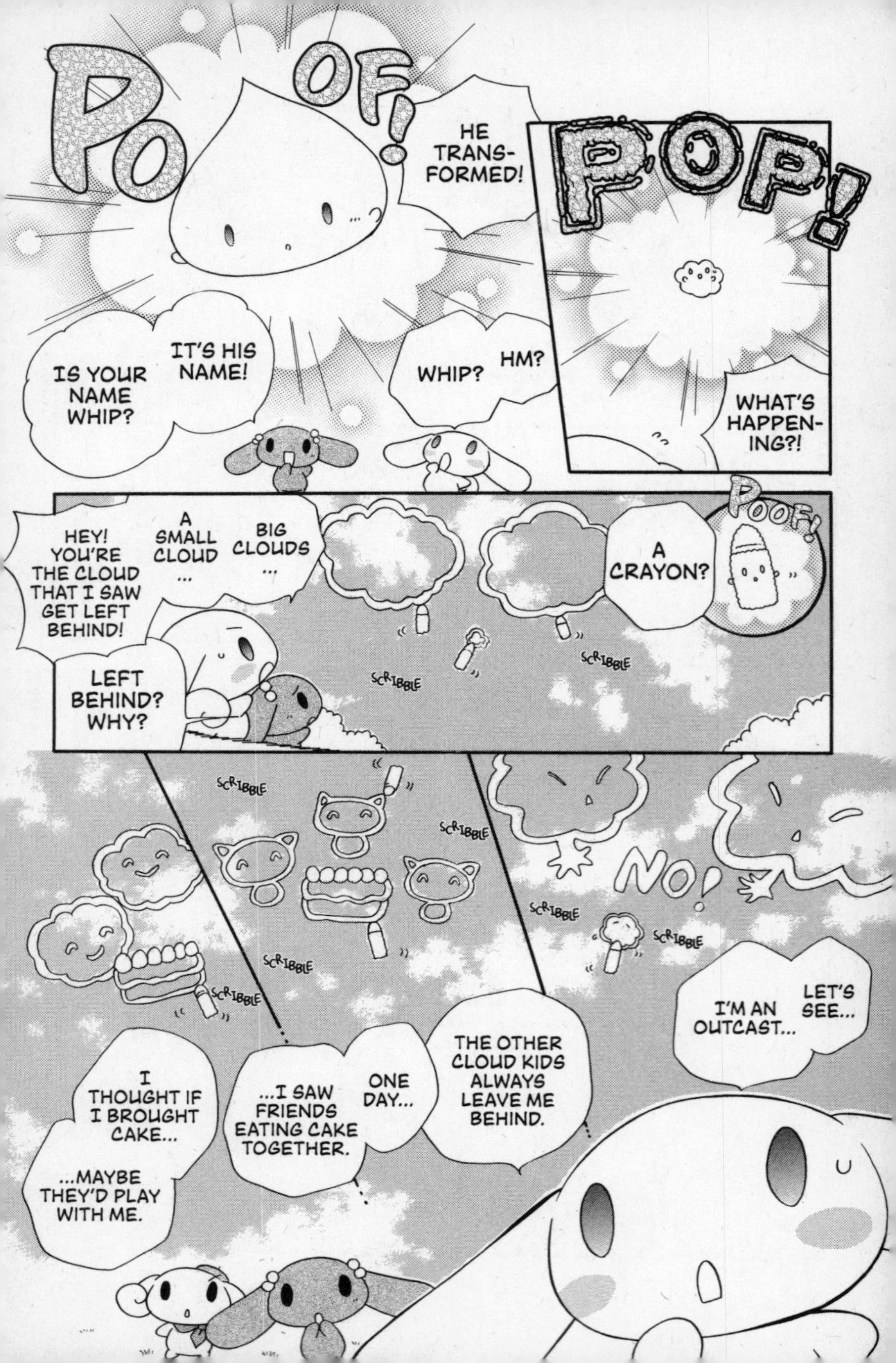
POP!
WHAT'S HAPPENING?!
POOF!
HE TRANSFORMED!
HM?
WHIP?
IT'S HIS NAME!
IS YOUR NAME WHIP?
POOF!
A CRAYON?
SCRIBBLE
SCRIBBLE
BIG CLOUDS...
A SMALL CLOUD...
HEY! YOU'RE THE CLOUD THAT I SAW GET LEFT BEHIND!
LEFT BEHIND? WHY?
LET'S SEE...
I'M AN OUTCAST...
NO!
SCRIBBLE
SCRIBBLE
SCRIBBLE
SCRIBBLE
SCRIBBLE
SCRIBBLE
THE OTHER CLOUD KIDS ALWAYS LEAVE ME BEHIND.
ONE DAY...
...I SAW FRIENDS EATING CAKE TOGETHER.
I THOUGHT IF I BROUGHT CAKE...
...MAYBE THEY'D PLAY WITH ME.

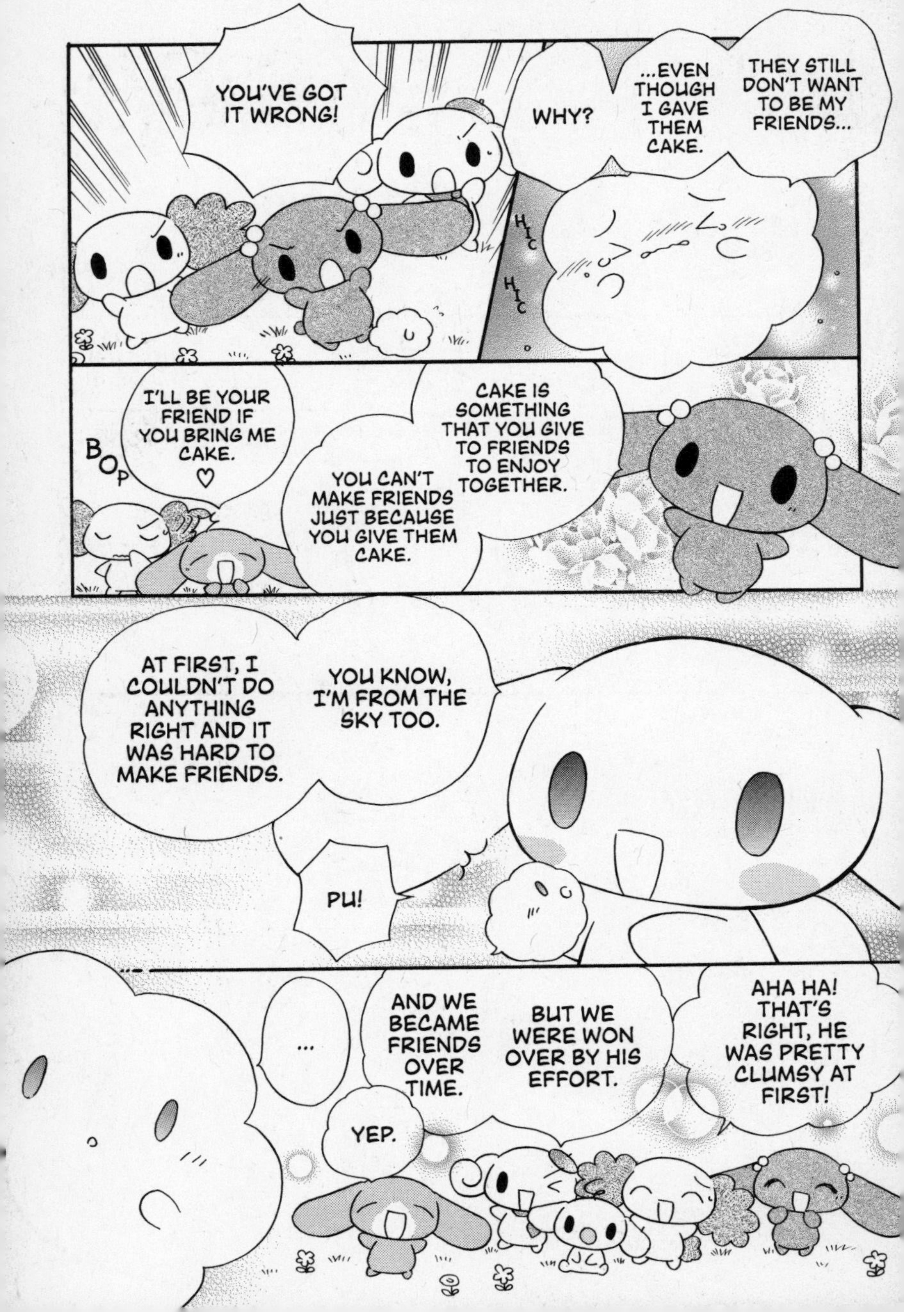
THEY STILL DON'T WANT TO BE MY FRIENDS...
...EVEN THOUGH I GAVE THEM CAKE.
WHY?
HIC HIC
YOU'VE GOT IT WRONG!
CAKE IS SOMETHING THAT YOU GIVE TO FRIENDS TO ENJOY TOGETHER.
YOU CAN'T MAKE FRIENDS JUST BECAUSE YOU GIVE THEM CAKE.
I'LL BE YOUR FRIEND IF YOU BRING ME CAKE. ♡
BOP
YOU KNOW, I'M FROM THE SKY TOO.
AT FIRST, I COULDN'T DO ANYTHING RIGHT AND IT WAS HARD TO MAKE FRIENDS.
PU!
AHA HA! THAT'S RIGHT, HE WAS PRETTY CLUMSY AT FIRST!
BUT WE WERE WON OVER BY HIS EFFORT.
AND WE BECAME FRIENDS OVER TIME.
YEP.
...

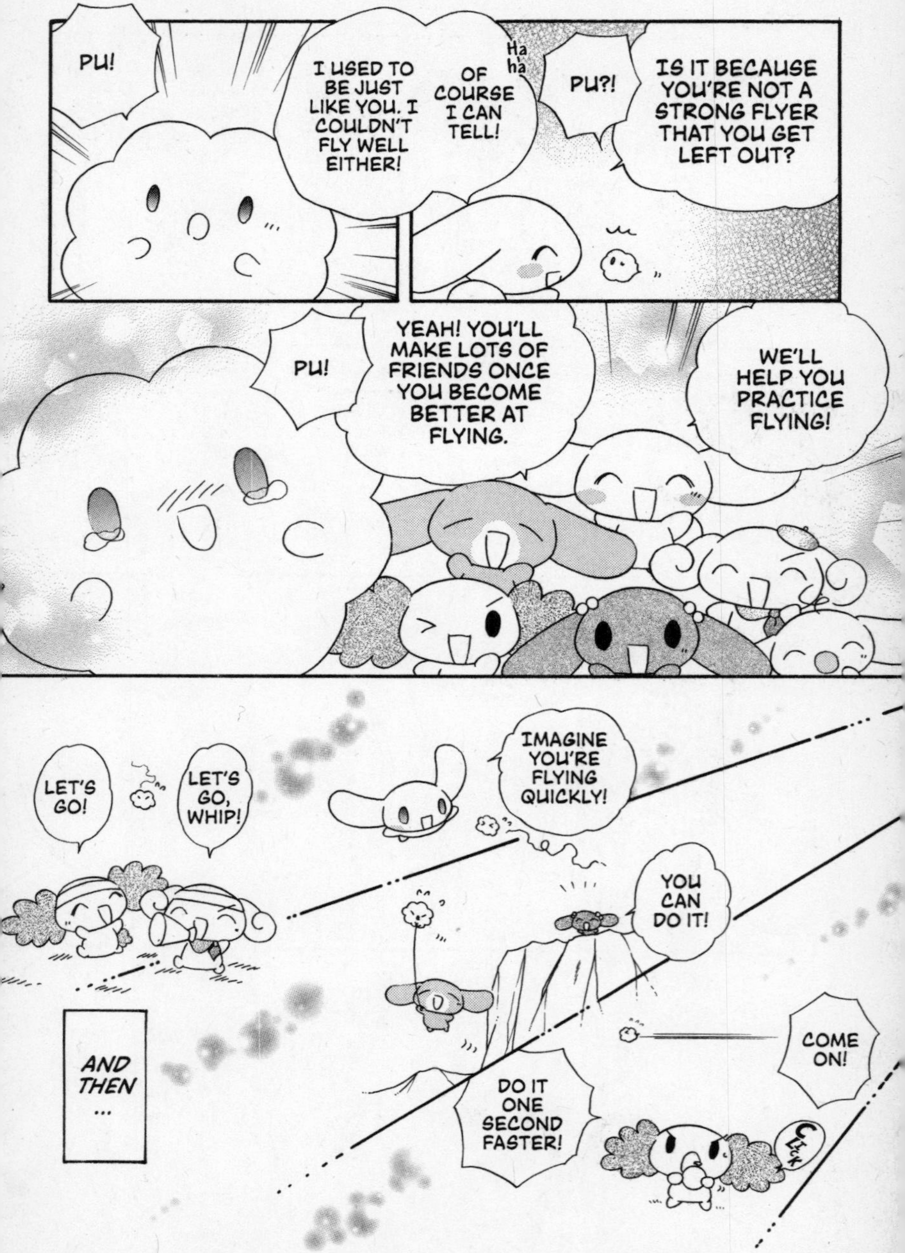
IS IT BECAUSE YOU'RE NOT A STRONG FLYER THAT YOU GET LEFT OUT?
PU?!
Ha ha
OF COURSE I CAN TELL!
I USED TO BE JUST LIKE YOU. I COULDN'T FLY WELL EITHER!
PU!
WE'LL HELP YOU PRACTICE FLYING!
YEAH! YOU'LL MAKE LOTS OF FRIENDS ONCE YOU BECOME BETTER AT FLYING.
PU!
IMAGINE YOU'RE FLYING QUICKLY!
LET'S GO, WHIP!
LET'S GO!
YOU CAN DO IT!
COME ON!
CLICK
DO IT ONE SECOND FASTER!
AND THEN ...

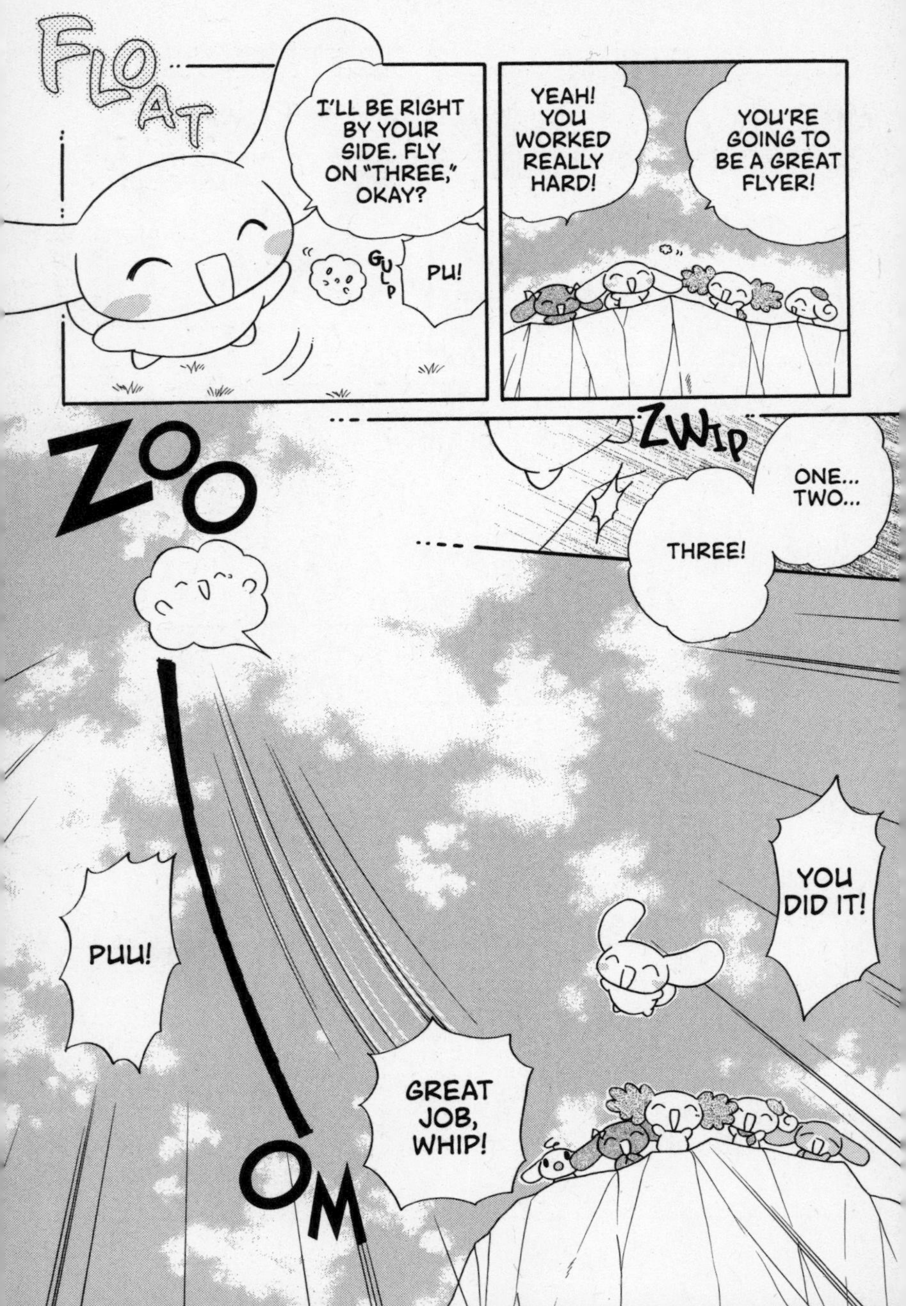
YOU'RE GOING TO BE A GREAT FLYER!
YEAH! YOU WORKED REALLY HARD!
FLOAT
I'LL BE RIGHT BY YOUR SIDE. FLY ON "THREE," OKAY?
PU!
GULP
ZWIP
ONE... TWO...
THREE!
ZOOOM
YOU DID IT!
PUU!
GREAT JOB, WHIP!

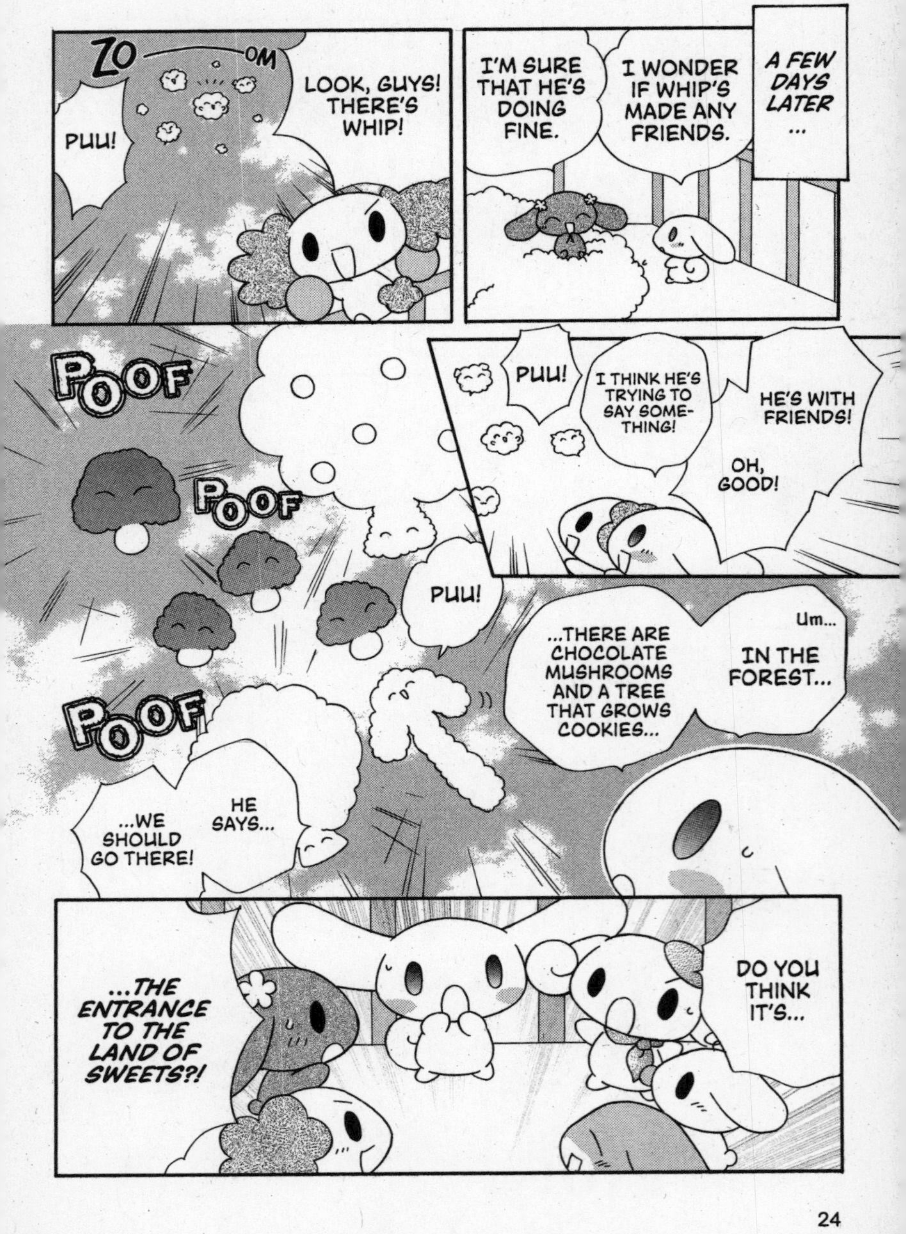
A FEW DAYS LATER ...
I WONDER IF WHIP'S MADE ANY FRIENDS.
I'M SURE THAT HE'S DOING FINE.
LOOK, GUYS! THERE'S WHIP!
ZO—OM
PUU!
HE'S WITH FRIENDS!
OH, GOOD!
I THINK HE'S TRYING TO SAY SOME-THING!
PUU!
POOF
POOF
PUU!
Um... IN THE FOREST...
...THERE ARE CHOCOLATE MUSHROOMS AND A TREE THAT GROWS COOKIES...
HE SAYS...
...WE SHOULD GO THERE!
POOF
DO YOU THINK IT'S...
...THE ENTRANCE TO THE LAND OF SWEETS?!

# Find the Tree That Grows Cookies!

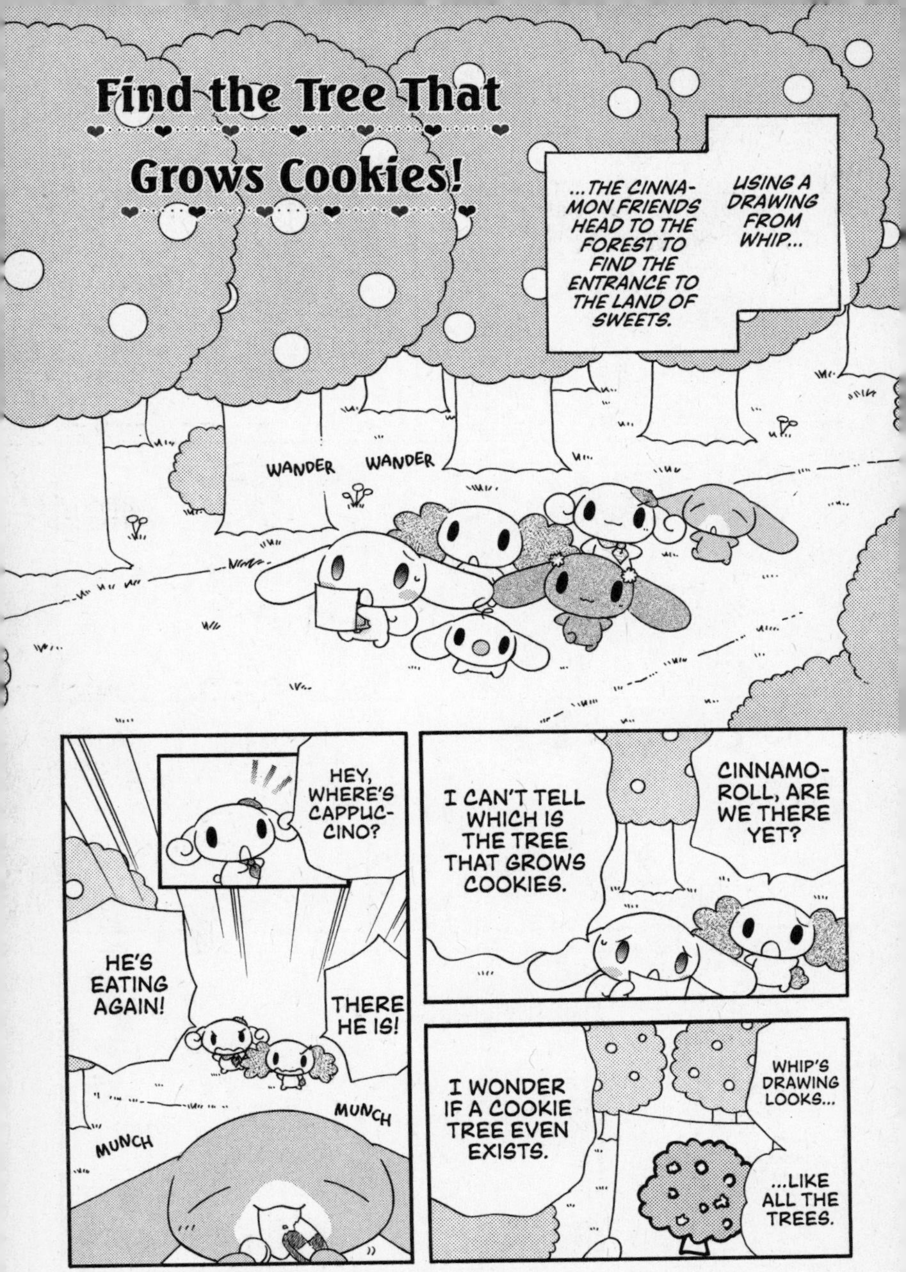
USING A DRAWING FROM WHIP...
...THE CINNAMON FRIENDS HEAD TO THE FOREST TO FIND THE ENTRANCE TO THE LAND OF SWEETS.
WANDER WANDER
CINNAMOROLL, ARE WE THERE YET?
I CAN'T TELL WHICH IS THE TREE THAT GROWS COOKIES.
WHIP'S DRAWING LOOKS...
...LIKE ALL THE TREES.
I WONDER IF A COOKIE TREE EVEN EXISTS.
HEY, WHERE'S CAPPUCCINO?
THERE HE IS!
HE'S EATING AGAIN!
MUNCH
MUNCH

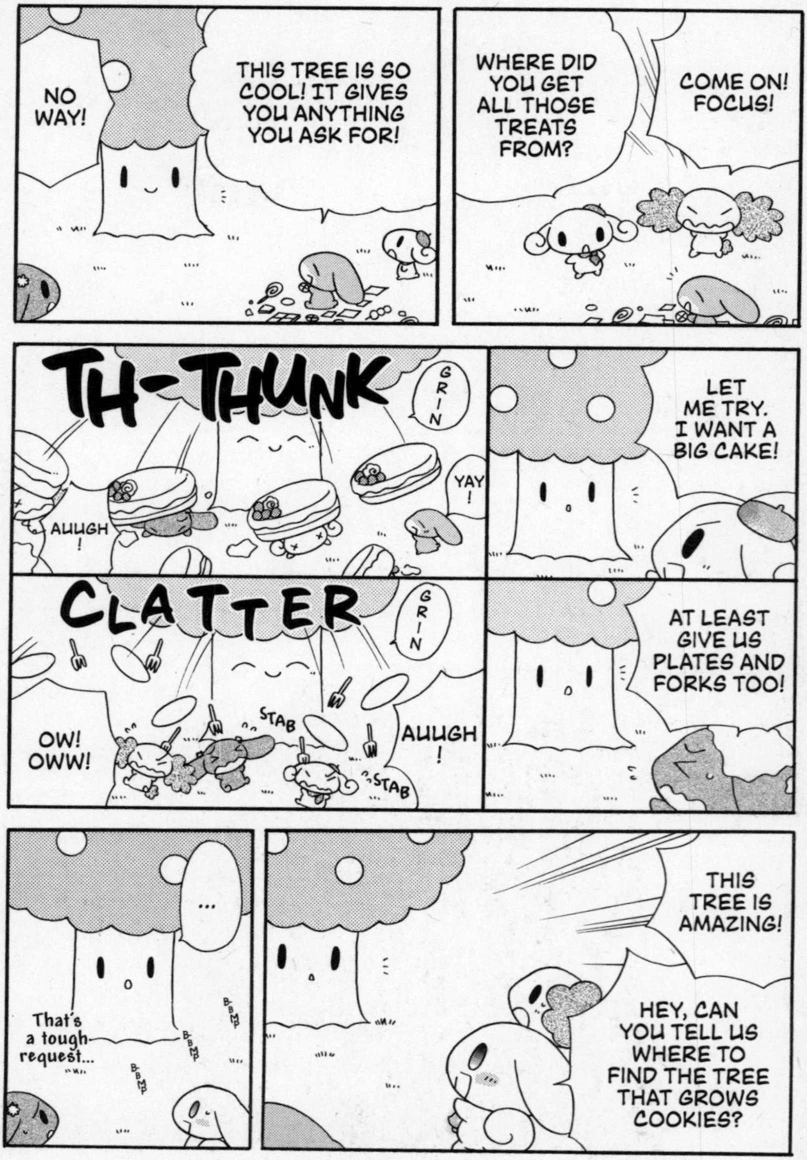
COME ON! FOCUS!
WHERE DID YOU GET ALL THOSE TREATS FROM?
THIS TREE IS SO COOL! IT GIVES YOU ANYTHING YOU ASK FOR!
NO WAY!
LET ME TRY. I WANT A BIG CAKE!
TH-THUNK
GRIN
YAY!
AUUGH!
AT LEAST GIVE US PLATES AND FORKS TOO!
CLATTER
GRIN
AUUGH!
STAB
STAB
OW! OWW!
THIS TREE IS AMAZING!
HEY, CAN YOU TELL US WHERE TO FIND THE TREE THAT GROWS COOKIES?
...
BBMP
BBMP
That's a tough request...
BBMP

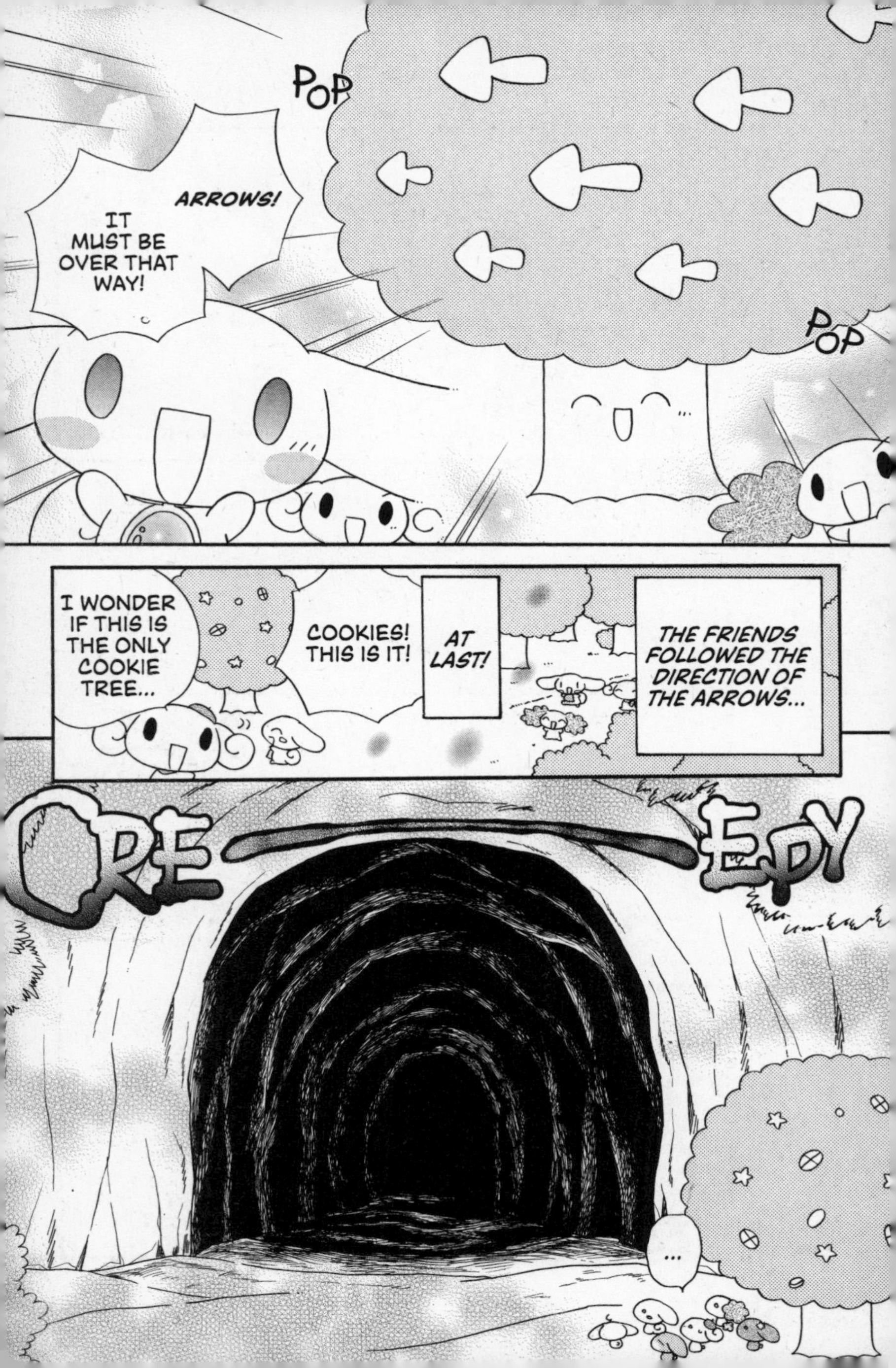
POP
POP
ARROWS!
IT MUST BE OVER THAT WAY!
THE FRIENDS FOLLOWED THE DIRECTION OF THE ARROWS...
AT LAST!
COOKIES! THIS IS IT!
I WONDER IF THIS IS THE ONLY COOKIE TREE...
CRE—EDY
...

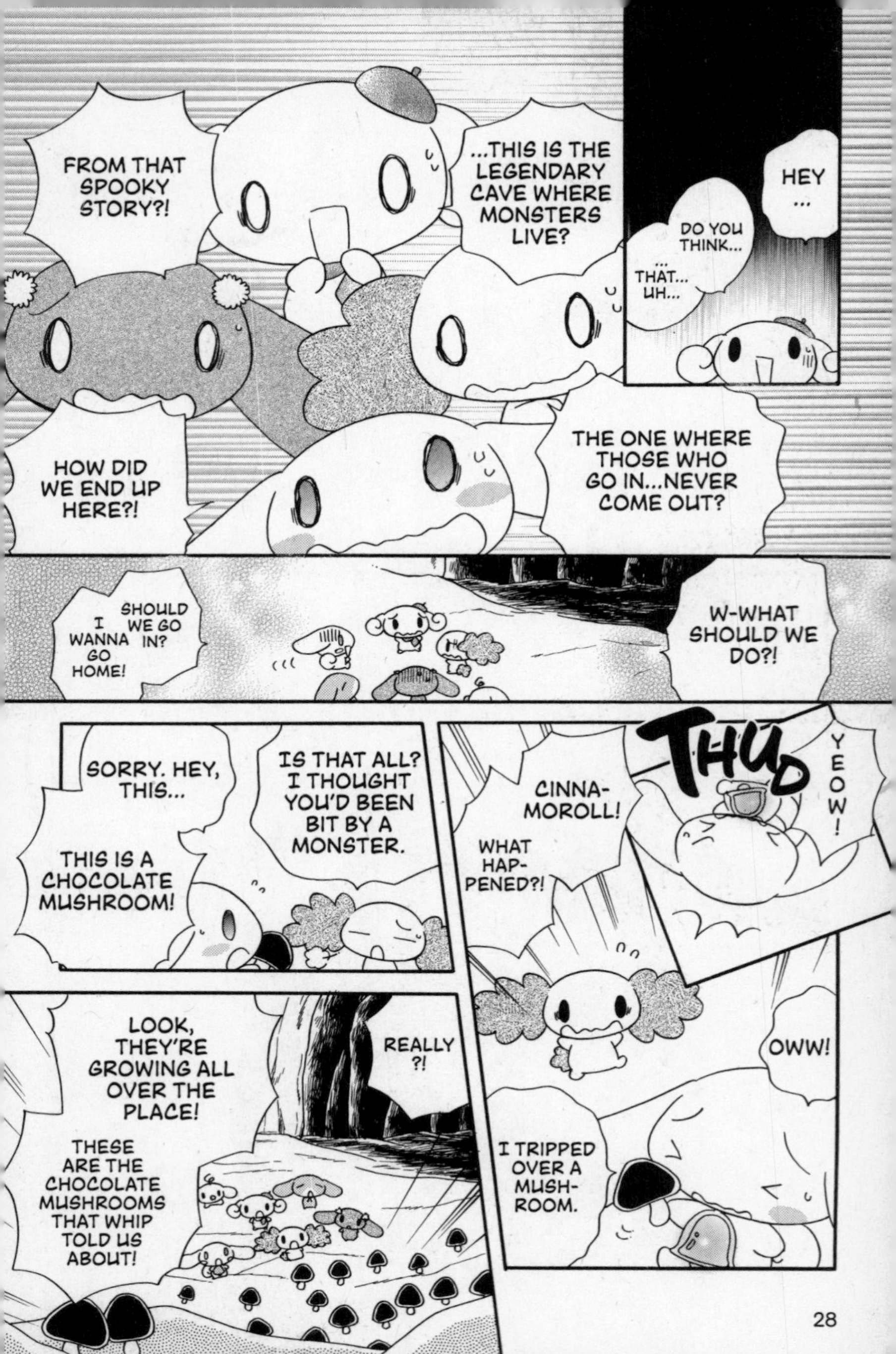
HEY ...
DO YOU THINK...
... THAT... UH...
...THIS IS THE LEGENDARY CAVE WHERE MONSTERS LIVE?
FROM THAT SPOOKY STORY?!
THE ONE WHERE THOSE WHO GO IN...NEVER COME OUT?
HOW DID WE END UP HERE?!
W-WHAT SHOULD WE DO?!
SHOULD WE GO IN?
I WANNA GO HOME!
THUD
YEOW!
CINNA-MOROLL!
WHAT HAP-PENED?!
OWW!
I TRIPPED OVER A MUSH-ROOM.
IS THAT ALL? I THOUGHT YOU'D BEEN BIT BY A MONSTER.
SORRY. HEY, THIS...
THIS IS A CHOCOLATE MUSHROOM!
REALLY ?!
LOOK, THEY'RE GROWING ALL OVER THE PLACE!
THESE ARE THE CHOCOLATE MUSHROOMS THAT WHIP TOLD US ABOUT!

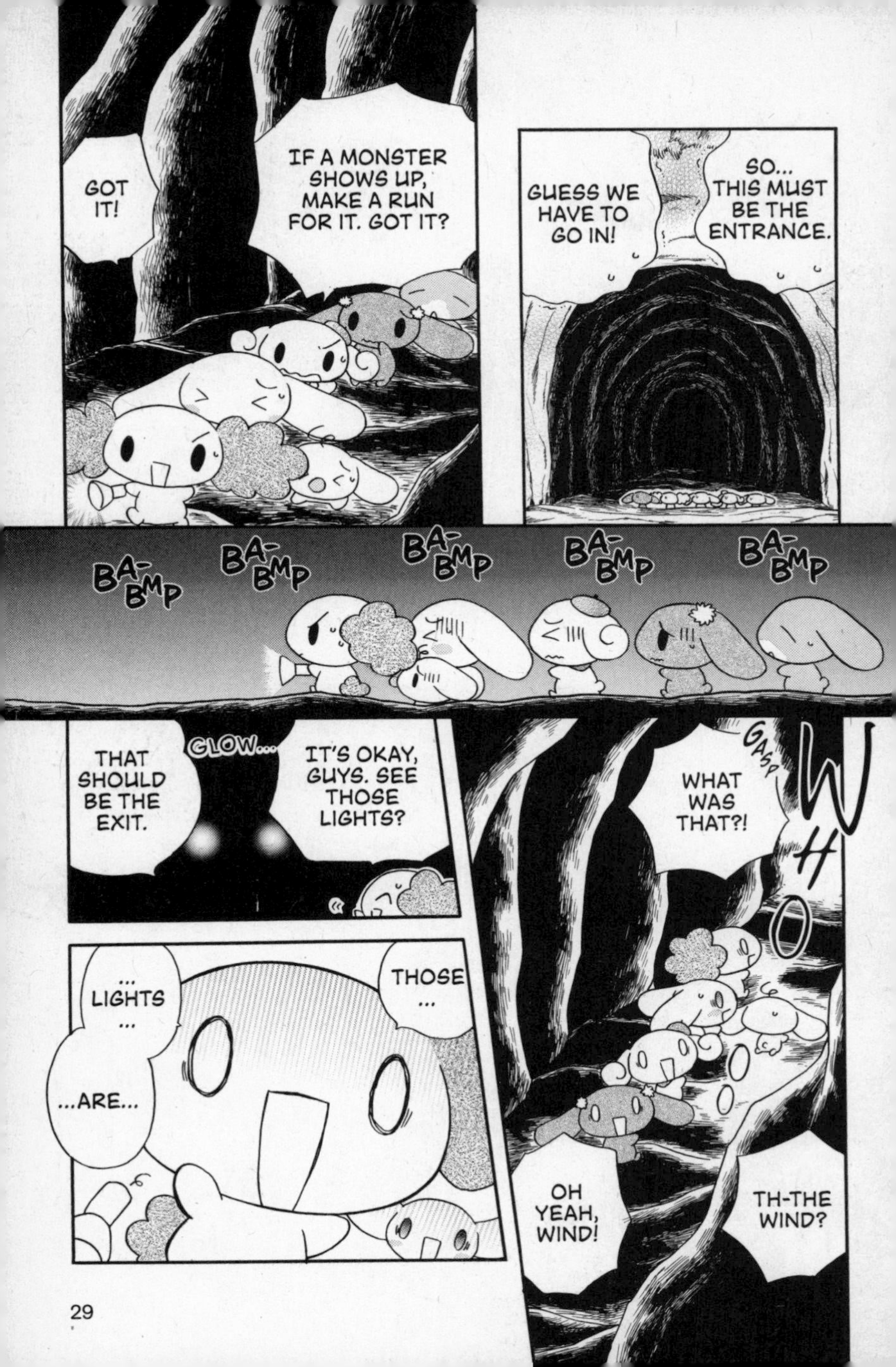
SO... THIS MUST BE THE ENTRANCE.
GUESS WE HAVE TO GO IN!
IF A MONSTER SHOWS UP, MAKE A RUN FOR IT. GOT IT?
GOT IT!
BA-BMP
BA-BMP
BA-BMP
BA-BMP
BA-BMP
GASP
WHAT WAS THAT?!
WHOO
TH-THE WIND?
OH YEAH, WIND!
IT'S OKAY, GUYS. SEE THOSE LIGHTS?
GLOW...
THAT SHOULD BE THE EXIT.
THOSE ...
... LIGHTS ...
...ARE...

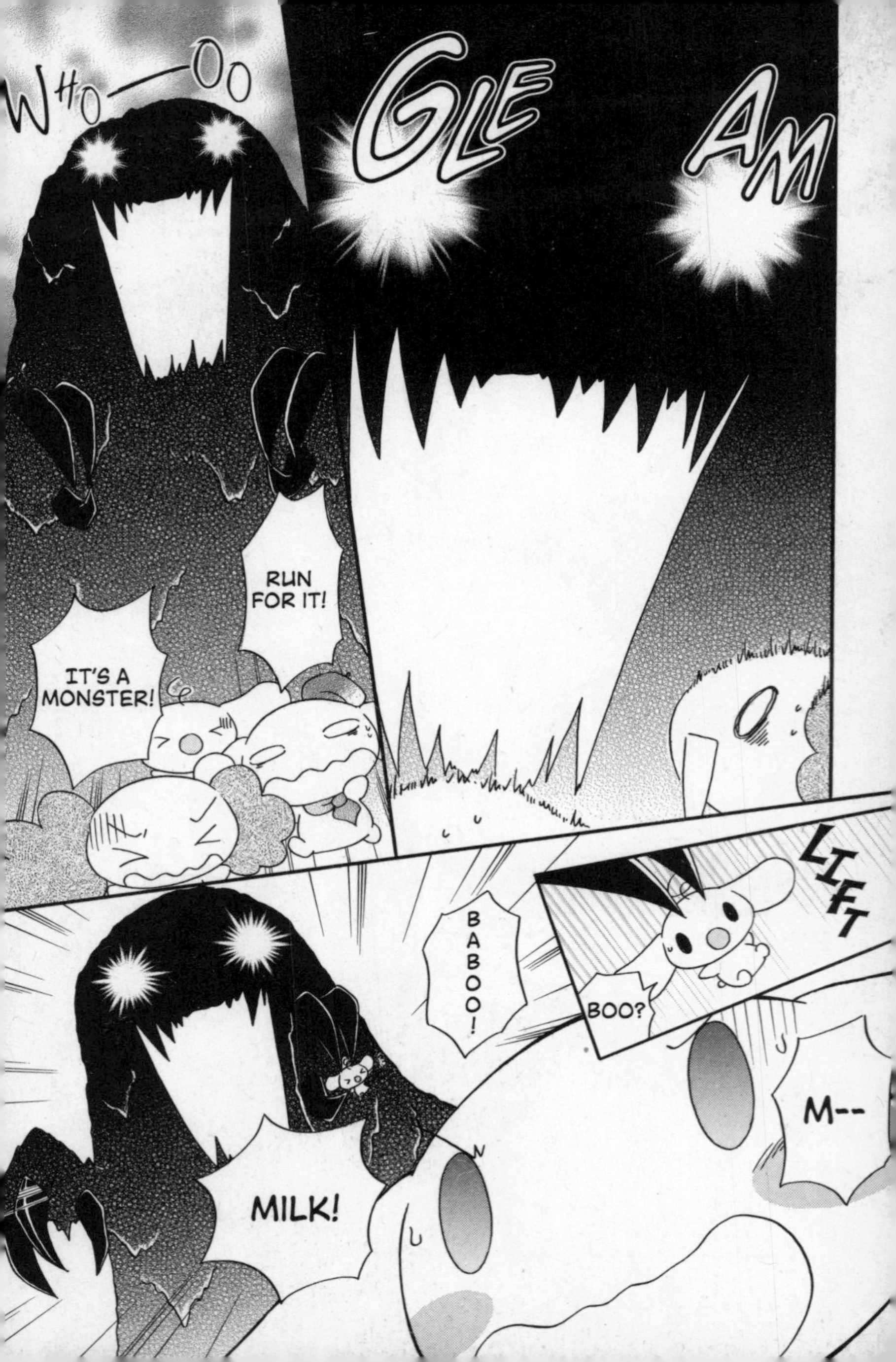
GLEAM
WHO——OO
RUN FOR IT!
IT'S A MONSTER!
LIFT
BOO?
BABOO!
M--
MILK!

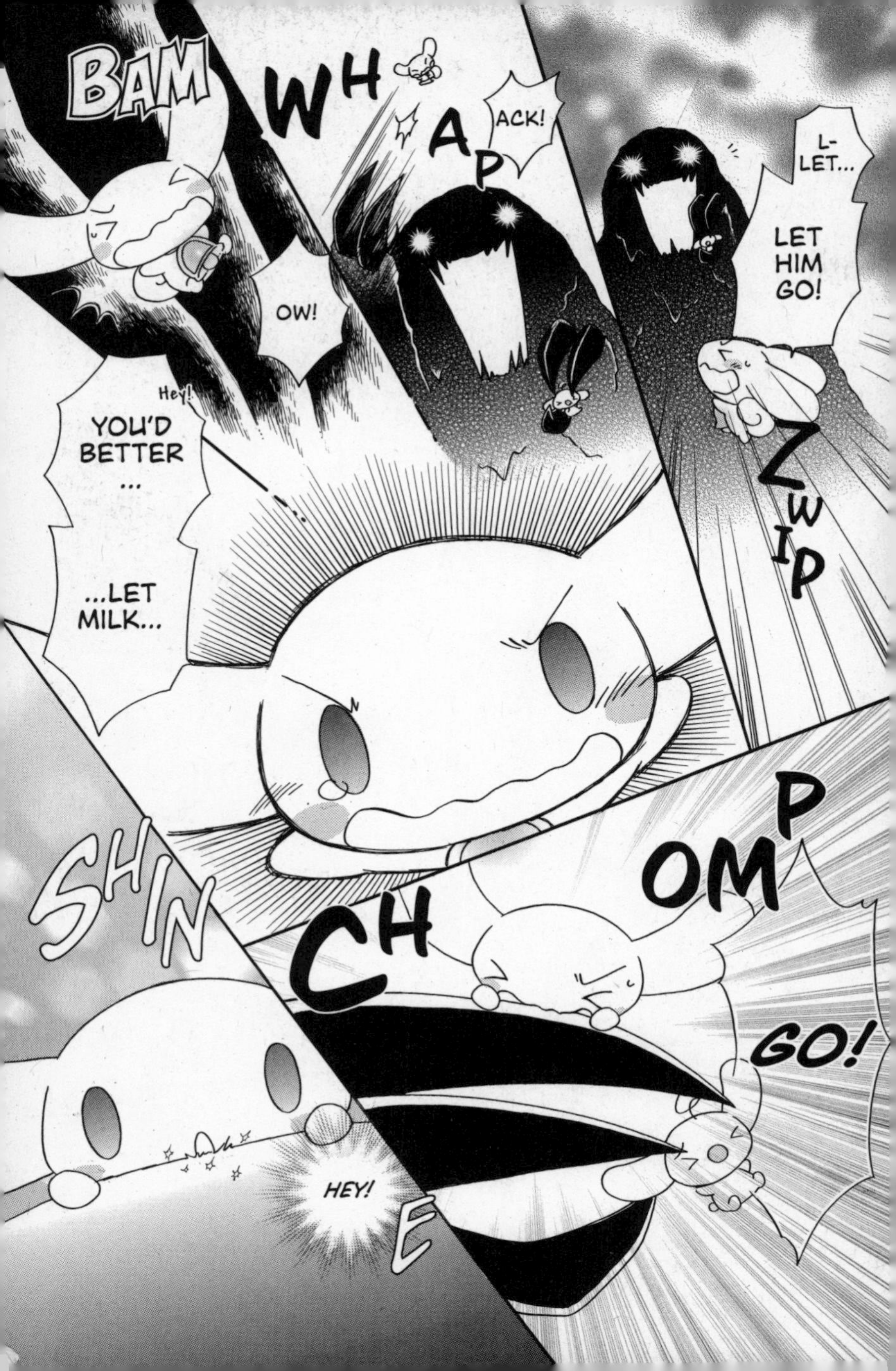
L-
LET...
LET HIM GO!
ZWIP
WHAP
ACK!
BAM
OW!
Hey!
YOU'D BETTER ...
...LET MILK...
CHOMP
GO!
SHIN
HEY!
E

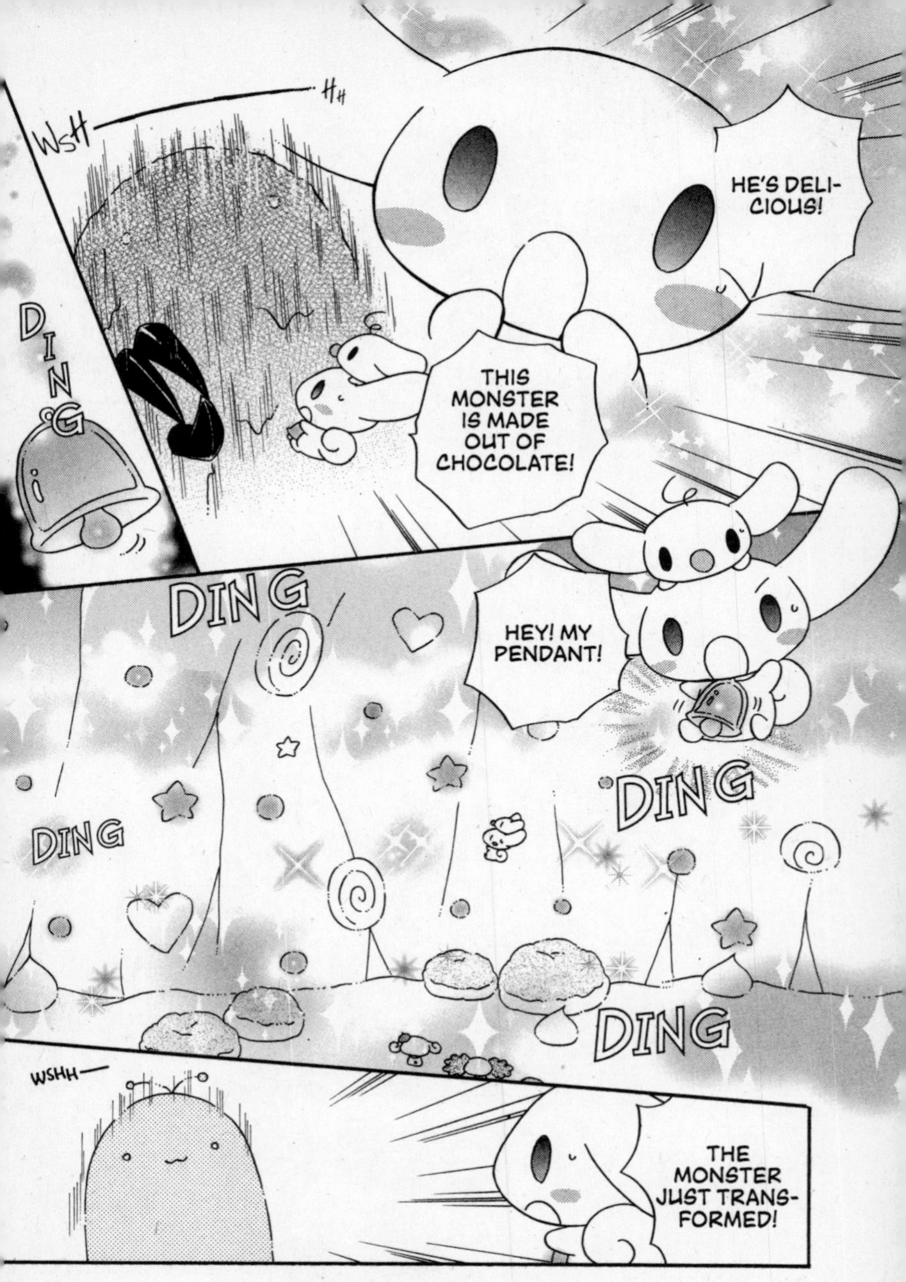
HE'S DELI-
CIOUS!
THIS MONSTER IS MADE OUT OF CHOCOLATE!
WSHH
DING
HEY! MY PENDANT!
DING
DING
DING
DING
THE MONSTER JUST TRANS-
FORMED!
WSHH—

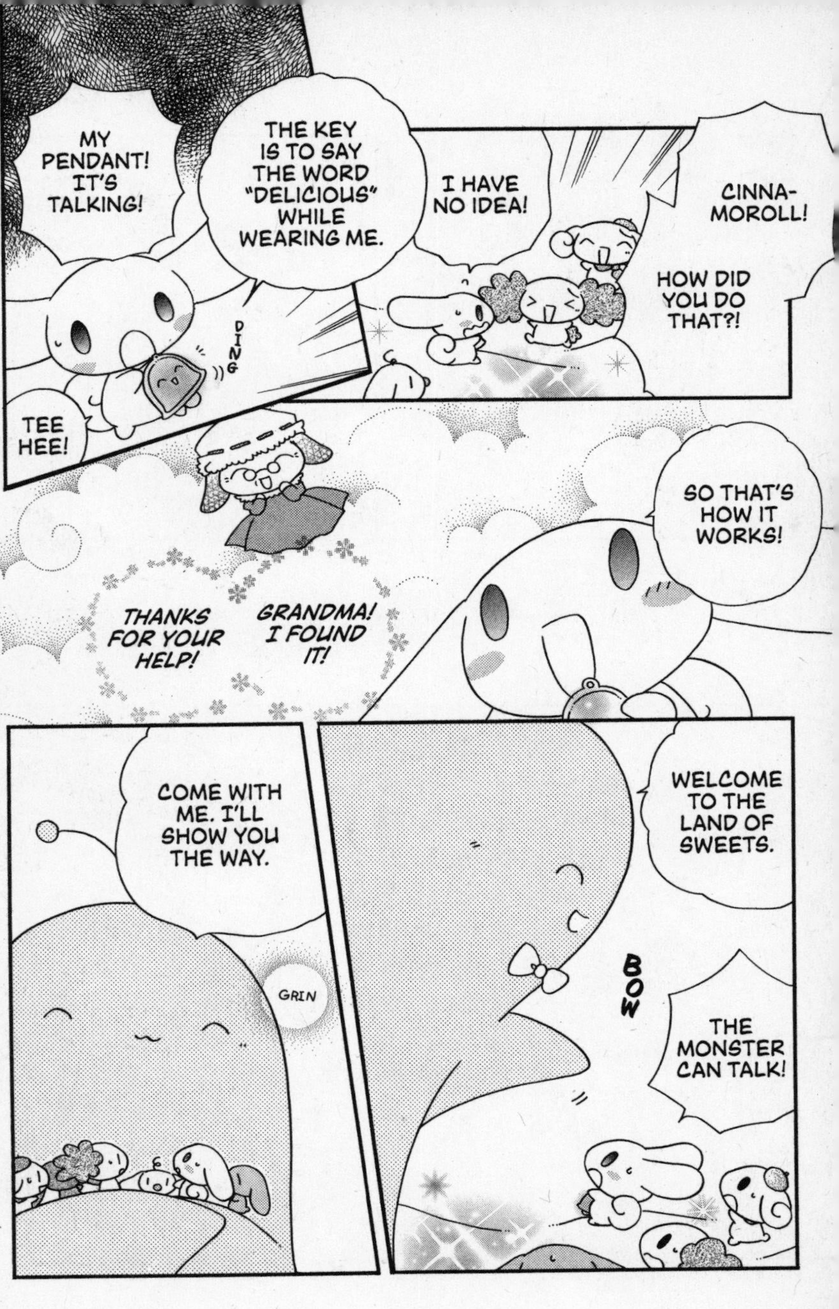
CINNA-MOROLL!
HOW DID YOU DO THAT?!
I HAVE NO IDEA!
THE KEY IS TO SAY THE WORD "DELICIOUS" WHILE WEARING ME.
MY PENDANT! IT'S TALKING!
DING
TEE HEE!
SO THAT'S HOW IT WORKS!
GRANDMA! I FOUND IT!
THANKS FOR YOUR HELP!
WELCOME TO THE LAND OF SWEETS.
BOW
THE MONSTER CAN TALK!
COME WITH ME. I'LL SHOW YOU THE WAY.
GRIN

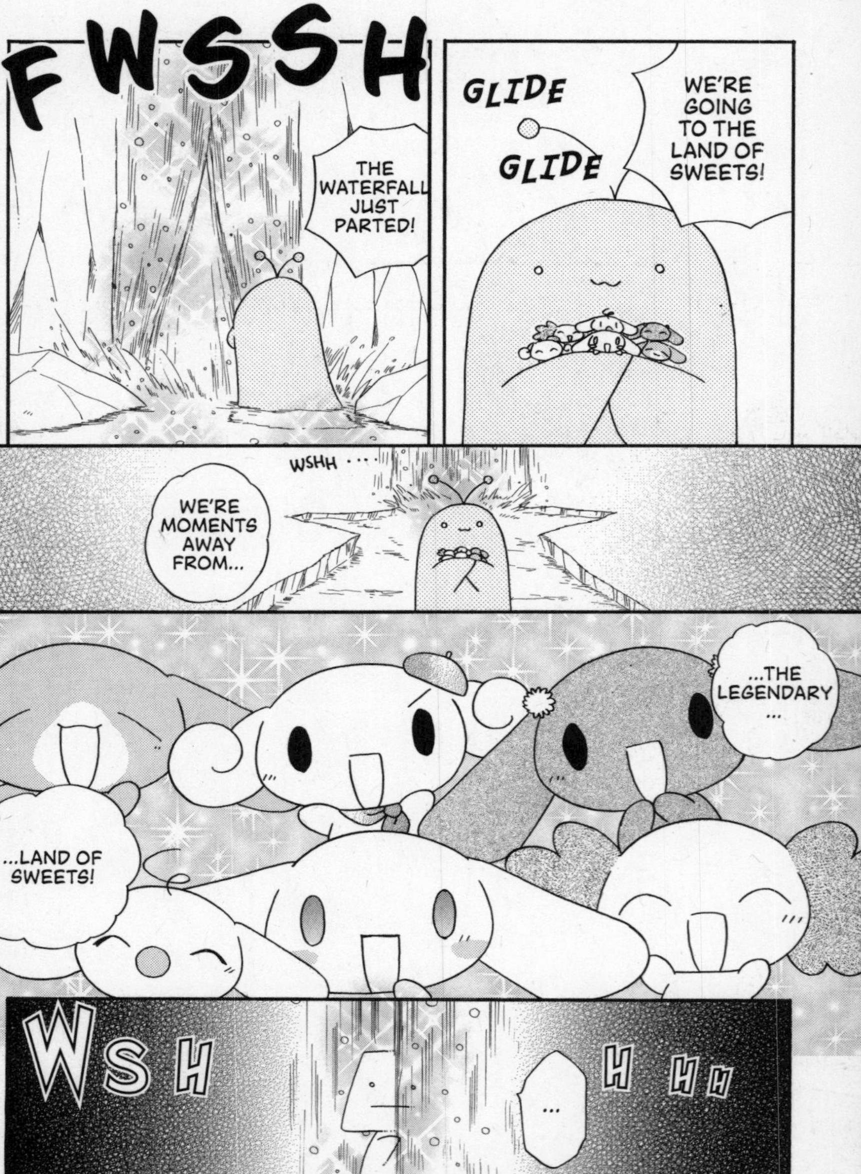
GLIDE
GLIDE
WE'RE GOING TO THE LAND OF SWEETS!
FWSSH
THE WATERFALL JUST PARTED!
WSHH...
WE'RE MOMENTS AWAY FROM...
...THE LEGENDARY ...
...LAND OF SWEETS!
WSH
H H H
...

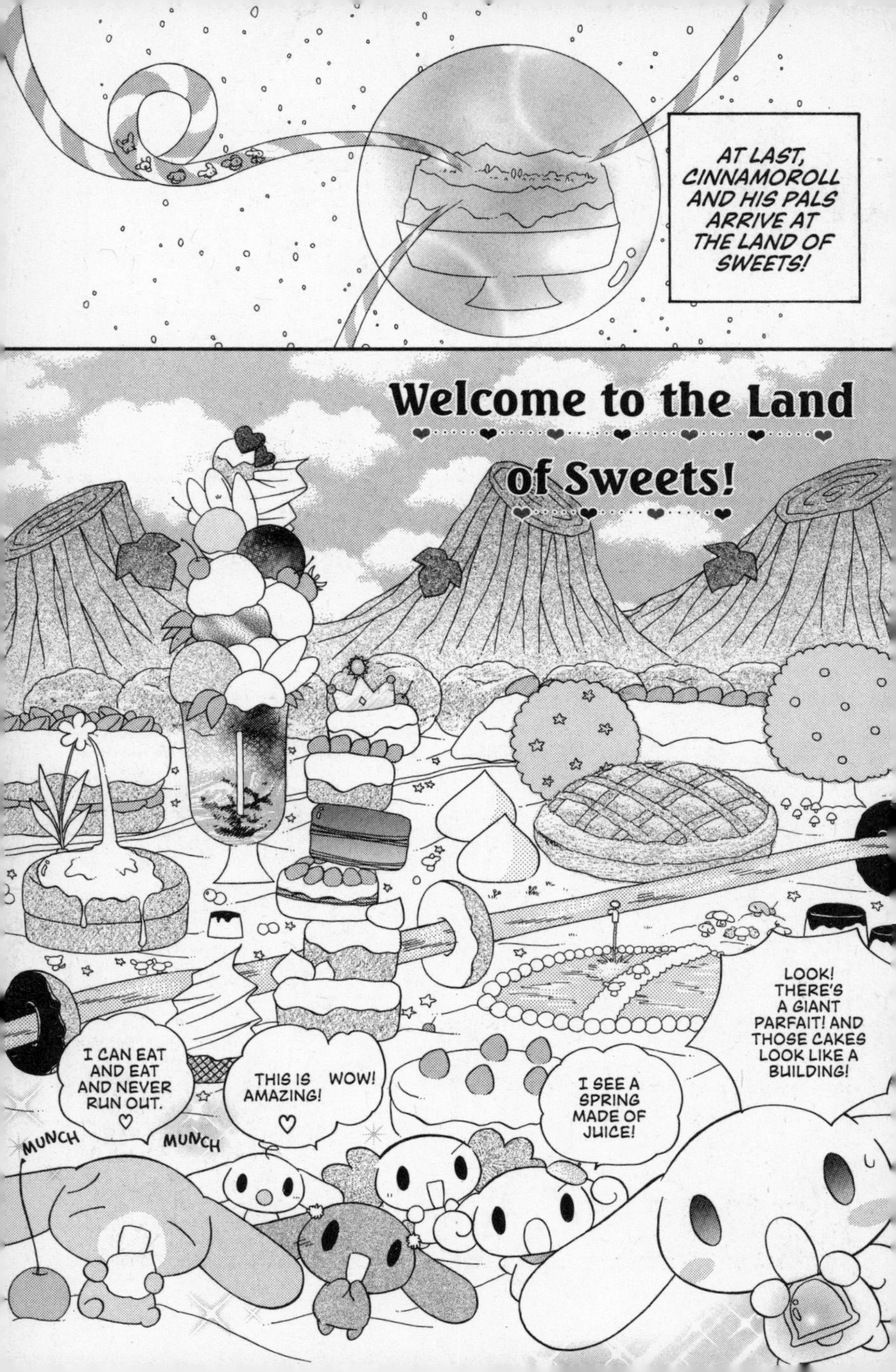
AT LAST, CINNAMOROLL AND HIS PALS ARRIVE AT THE LAND OF SWEETS!
Welcome to the Land of Sweets!
LOOK! THERE'S A GIANT PARFAIT! AND THOSE CAKES LOOK LIKE A BUILDING!
I SEE A SPRING MADE OF JUICE!
WOW!
THIS IS AMAZING! ♡
I CAN EAT AND EAT AND NEVER RUN OUT. ♡
MUNCH
MUNCH

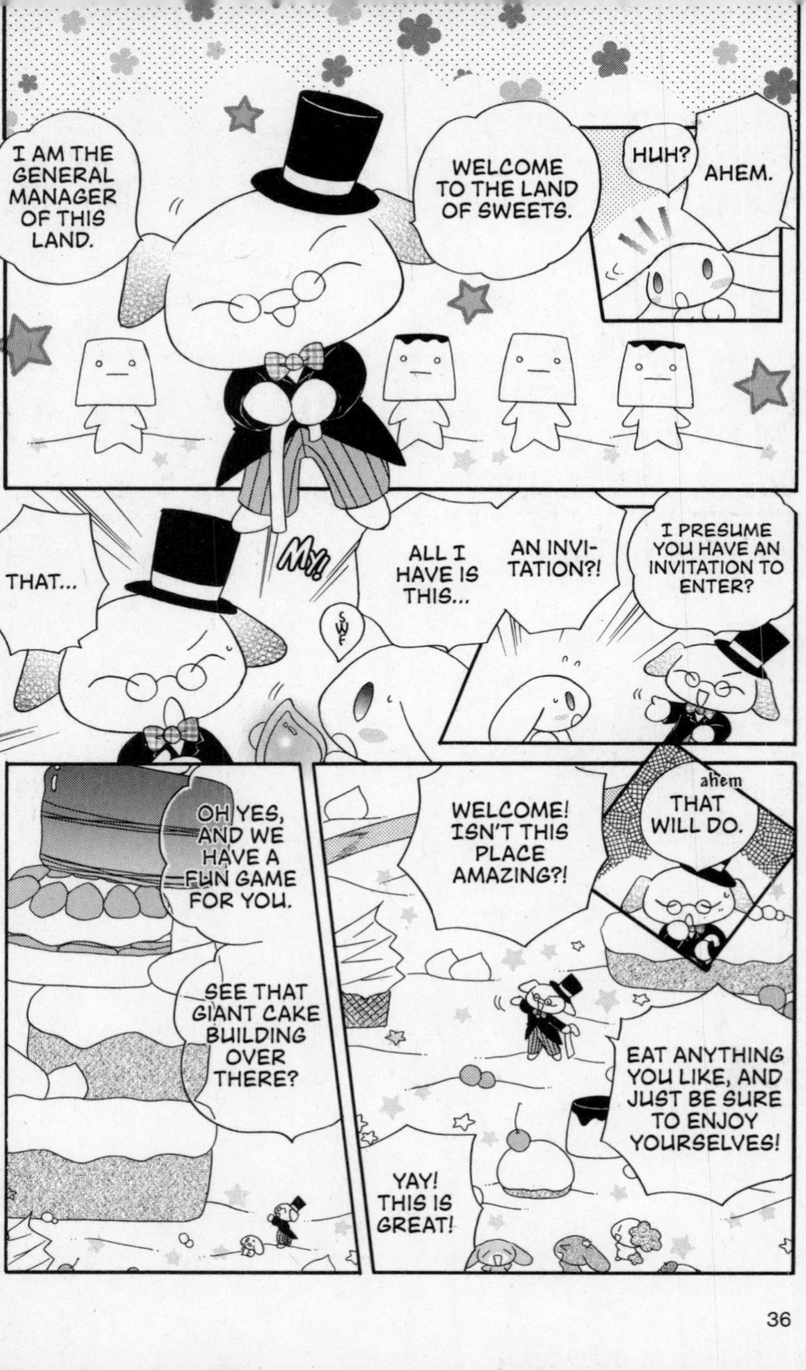
AHEM.
HUH?
WELCOME TO THE LAND OF SWEETS.
I AM THE GENERAL MANAGER OF THIS LAND.
I PRESUME YOU HAVE AN INVITATION TO ENTER?
AN INVITATION?!
ALL I HAVE IS THIS...
SWF
MY!
THAT...
ahem
THAT WILL DO.
WELCOME! ISN'T THIS PLACE AMAZING?!
EAT ANYTHING YOU LIKE, AND JUST BE SURE TO ENJOY YOURSELVES!
YAY! THIS IS GREAT!
OH YES, AND WE HAVE A FUN GAME FOR YOU.
SEE THAT GIANT CAKE BUILDING OVER THERE?

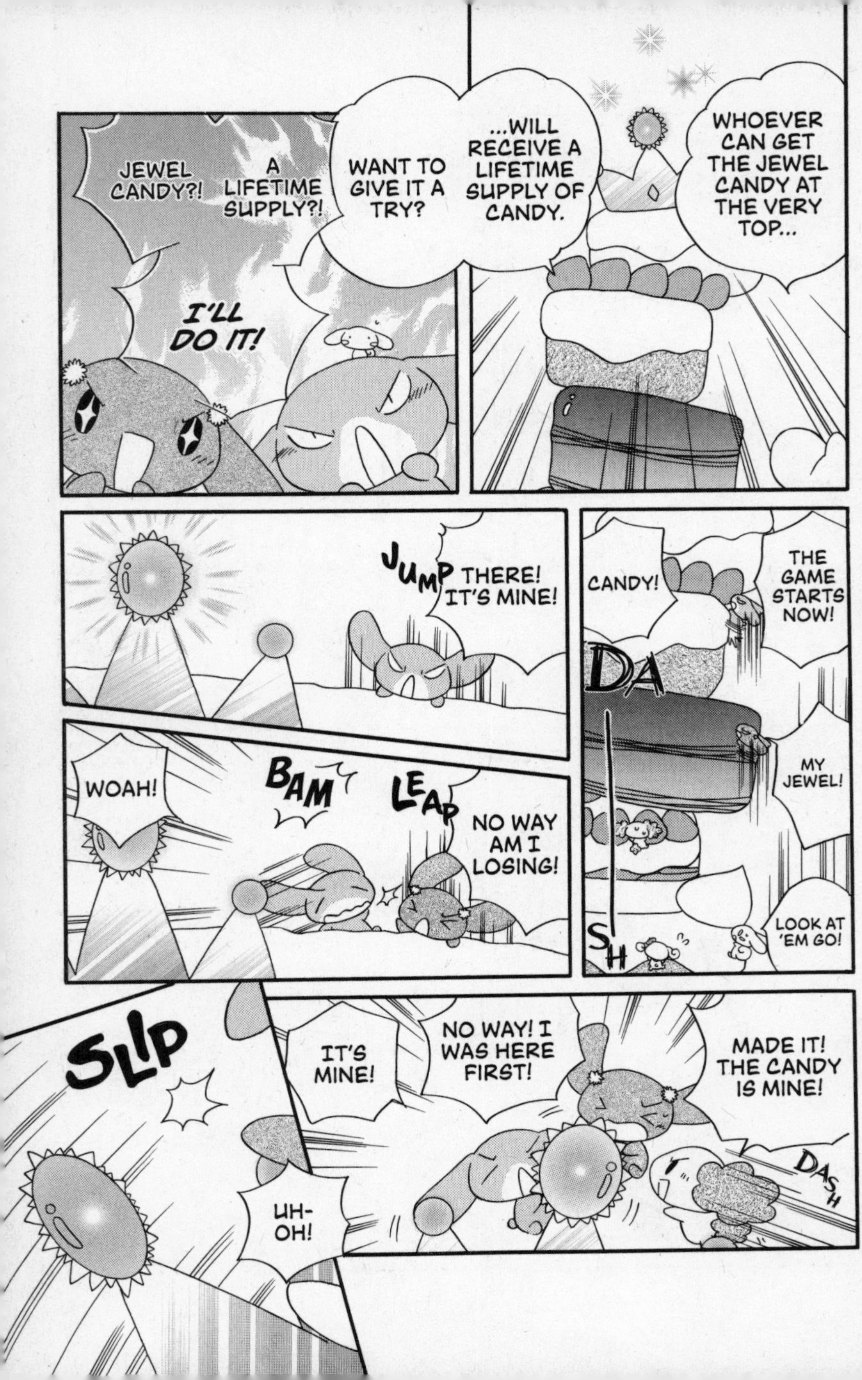
WHOEVER CAN GET THE JEWEL CANDY AT THE VERY TOP...
...WILL RECEIVE A LIFETIME SUPPLY OF CANDY.
WANT TO GIVE IT A TRY?
A LIFETIME SUPPLY?!
JEWEL CANDY?!
I'LL DO IT!
THE GAME STARTS NOW!
CANDY!
DA
MY JEWEL!
SH
LOOK AT 'EM GO!
JUMP
THERE! IT'S MINE!
NO WAY AM I LOSING!
LEAP
BAM
WOAH!
DASH
MADE IT! THE CANDY IS MINE!
NO WAY! I WAS HERE FIRST!
IT'S MINE!
UH-OH!
SLIP

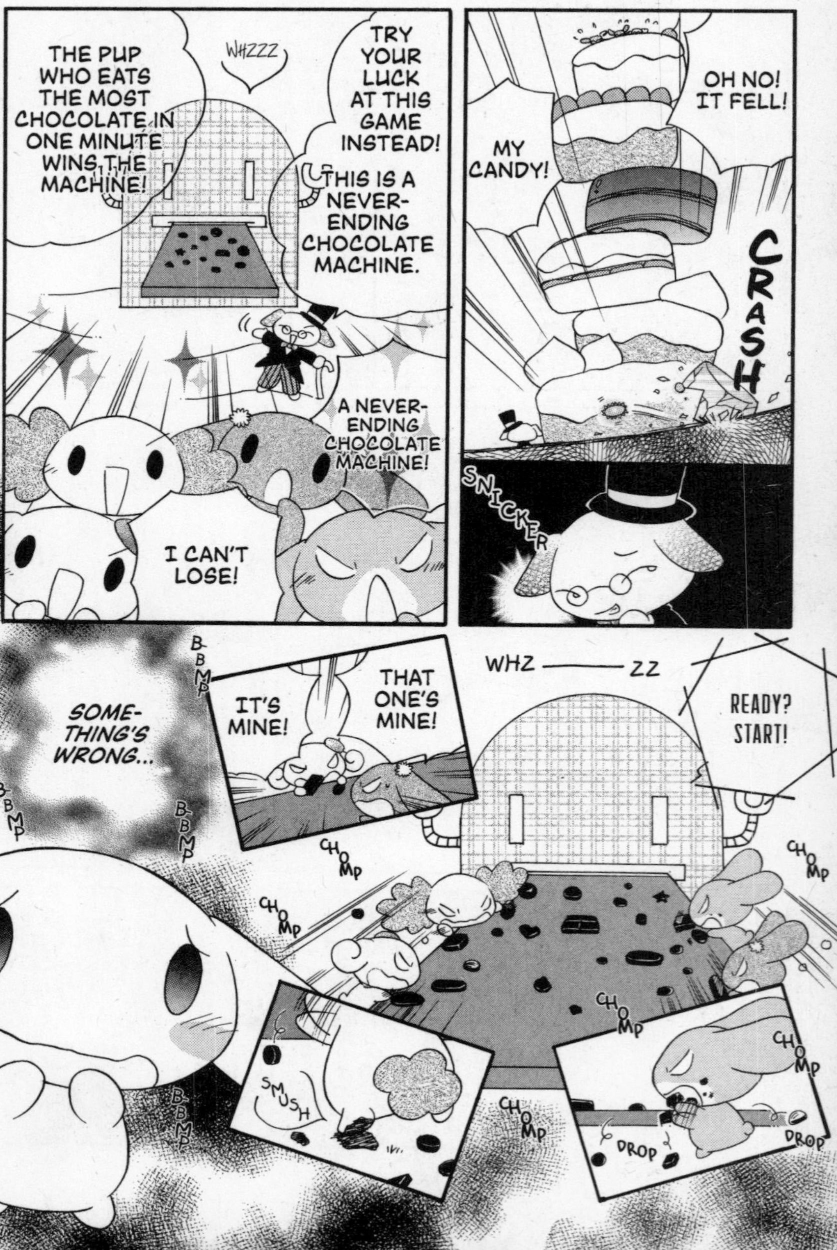
OH NO! IT FELL!
MY CANDY!
CRASH
SNICKER
TRY YOUR LUCK AT THIS GAME INSTEAD!
THIS IS A NEVER-ENDING CHOCOLATE MACHINE.
WHZZZ
THE PUP WHO EATS THE MOST CHOCOLATE IN ONE MINUTE WINS THE MACHINE!
A NEVER-ENDING CHOCOLATE MACHINE!
I CAN'T LOSE!
READY? START!
WHZ —— ZZ
THAT ONE'S MINE!
IT'S MINE!
B-B-MP
CHOMP
CHOMP
CHOMP
CHOMP
SOME-THING'S WRONG...
B-B-MP
B-B-MP
B-B-MP
CHOMP
DROP
DROP
SMUSH

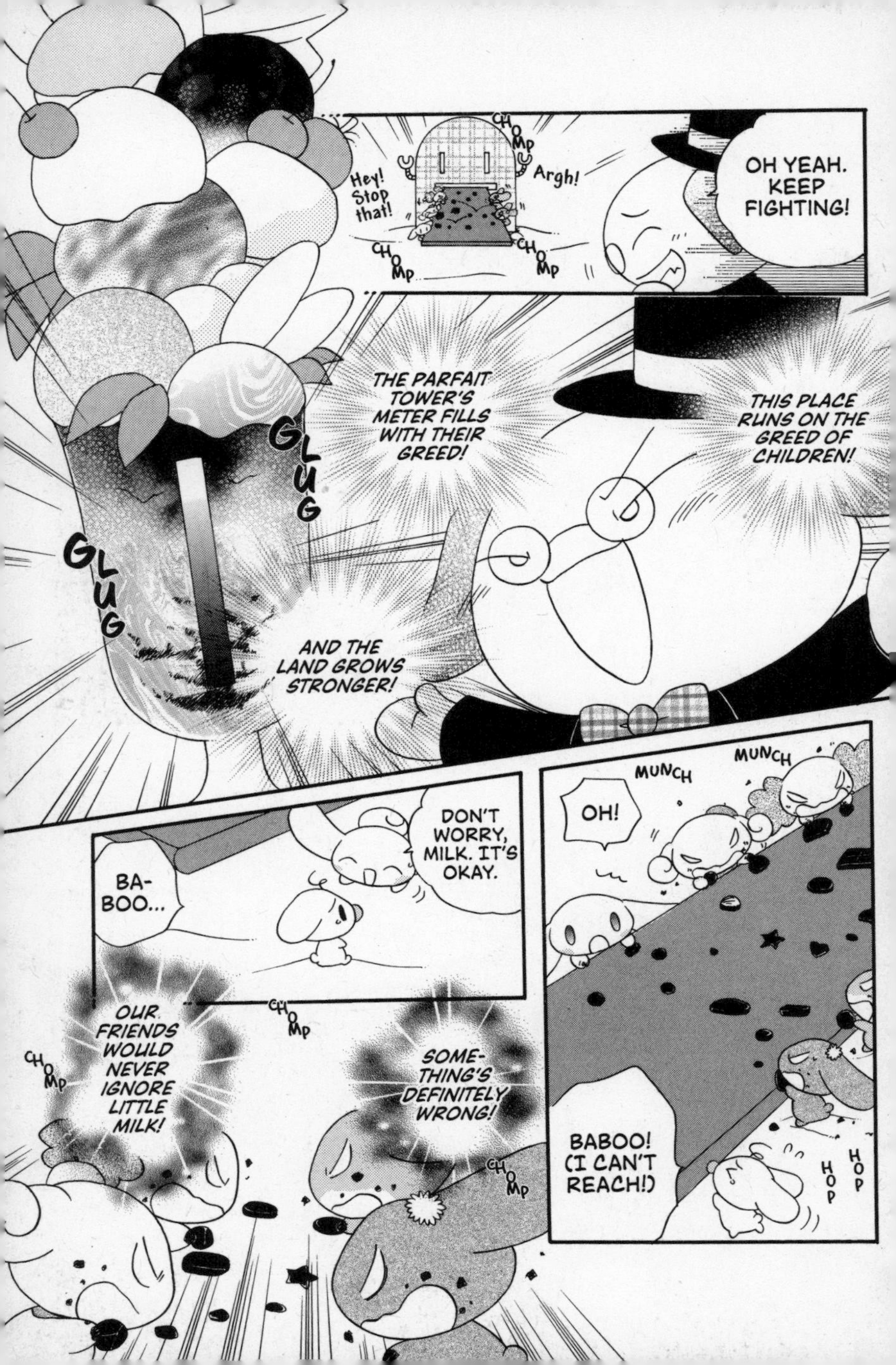
OH YEAH. KEEP FIGHTING!
CHOMP
Argh!
Hey! Stop that!
CHOMP
CHOMP
THIS PLACE RUNS ON THE GREED OF CHILDREN!
THE PARFAIT TOWER'S METER FILLS WITH THEIR GREED!
GLUG
AND THE LAND GROWS STRONGER!
GLUG
MUNCH
MUNCH
OH!
HOP HOP
BABOO! (I CAN'T REACH!)
DON'T WORRY, MILK. IT'S OKAY.
BA-BOO...
SOME-THING'S DEFINITELY WRONG!
CHOMP
CHOMP
OUR FRIENDS WOULD NEVER IGNORE LITTLE MILK!
CHOMP

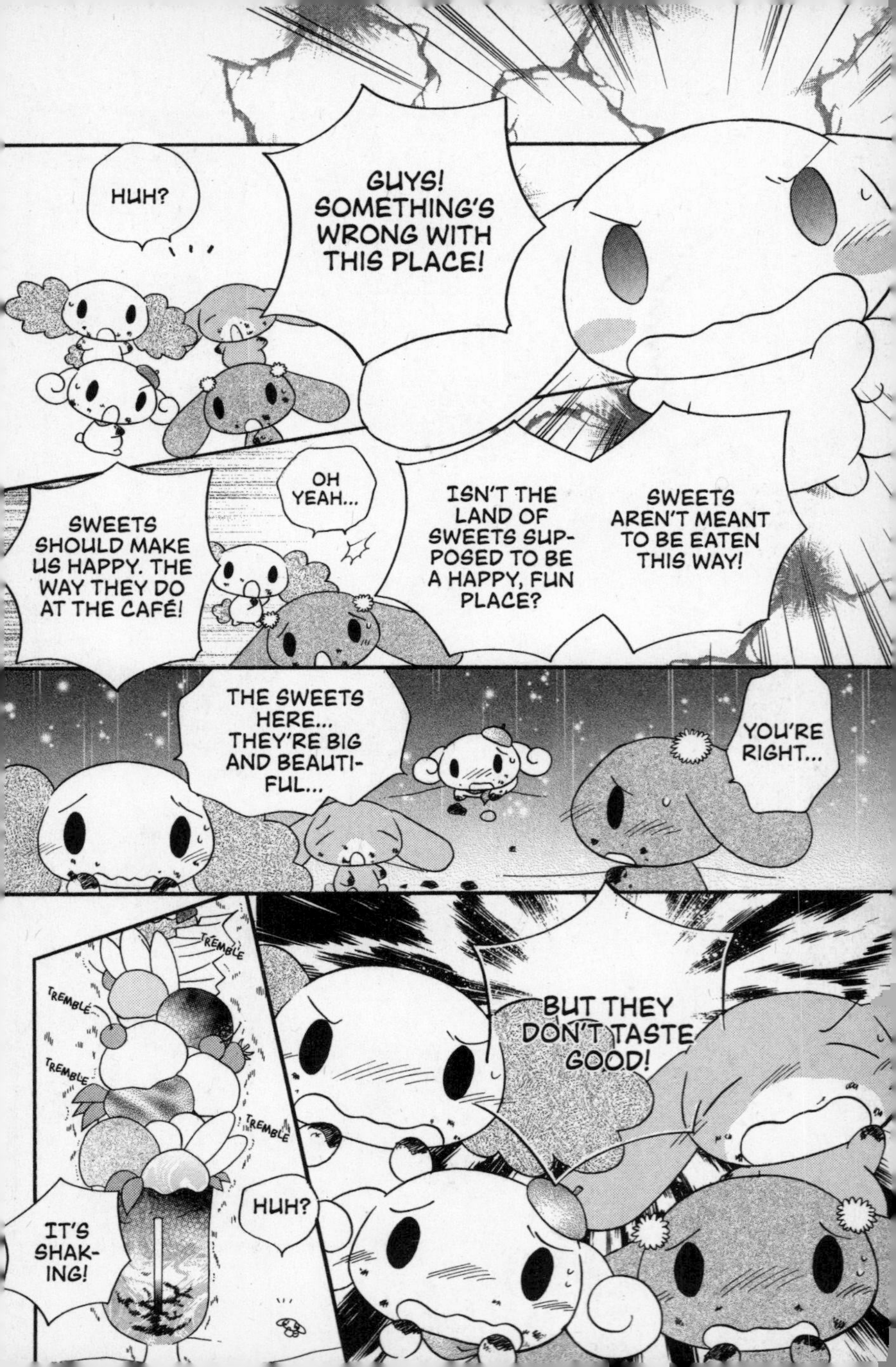
GUYS! SOMETHING'S WRONG WITH THIS PLACE!
HUH?
SWEETS AREN'T MEANT TO BE EATEN THIS WAY!
ISN'T THE LAND OF SWEETS SUP-POSED TO BE A HAPPY, FUN PLACE?
OH YEAH...
SWEETS SHOULD MAKE US HAPPY. THE WAY THEY DO AT THE CAFÉ!
YOU'RE RIGHT...
THE SWEETS HERE... THEY'RE BIG AND BEAUTI-FUL...
BUT THEY DON'T TASTE GOOD!
HUH?
TREMBLE
TREMBLE
TREMBLE
TREMBLE
IT'S SHAK-ING!

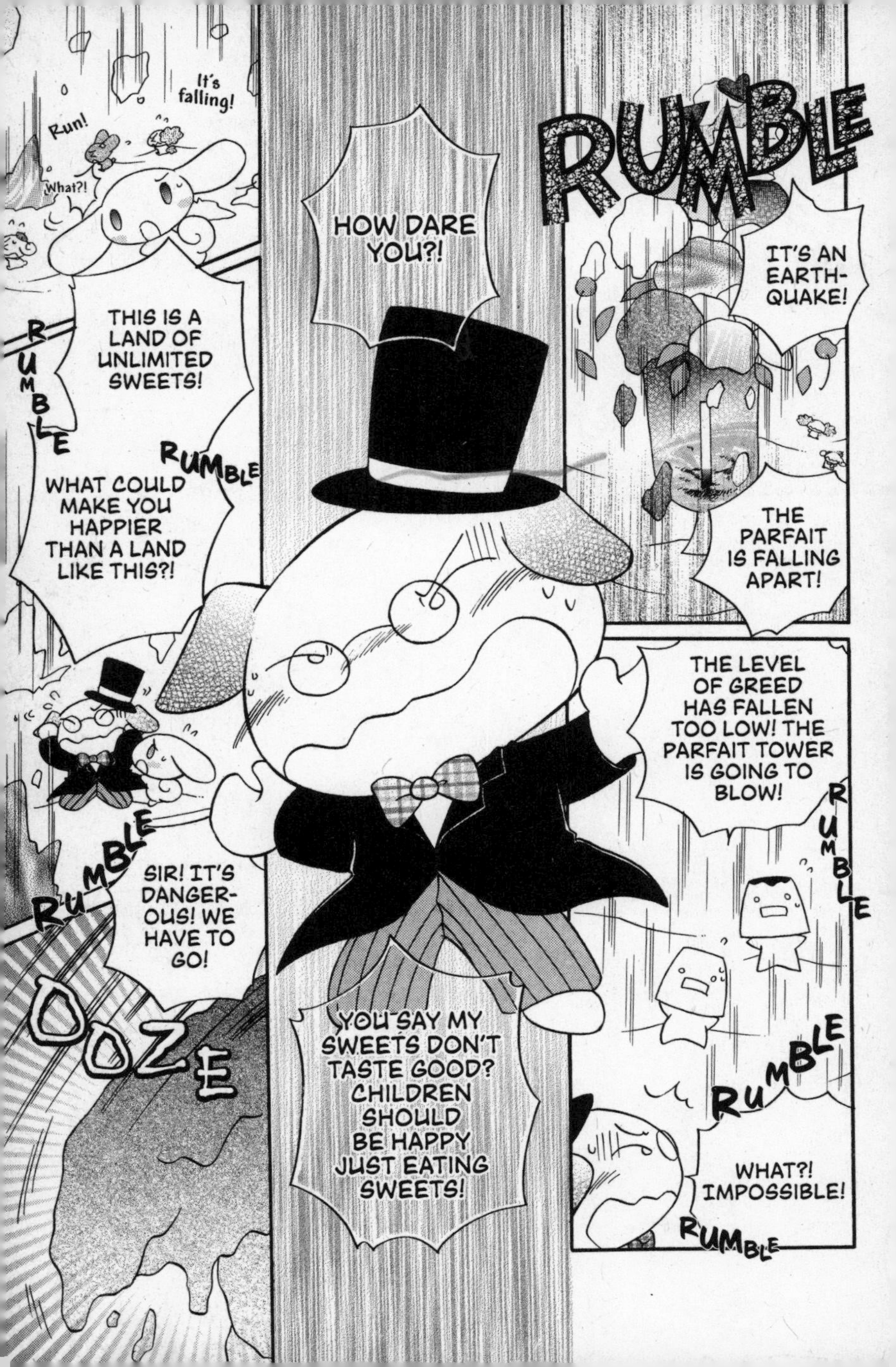
RUMBLE
IT'S AN EARTH-QUAKE!
THE PARFAIT IS FALLING APART!
THE LEVEL OF GREED HAS FALLEN TOO LOW! THE PARFAIT TOWER IS GOING TO BLOW!
RUMBLE
RUMBLE
WHAT?! IMPOSSIBLE!
RUMBLE
HOW DARE YOU?!
YOU SAY MY SWEETS DON'T TASTE GOOD? CHILDREN SHOULD BE HAPPY JUST EATING SWEETS!
It's falling!
Run!
What?!
THIS IS A LAND OF UNLIMITED SWEETS!
RUMBLE
RUMBLE
WHAT COULD MAKE YOU HAPPIER THAN A LAND LIKE THIS?!
RUMBLE
SIR! IT'S DANGER-OUS! WE HAVE TO GO!
OOZE

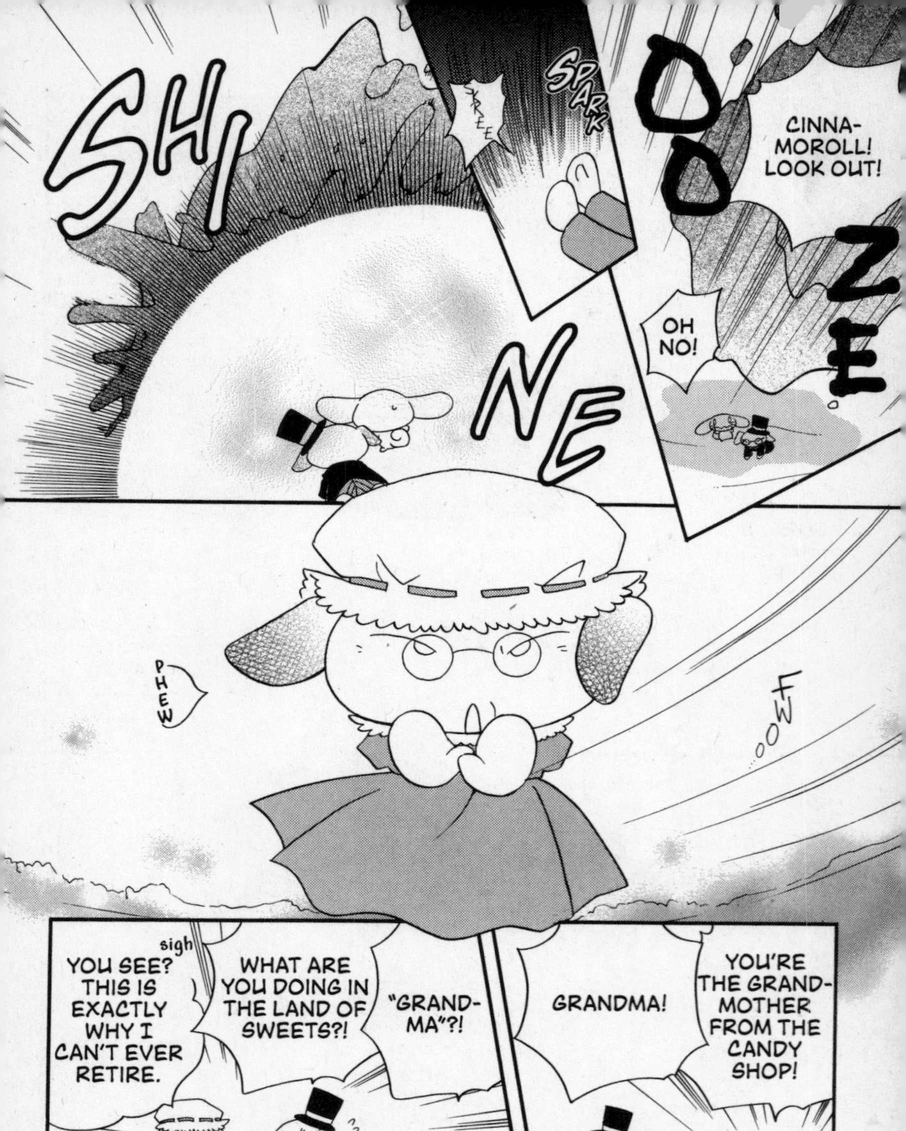
CINNA-
MOROLL!
LOOK OUT!
OH
NO!
DDZE
SPARK
SKREE
SHINE
PHEW
FWOO
YOU'RE
THE GRAND-
MOTHER
FROM THE
CANDY
SHOP!
GRANDMA!
"GRAND-
MA"?!
WHAT ARE
YOU DOING IN
THE LAND OF
SWEETS?!
sigh
YOU SEE?
THIS IS
EXACTLY
WHY I
CAN'T EVER
RETIRE.

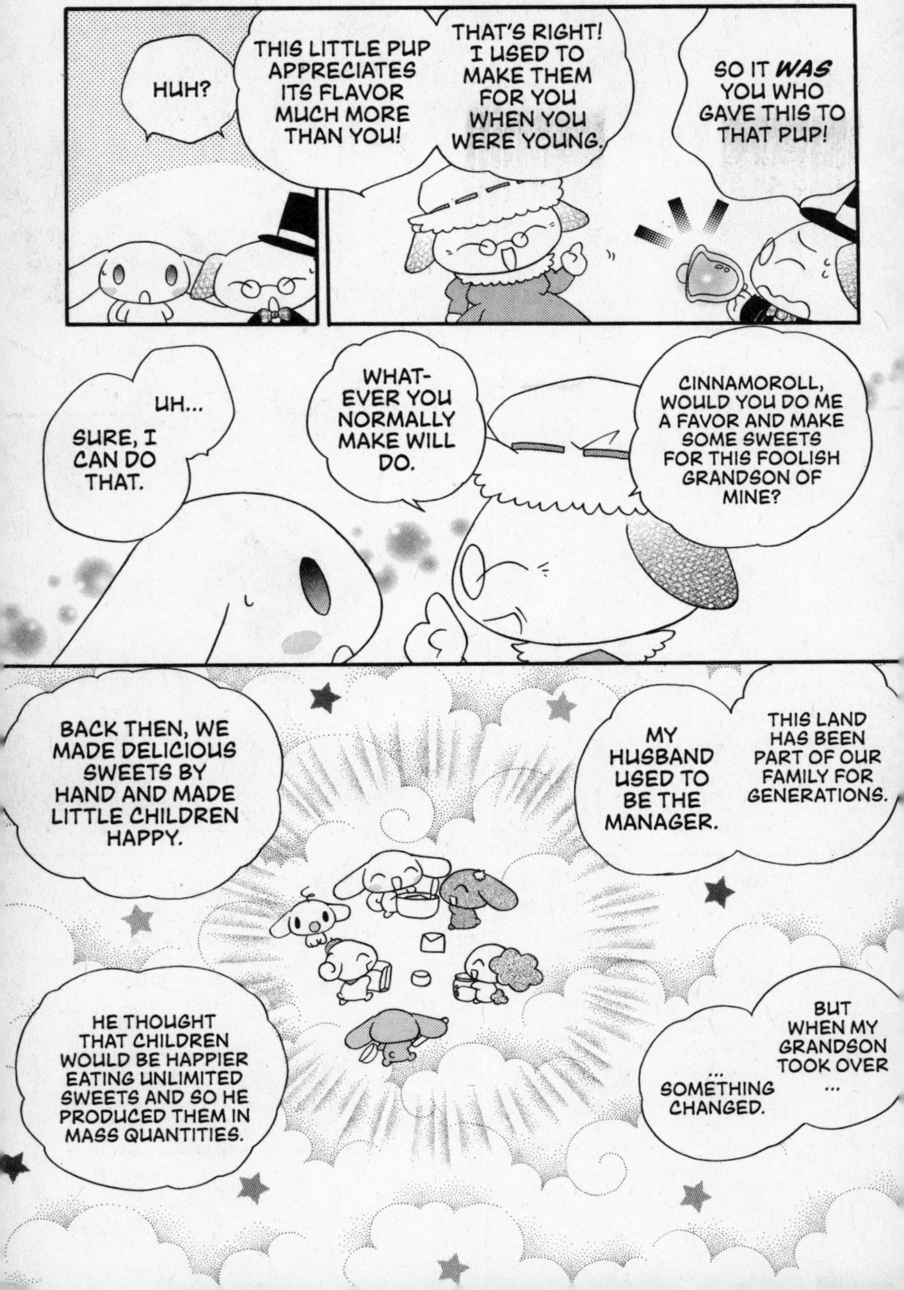
SO IT *WAS* YOU WHO GAVE THIS TO THAT PUP!
THAT'S RIGHT! I USED TO MAKE THEM FOR YOU WHEN YOU WERE YOUNG.
THIS LITTLE PUP APPRECIATES ITS FLAVOR MUCH MORE THAN YOU!
HUH?
CINNAMOROLL, WOULD YOU DO ME A FAVOR AND MAKE SOME SWEETS FOR THIS FOOLISH GRANDSON OF MINE?
WHATEVER YOU NORMALLY MAKE WILL DO.
UH... SURE, I CAN DO THAT.
THIS LAND HAS BEEN PART OF OUR FAMILY FOR GENERATIONS.
MY HUSBAND USED TO BE THE MANAGER.
BACK THEN, WE MADE DELICIOUS SWEETS BY HAND AND MADE LITTLE CHILDREN HAPPY.
BUT WHEN MY GRANDSON TOOK OVER ... ... SOMETHING CHANGED.
HE THOUGHT THAT CHILDREN WOULD BE HAPPIER EATING UNLIMITED SWEETS AND SO HE PRODUCED THEM IN MASS QUANTITIES.

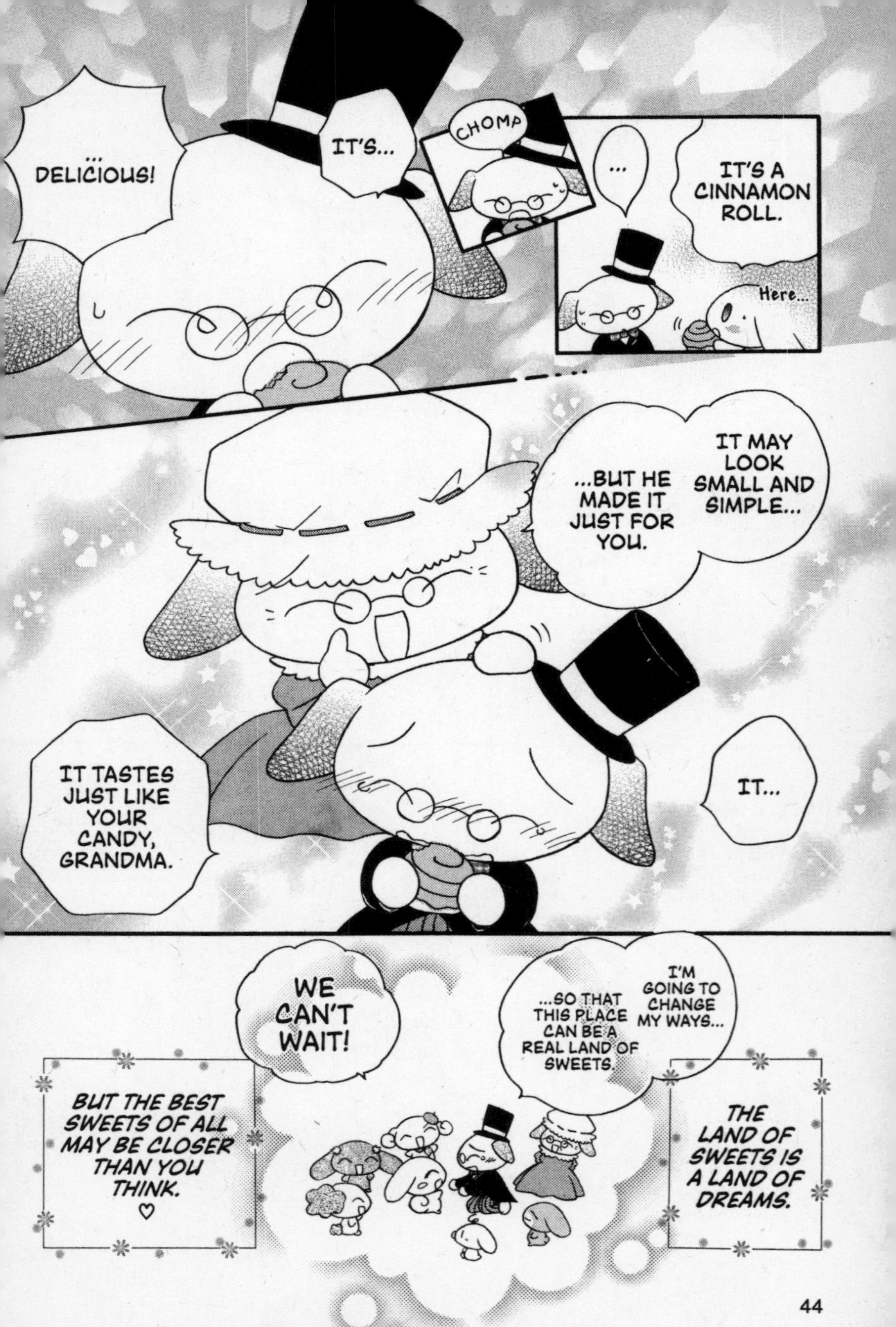
IT'S A CINNAMON ROLL.
...
Here...
CHOMP
IT'S...
...DELICIOUS!
IT MAY LOOK SMALL AND SIMPLE...
...BUT HE MADE IT JUST FOR YOU.
IT...
IT TASTES JUST LIKE YOUR CANDY, GRANDMA.
THE LAND OF SWEETS IS A LAND OF DREAMS.
I'M GOING TO CHANGE MY WAYS...
...SO THAT THIS PLACE CAN BE A REAL LAND OF SWEETS.
WE CAN'T WAIT!
BUT THE BEST SWEETS OF ALL MAY BE CLOSER THAN YOU THINK. ♡

★ Fluffy, Fluffy ♥ Cinnamoroll ★

# Meet the
# Mysterious
# Characters!
## ( PART 1 )

### Whip

A baby cloud that loves sweets. He's still learning to speak, but knows how to transform into all sorts of things.

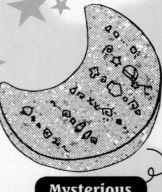

### Sweet Pendant

Bell-shaped candy. Special things can happen if used in times of trouble!

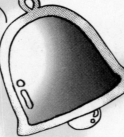

### Mysterious Stone Tablet

Cinnamoroll carried this from the sky in his treasure chest. It bears a mysterious message!

### Grandma Candy

She and her candy shop appear in town one day. What's her true identity?

Café in an Uproar!

# Manager for the Day! (Part 1)

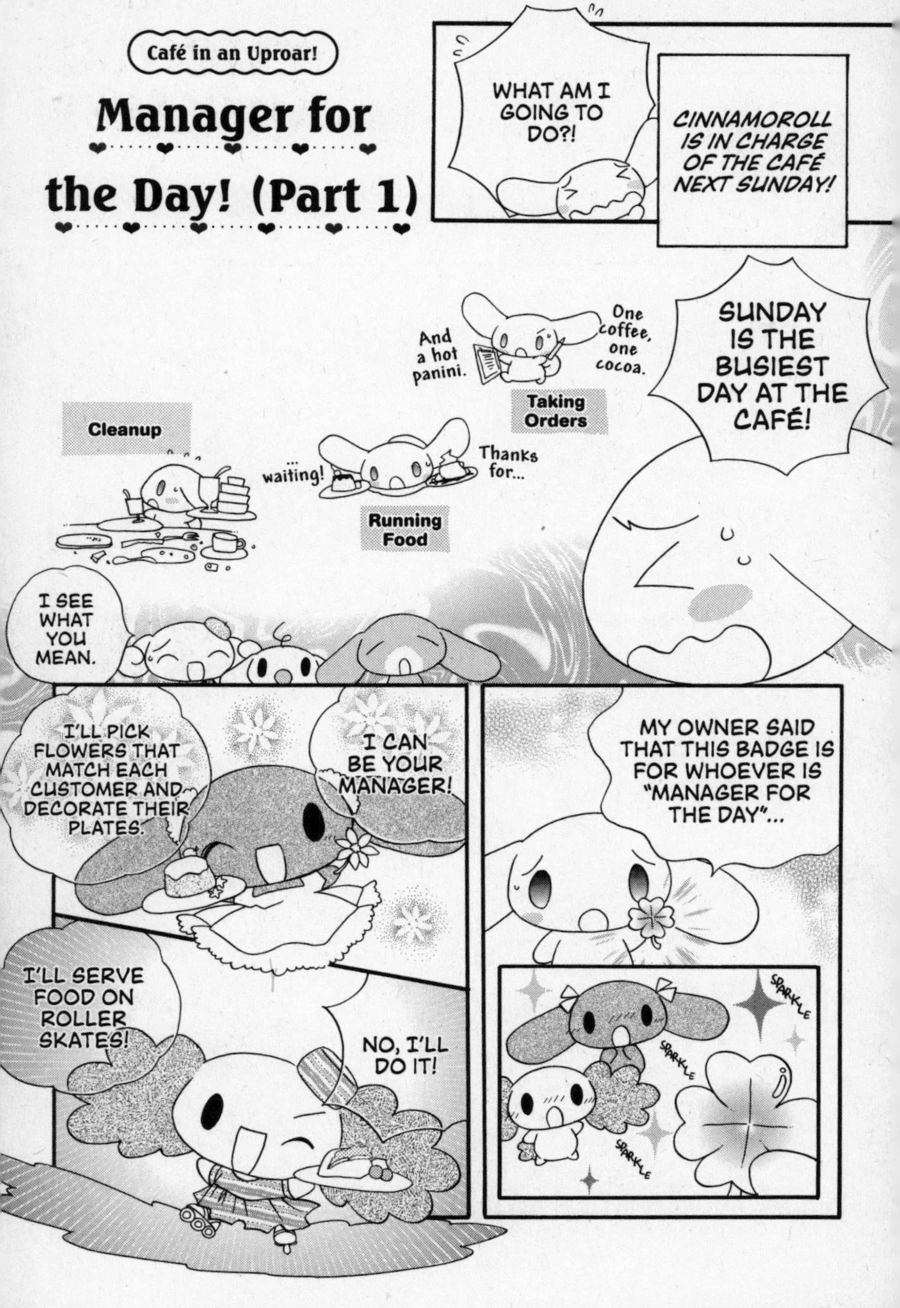
CINNAMOROLL IS IN CHARGE OF THE CAFÉ NEXT SUNDAY!
WHAT AM I GOING TO DO?!
SUNDAY IS THE BUSIEST DAY AT THE CAFÉ!
One coffee, one cocoa.
And a hot panini.
Taking Orders
Thanks for...
... waiting!
Running Food
Cleanup
I SEE WHAT YOU MEAN.
MY OWNER SAID THAT THIS BADGE IS FOR WHOEVER IS "MANAGER FOR THE DAY"...
SPARKLE
SPARKLE
SPARKLE
I CAN BE YOUR MANAGER!
I'LL PICK FLOWERS THAT MATCH EACH CUSTOMER AND DECORATE THEIR PLATES.
NO, I'LL DO IT!
I'LL SERVE FOOD ON ROLLER SKATES!

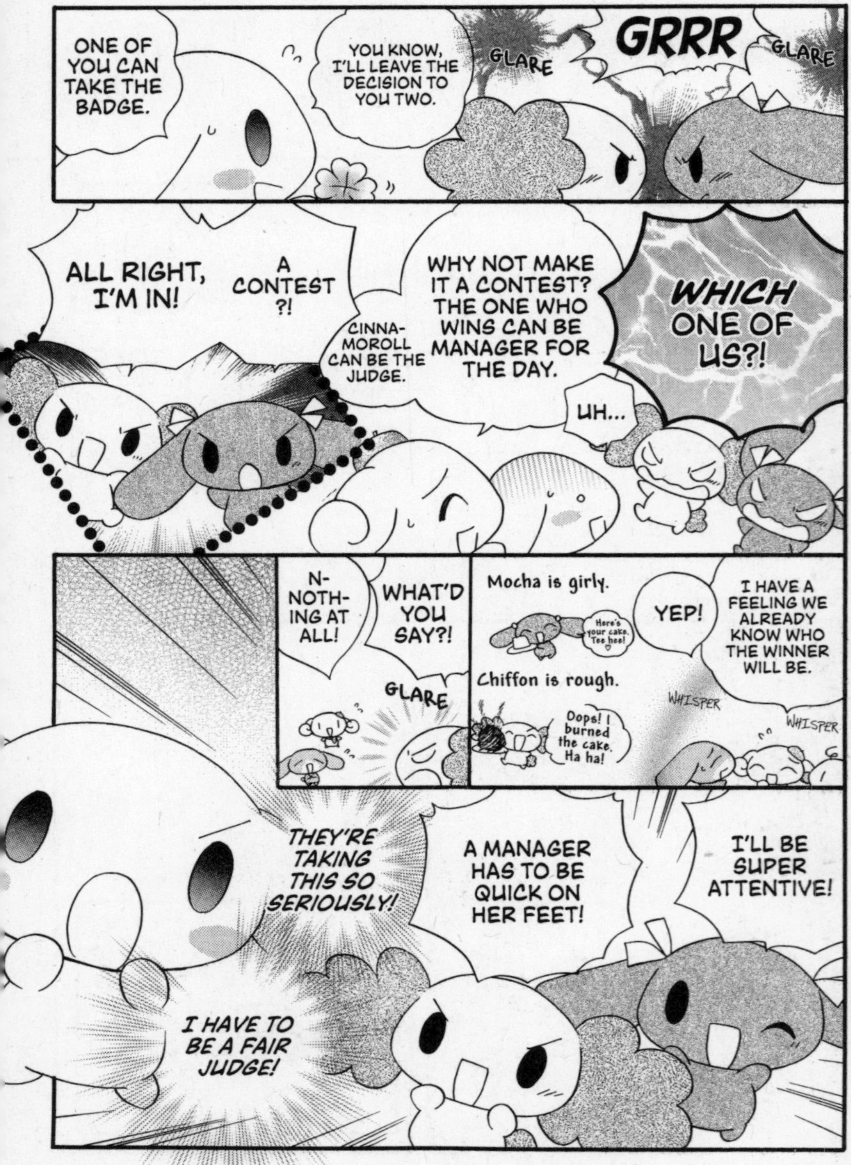
GLARE
GRRR
GLARE
YOU KNOW, I'LL LEAVE THE DECISION TO YOU TWO.
ONE OF YOU CAN TAKE THE BADGE.
WHICH ONE OF US?!
UH...
WHY NOT MAKE IT A CONTEST? THE ONE WHO WINS CAN BE MANAGER FOR THE DAY.
CINNAMOROLL CAN BE THE JUDGE.
A CONTEST?!
ALL RIGHT, I'M IN!
I HAVE A FEELING WE ALREADY KNOW WHO THE WINNER WILL BE.
YEP!
Mocha is girly.
Here's your cake. Tee hee! ♡
Chiffon is rough.
Oops! I burned the cake. Ha ha!
WHISPER
WHISPER
WHAT'D YOU SAY?!
N-NOTHING AT ALL!
GLARE
I'LL BE SUPER ATTENTIVE!
A MANAGER HAS TO BE QUICK ON HER FEET!
THEY'RE TAKING THIS SO SERIOUSLY!
I HAVE TO BE A FAIR JUDGE!

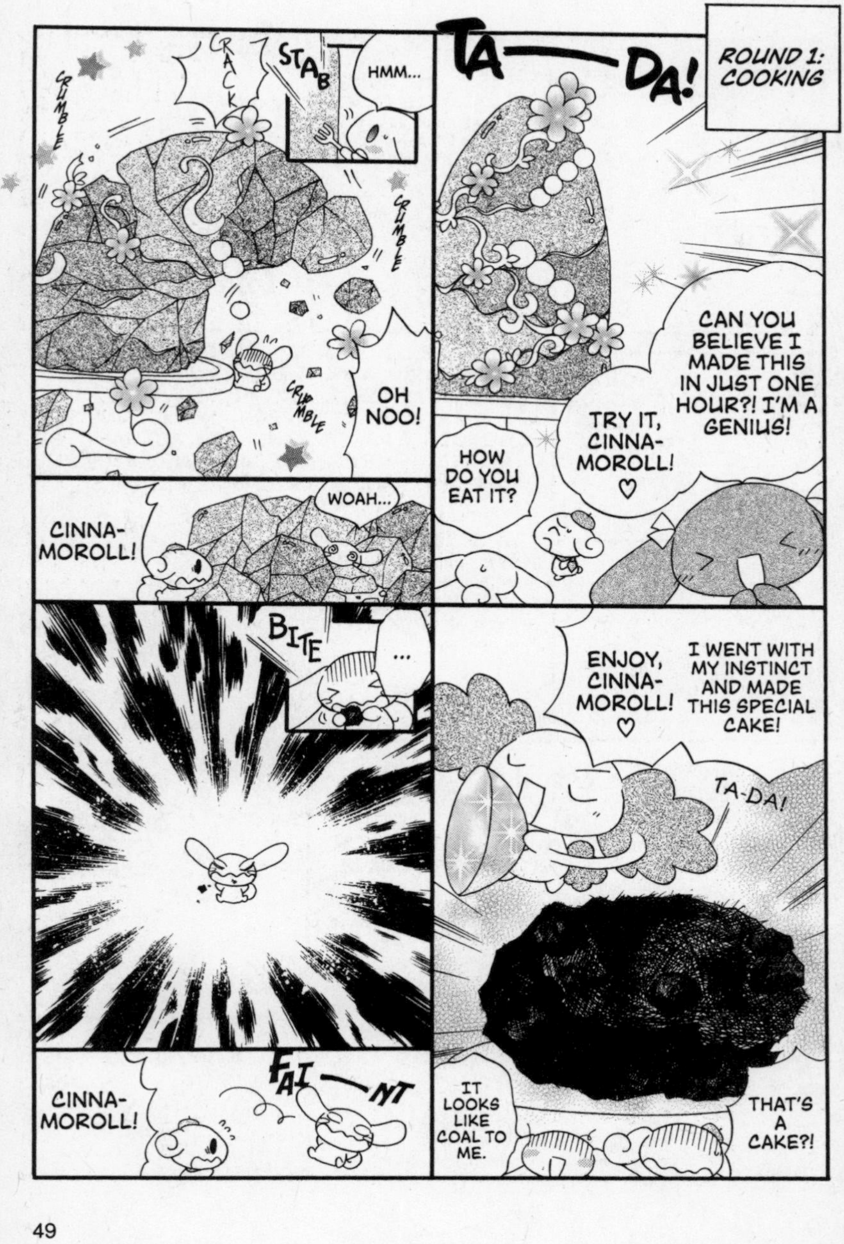
TA—DA!
ROUND 1: COOKING
CAN YOU BELIEVE I MADE THIS IN JUST ONE HOUR?! I'M A GENIUS!
TRY IT, CINNA-MOROLL! ♡
HOW DO YOU EAT IT?
HMM...
STAB
CRACK
CRUMBLE
CRUMBLE
OH NOO!
CRUMBLE
WOAH...
CINNA-MOROLL!
I WENT WITH MY INSTINCT AND MADE THIS SPECIAL CAKE!
ENJOY, CINNA-MOROLL! ♡
TA-DA!
THAT'S A CAKE?!
IT LOOKS LIKE COAL TO ME.
BITE
...
FAI—NT
CINNA-MOROLL!

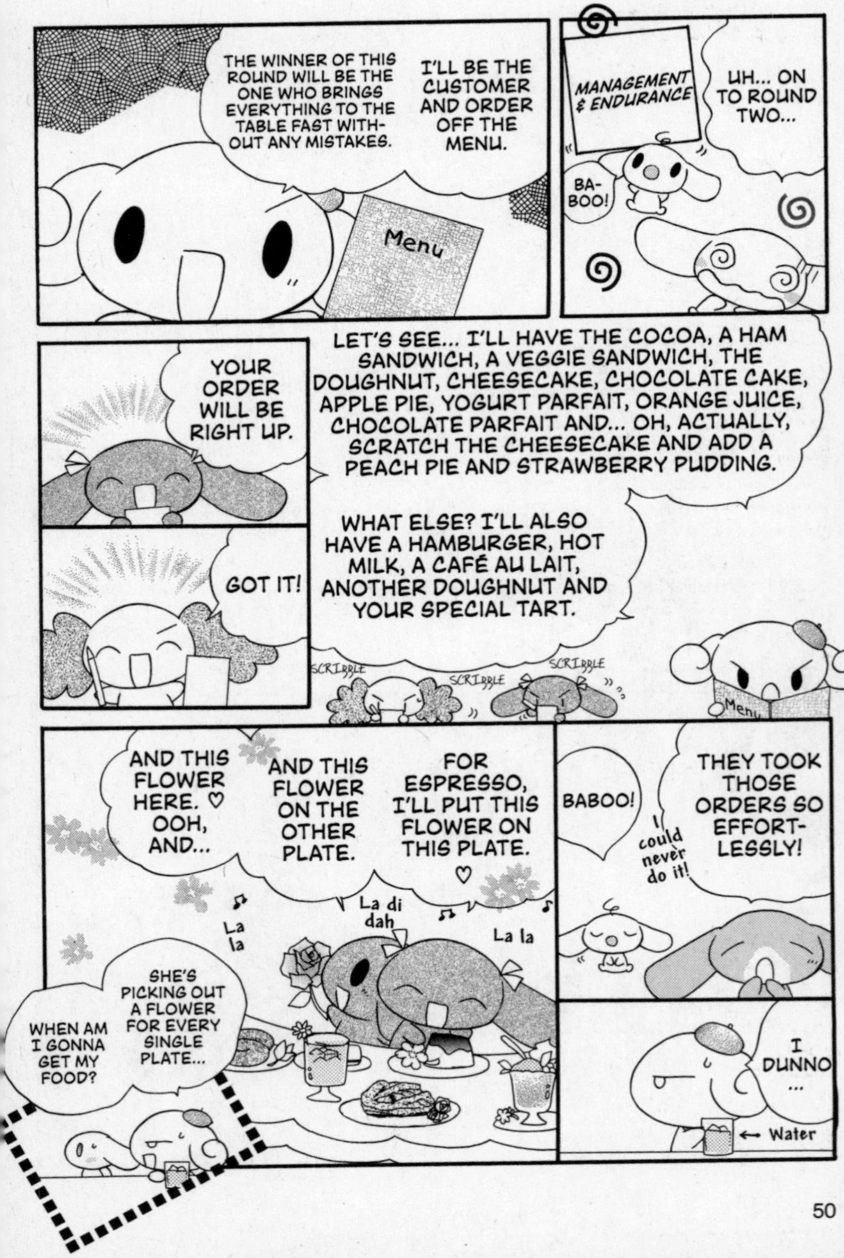
MANAGEMENT & ENDURANCE
UH... ON TO ROUND TWO...
BA-BOO!
I'LL BE THE CUSTOMER AND ORDER OFF THE MENU.
THE WINNER OF THIS ROUND WILL BE THE ONE WHO BRINGS EVERYTHING TO THE TABLE FAST WITH-OUT ANY MISTAKES.
Menu
LET'S SEE... I'LL HAVE THE COCOA, A HAM SANDWICH, A VEGGIE SANDWICH, THE DOUGHNUT, CHEESECAKE, CHOCOLATE CAKE, APPLE PIE, YOGURT PARFAIT, ORANGE JUICE, CHOCOLATE PARFAIT AND... OH, ACTUALLY, SCRATCH THE CHEESECAKE AND ADD A PEACH PIE AND STRAWBERRY PUDDING.
YOUR ORDER WILL BE RIGHT UP.
WHAT ELSE? I'LL ALSO HAVE A HAMBURGER, HOT MILK, A CAFÉ AU LAIT, ANOTHER DOUGHNUT AND YOUR SPECIAL TART.
GOT IT!
Menu
SCRIBBLE
SCRIBBLE
SCRIBBLE
THEY TOOK THOSE ORDERS SO EFFORT-LESSLY!
I could never do it!
BABOO!
I DUNNO...
Water
FOR ESPRESSO, I'LL PUT THIS FLOWER ON THIS PLATE. ♡
AND THIS FLOWER ON THE OTHER PLATE.
AND THIS FLOWER HERE. ♡ OOH, AND...
La la
La di dah
La la
SHE'S PICKING OUT A FLOWER FOR EVERY SINGLE PLATE...
WHEN AM I GONNA GET MY FOOD?

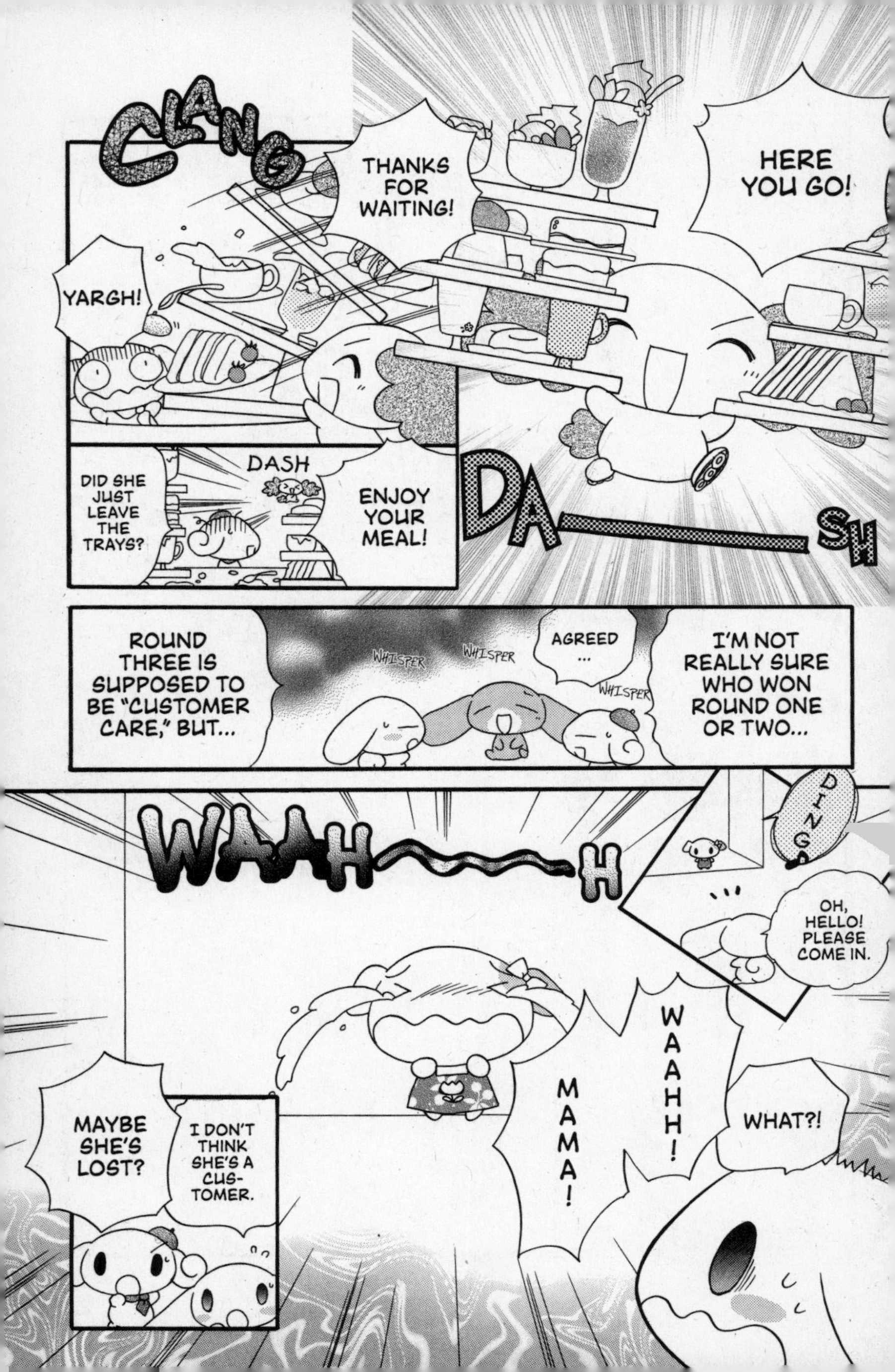
HERE YOU GO!
THANKS FOR WAITING!
DA——SH
CLANG
YARGH!
ENJOY YOUR MEAL!
DASH
DID SHE JUST LEAVE THE TRAYS?
I'M NOT REALLY SURE WHO WON ROUND ONE OR TWO...
WHISPER
AGREED...
WHISPER
WHISPER
ROUND THREE IS SUPPOSED TO BE "CUSTOMER CARE," BUT...
DING
OH, HELLO! PLEASE COME IN.
WAAAH——H
WHAT?!
WAAHH!
MAMA!
I DON'T THINK SHE'S A CUS-TOMER.
MAYBE SHE'S LOST?

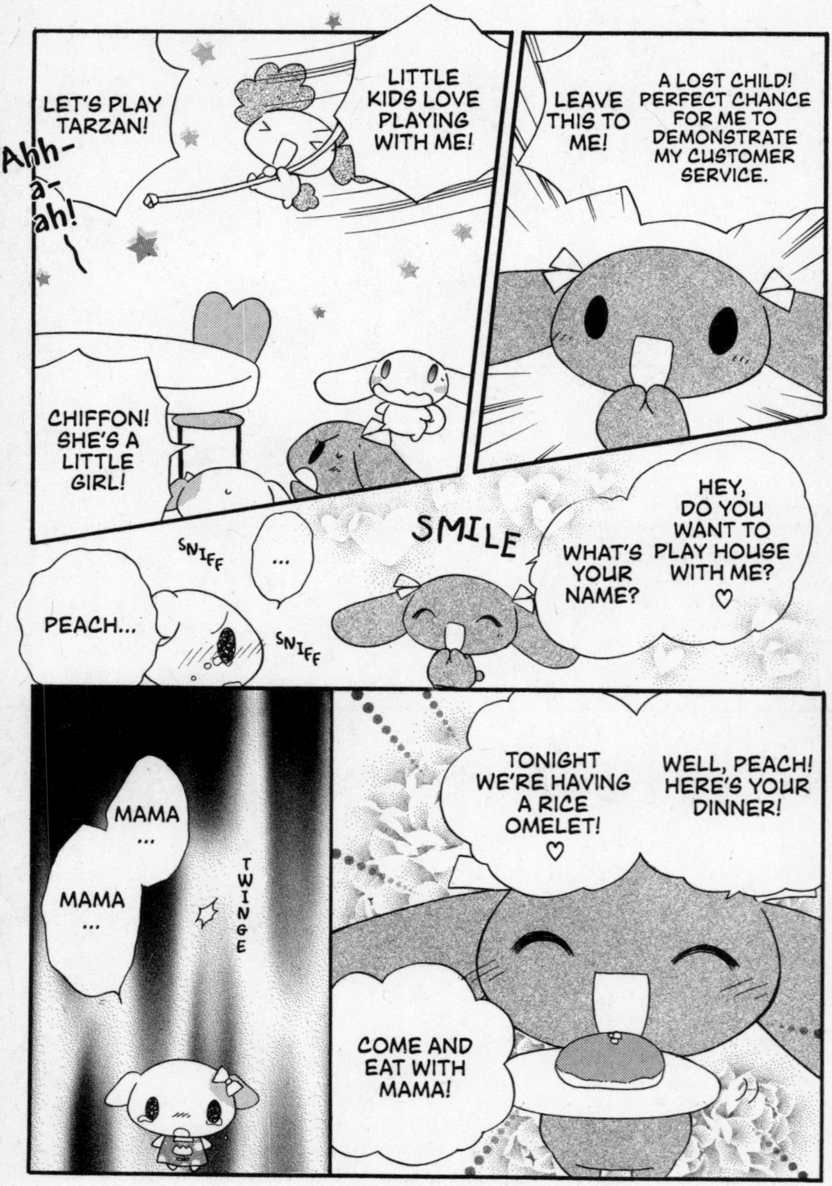
A LOST CHILD! PERFECT CHANCE FOR ME TO DEMONSTRATE MY CUSTOMER SERVICE.
LEAVE THIS TO ME!
LITTLE KIDS LOVE PLAYING WITH ME!
LET'S PLAY TARZAN!
Ahh-a-ah!
CHIFFON! SHE'S A LITTLE GIRL!
HEY, DO YOU WANT TO PLAY HOUSE WITH ME? ♡
WHAT'S YOUR NAME?
SMILE
...
SNIFF
PEACH...
SNIFF
WELL, PEACH! HERE'S YOUR DINNER!
TONIGHT WE'RE HAVING A RICE OMELET! ♡
COME AND EAT WITH MAMA!
MAMA ...
TWINGE
MAMA ...

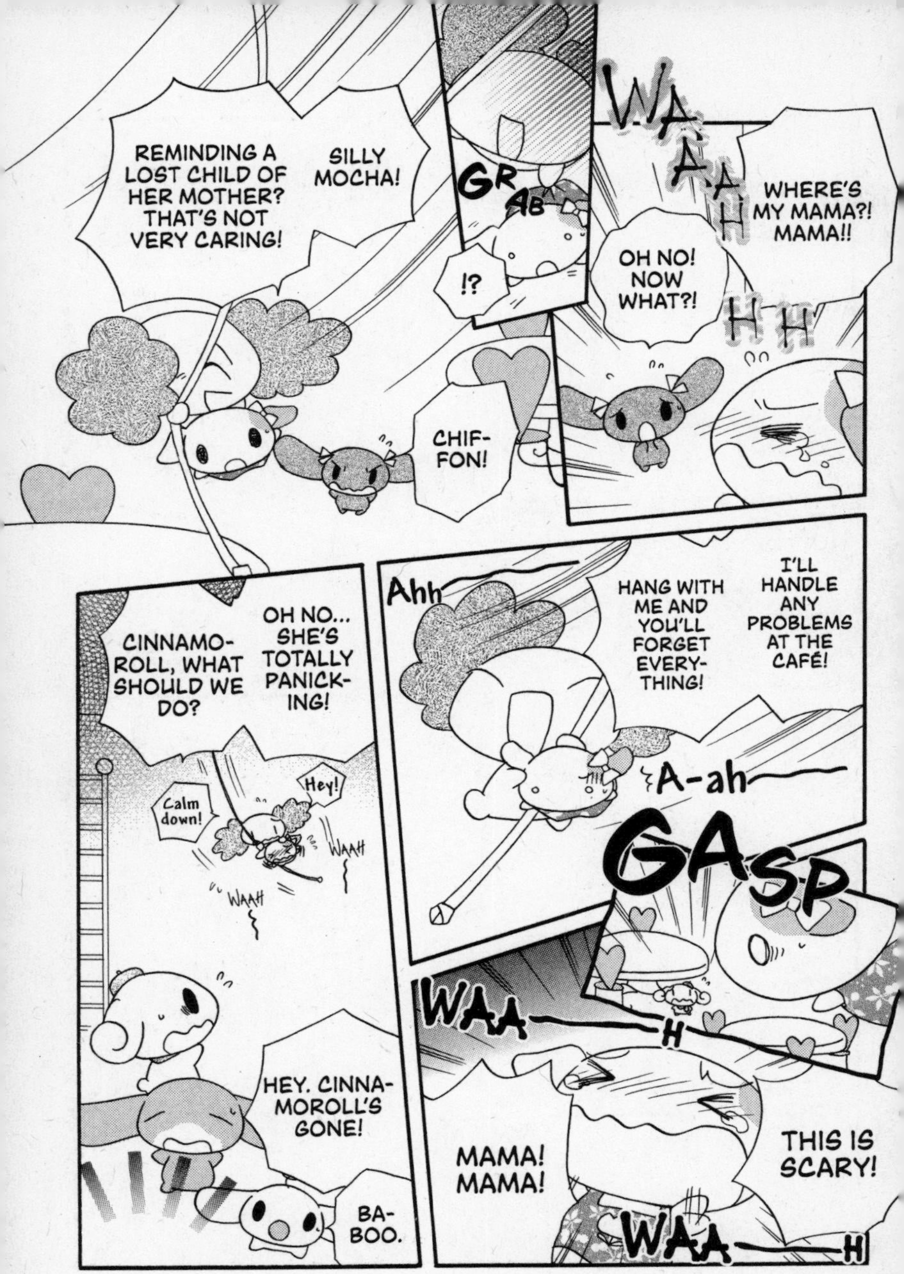
WAAAHHH
WHERE'S MY MAMA?! MAMA!!
OH NO! NOW WHAT?!
GRAB
!?
SILLY MOCHA!
REMINDING A LOST CHILD OF HER MOTHER? THAT'S NOT VERY CARING!
CHIF-FON!
I'LL HANDLE ANY PROBLEMS AT THE CAFÉ!
HANG WITH ME AND YOU'LL FORGET EVERY-THING!
Ahh
A-ah
GASP
THIS IS SCARY!
MAMA! MAMA!
WAAH
WAAH
OH NO... SHE'S TOTALLY PANICK-ING!
CINNAMO-ROLL, WHAT SHOULD WE DO?
Hey!
Calm down!
WAAH
WAAH
HEY. CINNA-MOROLL'S GONE!
BA-BOO.

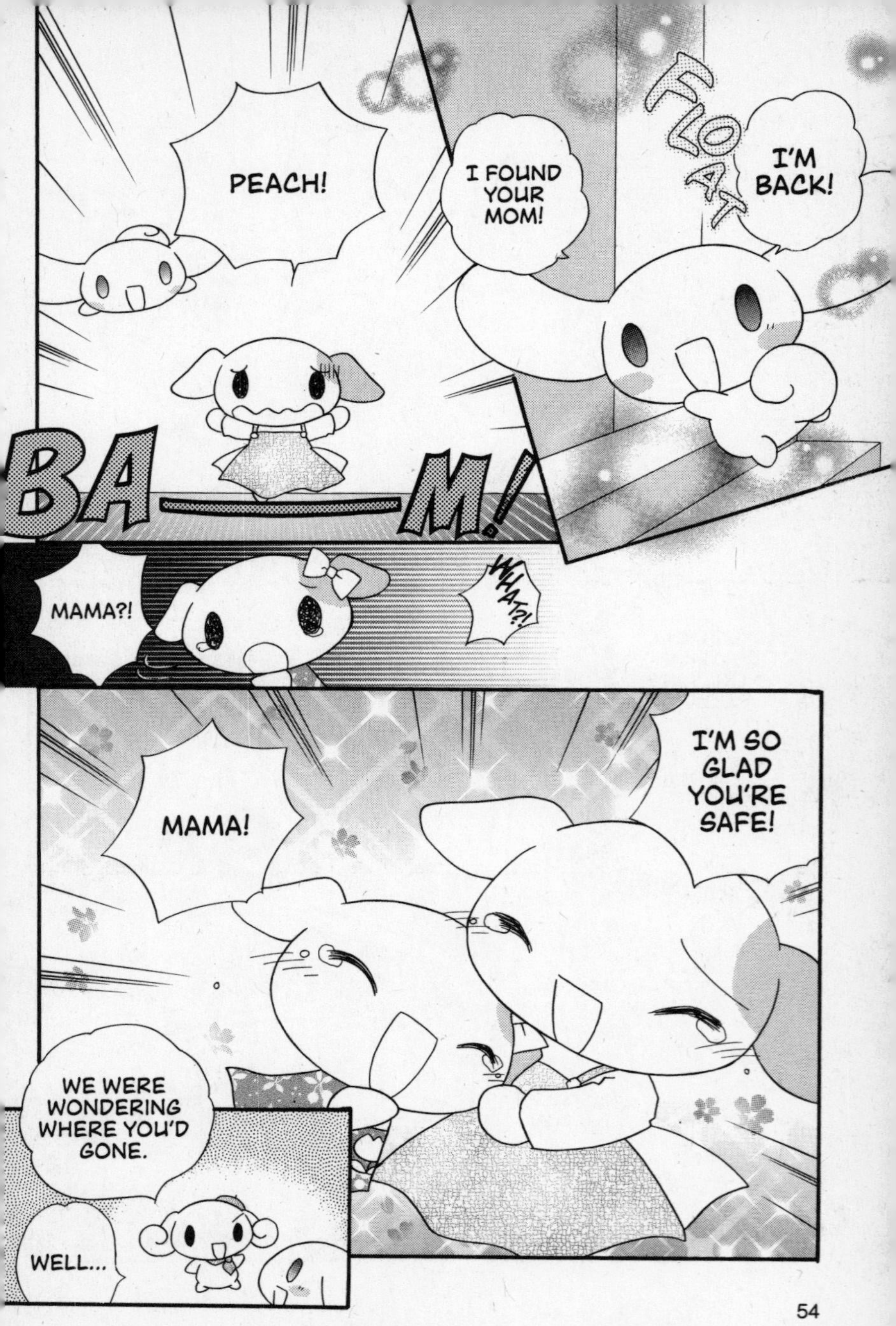
I'M BACK!
FLOAT
I FOUND YOUR MOM!
PEACH!
BA—M!
WHAT?!
MAMA?!
I'M SO GLAD YOU'RE SAFE!
MAMA!
WE WERE WONDERING WHERE YOU'D GONE.
WELL...

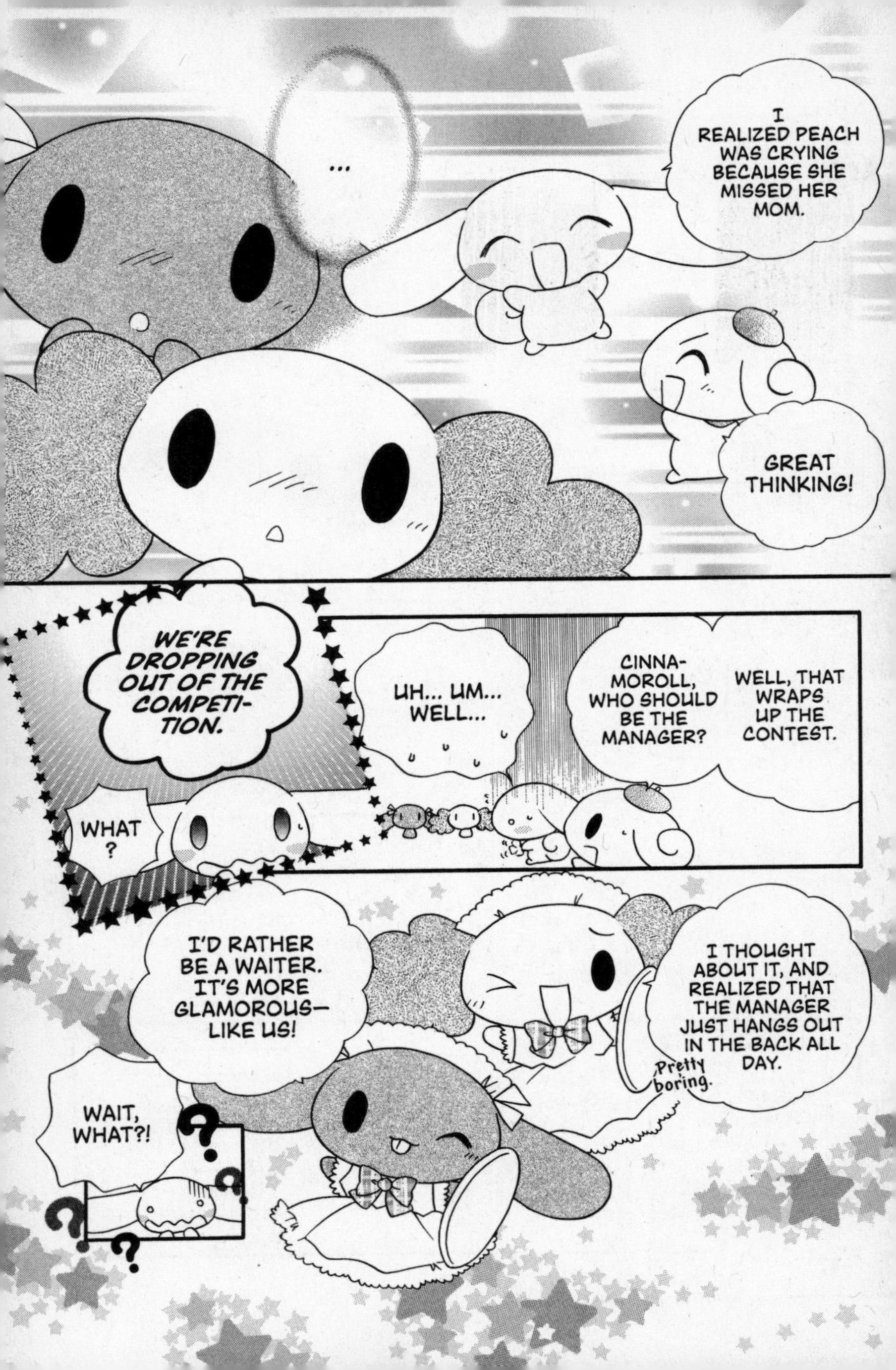
I REALIZED PEACH WAS CRYING BECAUSE SHE MISSED HER MOM.
GREAT THINKING!
...
WELL, THAT WRAPS UP THE CONTEST.
CINNA-MOROLL, WHO SHOULD BE THE MANAGER?
UH... UM... WELL...
WE'RE DROPPING OUT OF THE COMPETI-TION.
WHAT?
I THOUGHT ABOUT IT, AND REALIZED THAT THE MANAGER JUST HANGS OUT IN THE BACK ALL DAY.
Pretty boring.
I'D RATHER BE A WAITER. IT'S MORE GLAMOROUS—LIKE US!
WAIT, WHAT?!

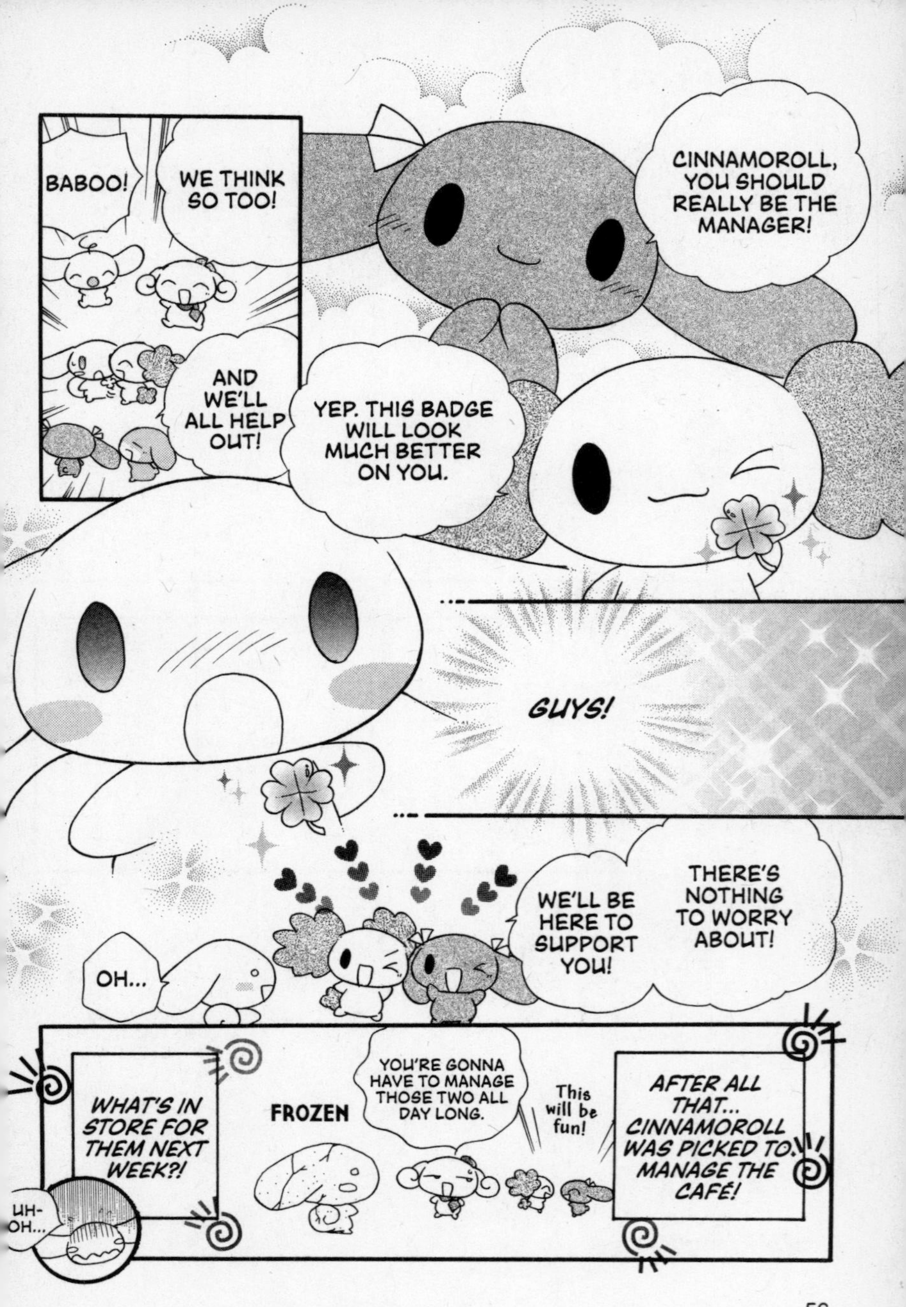
CINNAMOROLL, YOU SHOULD REALLY BE THE MANAGER!
YEP. THIS BADGE WILL LOOK MUCH BETTER ON YOU.
WE THINK SO TOO!
BABOO!
AND WE'LL ALL HELP OUT!
...
GUYS!
...
THERE'S NOTHING TO WORRY ABOUT!
WE'LL BE HERE TO SUPPORT YOU!
OH...
AFTER ALL THAT... CINNAMOROLL WAS PICKED TO MANAGE THE CAFÉ!
This will be fun!
YOU'RE GONNA HAVE TO MANAGE THOSE TWO ALL DAY LONG.
FROZEN
WHAT'S IN STORE FOR THEM NEXT WEEK?!
UH-OH...

# Manager for the Day! (Part 2)

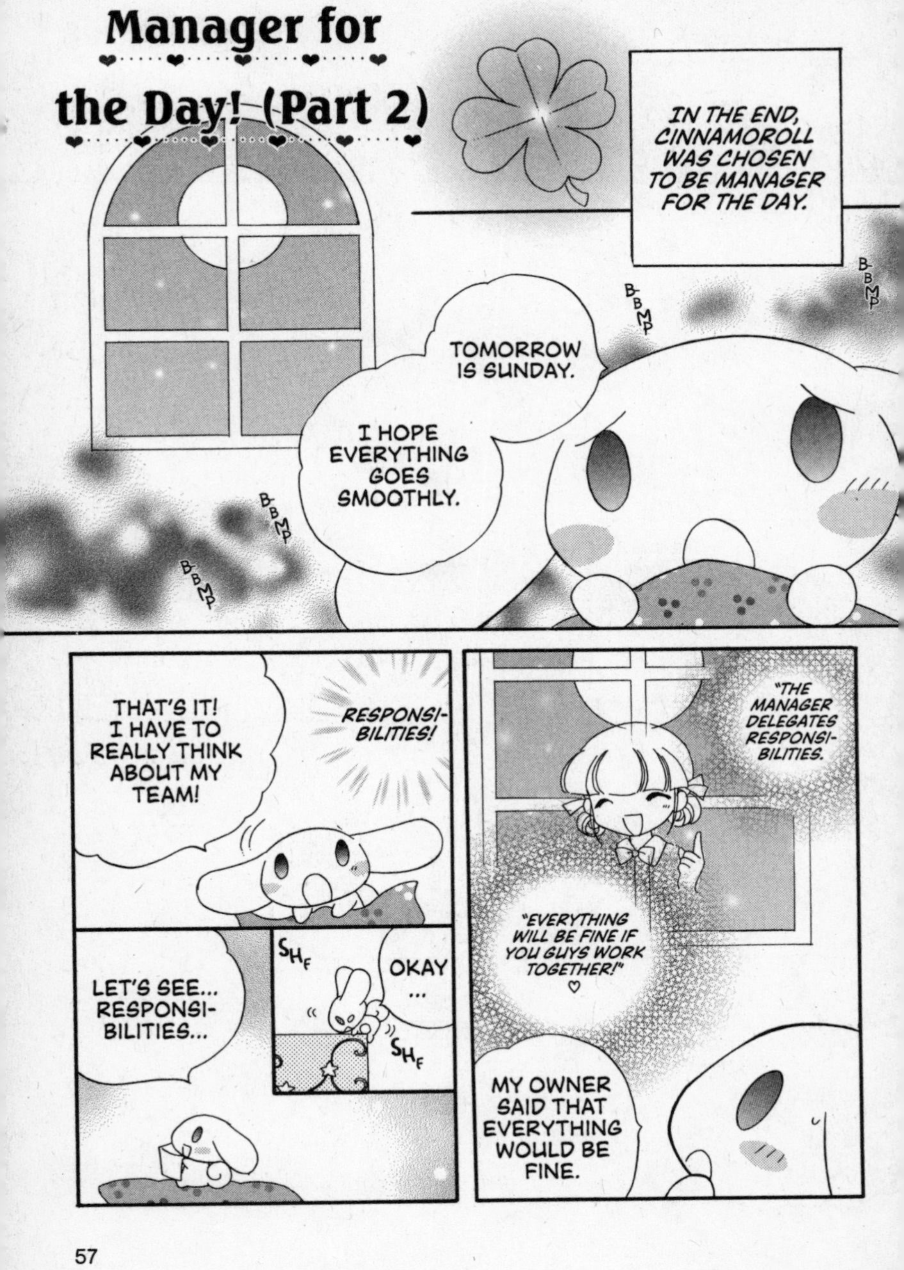

IN THE END, CINNAMOROLL WAS CHOSEN TO BE MANAGER FOR THE DAY.
B-BMP
B-BMP
TOMORROW IS SUNDAY.
I HOPE EVERYTHING GOES SMOOTHLY.
B-BMP
B-BMP
"THE MANAGER DELEGATES RESPONSI-BILITIES.
"EVERYTHING WILL BE FINE IF YOU GUYS WORK TOGETHER!" ♡
MY OWNER SAID THAT EVERYTHING WOULD BE FINE.
RESPONSI-BILITIES!
THAT'S IT! I HAVE TO REALLY THINK ABOUT MY TEAM!
OKAY ...
SHF
SHF
LET'S SEE... RESPONSI-BILITIES...

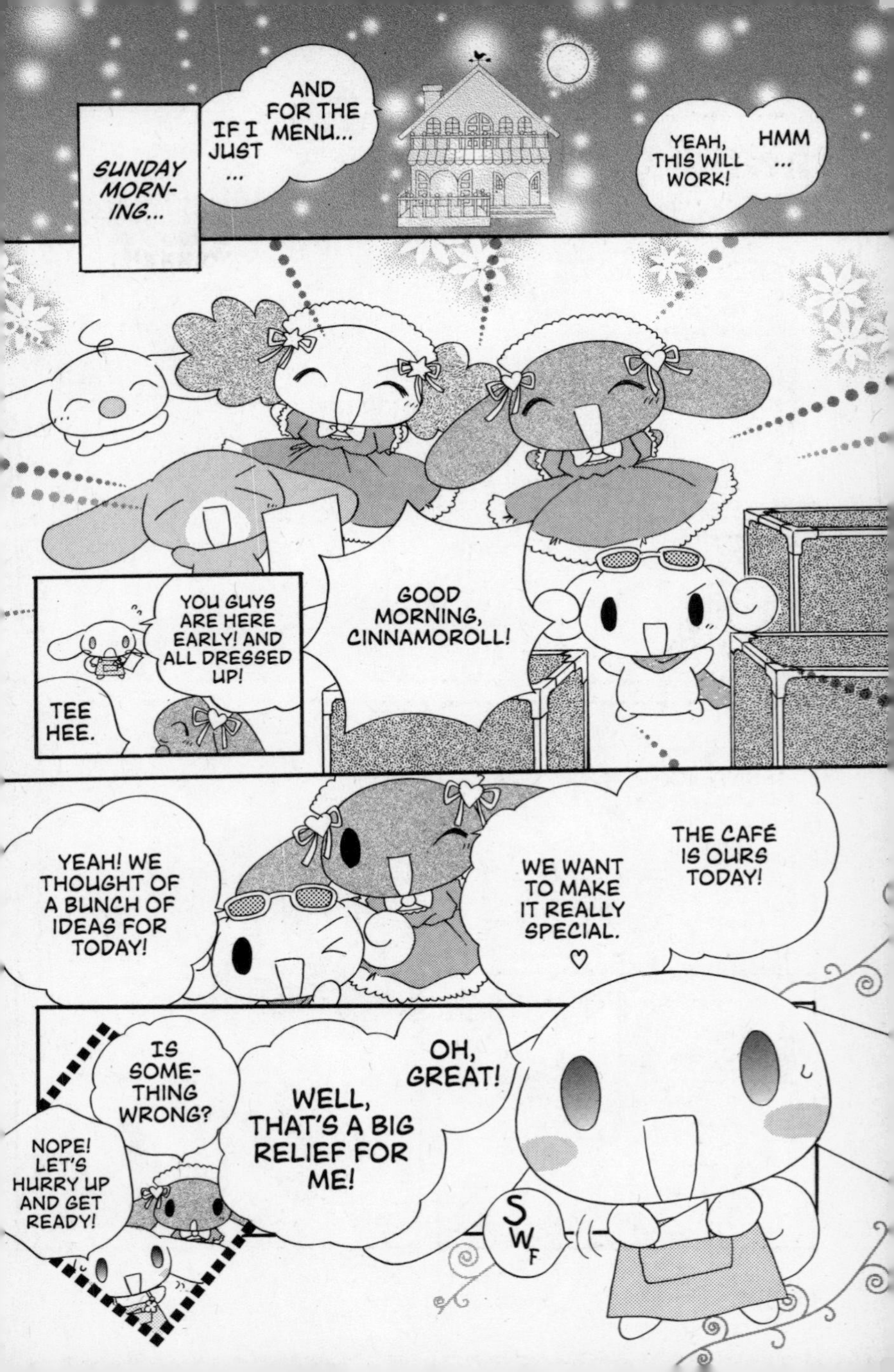
HMM ...
YEAH, THIS WILL WORK!
AND FOR THE MENU...
IF I JUST ...
SUNDAY MORNING...
GOOD MORNING, CINNAMOROLL!
YOU GUYS ARE HERE EARLY! AND ALL DRESSED UP!
TEE HEE.
THE CAFÉ IS OURS TODAY!
WE WANT TO MAKE IT REALLY SPECIAL. ♡
YEAH! WE THOUGHT OF A BUNCH OF IDEAS FOR TODAY!
OH, GREAT!
WELL, THAT'S A BIG RELIEF FOR ME!
SWF
IS SOMETHING WRONG?
NOPE! LET'S HURRY UP AND GET READY!

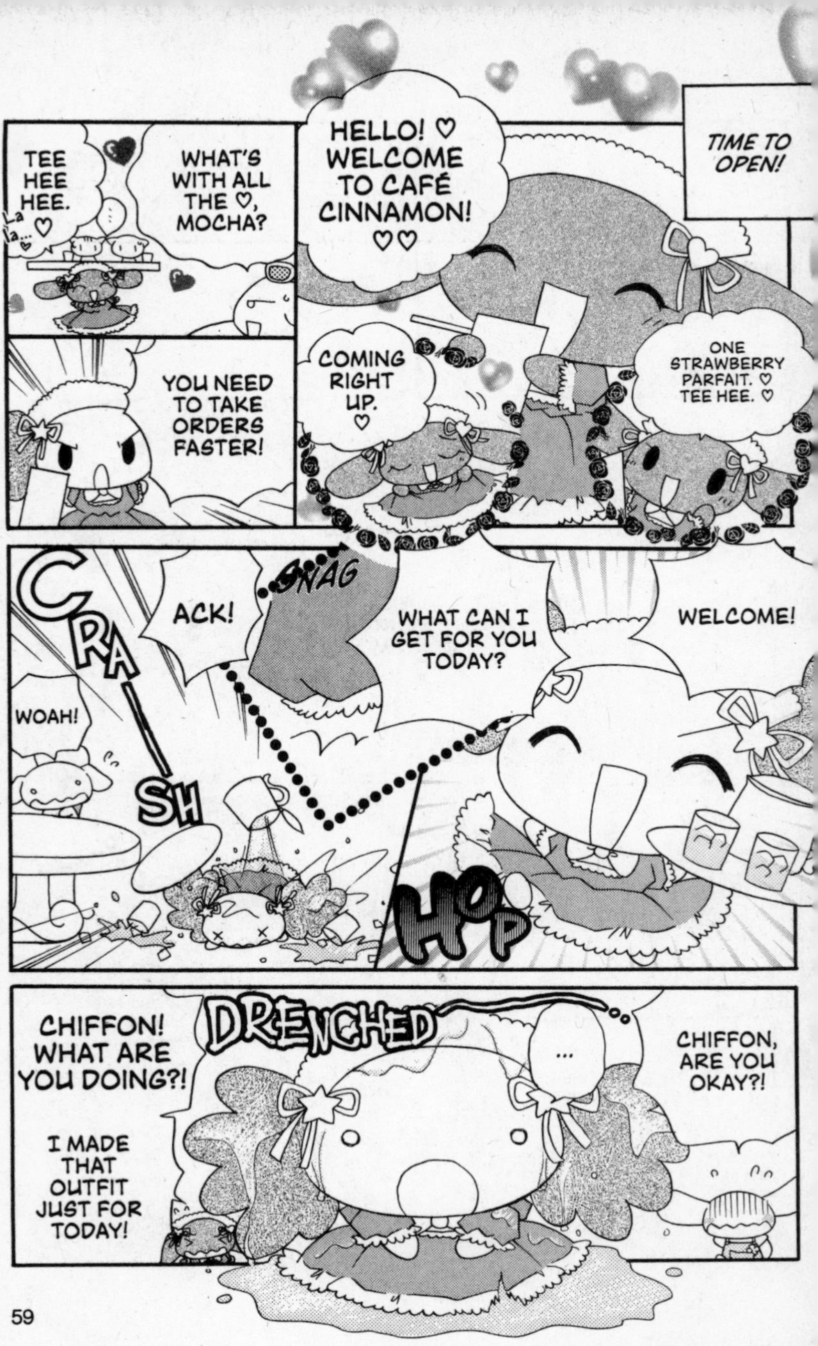
TIME TO OPEN!
HELLO! ♡ WELCOME TO CAFÉ CINNAMON! ♡♡
ONE STRAWBERRY PARFAIT. ♡ TEE HEE. ♡
COMING RIGHT UP. ♡
WHAT'S WITH ALL THE ♡, MOCHA?
TEE HEE HEE.
La la... ♡
YOU NEED TO TAKE ORDERS FASTER!
WELCOME!
WHAT CAN I GET FOR YOU TODAY?
HOP
SNAG
ACK!
CRASH
WOAH!
CHIFFON, ARE YOU OKAY?!
...
DRENCHED
CHIFFON! WHAT ARE YOU DOING?!
I MADE THAT OUTFIT JUST FOR TODAY!

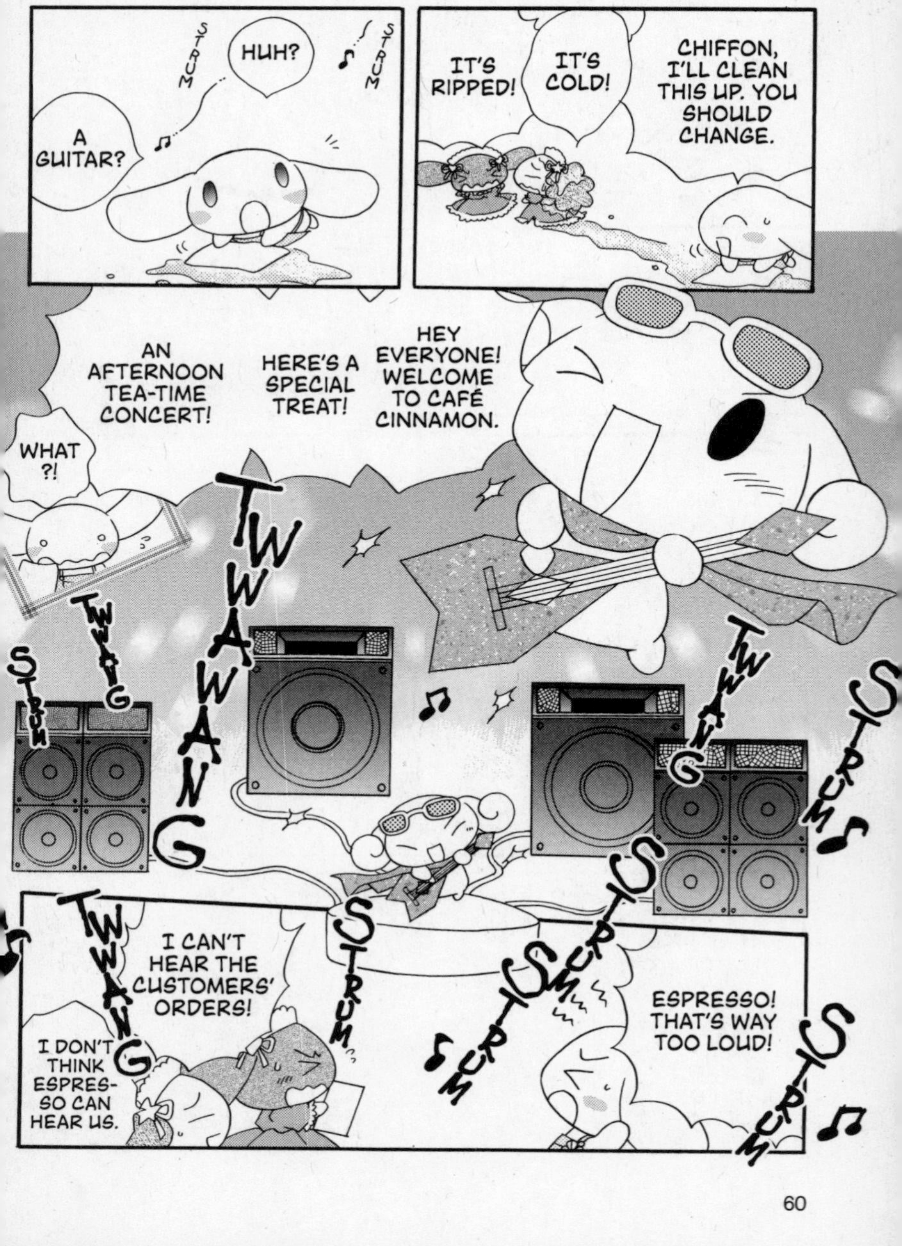
CHIFFON, I'LL CLEAN THIS UP. YOU SHOULD CHANGE.
IT'S COLD!
IT'S RIPPED!
STRUM
HUH?
STRUM
A GUITAR?
HEY EVERYONE! WELCOME TO CAFÉ CINNAMON.
HERE'S A SPECIAL TREAT!
AN AFTERNOON TEA-TIME CONCERT!
WHAT?!
STRUM
TWWANG
STRUM
TWWAWANG
TWWANG
STRUM
ESPRESSO! THAT'S WAY TOO LOUD!
STRUM
STRUM
STRUM
I CAN'T HEAR THE CUSTOMERS' ORDERS!
TWWANG
I DON'T THINK ESPRES-SO CAN HEAR US.

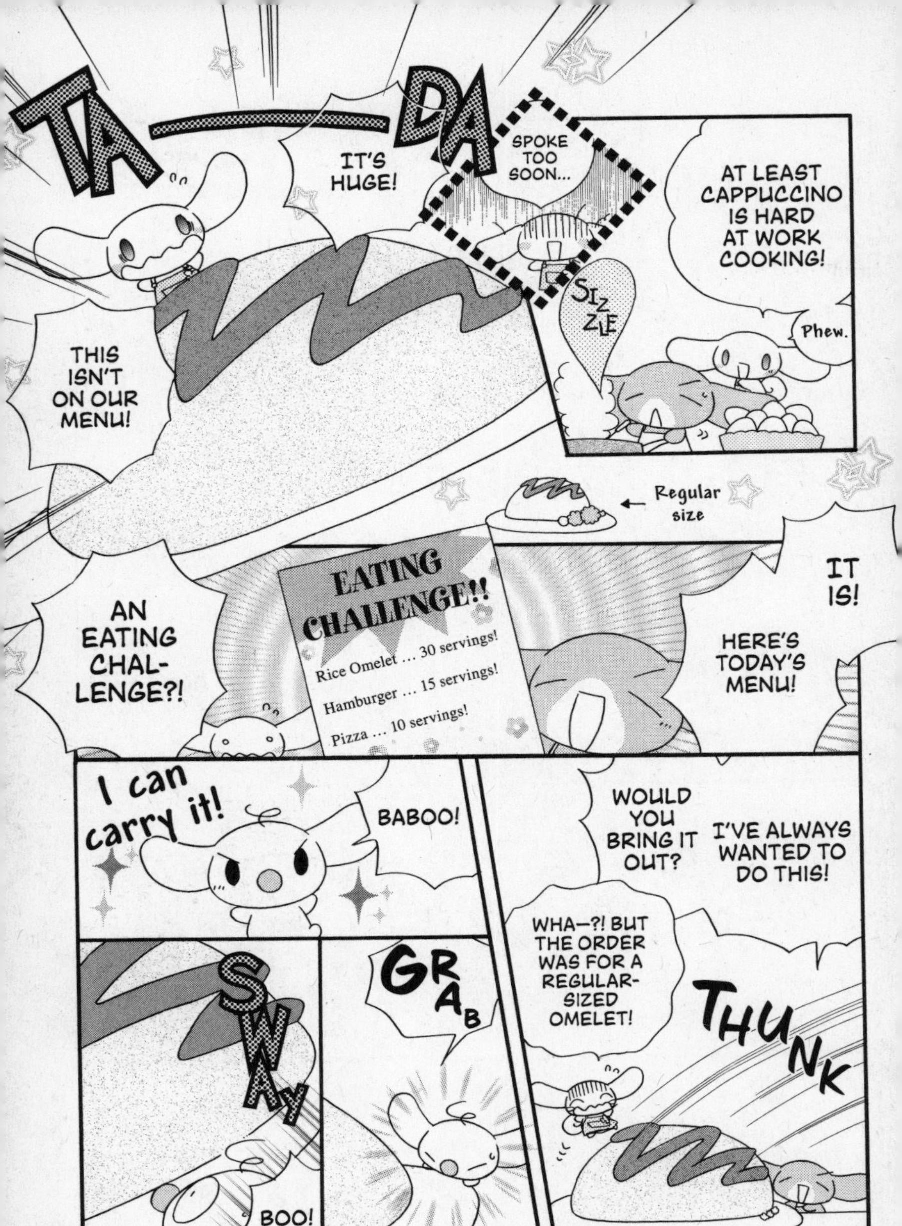
AT LEAST CAPPUCCINO IS HARD AT WORK COOKING!
Phew.
SIZZLE
SPOKE TOO SOON...
IT'S HUGE!
TA—DA
THIS ISN'T ON OUR MENU!
← Regular size
IT IS!
HERE'S TODAY'S MENU!
EATING CHALLENGE!!
Rice Omelet … 30 servings!
Hamburger … 15 servings!
Pizza … 10 servings!
AN EATING CHAL-LENGE?!
I'VE ALWAYS WANTED TO DO THIS!
WOULD YOU BRING IT OUT?
WHA—?! BUT THE ORDER WAS FOR A REGULAR-SIZED OMELET!
THUNK
BABOO!
I can carry it!
GRAB
SWAY
BOO!

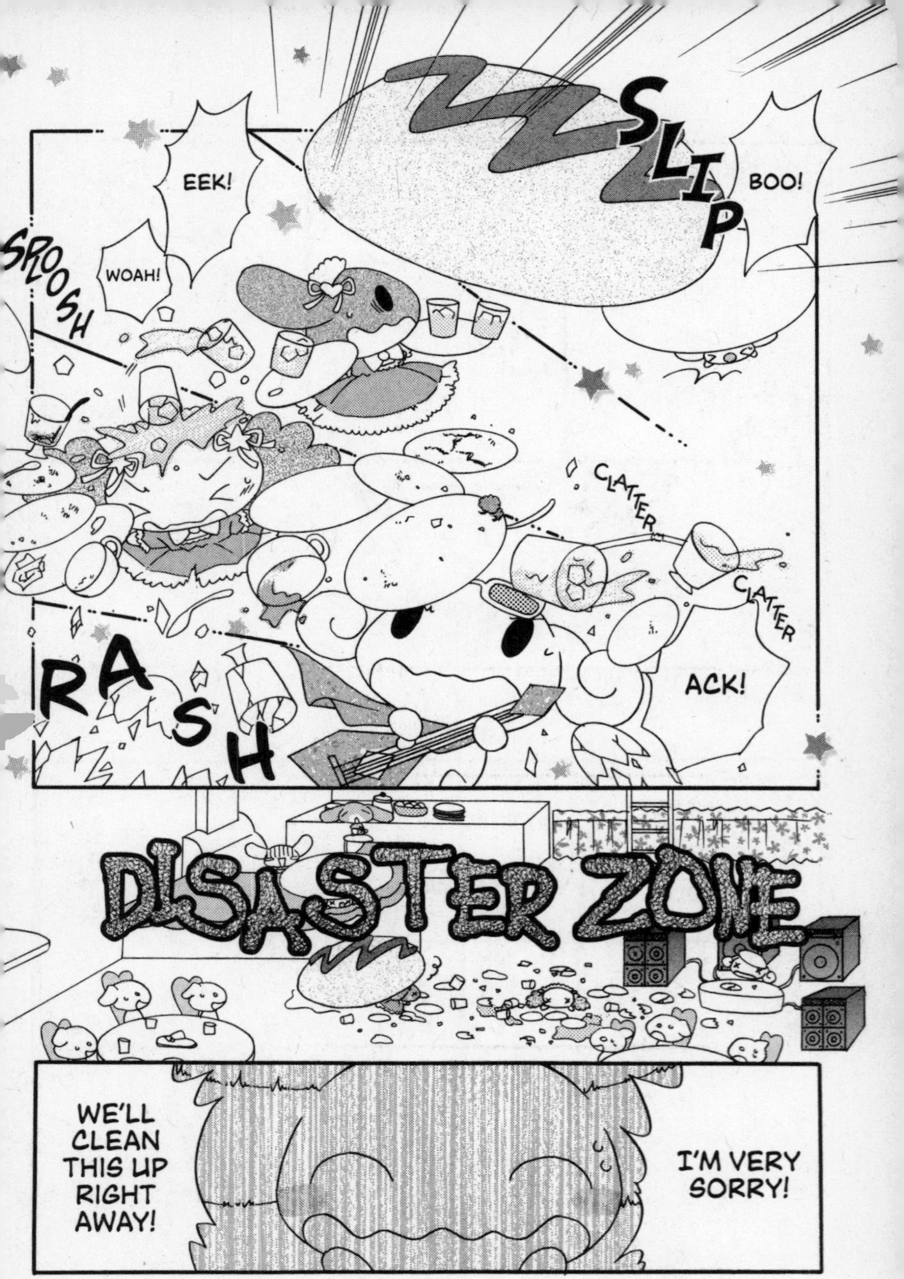
SLIP
BOO!
EEK!
WOAH!
SROOSH
CLATTER
CLATTER
ACK!
RASH
DISASTER ZONE
I'M VERY SORRY!
WE'LL CLEAN THIS UP RIGHT AWAY!

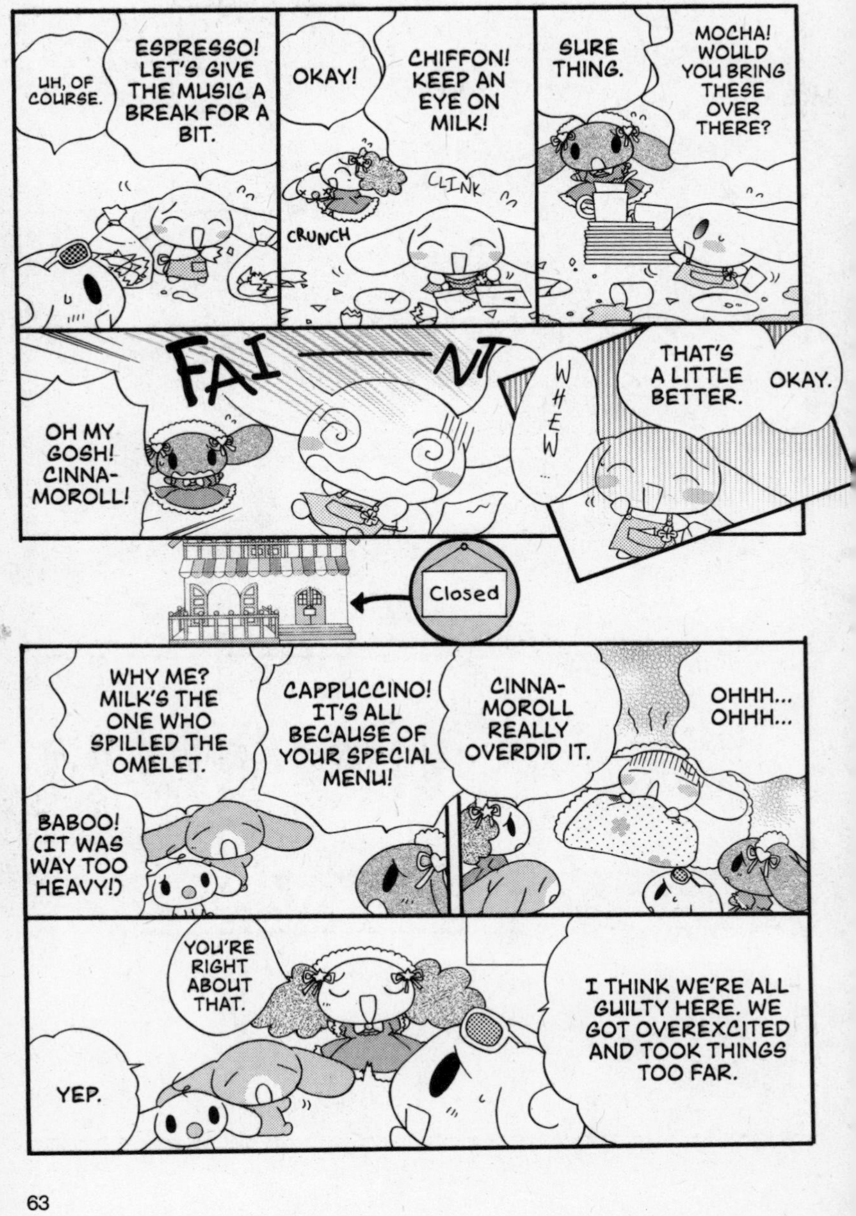
MOCHA! WOULD YOU BRING THESE OVER THERE?
SURE THING.
CHIFFON! KEEP AN EYE ON MILK!
OKAY!
CLINK
CRUNCH
ESPRESSO! LET'S GIVE THE MUSIC A BREAK FOR A BIT.
UH, OF COURSE.
THAT'S A LITTLE BETTER.
OKAY.
WHEW...
FAI——NT
OH MY GOSH! CINNAMOROLL!
Closed
OHHH... OHHH...
CINNAMOROLL REALLY OVERDID IT.
CAPPUCCINO! IT'S ALL BECAUSE OF YOUR SPECIAL MENU!
WHY ME? MILK'S THE ONE WHO SPILLED THE OMELET.
BABOO! (IT WAS WAY TOO HEAVY!)
I THINK WE'RE ALL GUILTY HERE. WE GOT OVEREXCITED AND TOOK THINGS TOO FAR.
YOU'RE RIGHT ABOUT THAT.
YEP.

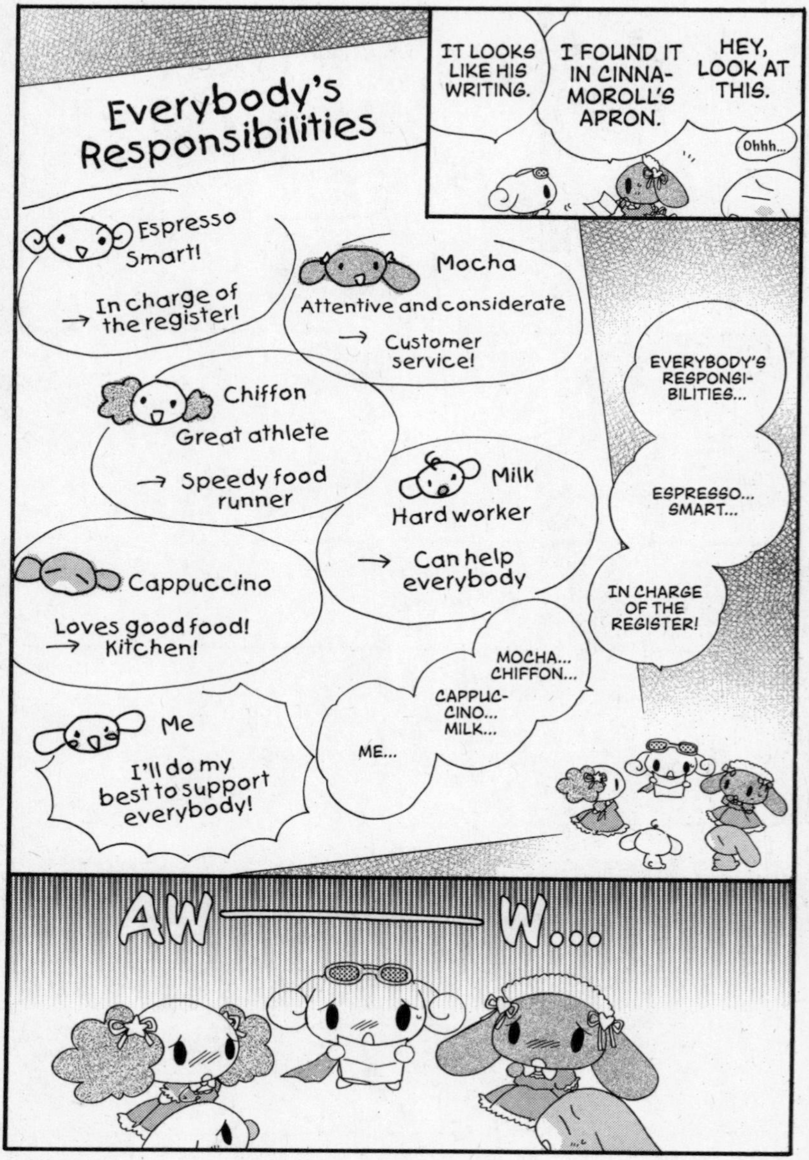
HEY, LOOK AT THIS.
I FOUND IT IN CINNA-MOROLL'S APRON.
IT LOOKS LIKE HIS WRITING.
Ohhh...
Everybody's Responsibilities
Espresso Smart! → In charge of the register!
Mocha Attentive and considerate → Customer service!
Chiffon Great athlete → Speedy food runner
Milk Hard worker → Can help everybody
Cappuccino Loves good food! → Kitchen!
Me I'll do my best to support everybody!
EVERYBODY'S RESPONSI-BILITIES...
ESPRESSO... SMART...
IN CHARGE OF THE REGISTER!
MOCHA... CHIFFON...
CAPPUC-CINO... MILK...
ME...
AW———W...

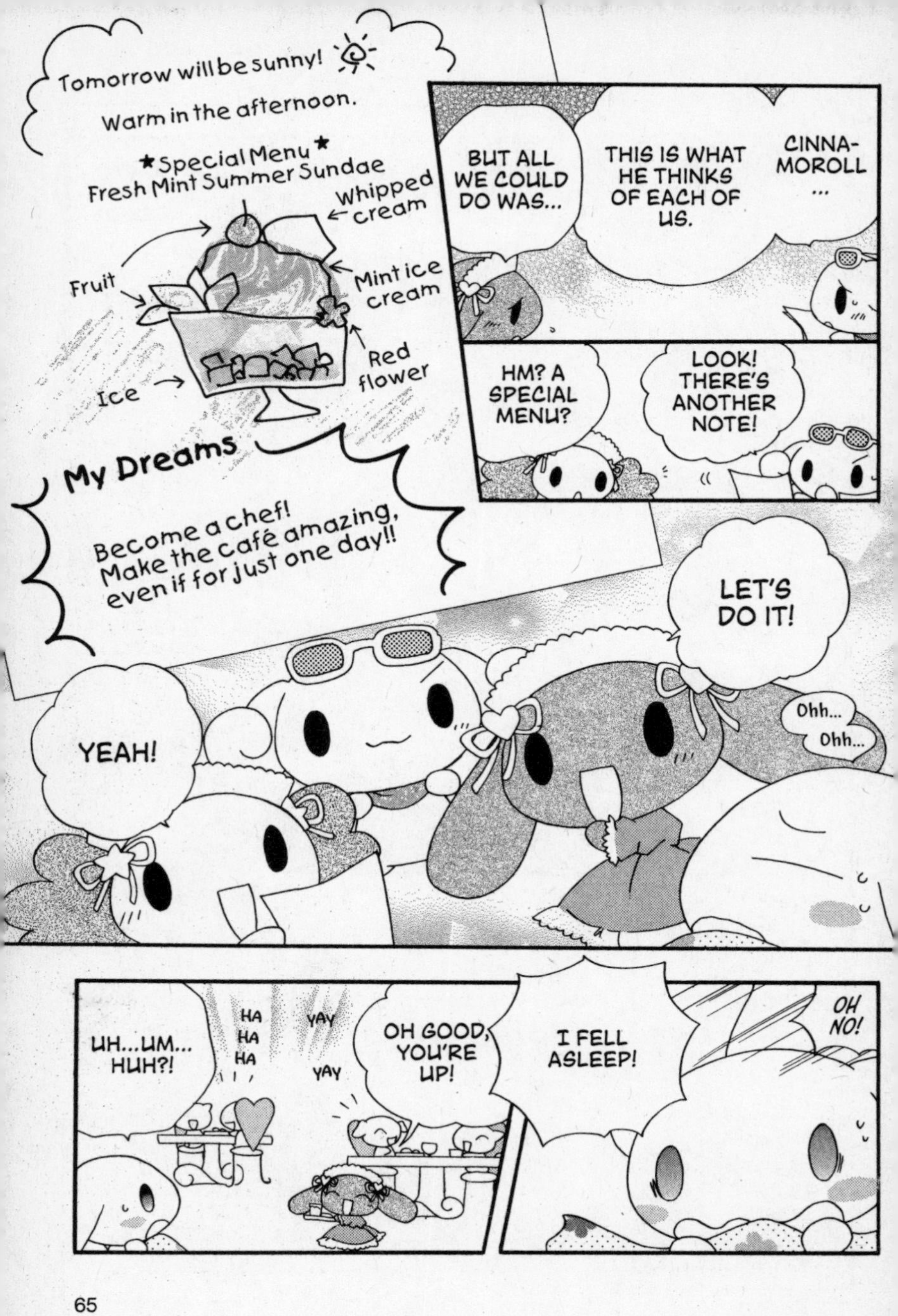
CINNA-MOROLL ...
THIS IS WHAT HE THINKS OF EACH OF US.
BUT ALL WE COULD DO WAS...
LOOK! THERE'S ANOTHER NOTE!
HM? A SPECIAL MENU?
Tomorrow will be sunny!
Warm in the afternoon.
★Special Menu★
Fresh Mint Summer Sundae
Whipped cream
Fruit
Mint ice cream
Red flower
Ice
My Dreams
Become a chef!
Make the café amazing, even if for just one day!!
LET'S DO IT!
Ohh... Ohh...
YEAH!
OH NO!
I FELL ASLEEP!
OH GOOD, YOU'RE UP!
YAY
YAY
HA HA HA
UH...UM... HUH?!

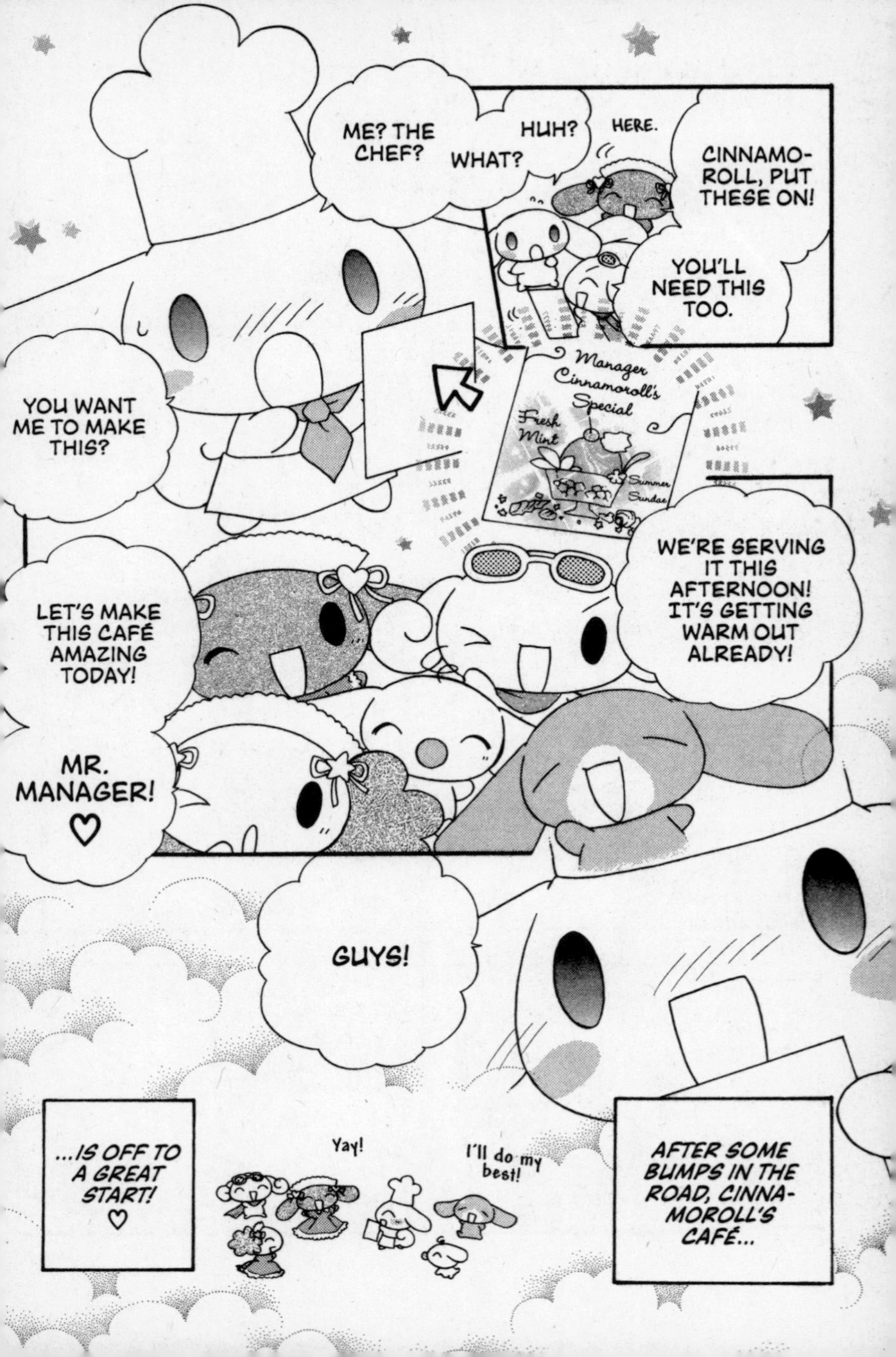
CINNAMO-ROLL, PUT THESE ON!
HERE.
YOU'LL NEED THIS TOO.
HUH?
WHAT?
ME? THE CHEF?
YOU WANT ME TO MAKE THIS?
Manager Cinnamoroll's Special
Fresh Mint
Summer Sundae
WE'RE SERVING IT THIS AFTERNOON! IT'S GETTING WARM OUT ALREADY!
LET'S MAKE THIS CAFÉ AMAZING TODAY!
MR. MANAGER! ♡
GUYS!
AFTER SOME BUMPS IN THE ROAD, CINNA-MOROLL'S CAFÉ...
I'll do my best!
Yay!
...IS OFF TO A GREAT START! ♡

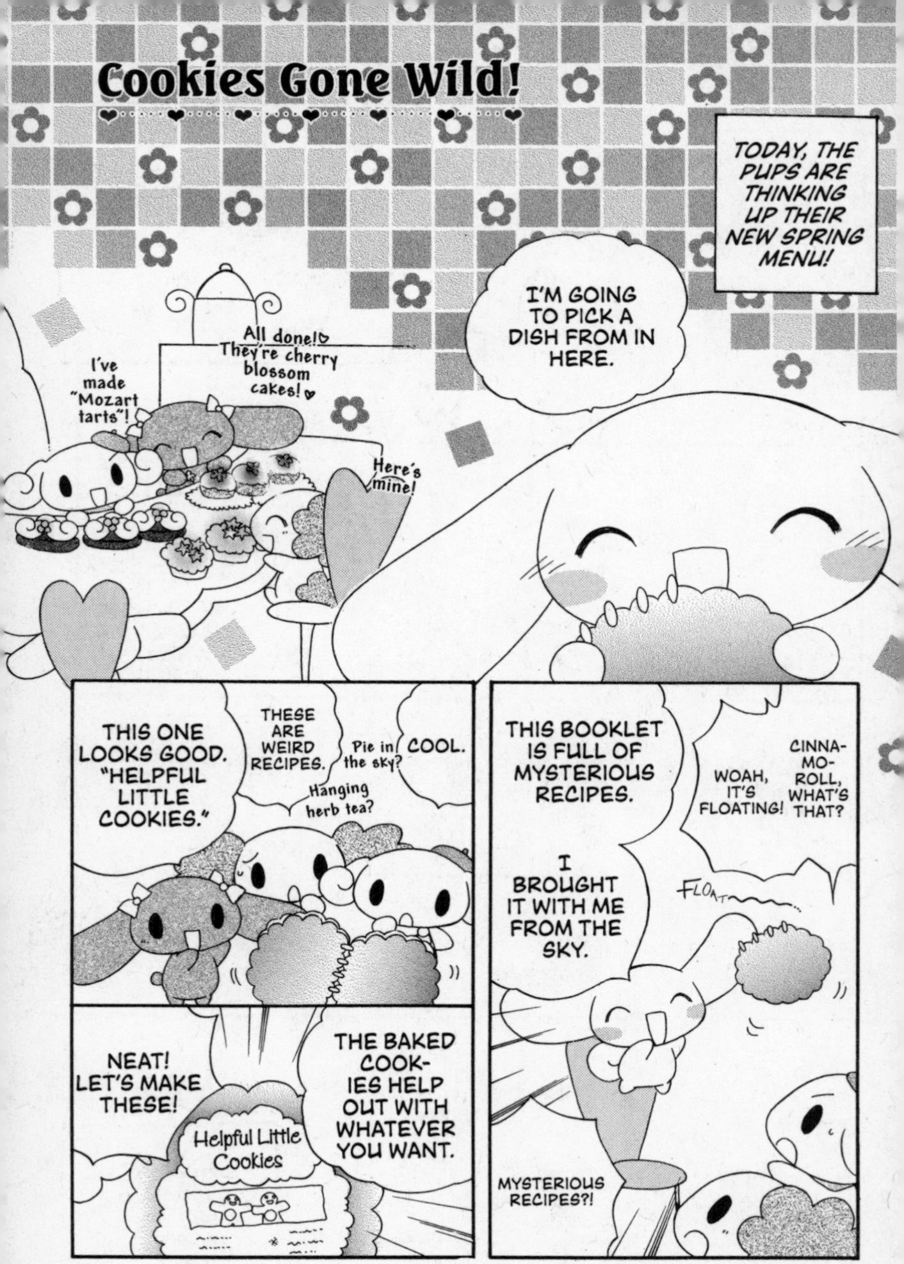
Cookies Gone Wild!
TODAY, THE PUPS ARE THINKING UP THEIR NEW SPRING MENU!
I'M GOING TO PICK A DISH FROM IN HERE.
Here's mine!
All done!♡ They're cherry blossom cakes!♡
I've made "Mozart tarts"!
CINNA-MO-ROLL, WHAT'S THAT?
WOAH, IT'S FLOATING!
THIS BOOKLET IS FULL OF MYSTERIOUS RECIPES.
I BROUGHT IT WITH ME FROM THE SKY.
FLOAT
MYSTERIOUS RECIPES?!
COOL.
Pie in the sky?
THESE ARE WEIRD RECIPES.
Hanging herb tea?
THIS ONE LOOKS GOOD. "HELPFUL LITTLE COOKIES."
THE BAKED COOK-IES HELP OUT WITH WHATEVER YOU WANT.
Helpful Little Cookies
NEAT! LET'S MAKE THESE!

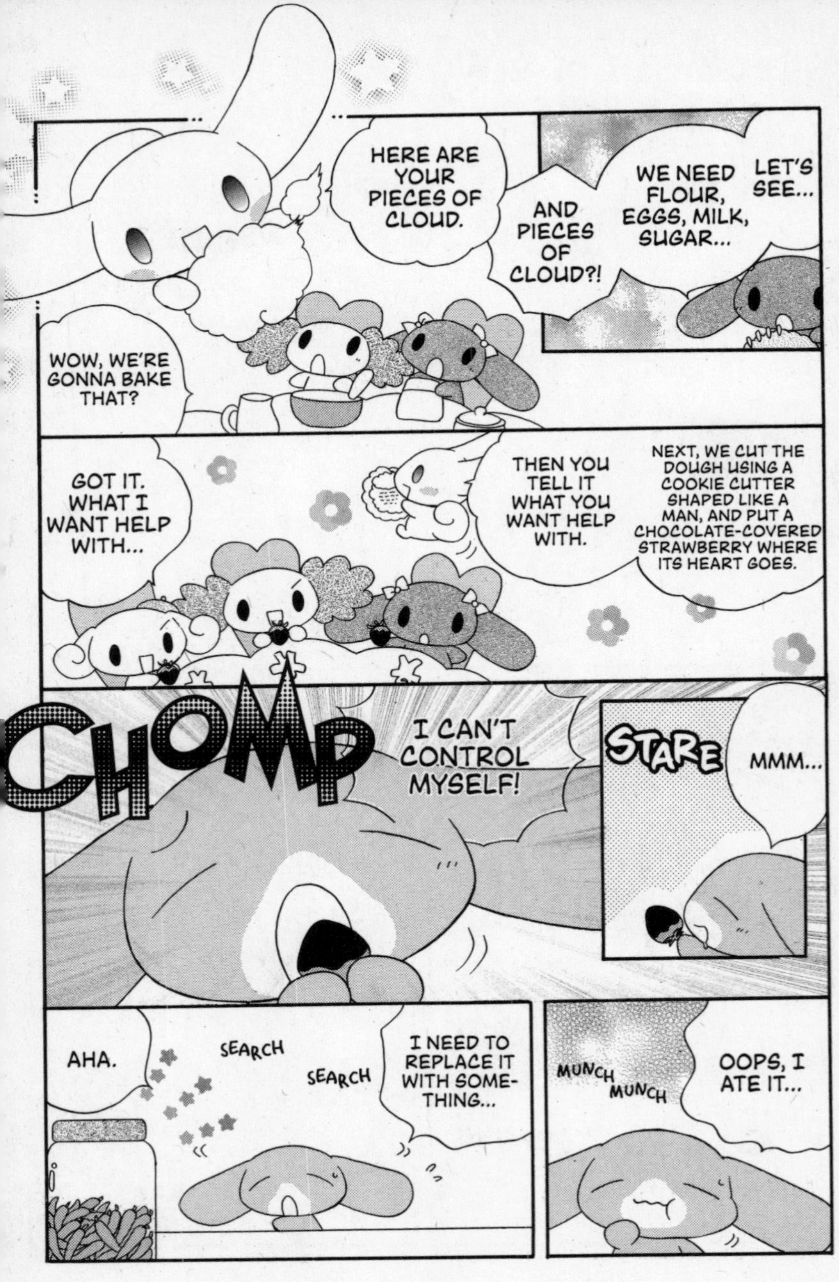
LET'S SEE...
WE NEED FLOUR, EGGS, MILK, SUGAR...
AND PIECES OF CLOUD?!
HERE ARE YOUR PIECES OF CLOUD.
WOW, WE'RE GONNA BAKE THAT?
NEXT, WE CUT THE DOUGH USING A COOKIE CUTTER SHAPED LIKE A MAN, AND PUT A CHOCOLATE-COVERED STRAWBERRY WHERE ITS HEART GOES.
THEN YOU TELL IT WHAT YOU WANT HELP WITH.
GOT IT. WHAT I WANT HELP WITH...
STARE
MMM...
CHOMP
I CAN'T CONTROL MYSELF!
OOPS, I ATE IT...
MUNCH MUNCH
I NEED TO REPLACE IT WITH SOME-THING...
SEARCH SEARCH
AHA.

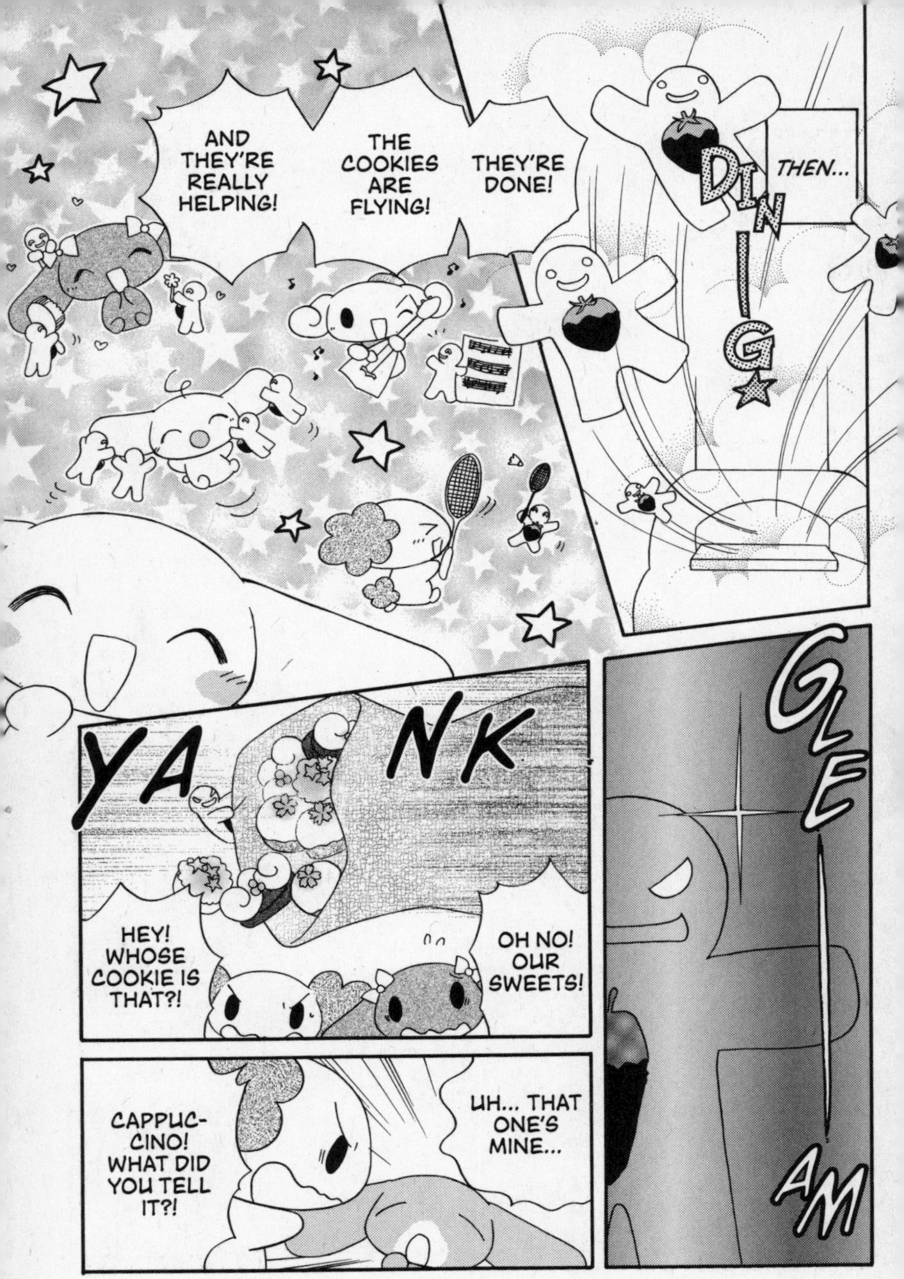
THEN...
DING
THEY'RE DONE!
THE COOKIES ARE FLYING!
AND THEY'RE REALLY HELPING!
GLEAM
YANK
OH NO! OUR SWEETS!
HEY! WHOSE COOKIE IS THAT?!
UH... THAT ONE'S MINE...
CAPPUCCINO! WHAT DID YOU TELL IT?!

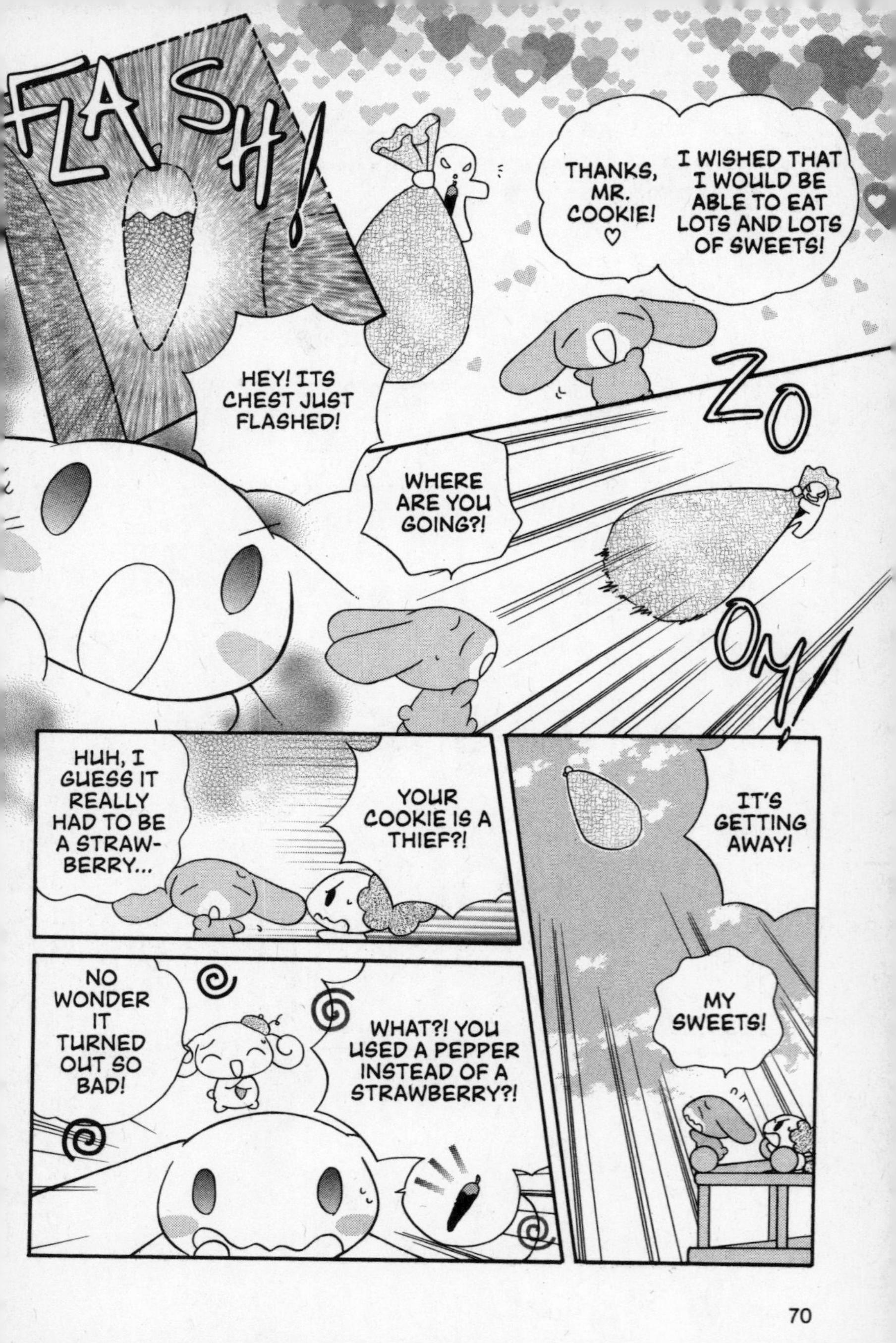
I WISHED THAT I WOULD BE ABLE TO EAT LOTS AND LOTS OF SWEETS!
THANKS, MR. COOKIE! ♡
FLASH!
HEY! ITS CHEST JUST FLASHED!
ZOOM!
WHERE ARE YOU GOING?!
IT'S GETTING AWAY!
MY SWEETS!
YOUR COOKIE IS A THIEF?!
HUH, I GUESS IT REALLY HAD TO BE A STRAW-BERRY...
WHAT?! YOU USED A PEPPER INSTEAD OF A STRAWBERRY?!
NO WONDER IT TURNED OUT SO BAD!

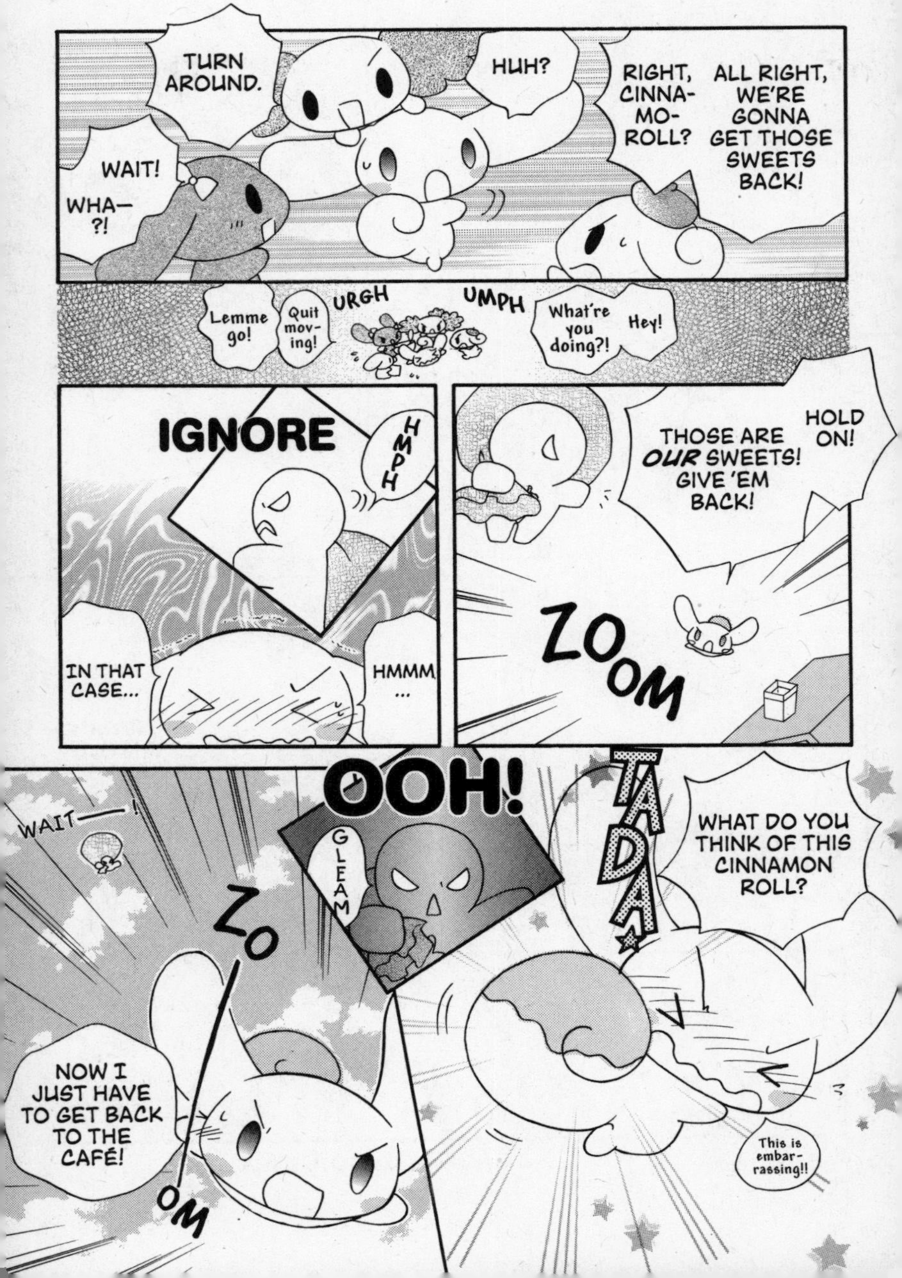
ALL RIGHT, WE'RE GONNA GET THOSE SWEETS BACK!
RIGHT, CINNA-MO-ROLL?
HUH?
TURN AROUND.
WAIT!
WHA—?!
Hey!
What're you doing?!
UMPH
URGH
Quit mov-ing!
Lemme go!
HOLD ON!
THOSE ARE OUR SWEETS! GIVE 'EM BACK!
ZOOM
HMPH
IGNORE
HMMM...
IN THAT CASE...
WHAT DO YOU THINK OF THIS CINNAMON ROLL?
TADA
This is embar-rassing!!
OOH!
GLEAM
WAIT——!
ZO
OM
NOW I JUST HAVE TO GET BACK TO THE CAFÉ!

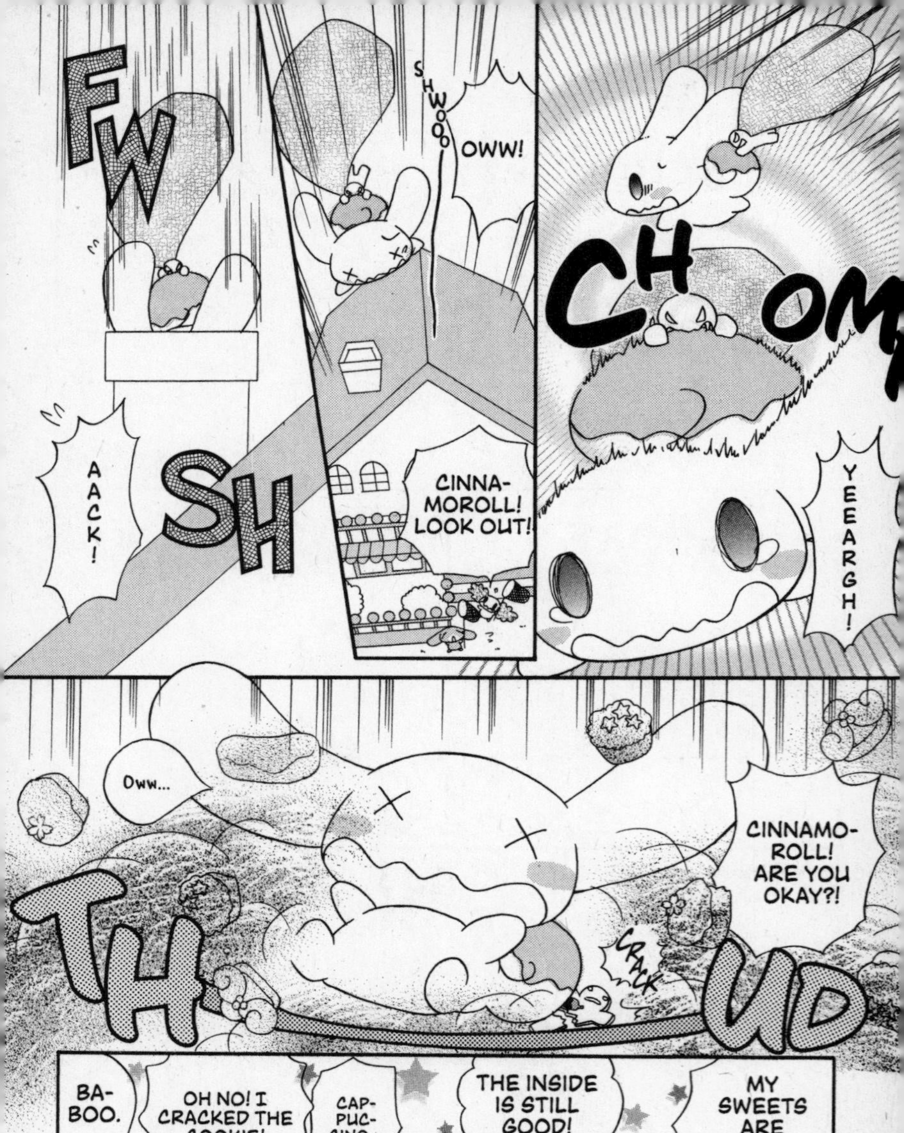
CHOMP
YEEARGH!
SHWOOO
OWW!
CINNAMOROLL! LOOK OUT!
FW
SH
AACK!
CINNAMOROLL! ARE YOU OKAY?!
Oww...
CRACK
THUD
MY SWEETS ARE RUINED!
Covered with soot!
SPLIT
THE INSIDE IS STILL GOOD!
CAPPUCCINO...
OH NO! I CRACKED THE COOKIE!
BABOO.

# Auditions at the Café!

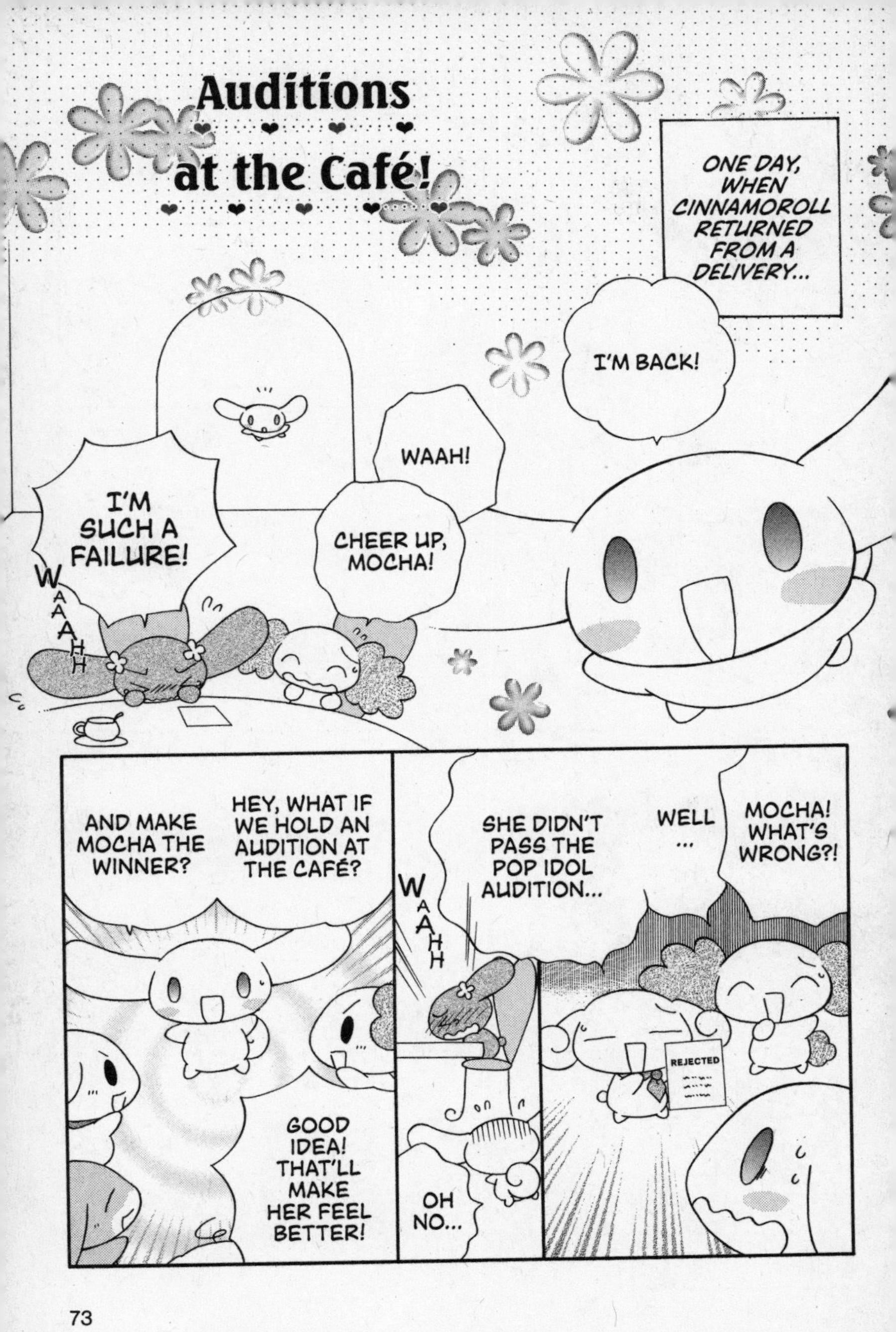
ONE DAY, WHEN CINNAMOROLL RETURNED FROM A DELIVERY...
I'M BACK!
WAAH!
CHEER UP, MOCHA!
I'M SUCH A FAILURE!
WAAAHH
MOCHA! WHAT'S WRONG?!
WELL ...
SHE DIDN'T PASS THE POP IDOL AUDITION...
REJECTED
WAAHH
OH NO...
HEY, WHAT IF WE HOLD AN AUDITION AT THE CAFÉ?
AND MAKE MOCHA THE WINNER?
GOOD IDEA! THAT'LL MAKE HER FEEL BETTER!

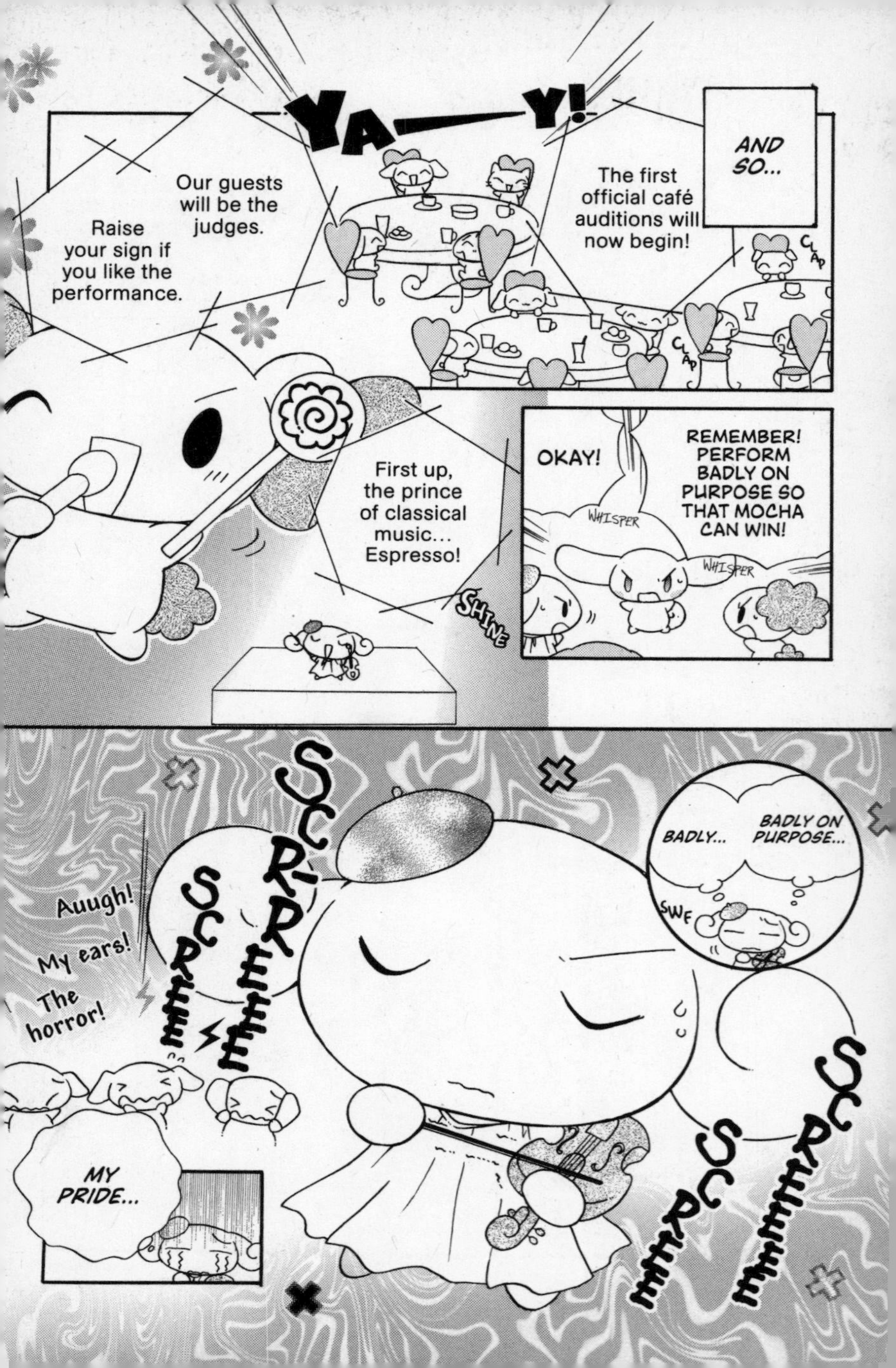

AND SO...
YA—Y!
The first official café auditions will now begin!
Our guests will be the judges.
Raise your sign if you like the performance.
CLAP
CLAP
REMEMBER! PERFORM BADLY ON PURPOSE SO THAT MOCHA CAN WIN!
WHISPER
OKAY!
WHISPER
First up, the prince of classical music... Espresso!
SHINE
SCREEEE
SCREEEE
BADLY... BADLY ON PURPOSE...
SWF
SCRREEEE
SCREEEE
Auugh! My ears! The horror!
MY PRIDE...

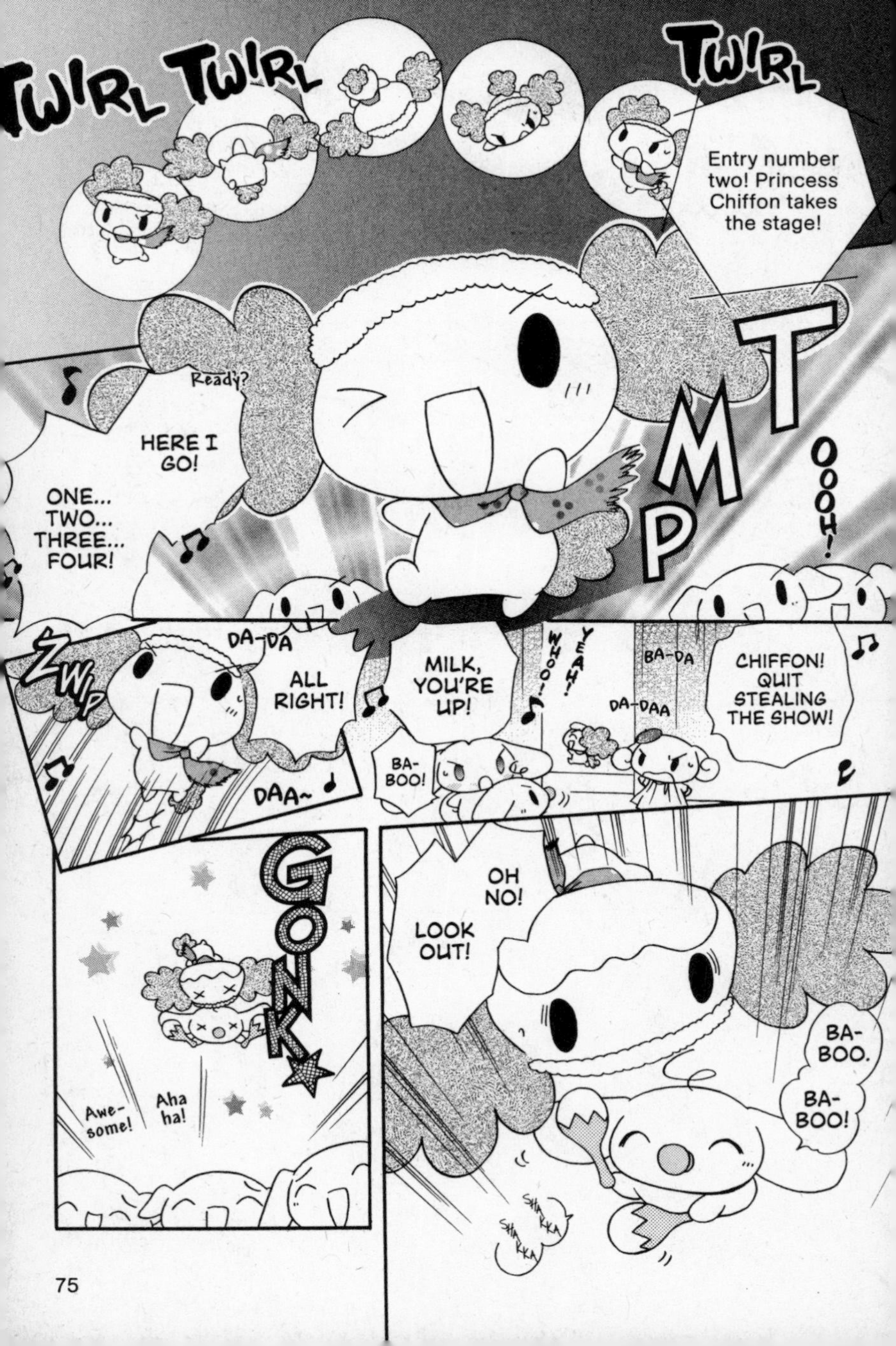
TWIRL
Entry number two! Princess Chiffon takes the stage!
TWIRL TWIRL
OOOH!
TMP
Ready?
HERE I GO!
ONE... TWO... THREE... FOUR!
CHIFFON! QUIT STEALING THE SHOW!
BA-DA
DA-DAA
YEAH!
WHOO!
MILK, YOU'RE UP!
BA-BOO!
DA-DA
ALL RIGHT!
ZWIP
DAA~
OH NO!
LOOK OUT!
BA-BOO.
BA-BOO!
SHAKKA
SHAKKA
GONK
Aha ha!
Awe-some!

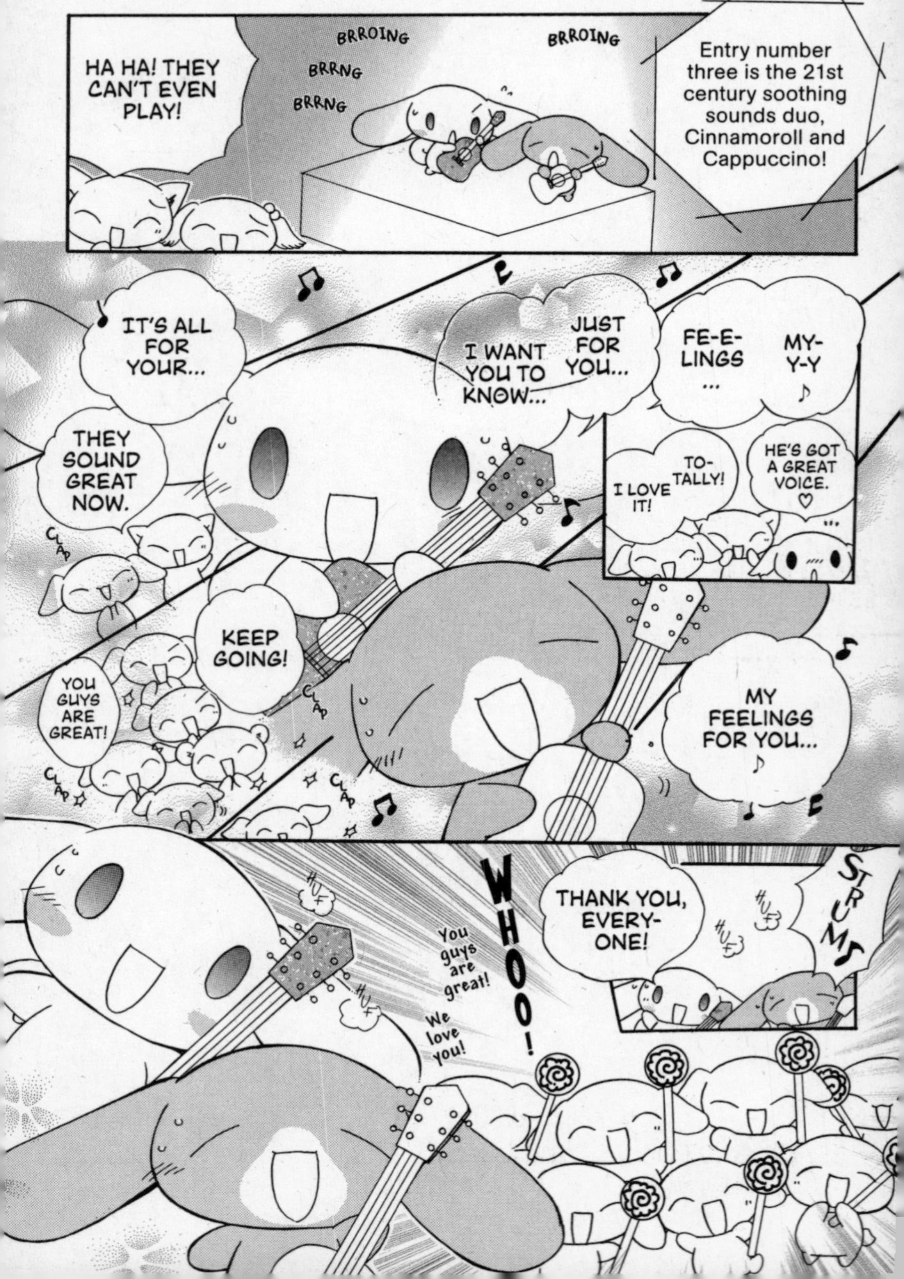
Entry number three is the 21st century soothing sounds duo, Cinnamoroll and Cappuccino!
BRROING
BRROING
BRRNG
BRRNG
HA HA! THEY CAN'T EVEN PLAY!
MY-Y-Y ♪
FE-E-LINGS...
JUST FOR YOU...
I WANT YOU TO KNOW...
IT'S ALL FOR YOUR...
HE'S GOT A GREAT VOICE. ♡
TO-TALLY!
I LOVE IT!
THEY SOUND GREAT NOW.
CLAP
MY FEELINGS FOR YOU... ♪
KEEP GOING!
CLAP
YOU GUYS ARE GREAT!
CLAP
CLAP
STRUMS
HUF
HUF
THANK YOU, EVERY-ONE!
WHOOO!
You guys are great!
We love you!
HUF
HUF

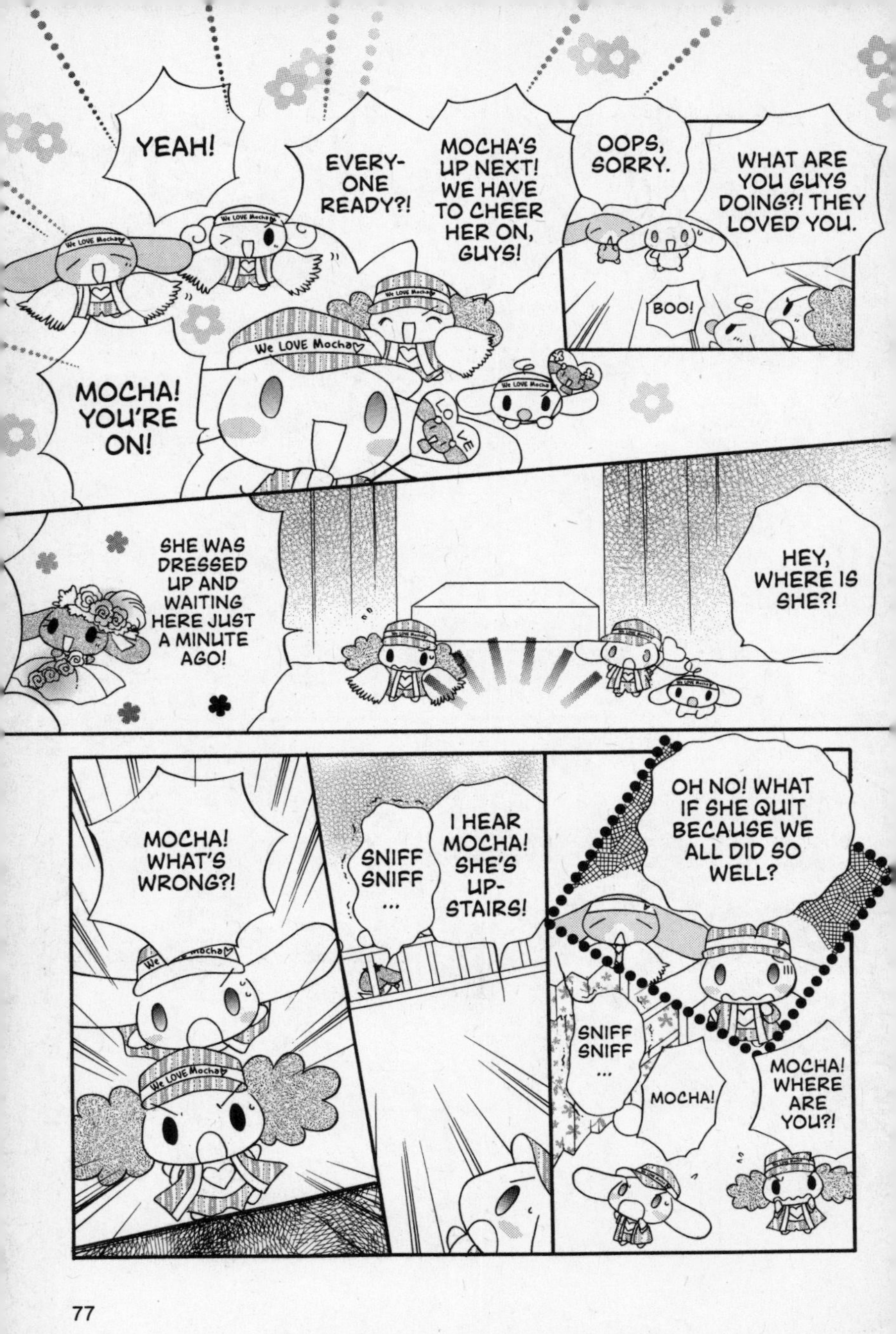
WHAT ARE YOU GUYS DOING?! THEY LOVED YOU.
OOPS, SORRY.
BOO!
MOCHA'S UP NEXT! WE HAVE TO CHEER HER ON, GUYS!
EVERY-ONE READY?!
YEAH!
We LOVE Mocha
MOCHA! YOU'RE ON!
LOVE
HEY, WHERE IS SHE?!
SHE WAS DRESSED UP AND WAITING HERE JUST A MINUTE AGO!
OH NO! WHAT IF SHE QUIT BECAUSE WE ALL DID SO WELL?
MOCHA! WHERE ARE YOU?!
MOCHA!
SNIFF SNIFF ...
I HEAR MOCHA! SHE'S UP-STAIRS!
SNIFF SNIFF ...
MOCHA! WHAT'S WRONG?!

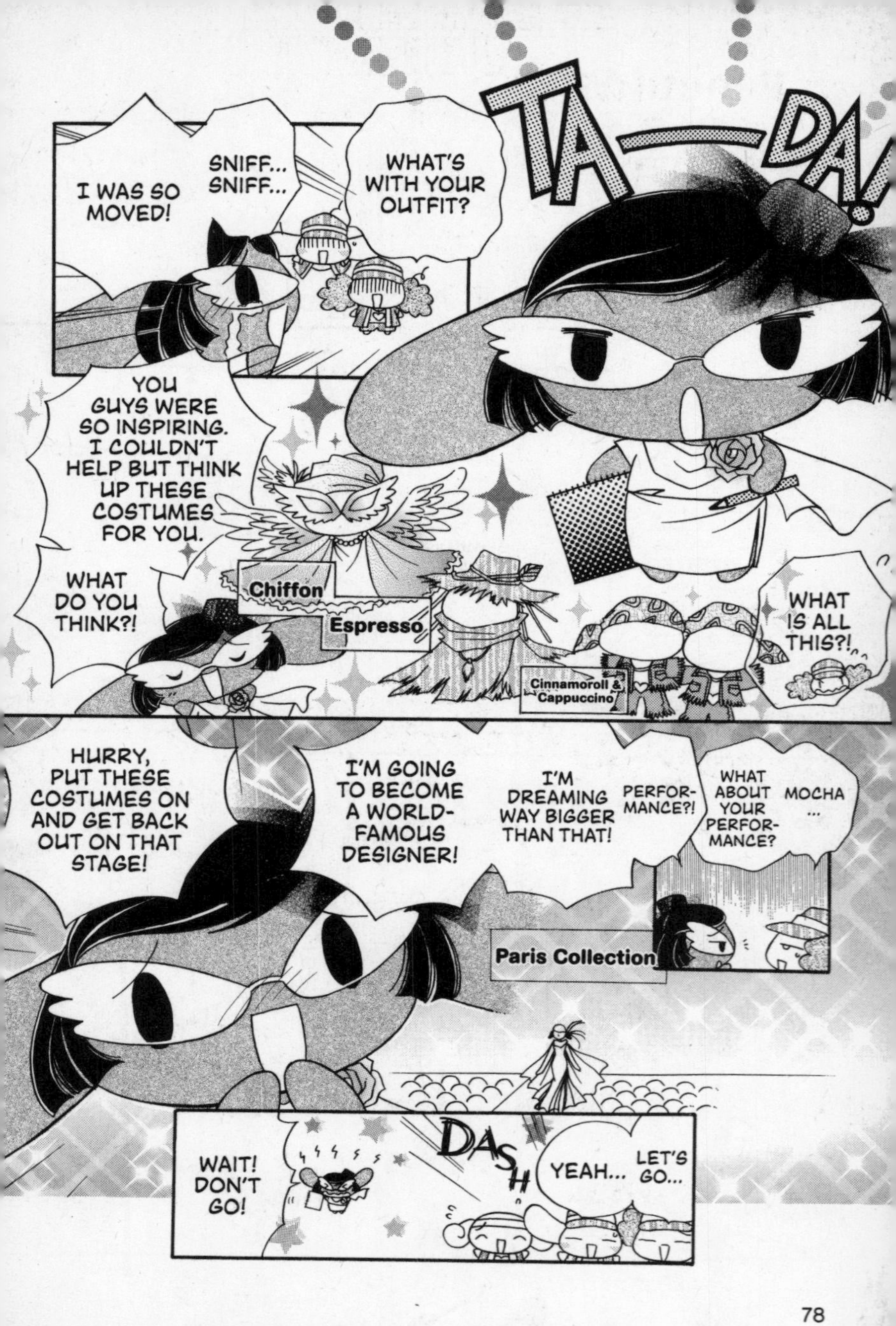
TA—DA!
WHAT'S WITH YOUR OUTFIT?
SNIFF... SNIFF...
I WAS SO MOVED!
WHAT IS ALL THIS?!
YOU GUYS WERE SO INSPIRING. I COULDN'T HELP BUT THINK UP THESE COSTUMES FOR YOU.
WHAT DO YOU THINK?!
Chiffon
Espresso
Cinnamoroll & Cappuccino
MOCHA ...
WHAT ABOUT YOUR PERFORMANCE?
PERFORMANCE?!
I'M DREAMING WAY BIGGER THAN THAT!
I'M GOING TO BECOME A WORLD-FAMOUS DESIGNER!
Paris Collection
HURRY, PUT THESE COSTUMES ON AND GET BACK OUT ON THAT STAGE!
LET'S GO...
YEAH...
DASH
WAIT! DON'T GO!

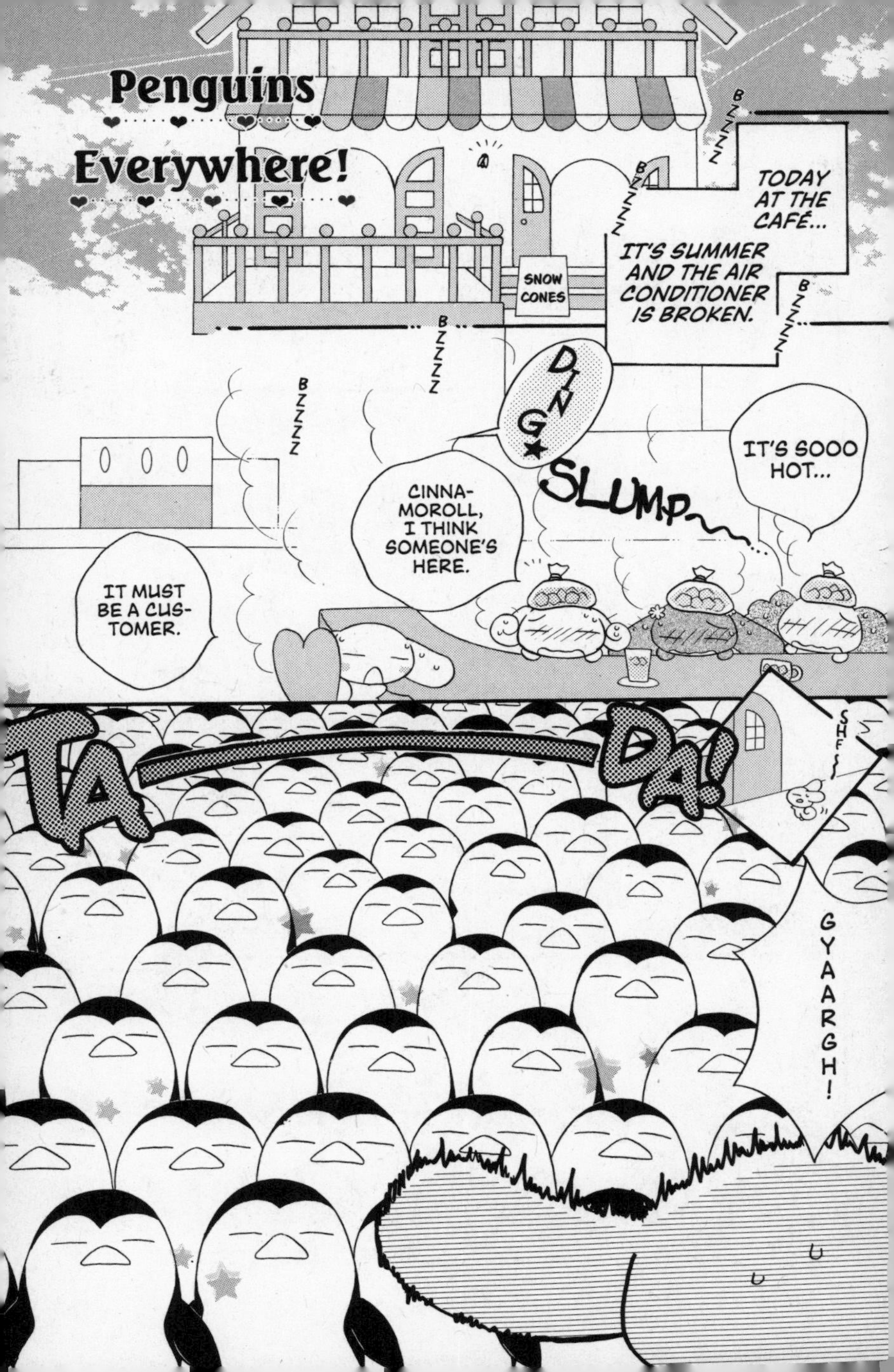
Penguins Everywhere!
TODAY AT THE CAFÉ...
IT'S SUMMER AND THE AIR CONDITIONER IS BROKEN.
BZZZZ
SNOW CONES
BZZZZ
IT'S SOOO HOT...
SLUMP
DING★
CINNA-MOROLL, I THINK SOMEONE'S HERE.
IT MUST BE A CUS-TOMER.
SHF
TA—DA!
GYAARGH!

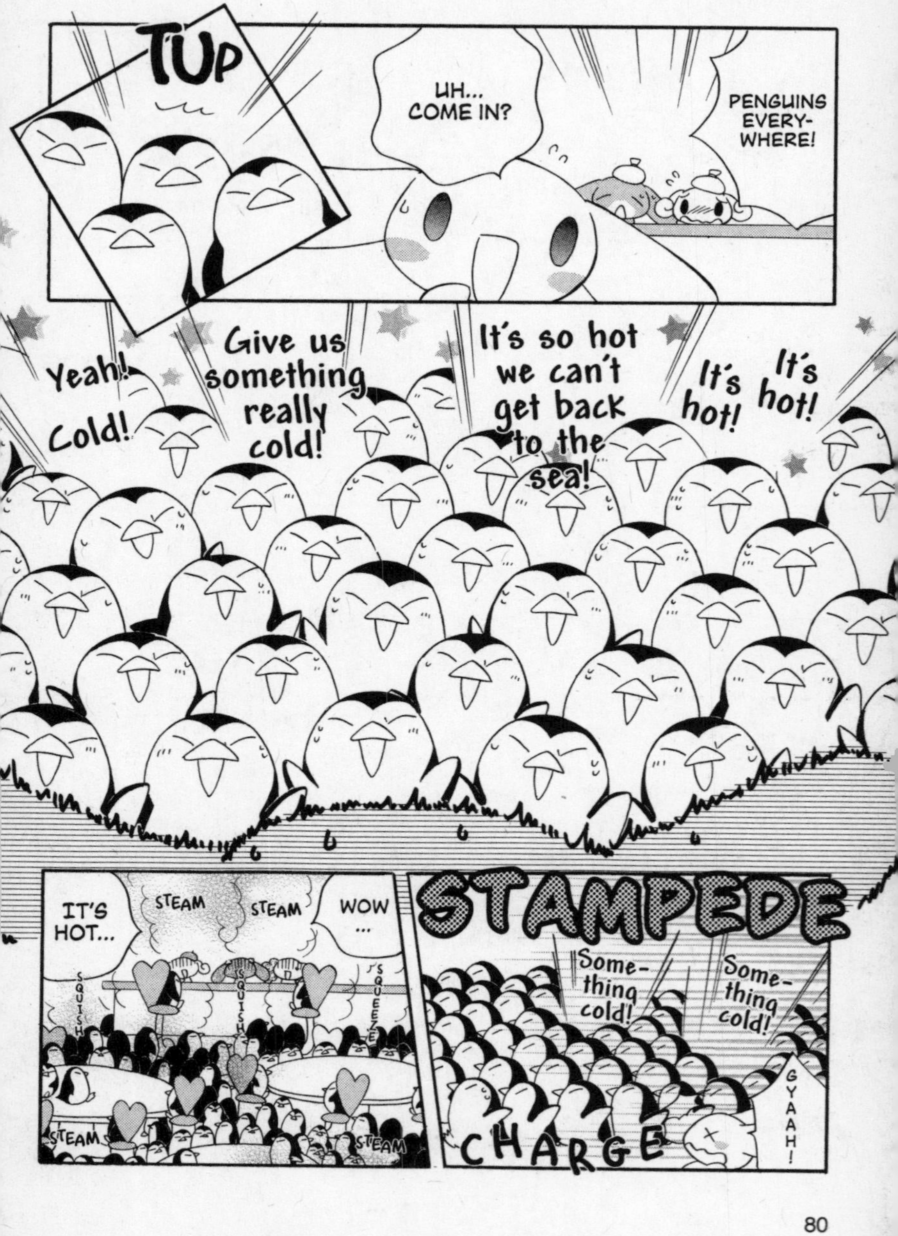
PENGUINS EVERY-WHERE!
UH... COME IN?
TUP
It's hot!
It's hot!
It's so hot we can't get back to the sea!
Give us something really cold!
Yeah! Cold!
STAMPEDE
Some-thing cold!
Some-thing cold!
GYAAH!
CHARGE
WOW ...
STEAM
STEAM
IT'S HOT...
SQUEEZE
SQUISH
SQUISH
STEAM
STEAM

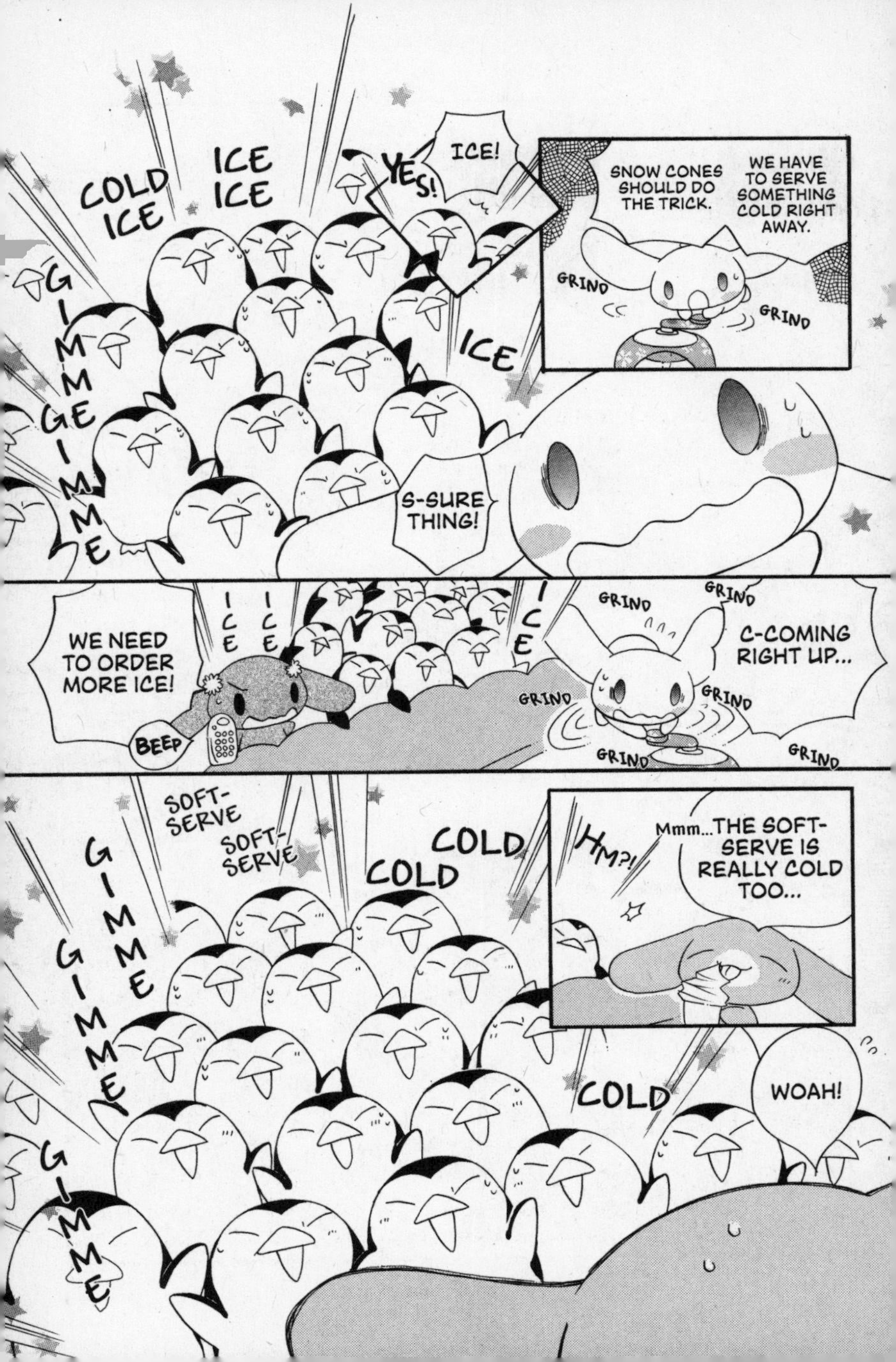
WE HAVE TO SERVE SOMETHING COLD RIGHT AWAY.
SNOW CONES SHOULD DO THE TRICK.
GRIND
GRIND
ICE!
YES!
ICE ICE
COLD ICE
GIMME GIMME
ICE
S-SURE THING!
GRIND
GRIND
C-COMING RIGHT UP...
GRIND
GRIND
GRIND
GRIND
ICE
ICE
ICE
WE NEED TO ORDER MORE ICE!
BEEP
Mmm...THE SOFT-SERVE IS REALLY COLD TOO...
HM?!
COLD
COLD
SOFT-SERVE
SOFT-SERVE
GIMME
GIMME
WOAH!
COLD
GIMME

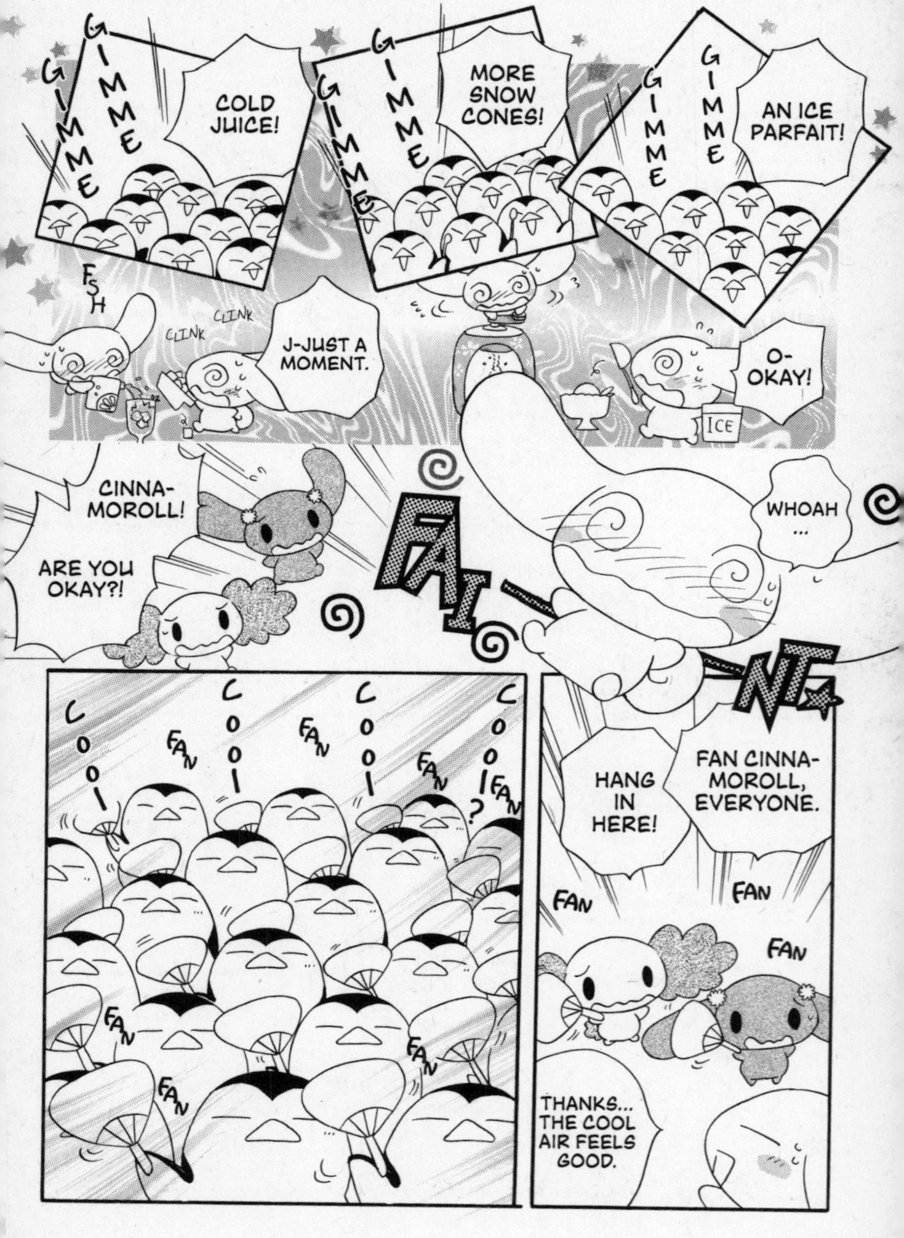
GIMME
GIMME
AN ICE PARFAIT!
GIMME
GIMME
MORE SNOW CONES!
GIMME
GIMME
COLD JUICE!
O-OKAY!
ICE
J-JUST A MOMENT.
CLINK
CLINK
FSH
WHOAH ...
FAINT
CINNA-MOROLL!
ARE YOU OKAY?!
FAN CINNA-MOROLL, EVERYONE.
HANG IN HERE!
FAN
FAN
FAN
THANKS... THE COOL AIR FEELS GOOD.
COOOL?
FAN
COOOL
FAN
COOOL
FAN
COOOL
FAN
FAN
FAN
FAN

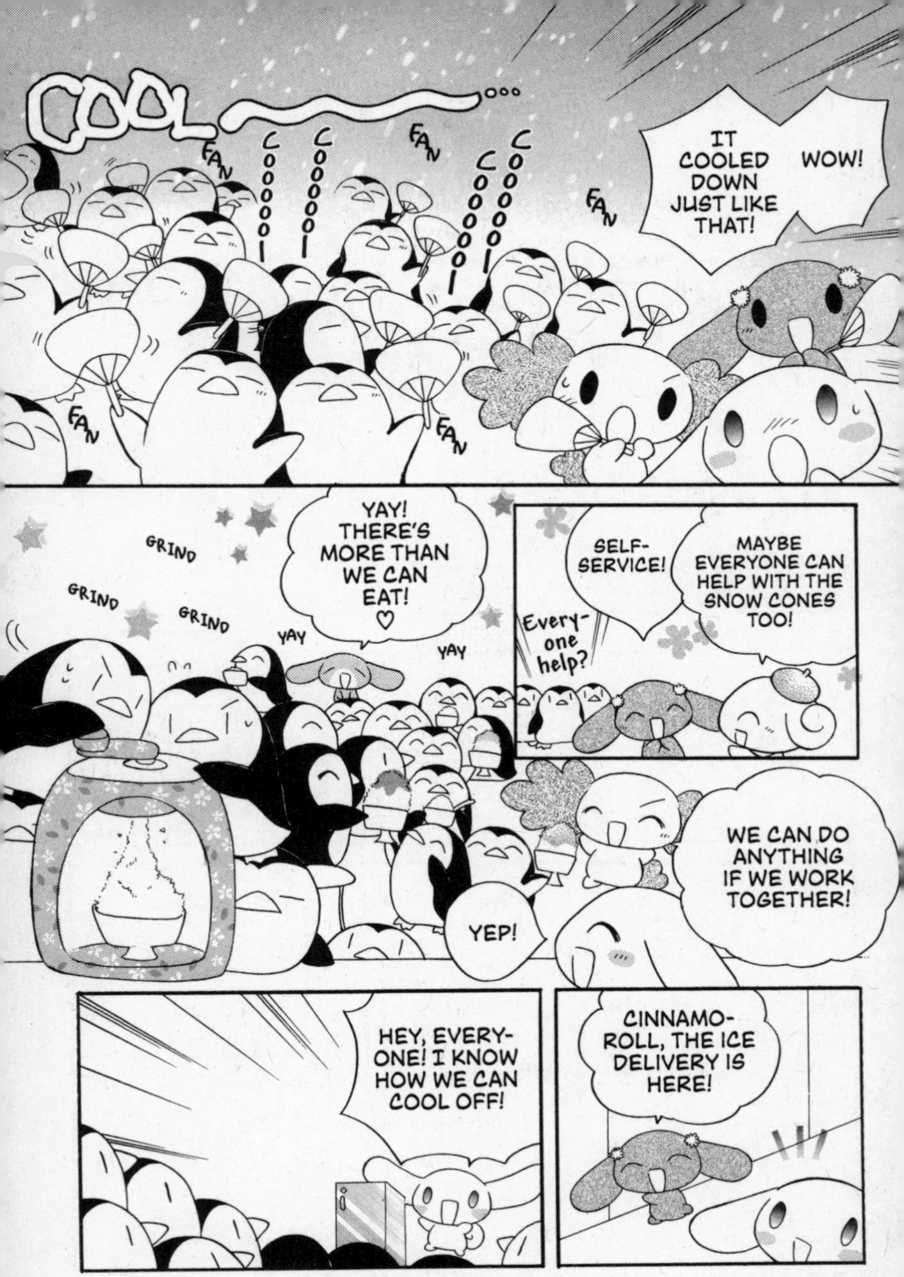
WOW!
IT COOLED DOWN JUST LIKE THAT!
COOL~~~...
COOOOOL
COOOOOL
COOOOOL
COOOOOL
FAN
FAN
FAN
FAN
FAN
MAYBE EVERYONE CAN HELP WITH THE SNOW CONES TOO!
SELF-SERVICE!
Every-one help?
YAY! THERE'S MORE THAN WE CAN EAT! ♡
GRIND
GRIND
GRIND
YAY
YAY
WE CAN DO ANYTHING IF WE WORK TOGETHER!
YEP!
CINNAMO-ROLL, THE ICE DELIVERY IS HERE!
HEY, EVERY-ONE! I KNOW HOW WE CAN COOL OFF!

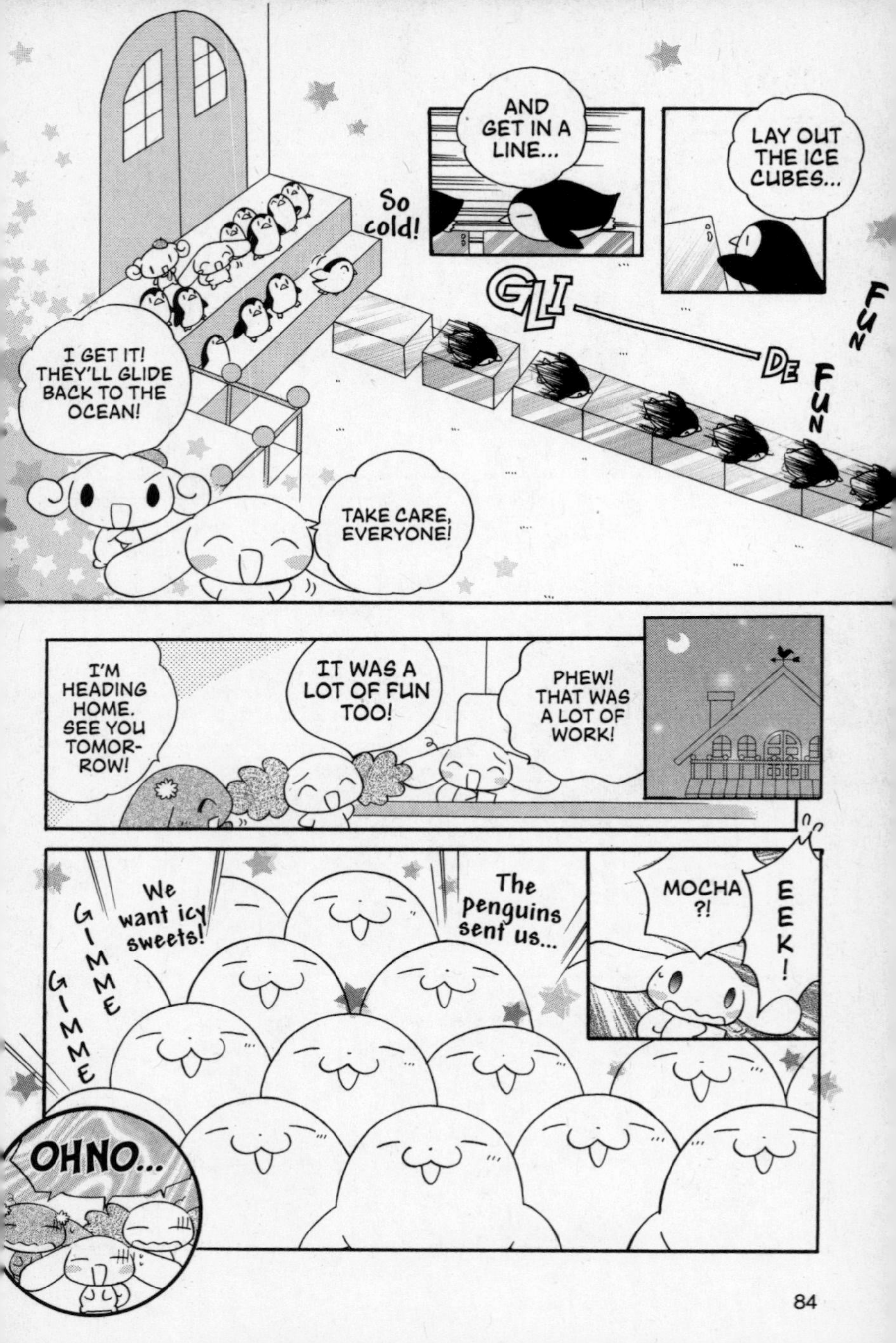

LAY OUT THE ICE CUBES...
AND GET IN A LINE...
So cold!
GLI DE
FUN FUN
I GET IT! THEY'LL GLIDE BACK TO THE OCEAN!
TAKE CARE, EVERYONE!
PHEW! THAT WAS A LOT OF WORK!
IT WAS A LOT OF FUN TOO!
I'M HEADING HOME. SEE YOU TOMOR-ROW!
EEK!
MOCHA ?!
The penguins sent us...
We want icy sweets!
GIMME
GIMME
OHNO...

# Mocha's Fortune

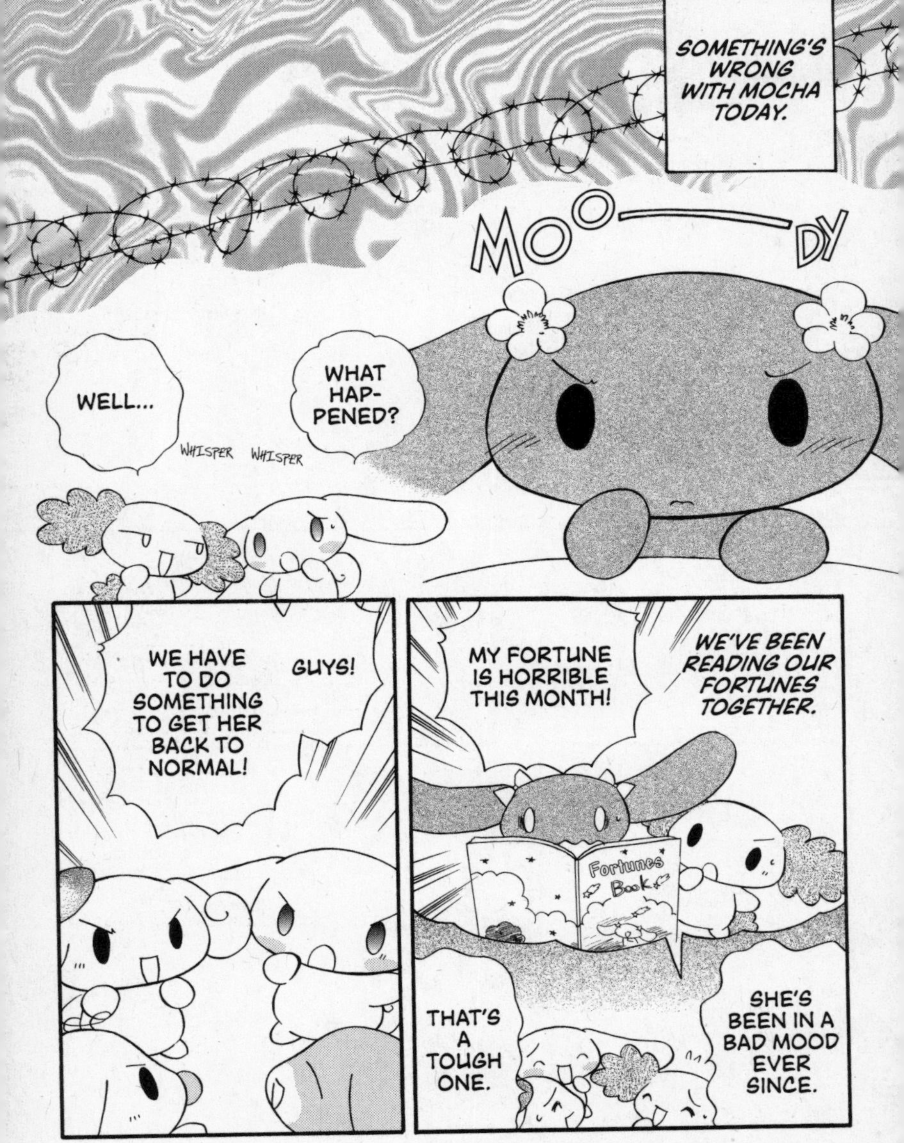
SOMETHING'S WRONG WITH MOCHA TODAY.
MOO—DY
WHAT HAP-PENED?
WELL...
WHISPER WHISPER
WE'VE BEEN READING OUR FORTUNES TOGETHER.
MY FORTUNE IS HORRIBLE THIS MONTH!
Fortunes Book
SHE'S BEEN IN A BAD MOOD EVER SINCE.
THAT'S A TOUGH ONE.
GUYS!
WE HAVE TO DO SOMETHING TO GET HER BACK TO NORMAL!

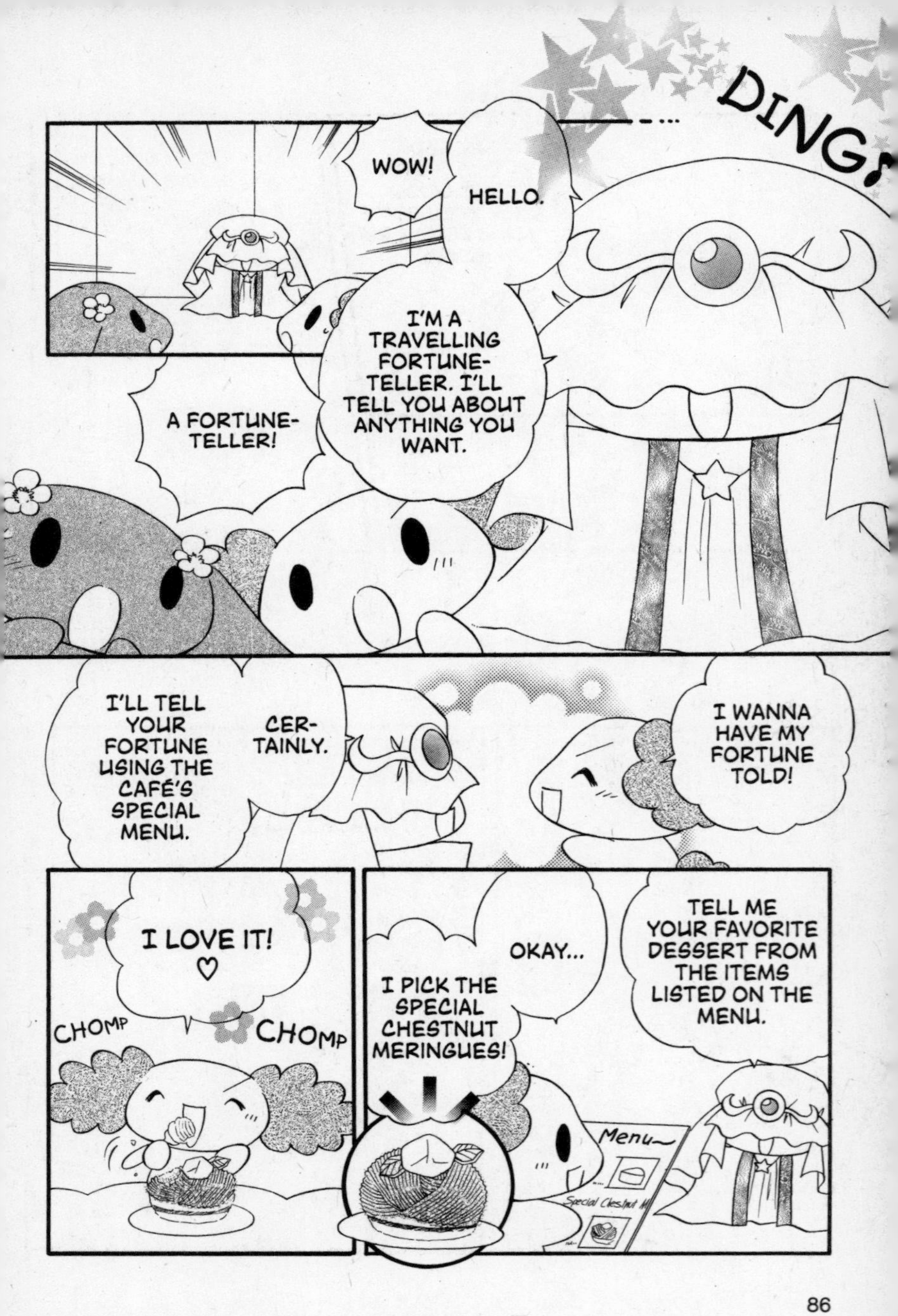
DING♪
HELLO.
I'M A TRAVELLING FORTUNE-TELLER. I'LL TELL YOU ABOUT ANYTHING YOU WANT.
WOW!
A FORTUNE-TELLER!
I WANNA HAVE MY FORTUNE TOLD!
CER-TAINLY.
I'LL TELL YOUR FORTUNE USING THE CAFÉ'S SPECIAL MENU.
TELL ME YOUR FAVORITE DESSERT FROM THE ITEMS LISTED ON THE MENU.
OKAY...
I PICK THE SPECIAL CHESTNUT MERINGUES!
Menu~
I LOVE IT! ♡
CHOMP
CHOMP

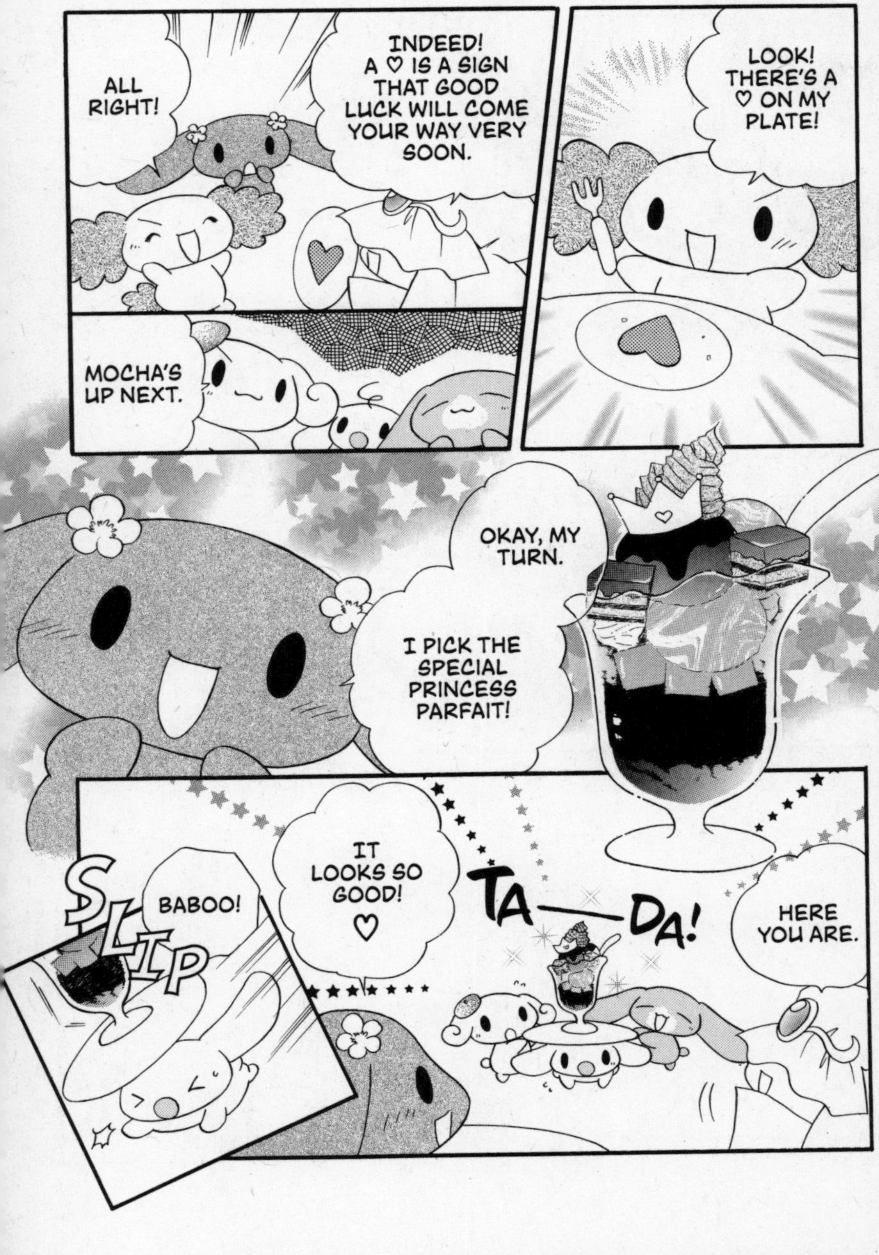
LOOK! THERE'S A ♡ ON MY PLATE!
INDEED! A ♡ IS A SIGN THAT GOOD LUCK WILL COME YOUR WAY VERY SOON.
ALL RIGHT!
MOCHA'S UP NEXT.
OKAY, MY TURN.
I PICK THE SPECIAL PRINCESS PARFAIT!
HERE YOU ARE.
TA—DA!
IT LOOKS SO GOOD! ♡
BABOO!
SLIP

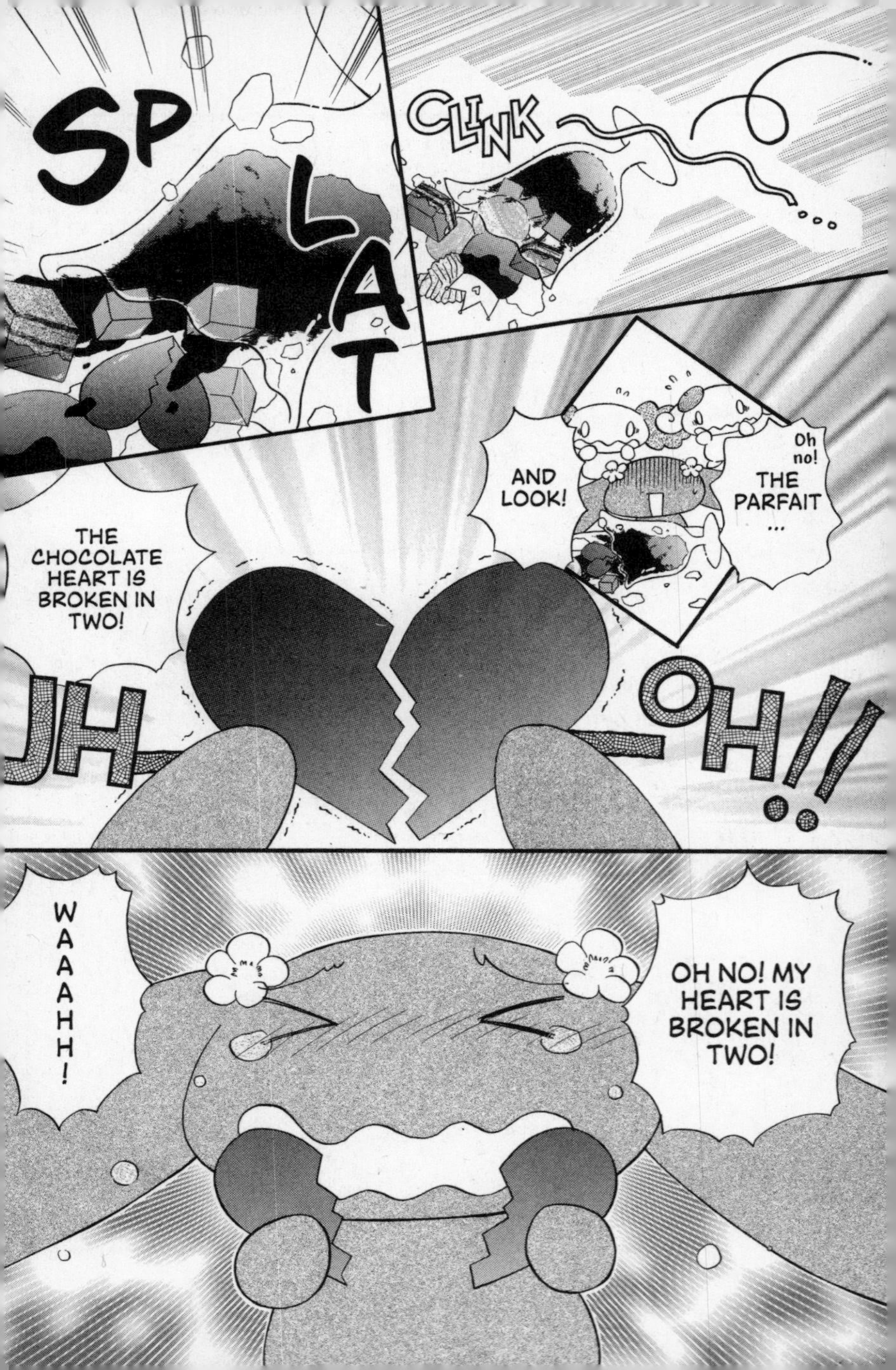
CLINK
...
SPLAT
Oh no! THE PARFAIT...
AND LOOK!
THE CHOCOLATE HEART IS BROKEN IN TWO!
JH—OH!!
OH NO! MY HEART IS BROKEN IN TWO!
WAAAHH!

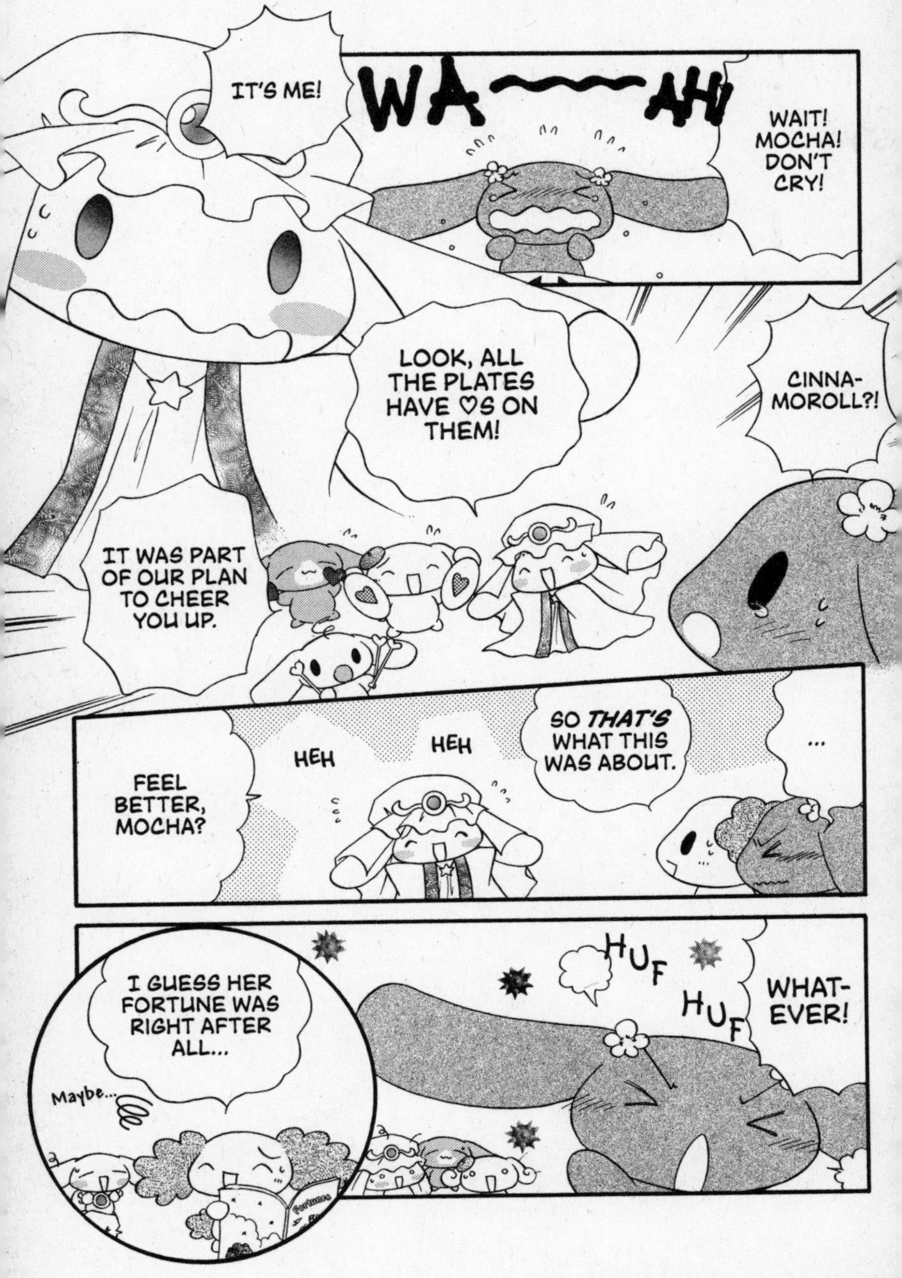
WA——AH!
WAIT! MOCHA! DON'T CRY!
CINNA-MOROLL?!
IT'S ME!
LOOK, ALL THE PLATES HAVE ♡S ON THEM!
IT WAS PART OF OUR PLAN TO CHEER YOU UP.
...
SO *THAT'S* WHAT THIS WAS ABOUT.
HEH HEH
FEEL BETTER, MOCHA?
WHAT-EVER!
HUF HUF
I GUESS HER FORTUNE WAS RIGHT AFTER ALL...
Maybe...

★ Fluffy, Fluffy ♥ Cinnamoroll ★

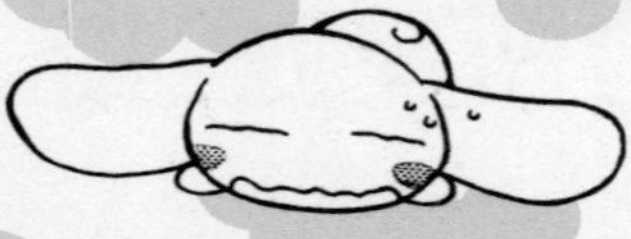

# A Halloween Ghost

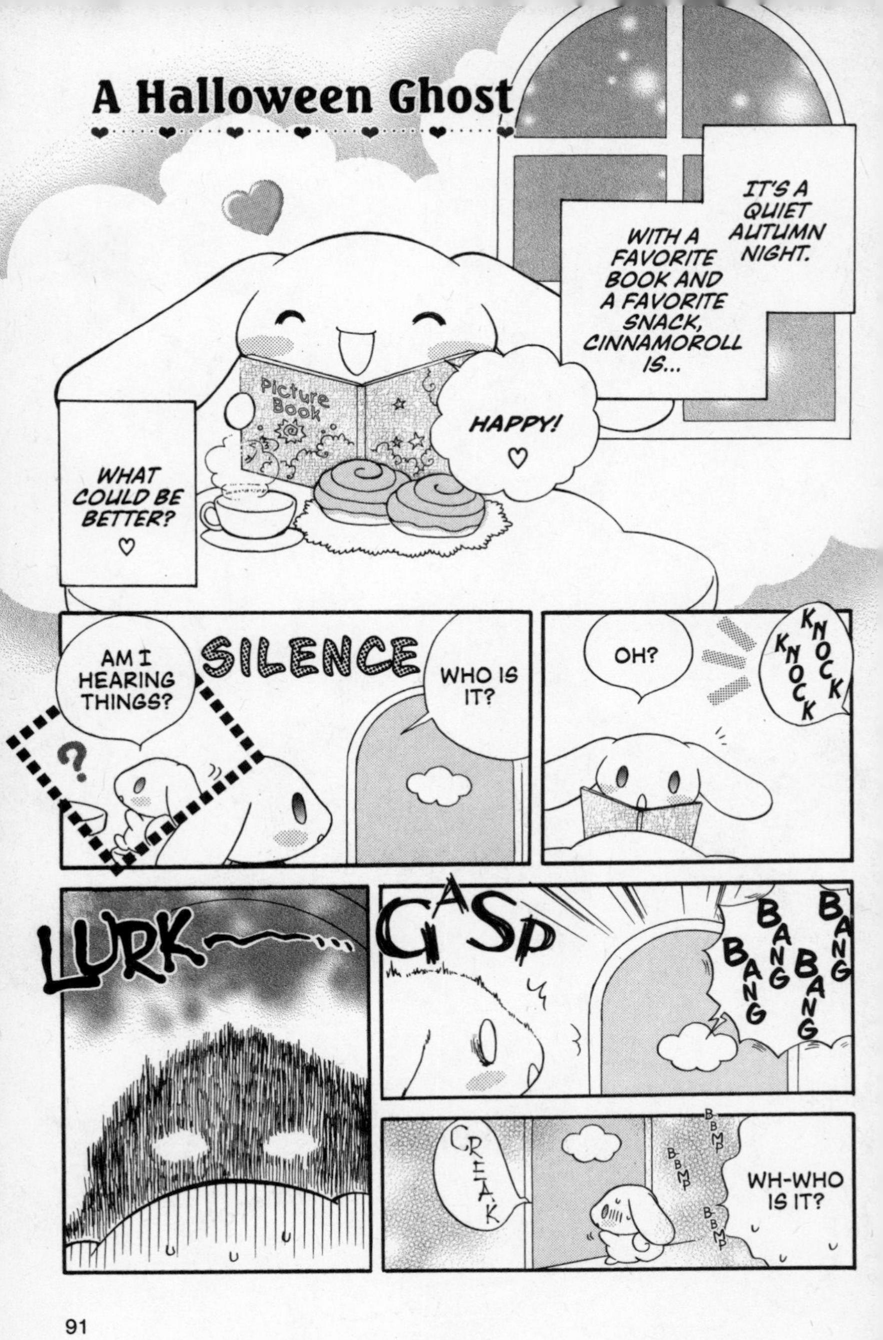
IT'S A QUIET AUTUMN NIGHT.
WITH A FAVORITE BOOK AND A FAVORITE SNACK, CINNAMOROLL IS...
HAPPY! ♡
WHAT COULD BE BETTER? ♡
Picture Book
KNOCK KNOCK
OH?
WHO IS IT?
SILENCE
AM I HEARING THINGS?
?
BANG BANG BANG BANG
GASP
WH-WHO IS IT?
BBMP BBMP BBMP
CREAK
LURK—...

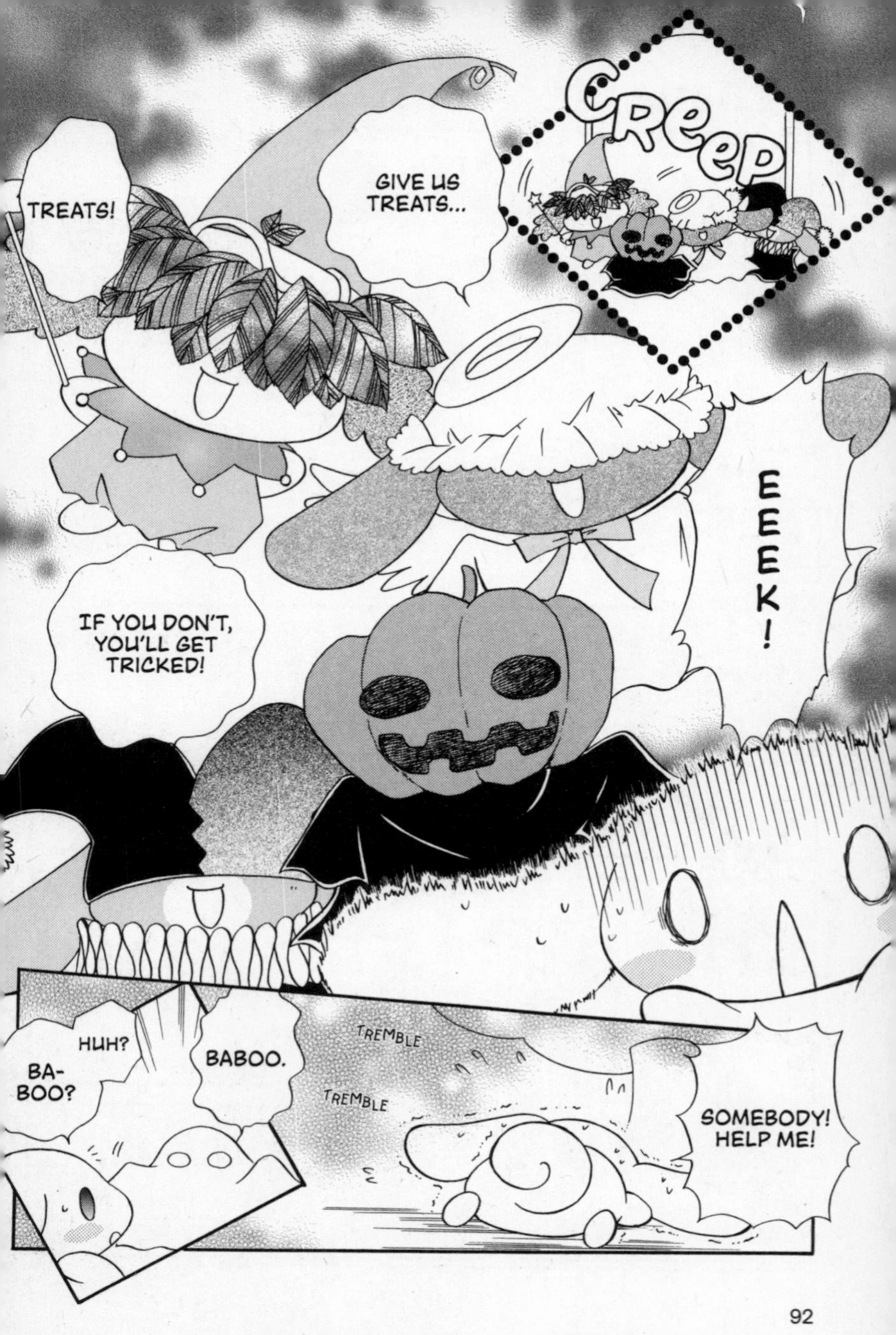

CREEP
GIVE US TREATS...
TREATS!
IF YOU DON'T, YOU'LL GET TRICKED!
EEEK!
SOMEBODY! HELP ME!
TREMBLE
TREMBLE
BABOO.
HUH?
BA-BOO?

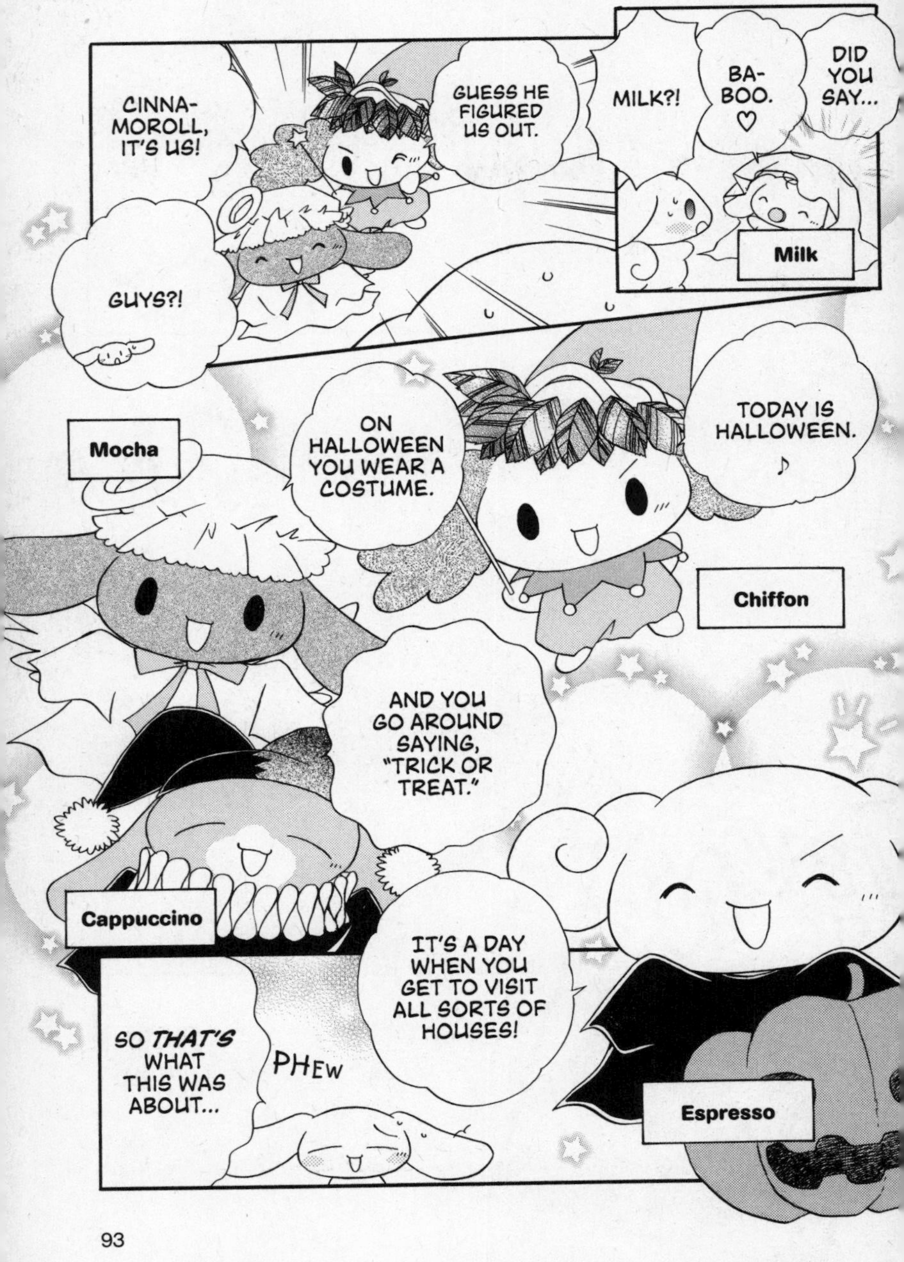
DID YOU SAY...
BA-BOO. ♡
MILK?!
Milk
GUESS HE FIGURED US OUT.
CINNA-MOROLL, IT'S US!
GUYS?!
TODAY IS HALLOWEEN. ♪
Chiffon
ON HALLOWEEN YOU WEAR A COSTUME.
Mocha
AND YOU GO AROUND SAYING, "TRICK OR TREAT."
IT'S A DAY WHEN YOU GET TO VISIT ALL SORTS OF HOUSES!
Espresso
Cappuccino
PHEW
SO *THAT'S* WHAT THIS WAS ABOUT...

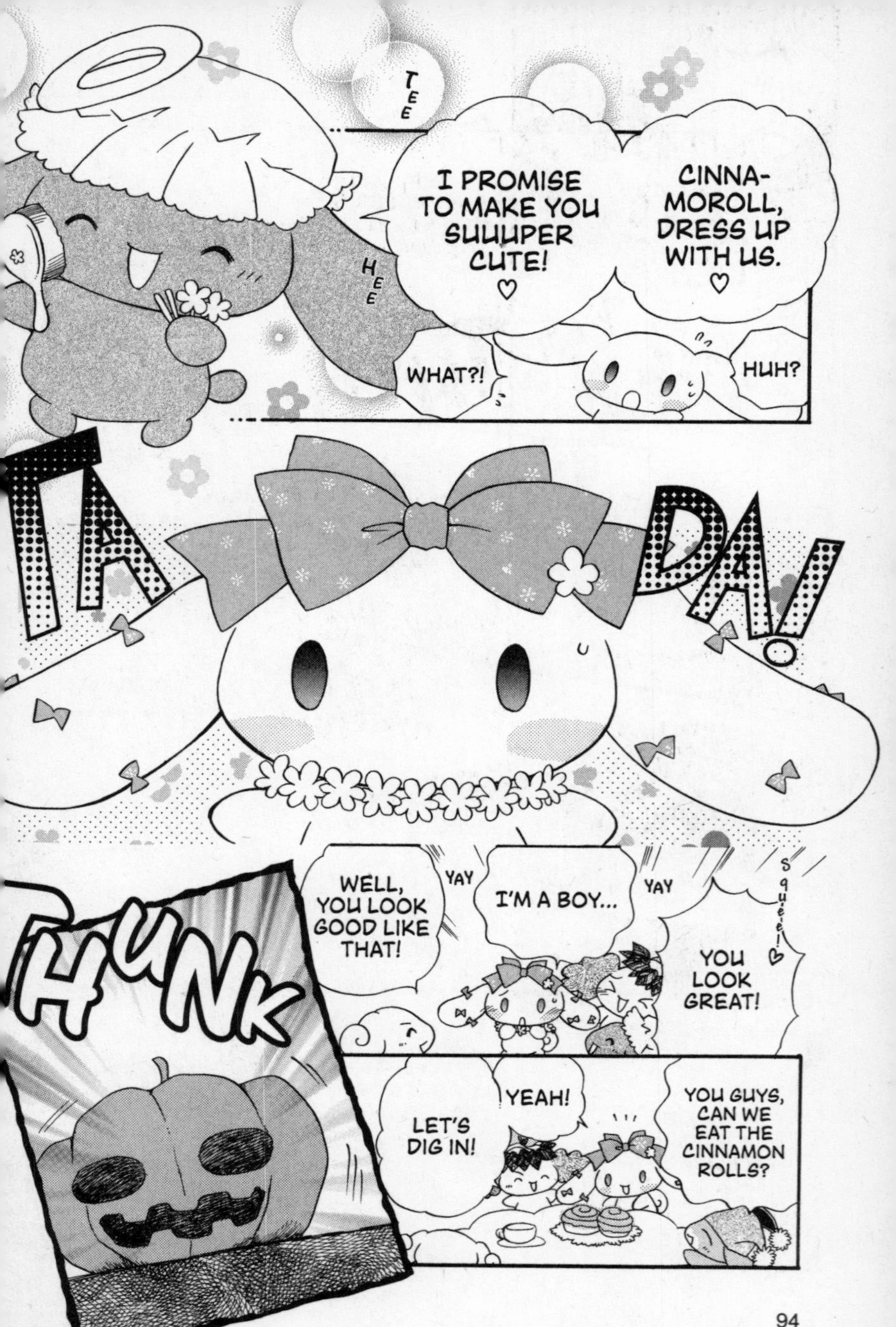
CINNA-MOROLL, DRESS UP WITH US. ♡
I PROMISE TO MAKE YOU SUUUPER CUTE! ♡
TEE HEE
HUH?
WHAT?!
TA DA!
YOU LOOK GREAT! ♡
Squeee!
YAY
I'M A BOY...
YAY
WELL, YOU LOOK GOOD LIKE THAT!
YOU GUYS, CAN WE EAT THE CINNAMON ROLLS?
YEAH!
LET'S DIG IN!
THUNK

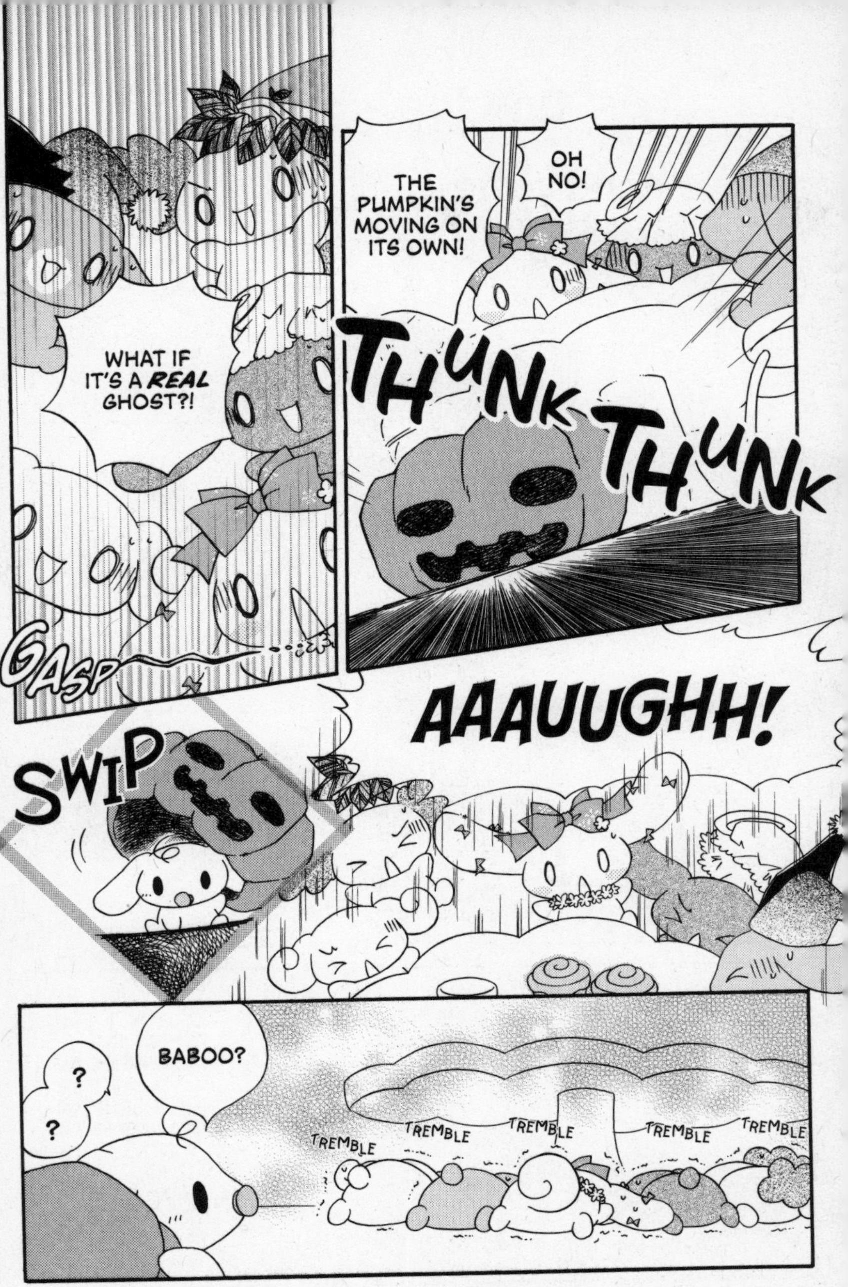
OH NO!
THE PUMPKIN'S MOVING ON ITS OWN!
THUNK THUNK
WHAT IF IT'S A *REAL* GHOST?!
GASP
AAAUUGHH!
SWIP
TREMBLE
TREMBLE
TREMBLE
TREMBLE
TREMBLE
BABOO?
? ?

# Girls' Day for Everyone

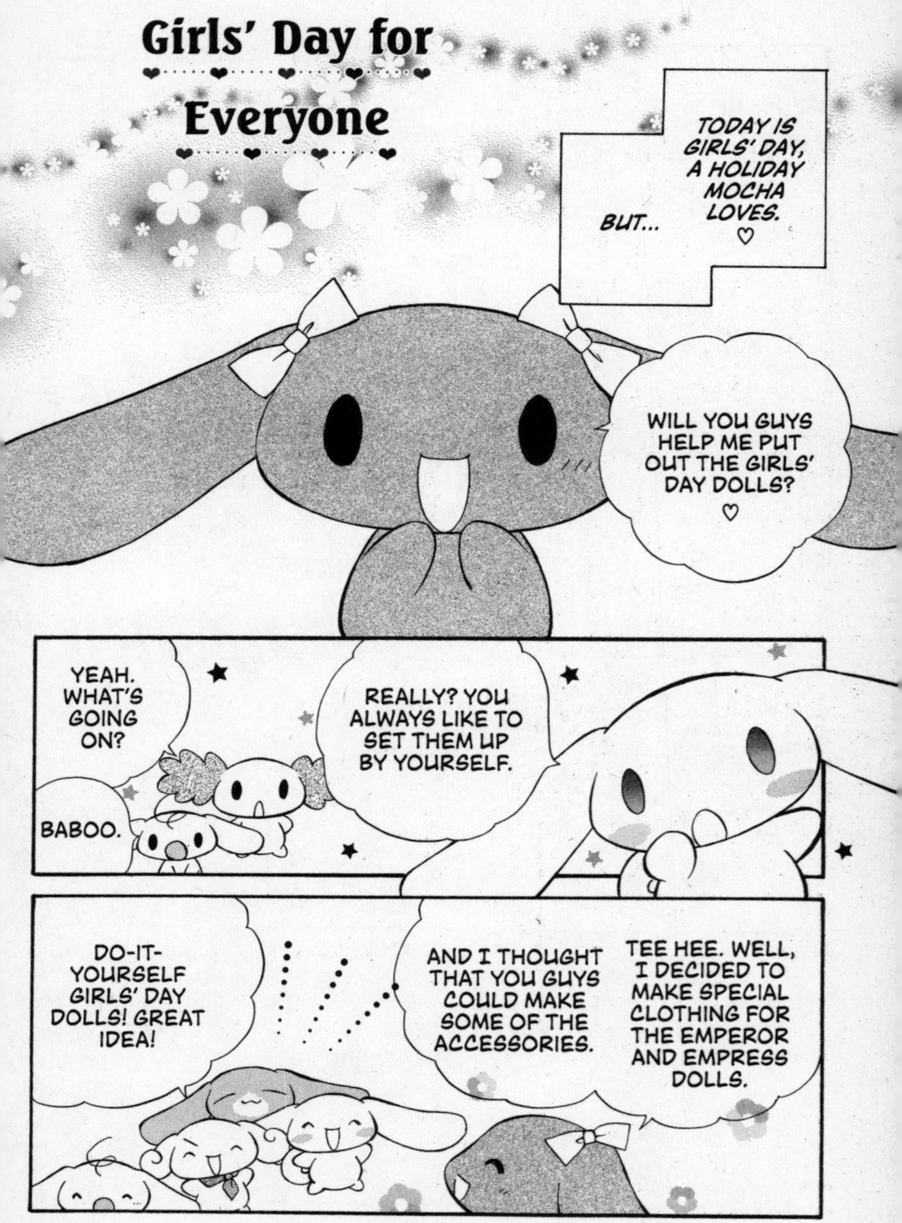
TODAY IS GIRLS' DAY, A HOLIDAY MOCHA LOVES. ♡
BUT...
WILL YOU GUYS HELP ME PUT OUT THE GIRLS' DAY DOLLS? ♡
REALLY? YOU ALWAYS LIKE TO SET THEM UP BY YOURSELF.
YEAH. WHAT'S GOING ON?
BABOO.
TEE HEE. WELL, I DECIDED TO MAKE SPECIAL CLOTHING FOR THE EMPEROR AND EMPRESS DOLLS.
AND I THOUGHT THAT YOU GUYS COULD MAKE SOME OF THE ACCESSORIES.
DO-IT-YOURSELF GIRLS' DAY DOLLS! GREAT IDEA!

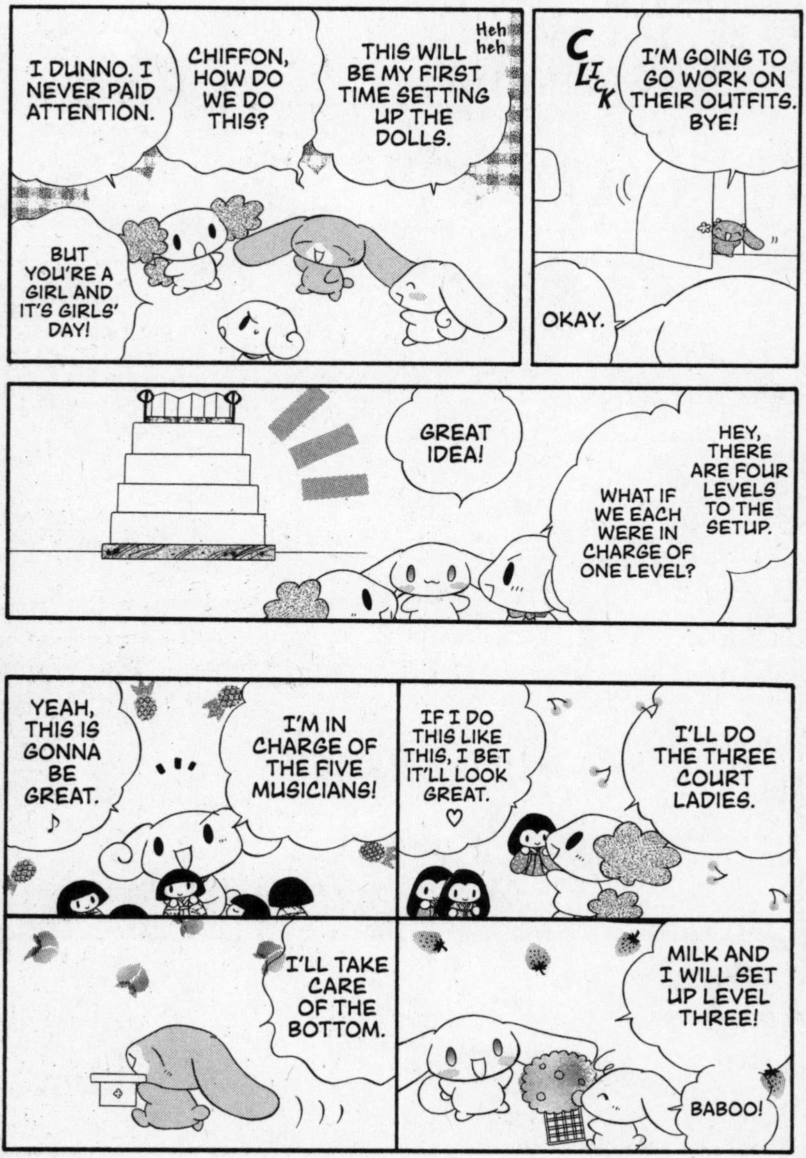
CLICK
I'M GOING TO GO WORK ON THEIR OUTFITS. BYE!
OKAY.
Heh heh
THIS WILL BE MY FIRST TIME SETTING UP THE DOLLS.
CHIFFON, HOW DO WE DO THIS?
I DUNNO. I NEVER PAID ATTENTION.
BUT YOU'RE A GIRL AND IT'S GIRLS' DAY!
HEY, THERE ARE FOUR LEVELS TO THE SETUP.
WHAT IF WE EACH WERE IN CHARGE OF ONE LEVEL?
GREAT IDEA!
I'LL DO THE THREE COURT LADIES.
IF I DO THIS LIKE THIS, I BET IT'LL LOOK GREAT. ♡
I'M IN CHARGE OF THE FIVE MUSICIANS!
YEAH, THIS IS GONNA BE GREAT. ♪
MILK AND I WILL SET UP LEVEL THREE!
BABOO!
I'LL TAKE CARE OF THE BOTTOM.

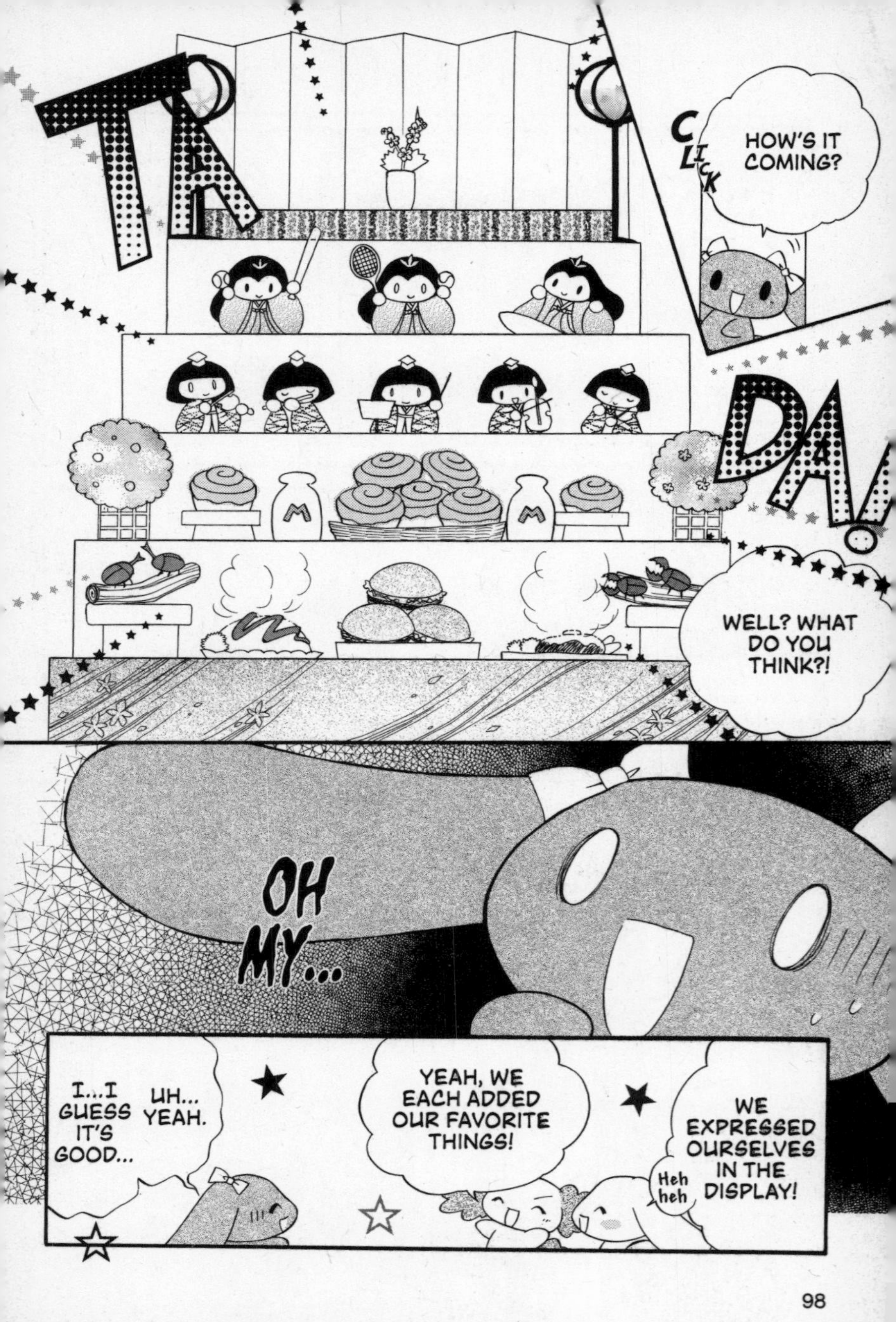
CLICK
HOW'S IT COMING?
TA-DA!
WELL? WHAT DO YOU THINK?!
OH MY...
WE EXPRESSED OURSELVES IN THE DISPLAY!
Heh heh
YEAH, WE EACH ADDED OUR FAVORITE THINGS!
UH... YEAH.
I...I GUESS IT'S GOOD...

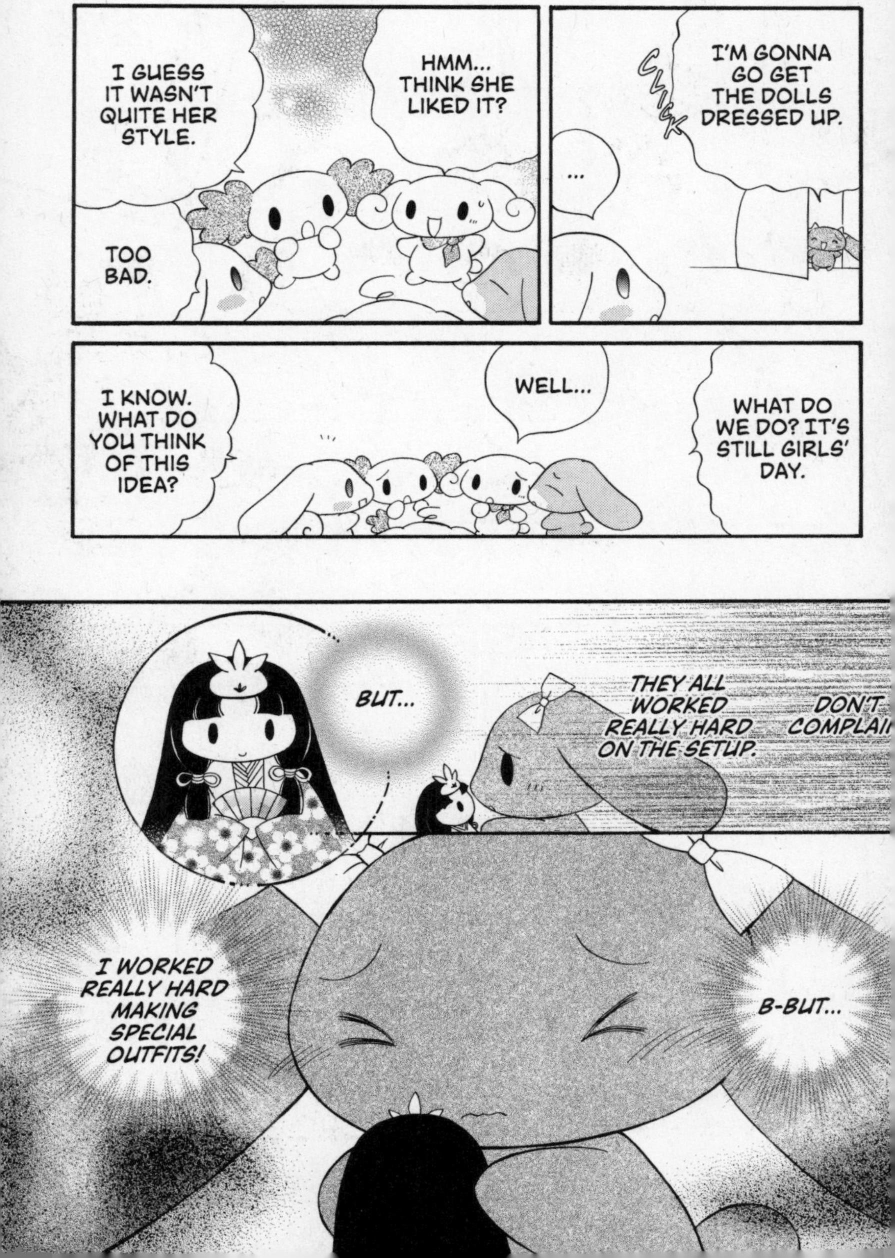
I'M GONNA GO GET THE DOLLS DRESSED UP.
CLICK
...
HMM... THINK SHE LIKED IT?
I GUESS IT WASN'T QUITE HER STYLE.
TOO BAD.
WHAT DO WE DO? IT'S STILL GIRLS' DAY.
WELL...
I KNOW. WHAT DO YOU THINK OF THIS IDEA?
DON'T COMPLAI
THEY ALL WORKED REALLY HARD ON THE SETUP.
BUT...
B-BUT...
I WORKED REALLY HARD MAKING SPECIAL OUTFITS!

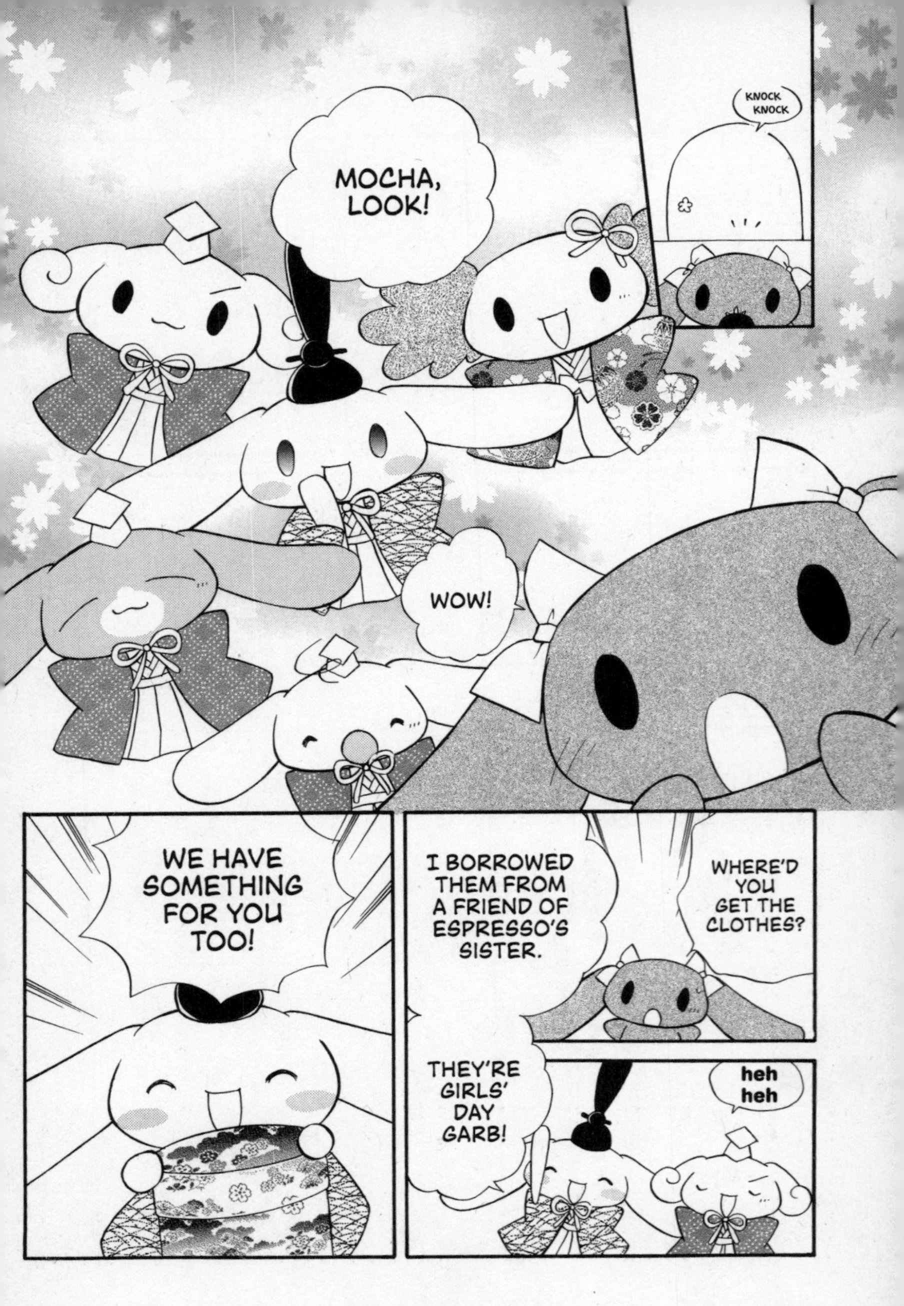
KNOCK KNOCK
MOCHA, LOOK!
WOW!
WHERE'D YOU GET THE CLOTHES?
I BORROWED THEM FROM A FRIEND OF ESPRESSO'S SISTER.
heh heh
THEY'RE GIRLS' DAY GARB!
WE HAVE SOMETHING FOR YOU TOO!

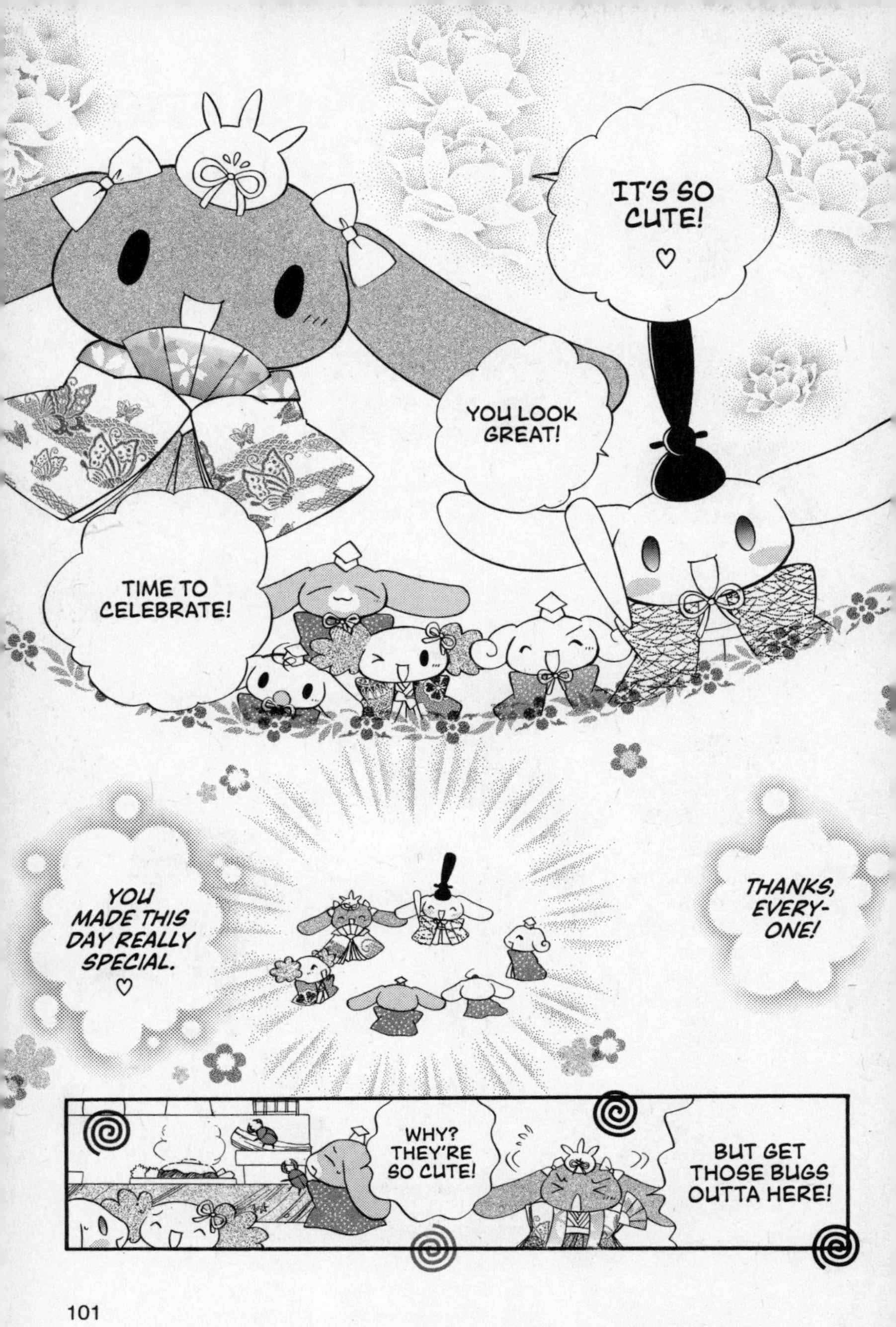
IT'S SO CUTE! ♡
YOU LOOK GREAT!
TIME TO CELEBRATE!
THANKS, EVERY-ONE!
YOU MADE THIS DAY REALLY SPECIAL. ♡
BUT GET THOSE BUGS OUTTA HERE!
WHY? THEY'RE SO CUTE!

# Meet the Mysterious Characters!
( PART 2 )

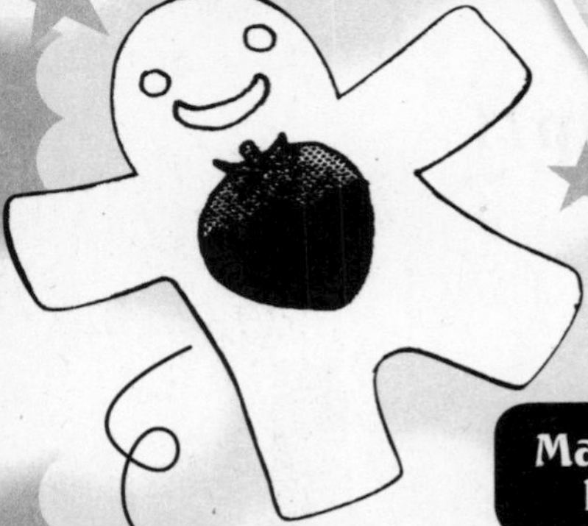

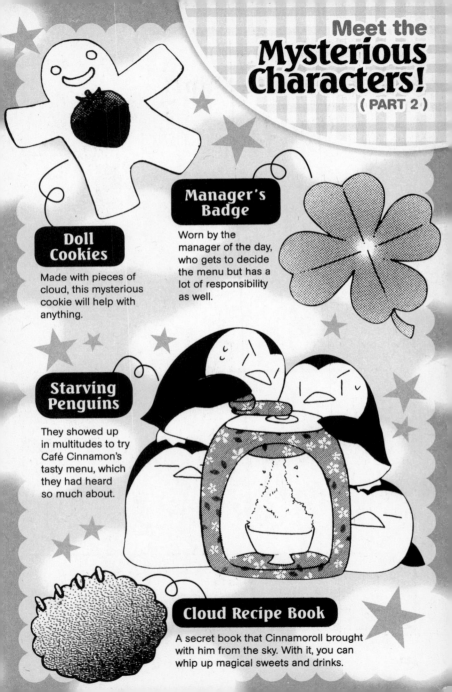

## Doll Cookies

Made with pieces of cloud, this mysterious cookie will help with anything.

## Manager's Badge

Worn by the manager of the day, who gets to decide the menu but has a lot of responsibility as well.

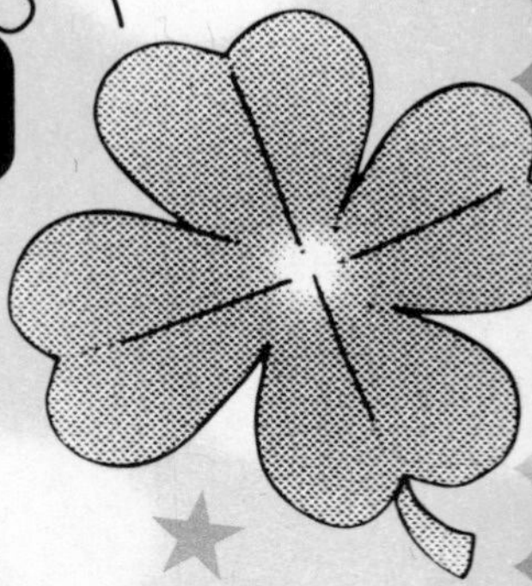

## Starving Penguins

They showed up in multitudes to try Café Cinnamon's tasty menu, which they had heard so much about.

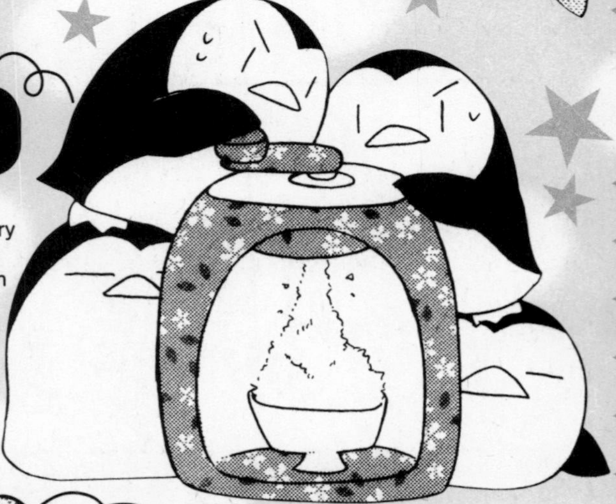

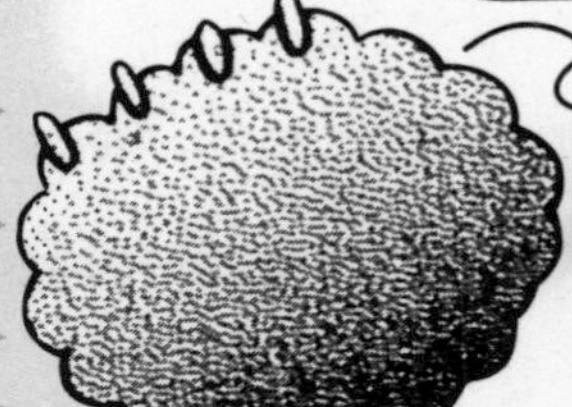

## Cloud Recipe Book

A secret book that Cinnamoroll brought with him from the sky. With it, you can whip up magical sweets and drinks.

It's Summer! Time for Fun!

# A Sunken Cruise Ship?!

## (Part 1)

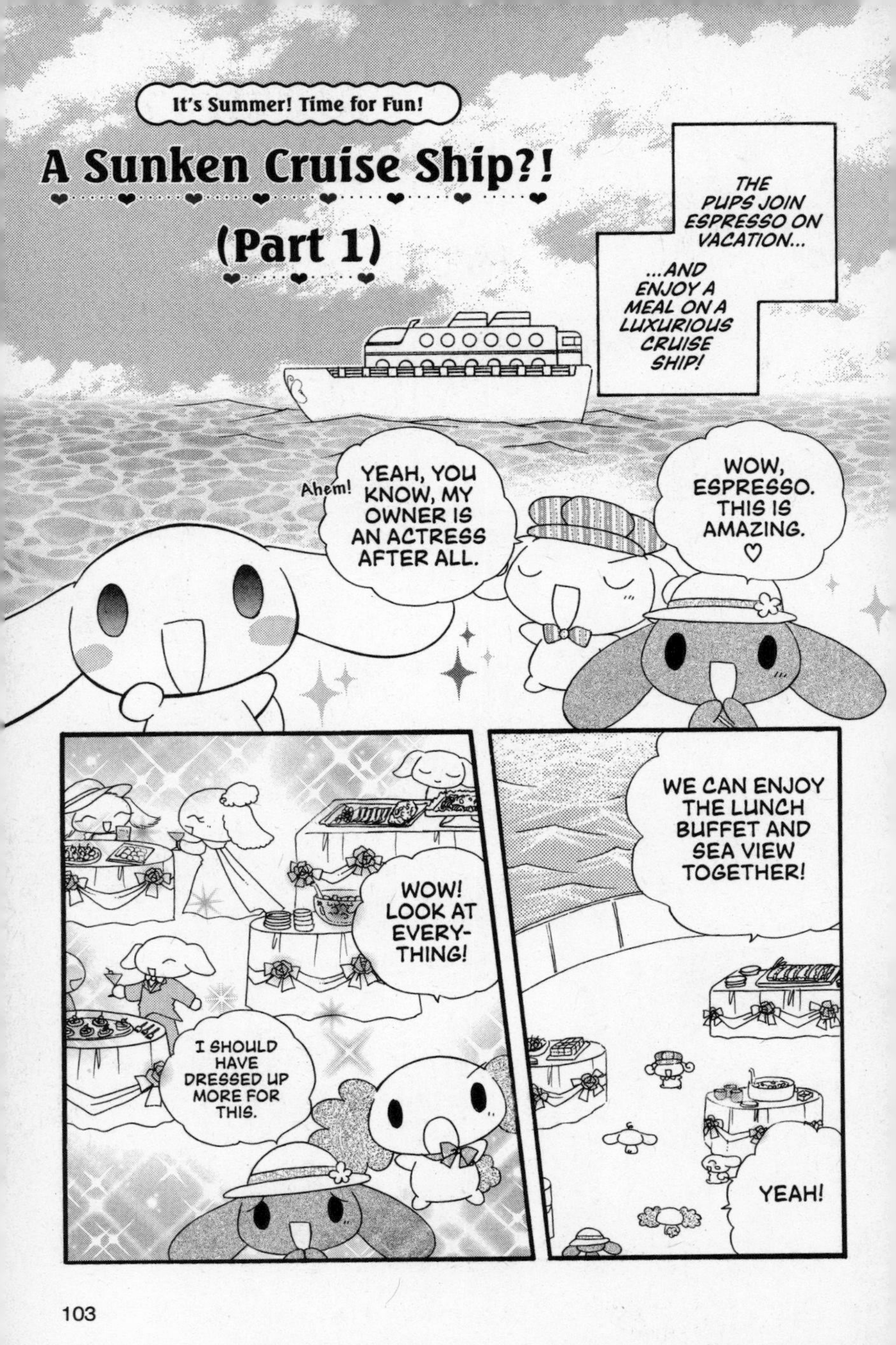

THE PUPS JOIN ESPRESSO ON VACATION...
...AND ENJOY A MEAL ON A LUXURIOUS CRUISE SHIP!
WOW, ESPRESSO. THIS IS AMAZING. ♡
Ahem!
YEAH, YOU KNOW, MY OWNER IS AN ACTRESS AFTER ALL.
WE CAN ENJOY THE LUNCH BUFFET AND SEA VIEW TOGETHER!
YEAH!
WOW! LOOK AT EVERY-THING!
I SHOULD HAVE DRESSED UP MORE FOR THIS.

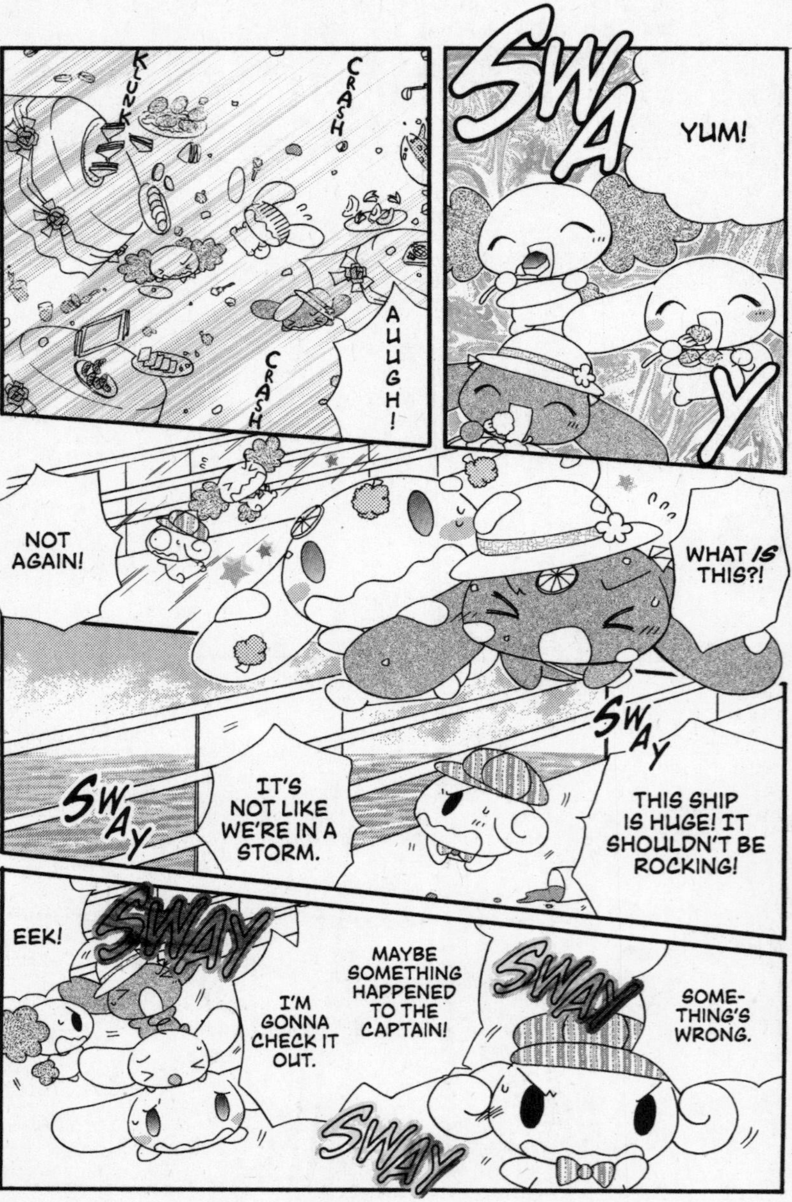
SWAY
YUM!
CRASH
KLUNK
AUUGH!
CRASH
WHAT *IS* THIS?!
NOT AGAIN!
SWAY
THIS SHIP IS HUGE! IT SHOULDN'T BE ROCKING!
IT'S NOT LIKE WE'RE IN A STORM.
SWAY
SOMETHING'S WRONG.
SWAY
MAYBE SOMETHING HAPPENED TO THE CAPTAIN!
I'M GONNA CHECK IT OUT.
SWAY
EEK!
SWAY

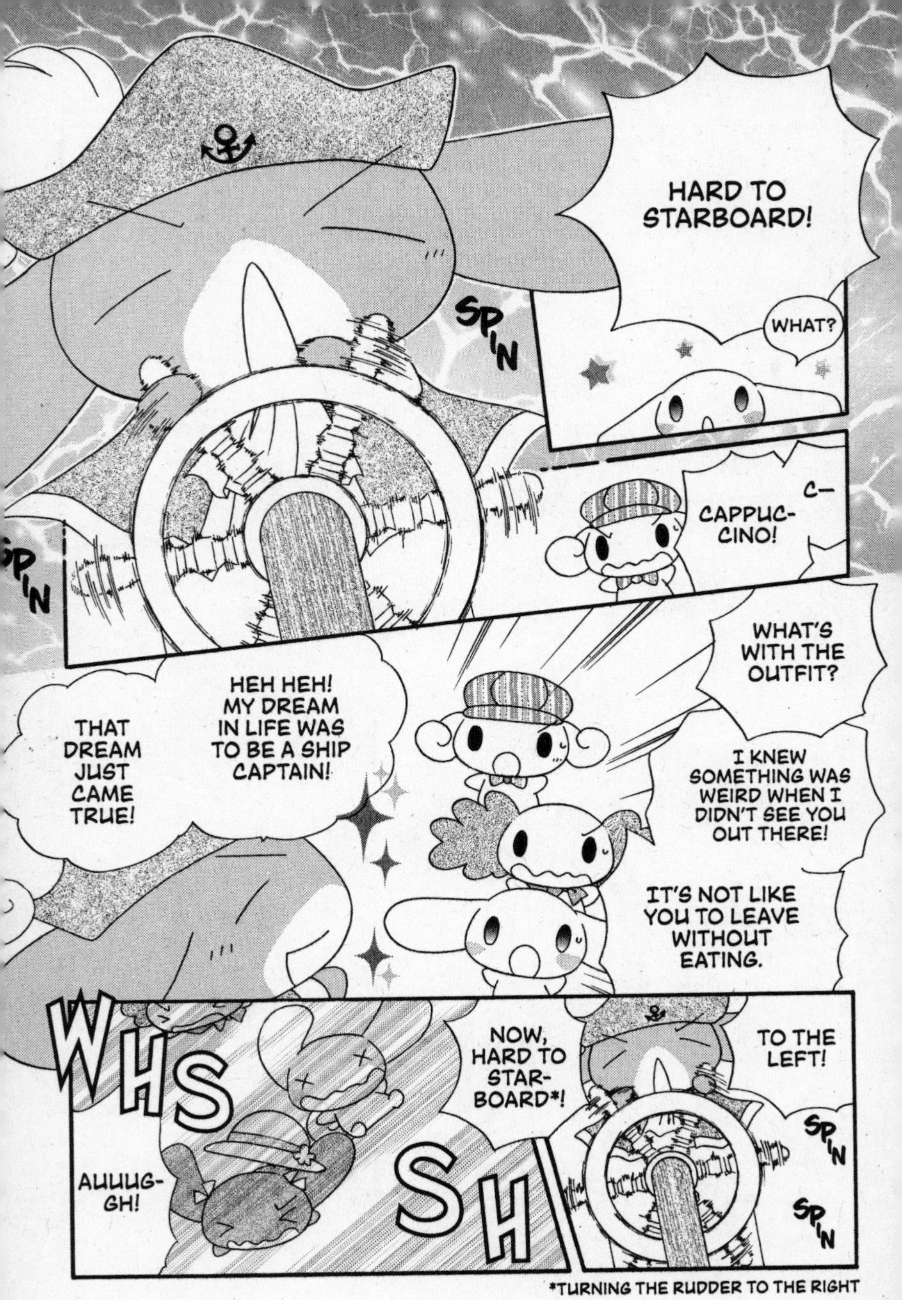
HARD TO STARBOARD!
SPIN
WHAT?
C— CAPPUC-CINO!
SPIN
WHAT'S WITH THE OUTFIT?
I KNEW SOMETHING WAS WEIRD WHEN I DIDN'T SEE YOU OUT THERE!
IT'S NOT LIKE YOU TO LEAVE WITHOUT EATING.
HEH HEH! MY DREAM IN LIFE WAS TO BE A SHIP CAPTAIN!
THAT DREAM JUST CAME TRUE!
TO THE LEFT!
SPIN
SPIN
NOW, HARD TO STAR-BOARD*!
WHSSH
AUUUG-GH!

*TURNING THE RUDDER TO THE RIGHT

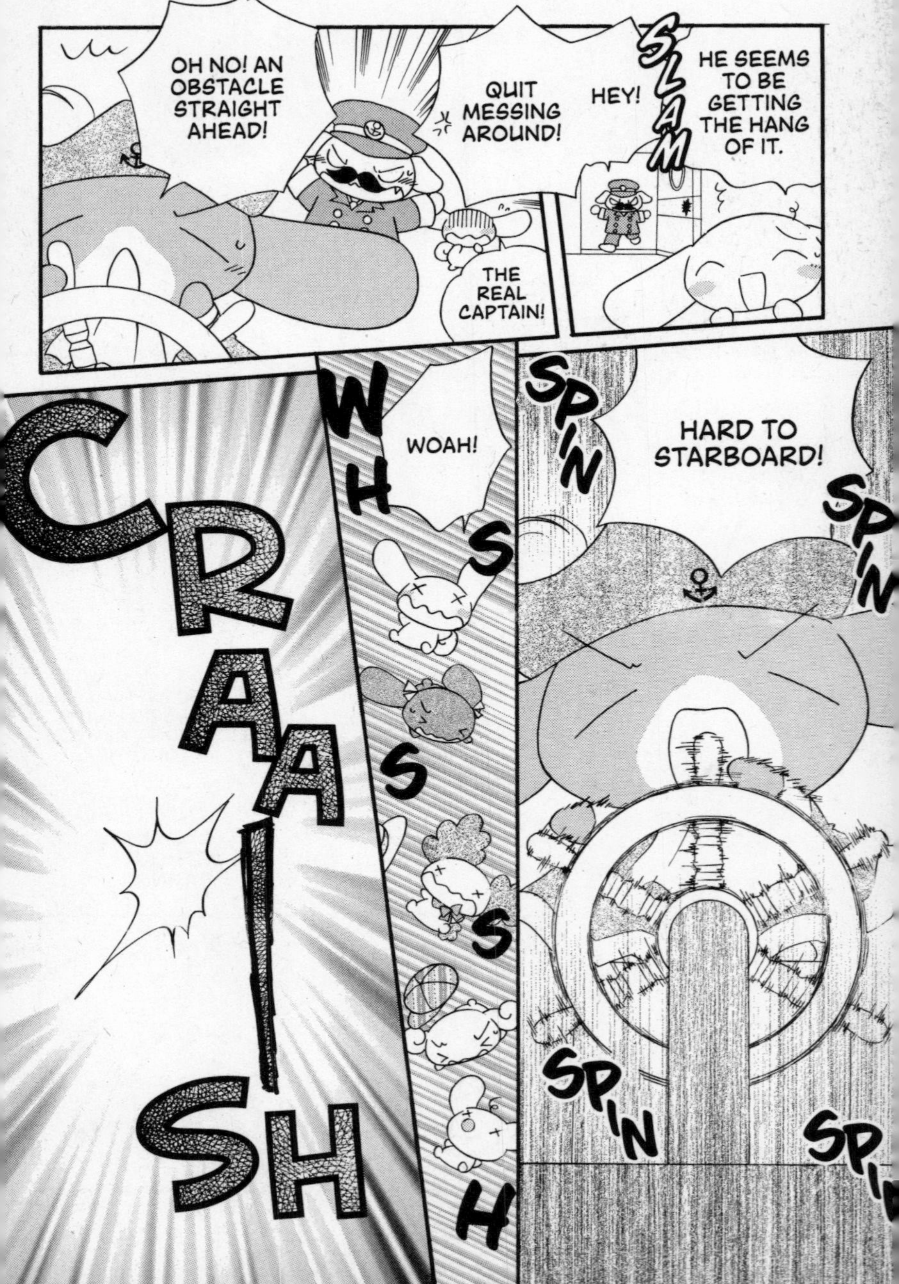
HE SEEMS TO BE GETTING THE HANG OF IT.
SLAM
HEY!
QUIT MESSING AROUND!
THE REAL CAPTAIN!
OH NO! AN OBSTACLE STRAIGHT AHEAD!
HARD TO STARBOARD!
SPIN
SPIN
SPIN
WOAH!
WHSSSSH
CRAAASH

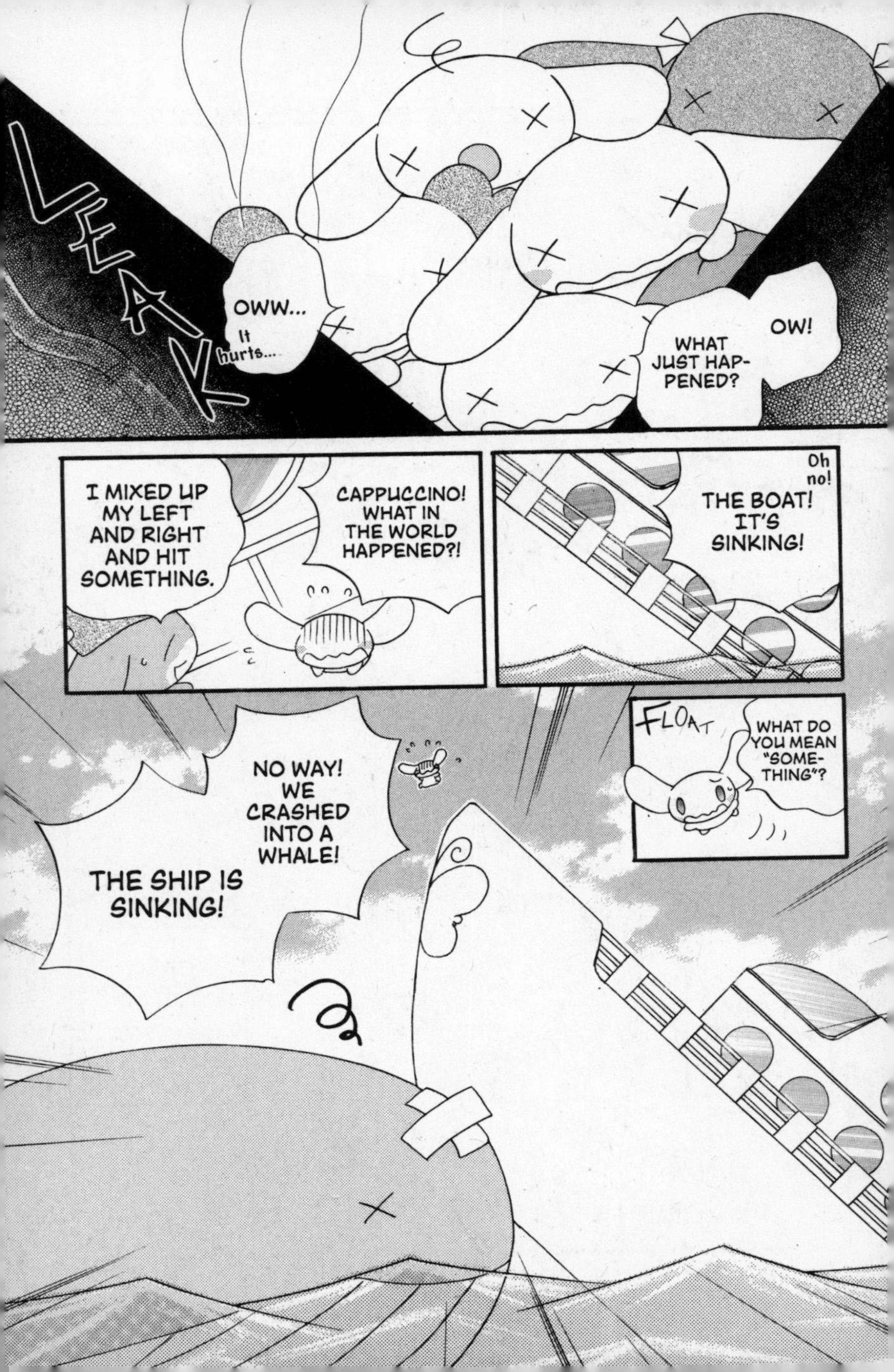
OW!
WHAT JUST HAP-PENED?
OWW... It hurts...
LEAK
Oh no!
THE BOAT! IT'S SINKING!
CAPPUCCINO! WHAT IN THE WORLD HAPPENED?!
I MIXED UP MY LEFT AND RIGHT AND HIT SOMETHING.
FLOAT
WHAT DO YOU MEAN "SOME-THING"?
NO WAY! WE CRASHED INTO A WHALE!
THE SHIP IS SINKING!

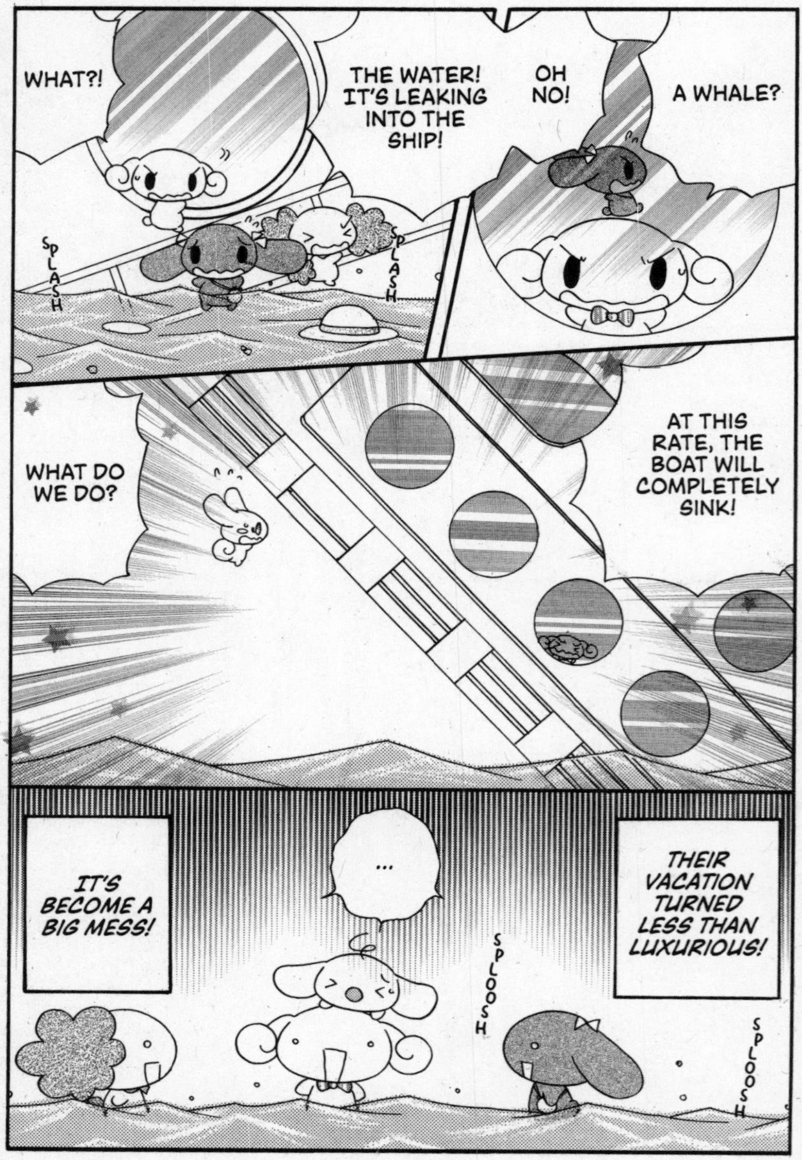
A WHALE?
OH NO!
THE WATER! IT'S LEAKING INTO THE SHIP!
WHAT?!
SPLASH
SPLASH
AT THIS RATE, THE BOAT WILL COMPLETELY SINK!
WHAT DO WE DO?
THEIR VACATION TURNED LESS THAN LUXURIOUS!
SPLOOSH
SPLOOSH
...
IT'S BECOME A BIG MESS!

# A Sunken Cruise Ship?!
## (Part 2)

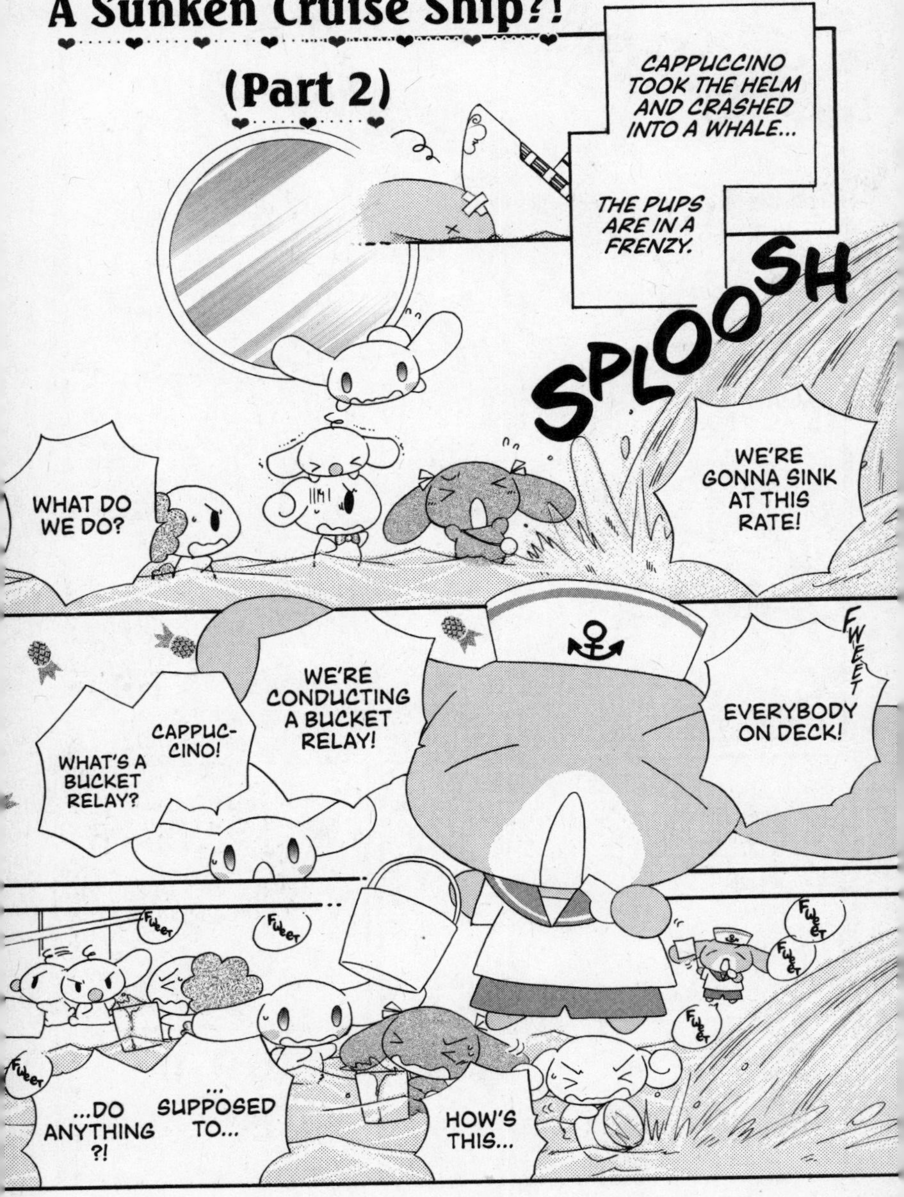
CAPPUCCINO TOOK THE HELM AND CRASHED INTO A WHALE...
THE PUPS ARE IN A FRENZY.
SPLOOSH
WE'RE GONNA SINK AT THIS RATE!
WHAT DO WE DO?
FWEET
EVERYBODY ON DECK!
WE'RE CONDUCTING A BUCKET RELAY!
CAPPUC-CINO!
WHAT'S A BUCKET RELAY?
Fweet
Fweet
Fweet
Fweet
Fweet
Fweet
HOW'S THIS...
... SUPPOSED TO...
...DO ANYTHING ?!

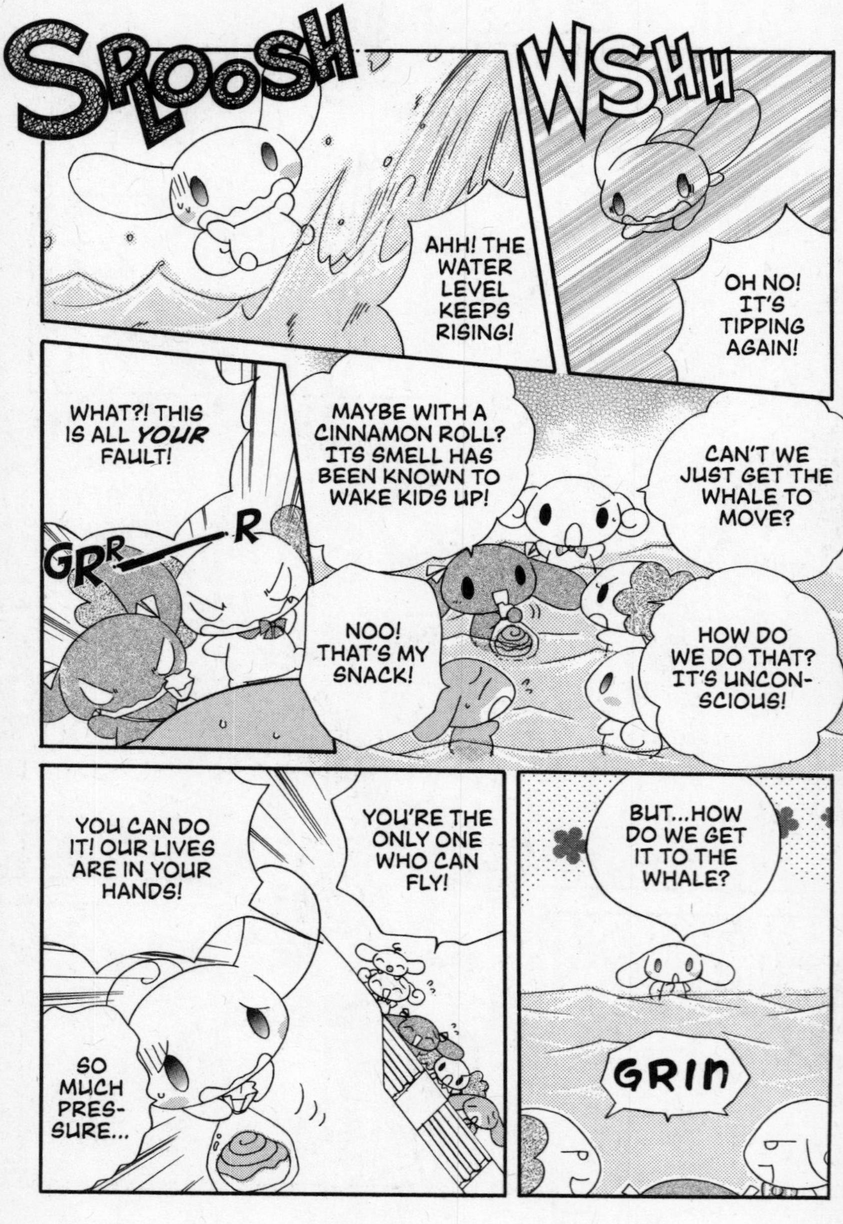
WSHH
OH NO! IT'S TIPPING AGAIN!
SPLOOSH
AHH! THE WATER LEVEL KEEPS RISING!
CAN'T WE JUST GET THE WHALE TO MOVE?
HOW DO WE DO THAT? IT'S UNCONSCIOUS!
MAYBE WITH A CINNAMON ROLL? ITS SMELL HAS BEEN KNOWN TO WAKE KIDS UP!
NOO! THAT'S MY SNACK!
WHAT?! THIS IS ALL *YOUR* FAULT!
GRR—R
BUT...HOW DO WE GET IT TO THE WHALE?
GRIN
YOU'RE THE ONLY ONE WHO CAN FLY!
YOU CAN DO IT! OUR LIVES ARE IN YOUR HANDS!
SO MUCH PRES-SURE...

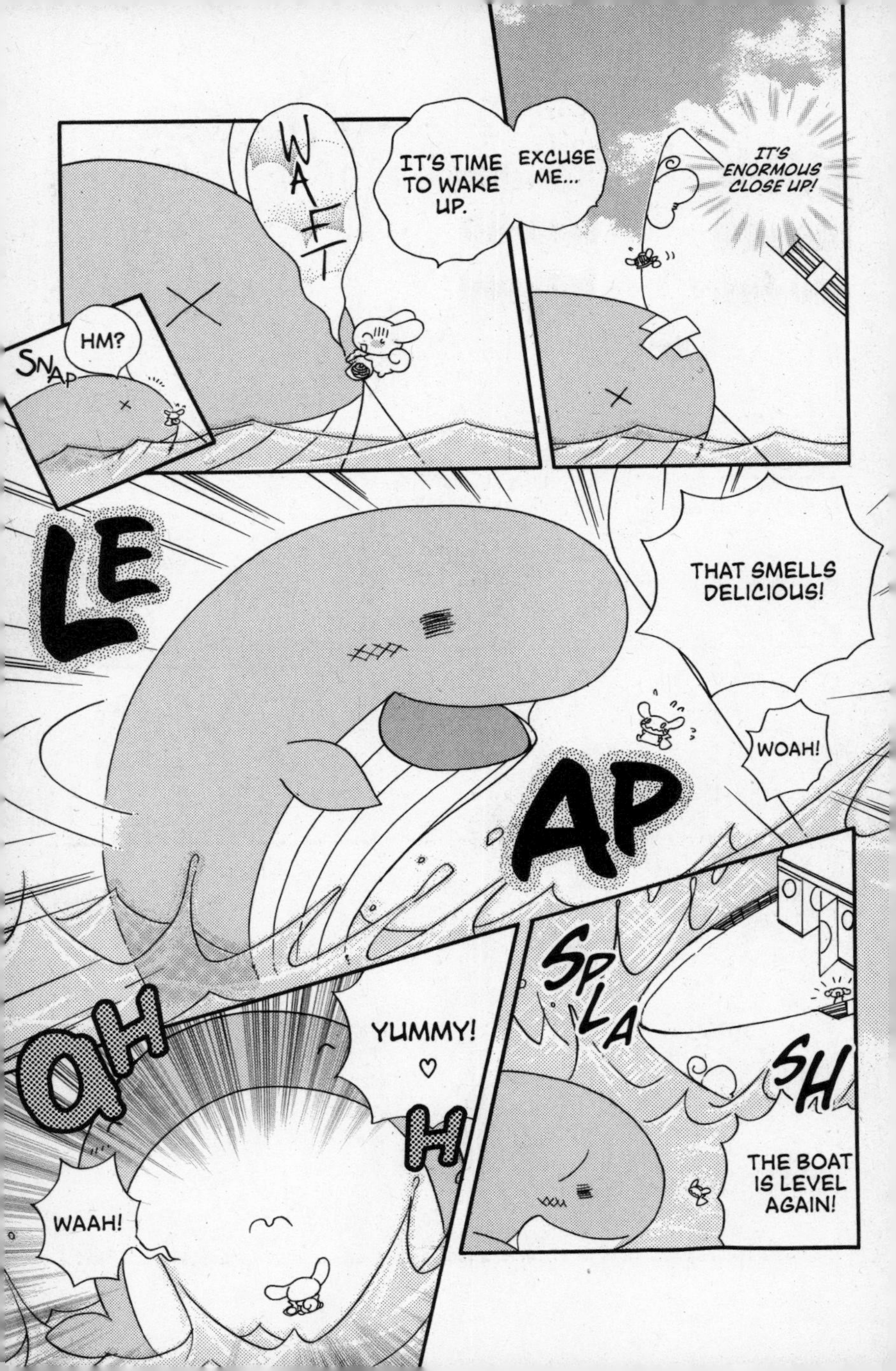
IT'S ENORMOUS CLOSE UP!
EXCUSE ME...
IT'S TIME TO WAKE UP.
WAFT
HM?
SNAP
THAT SMELLS DELICIOUS!
WOAH!
LE
AP
SPLA
SH
THE BOAT IS LEVEL AGAIN!
YUMMY! ♡
OH
H
WAAH!

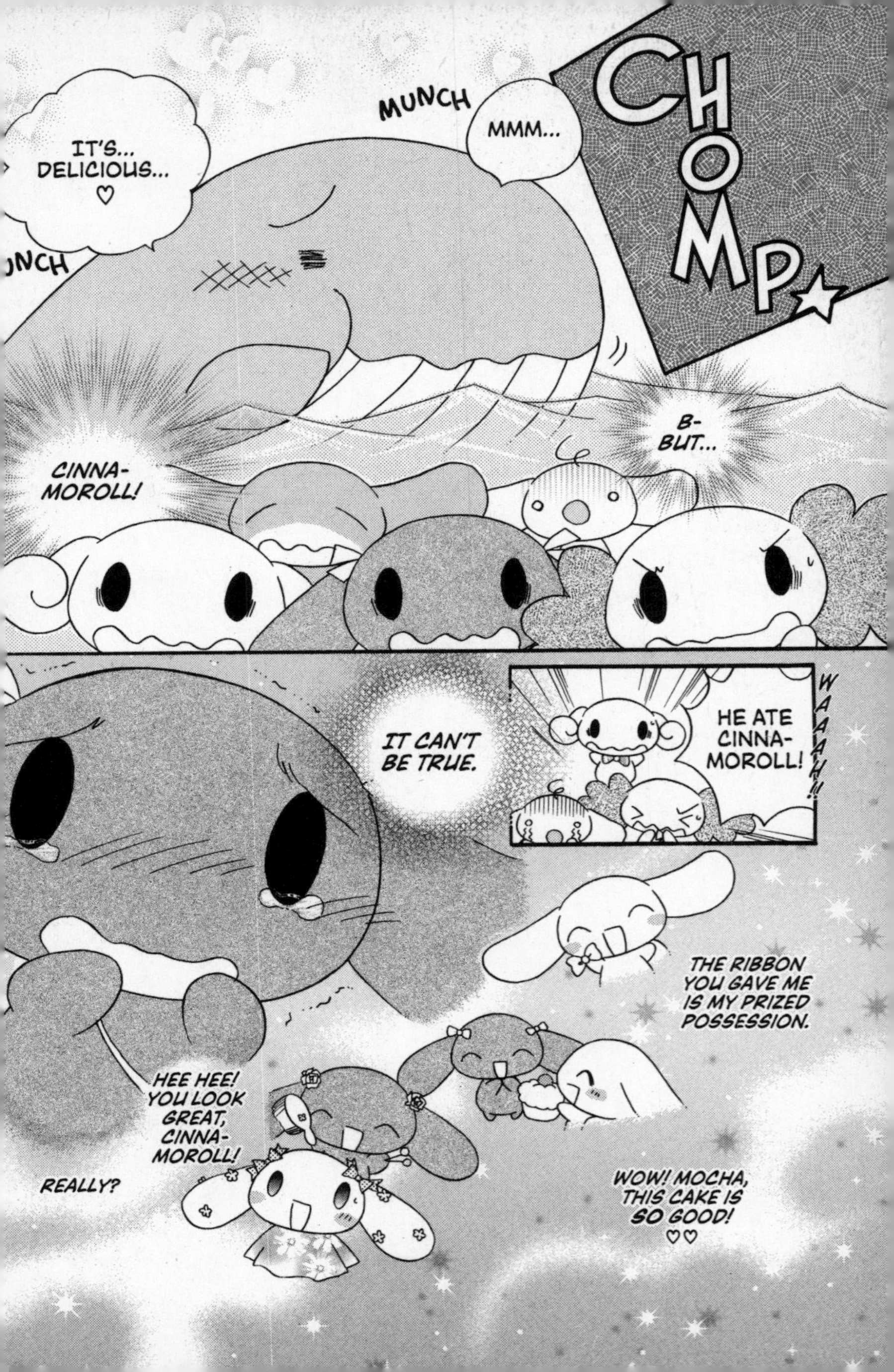
CHOMP★
MMM...
MUNCH
IT'S... DELICIOUS... ♡
UNCH
B-BUT...
CINNA-MOROLL!
WAAAAH!!
HE ATE CINNA-MOROLL!
IT CAN'T BE TRUE.
THE RIBBON YOU GAVE ME IS MY PRIZED POSSESSION.
WOW! MOCHA, THIS CAKE IS SO GOOD! ♡♡
HEE HEE! YOU LOOK GREAT, CINNA-MOROLL!
REALLY?

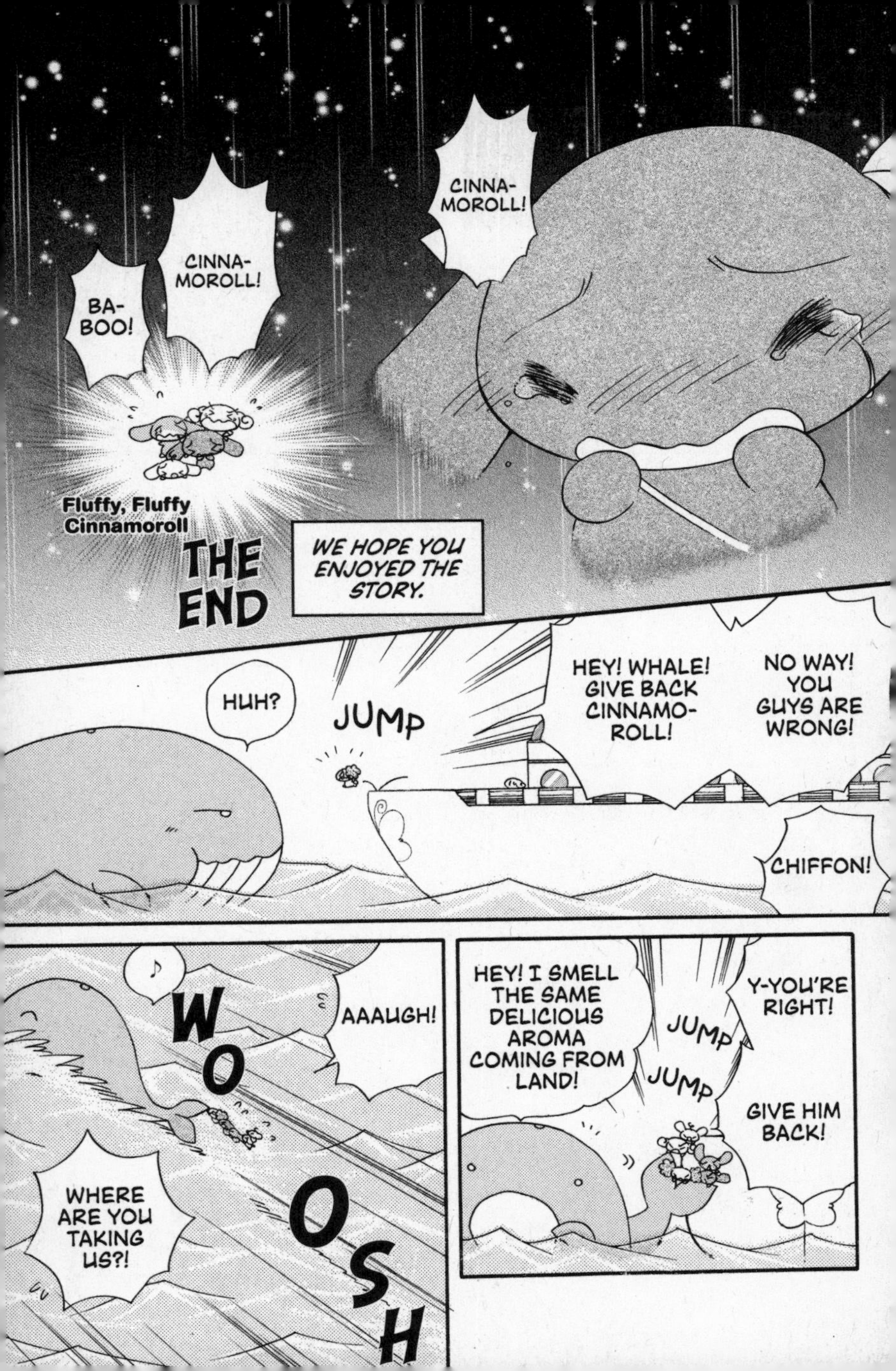
CINNA-MOROLL!
CINNA-MOROLL!
BA-BOO!
Fluffy, Fluffy Cinnamoroll
THE END
WE HOPE YOU ENJOYED THE STORY.
NO WAY! YOU GUYS ARE WRONG!
HEY! WHALE! GIVE BACK CINNAMO-ROLL!
CHIFFON!
JUMP
HUH?
Y-YOU'RE RIGHT!
HEY! I SMELL THE SAME DELICIOUS AROMA COMING FROM LAND!
JUMP
JUMP
GIVE HIM BACK!
♪
AAAUGH!
WOOSH
WHERE ARE YOU TAKING US?!

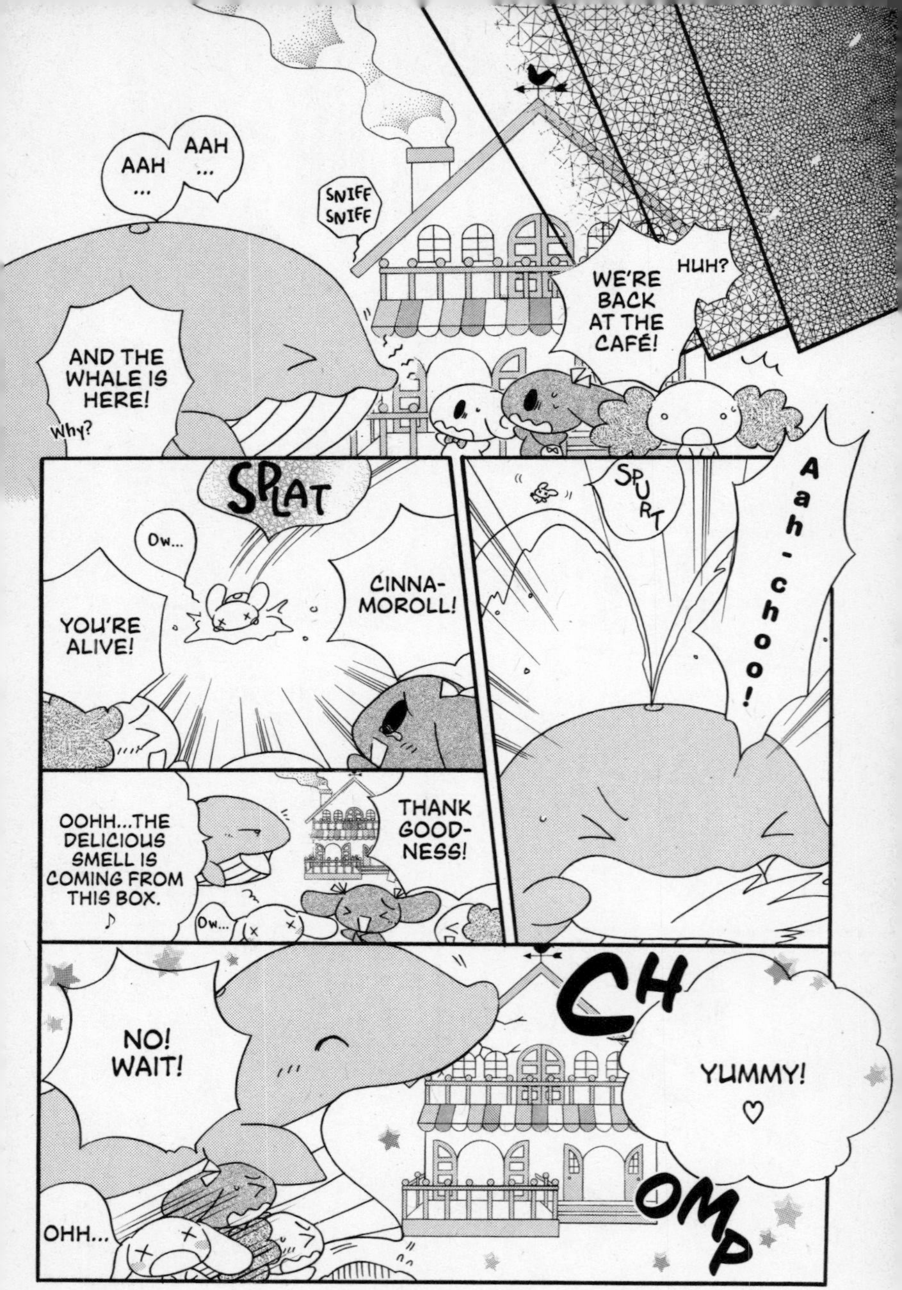
HUH?
WE'RE BACK AT THE CAFÉ!
SNIFF SNIFF
AAH ...
AAH ...
AND THE WHALE IS HERE!
Why?
Aah-choo!
SPURT
SPLAT
CINNA-MOROLL!
Ow...
YOU'RE ALIVE!
THANK GOODNESS!
OOHH...THE DELICIOUS SMELL IS COMING FROM THIS BOX. ♪
Ow...
CHOMP
YUMMY! ♡
NO! WAIT!
OHH...

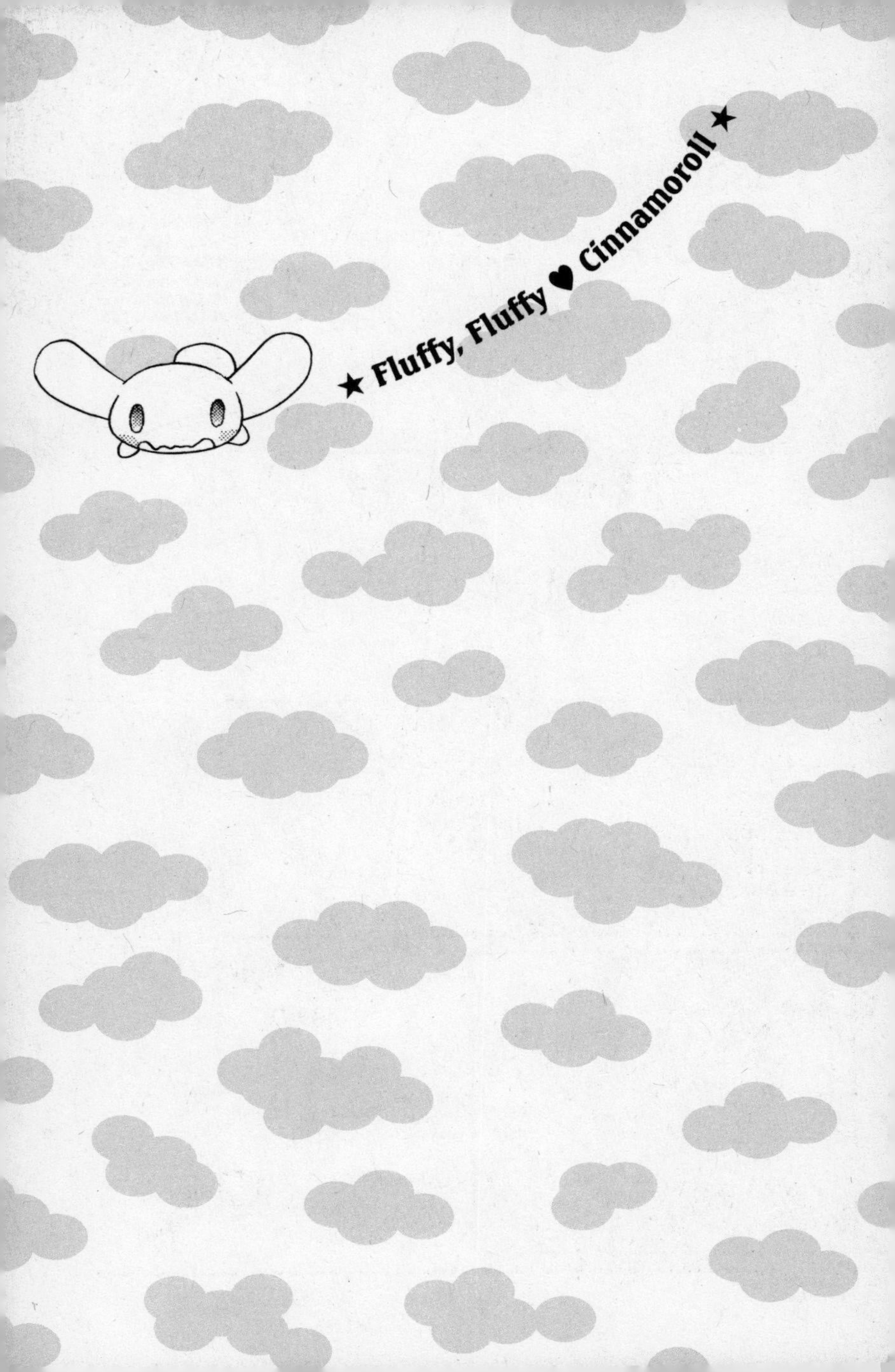
★ Fluffy, Fluffy ♥ Cinnamoroll ★

# Caught on a Deserted Island!

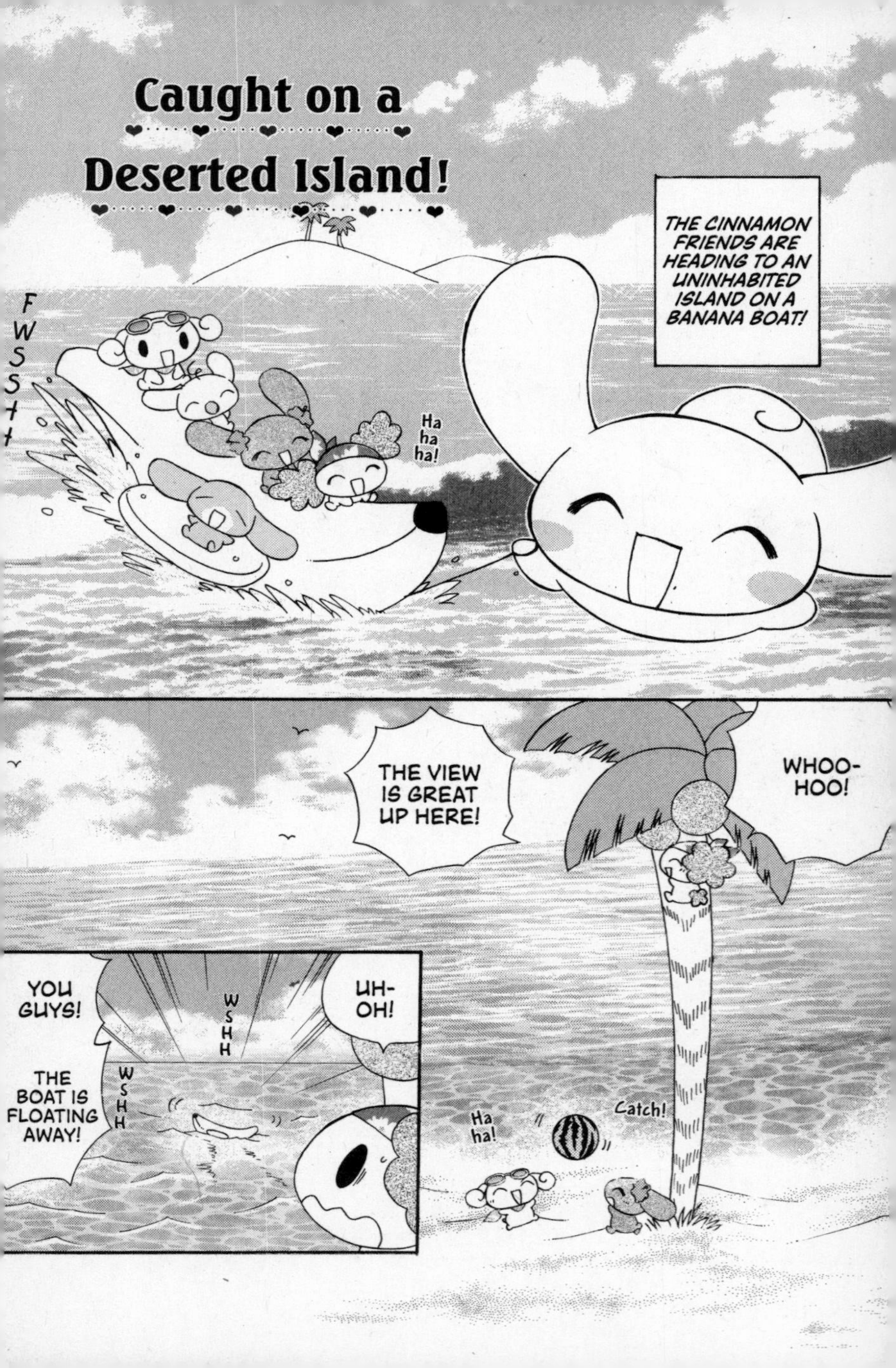
THE CINNAMON FRIENDS ARE HEADING TO AN UNINHABITED ISLAND ON A BANANA BOAT!
Ha ha ha!
FWSSTT
WHOO-HOO!
THE VIEW IS GREAT UP HERE!
Catch!
Ha ha!
UH-OH!
WSHH
YOU GUYS!
WSHH
THE BOAT IS FLOATING AWAY!

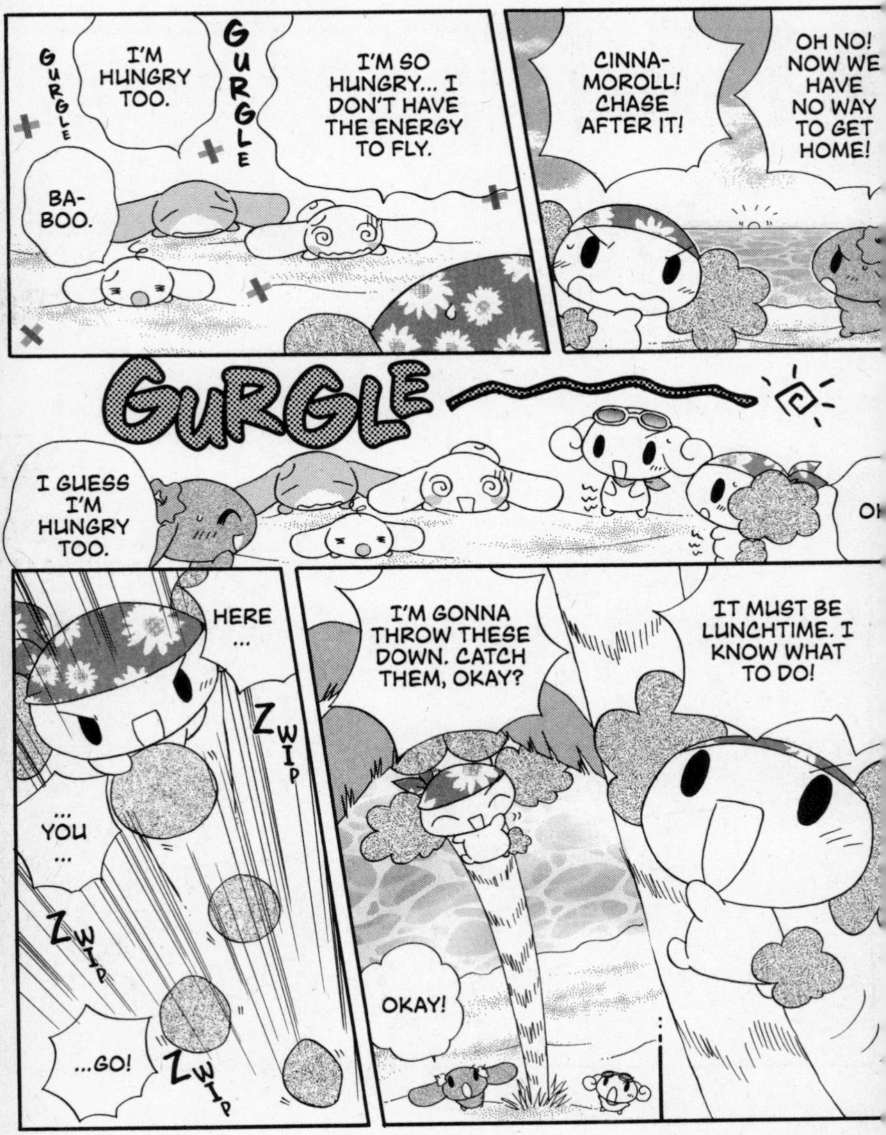
OH NO! NOW WE HAVE NO WAY TO GET HOME!
CINNA-MOROLL! CHASE AFTER IT!
I'M SO HUNGRY... I DON'T HAVE THE ENERGY TO FLY.
GURGLE
I'M HUNGRY TOO.
GURGLE
BA-BOO.
GURGLE
I GUESS I'M HUNGRY TOO.
IT MUST BE LUNCHTIME. I KNOW WHAT TO DO!
I'M GONNA THROW THESE DOWN. CATCH THEM, OKAY?
OKAY!
HERE ...
ZWIP
... YOU ...
ZWIP
...GO!
ZWIP

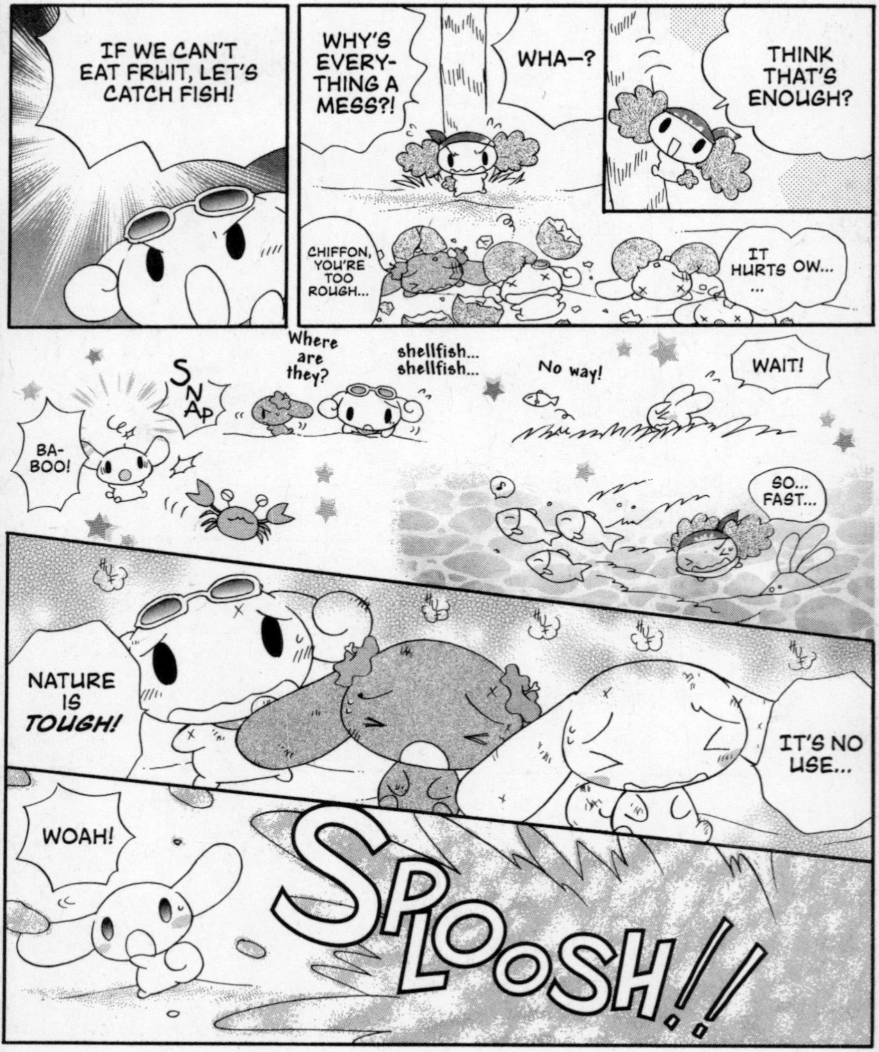
THINK THAT'S ENOUGH?
WHA—?
WHY'S EVERY-THING A MESS?!
IT HURTS OW... ...
CHIFFON, YOU'RE TOO ROUGH...
IF WE CAN'T EAT FRUIT, LET'S CATCH FISH!
WAIT!
No way!
shellfish... shellfish...
Where are they?
SNAP
SO... FAST...
BA-BOO!
IT'S NO USE...
NATURE IS TOUGH!
SPLOOSH!!
WOAH!

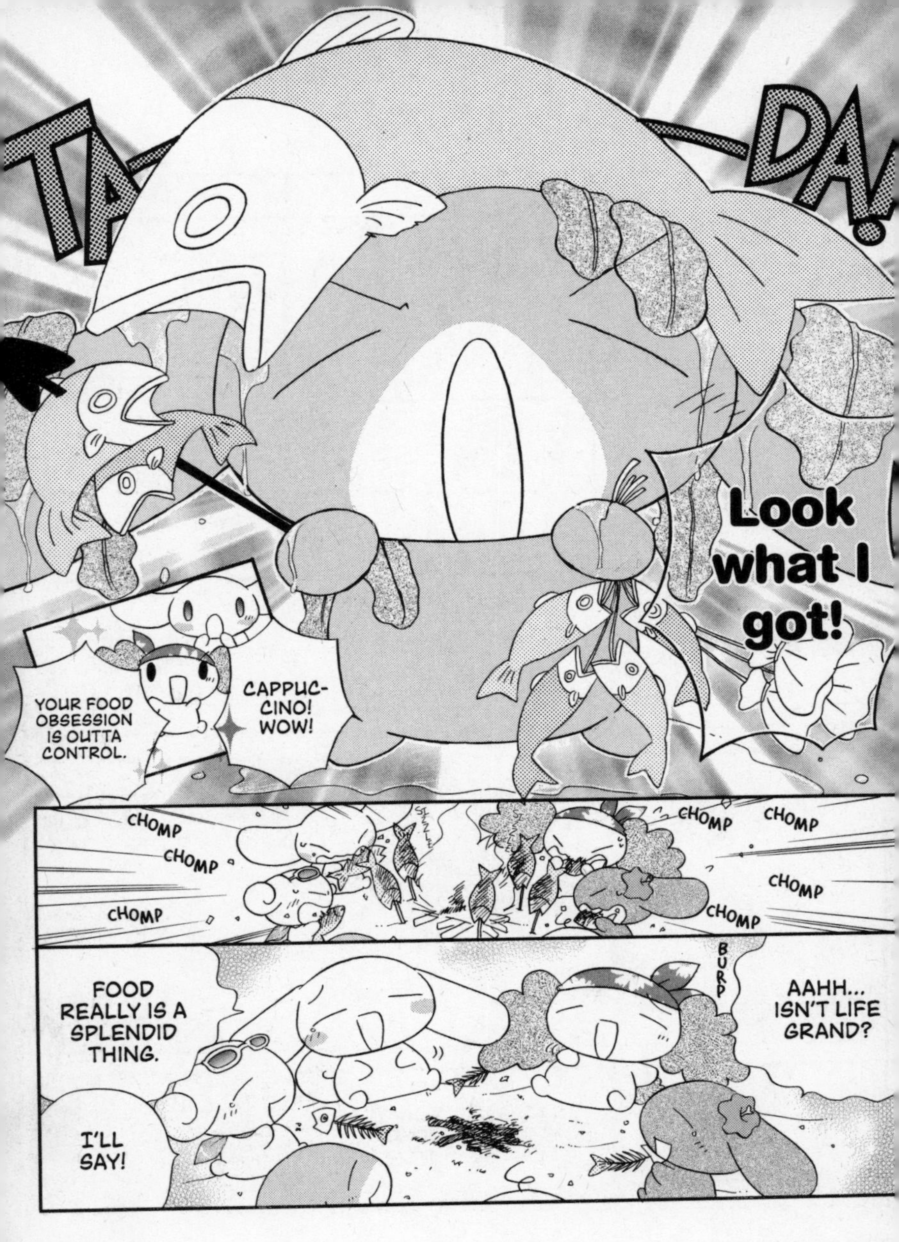
TA-DA!
Look what I got!
CAPPUC-CINO! WOW!
YOUR FOOD OBSESSION IS OUTTA CONTROL.
CHOMP CHOMP
CHOMP CHOMP
CHOMP
CHOMP CHOMP
CHOMP
BURP
AAHH... ISN'T LIFE GRAND?
FOOD REALLY IS A SPLENDID THING.
I'LL SAY!

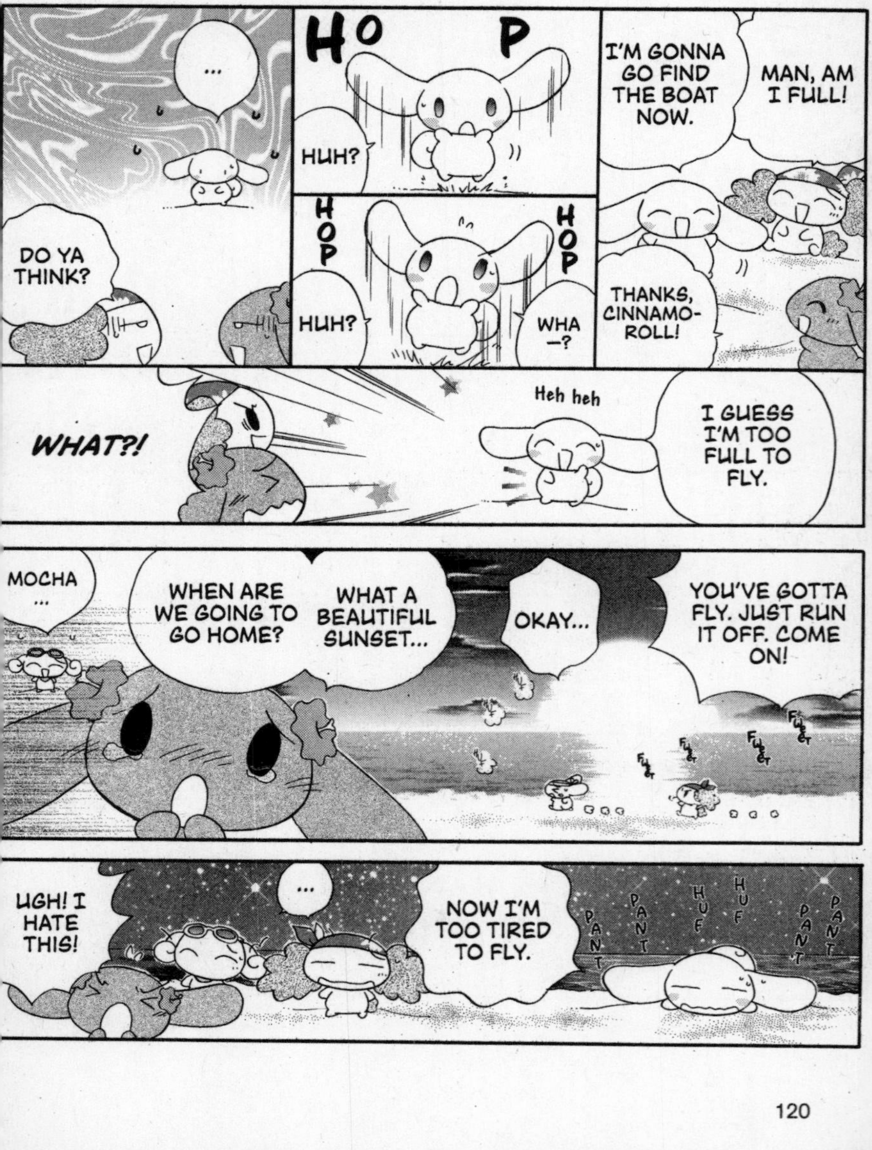
MAN, AM I FULL!
I'M GONNA GO FIND THE BOAT NOW.
THANKS, CINNAMO-ROLL!
HOP
HUH?
HOP
HOP
WHA—?
HUH?
...
DO YA THINK?
I GUESS I'M TOO FULL TO FLY.
Heh heh
WHAT?!
YOU'VE GOTTA FLY. JUST RUN IT OFF. COME ON!
OKAY...
WHAT A BEAUTIFUL SUNSET...
WHEN ARE WE GOING TO GO HOME?
MOCHA ...
PANT
PANT
HUF
HUF
PANT
PANT
NOW I'M TOO TIRED TO FLY.
...
UGH! I HATE THIS!

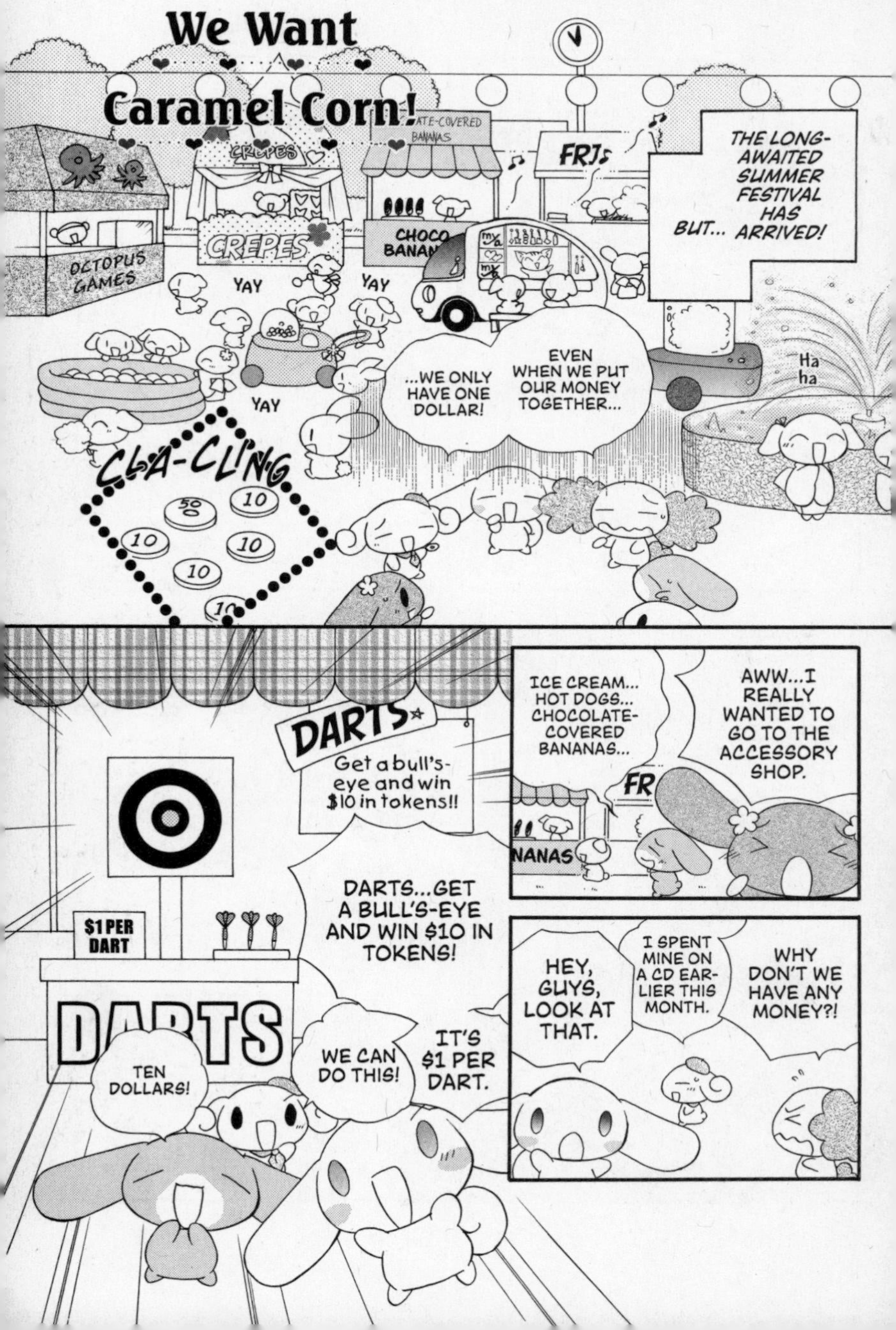
We Want Caramel Corn!
THE LONG-AWAITED SUMMER FESTIVAL HAS ARRIVED!
BUT...
FRJs
ATE-COVERED BANANAS
CHOCO BANANA
CREPES
OCTOPUS GAMES
EVEN WHEN WE PUT OUR MONEY TOGETHER...
...WE ONLY HAVE ONE DOLLAR!
Ha ha
YAY
YAY
YAY
CLA-CLING
AWW...I REALLY WANTED TO GO TO THE ACCESSORY SHOP.
ICE CREAM... HOT DOGS... CHOCOLATE-COVERED BANANAS...
FR
NANAS
WHY DON'T WE HAVE ANY MONEY?!
I SPENT MINE ON A CD EARLIER THIS MONTH.
HEY, GUYS, LOOK AT THAT.
DARTS
Get a bull's-eye and win $10 in tokens!!
DARTS...GET A BULL'S-EYE AND WIN $10 IN TOKENS!
IT'S $1 PER DART.
WE CAN DO THIS!
TEN DOLLARS!
$1 PER DART
DARTS

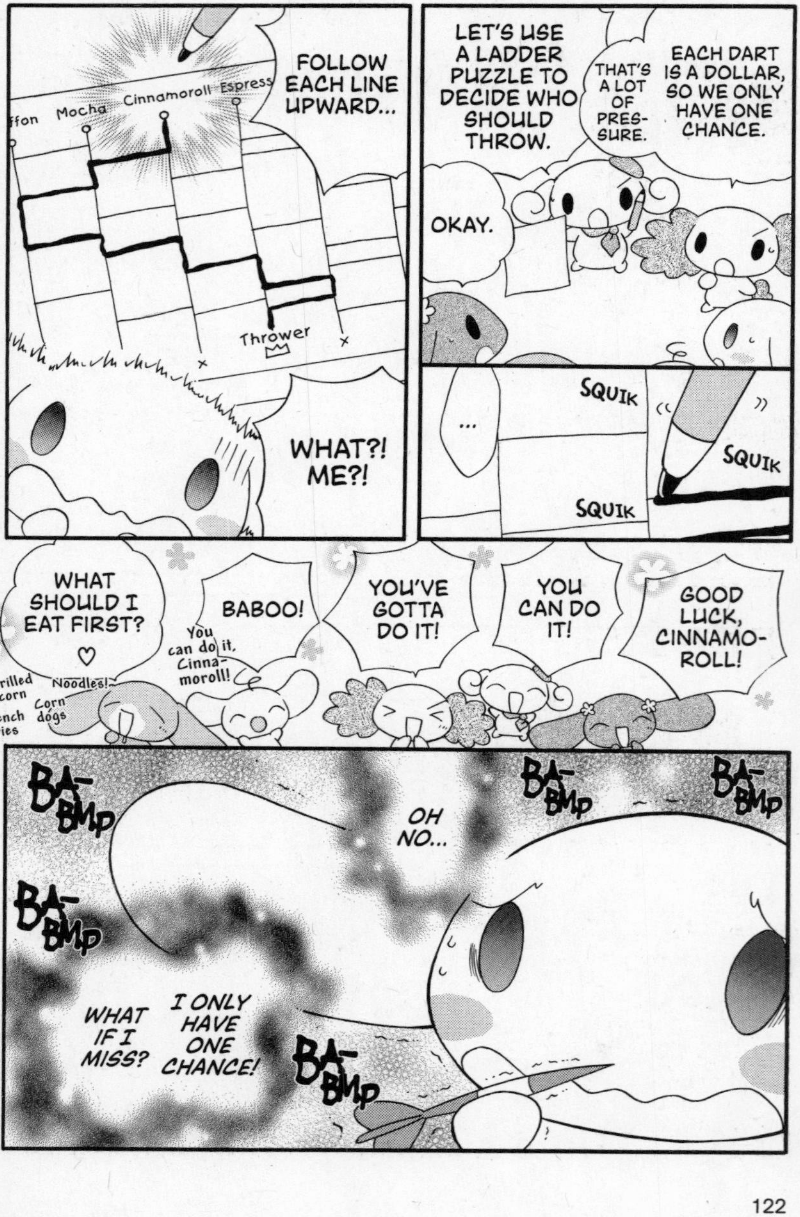
EACH DART IS A DOLLAR, SO WE ONLY HAVE ONE CHANCE.
THAT'S A LOT OF PRESSURE.
LET'S USE A LADDER PUZZLE TO DECIDE WHO SHOULD THROW.
OKAY.
SQUIK
...
SQUIK
SQUIK
FOLLOW EACH LINE UPWARD...
ffon
Mocha
Cinnamoroll
Espress
Thrower
WHAT?! ME?!
GOOD LUCK, CINNAMOROLL!
YOU CAN DO IT!
YOU'VE GOTTA DO IT!
BABOO!
You can do it, Cinnamoroll!
WHAT SHOULD I EAT FIRST? ♡
Noodles!
Grilled corn
Corn dogs
French fries
BA-BMP
BA-BMP
OH NO...
BA-BMP
BA-BMP
I ONLY HAVE ONE CHANCE!
WHAT IF I MISS?
BA-BMP

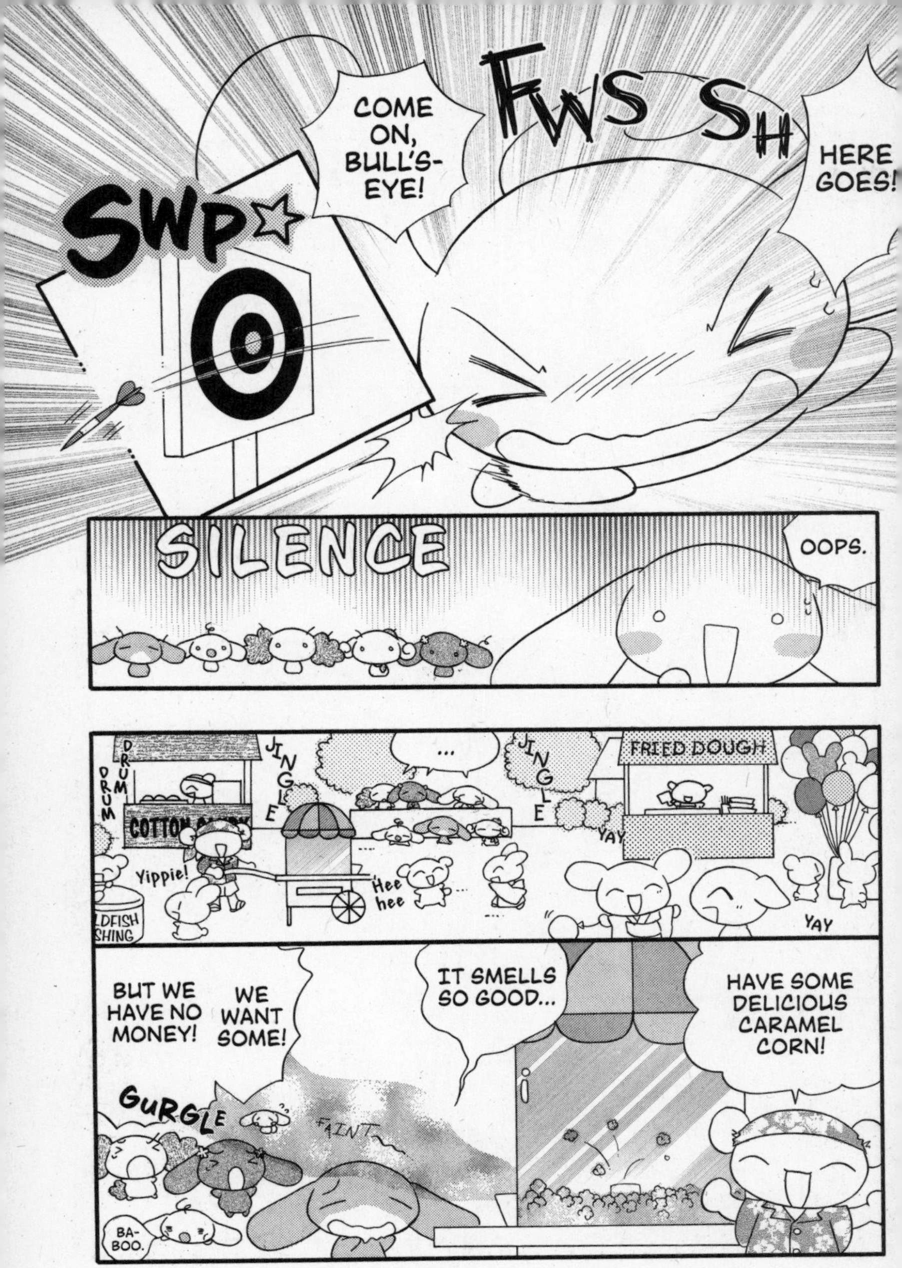
HERE GOES!
FWS SH
COME ON, BULL'S-EYE!
SWP☆
OOPS.
SILENCE
FRIED DOUGH
YAY
YAY
JINGLE
...
JINGLE
DRUM DRUM
Yippie!
Hee hee
HAVE SOME DELICIOUS CARAMEL CORN!
IT SMELLS SO GOOD...
WE WANT SOME!
BUT WE HAVE NO MONEY!
GURGLE
FAINT
BA-BOO.

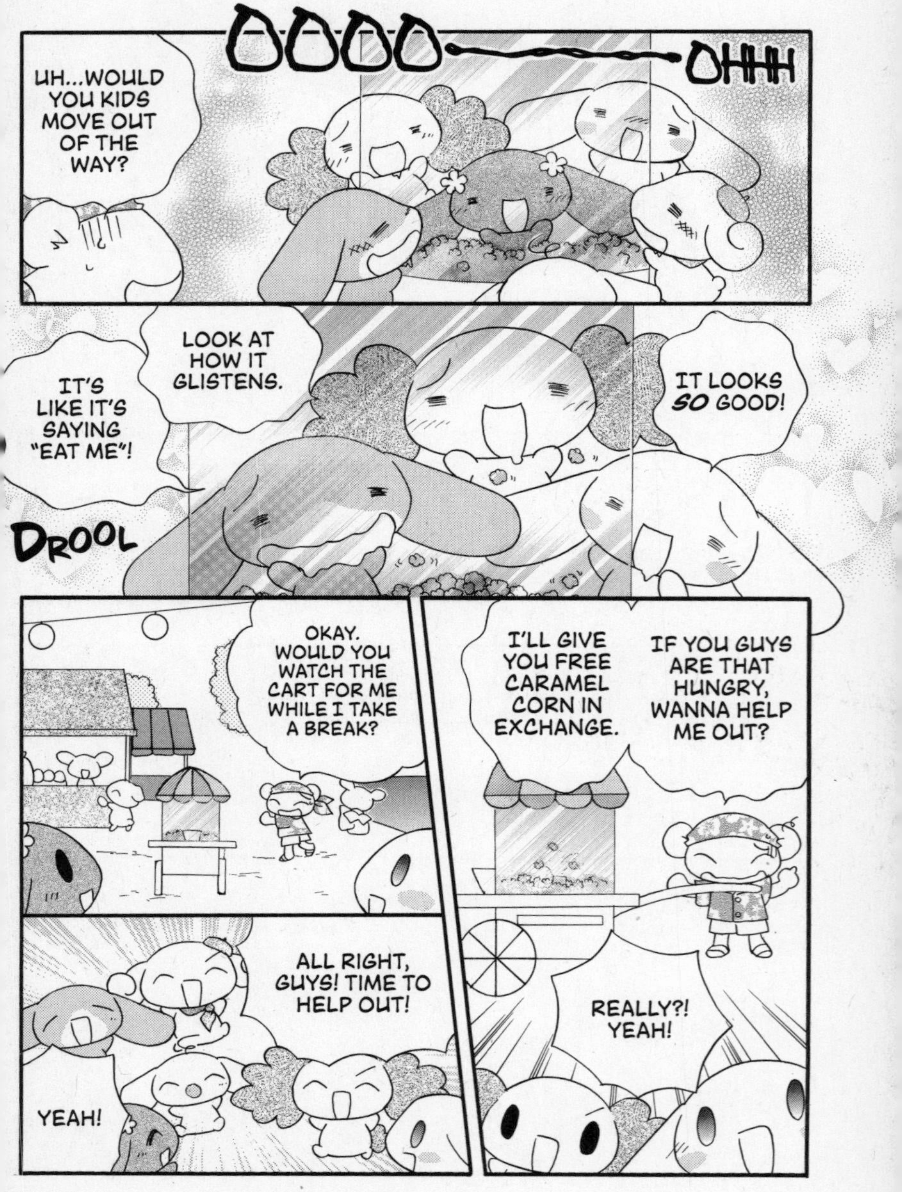
OOOO——OHHH
UH...WOULD YOU KIDS MOVE OUT OF THE WAY?
IT LOOKS *SO* GOOD!
LOOK AT HOW IT GLISTENS.
IT'S LIKE IT'S SAYING "EAT ME"!
DROOL
IF YOU GUYS ARE THAT HUNGRY, WANNA HELP ME OUT?
I'LL GIVE YOU FREE CARAMEL CORN IN EXCHANGE.
REALLY?! YEAH!
OKAY. WOULD YOU WATCH THE CART FOR ME WHILE I TAKE A BREAK?
ALL RIGHT, GUYS! TIME TO HELP OUT!
YEAH!

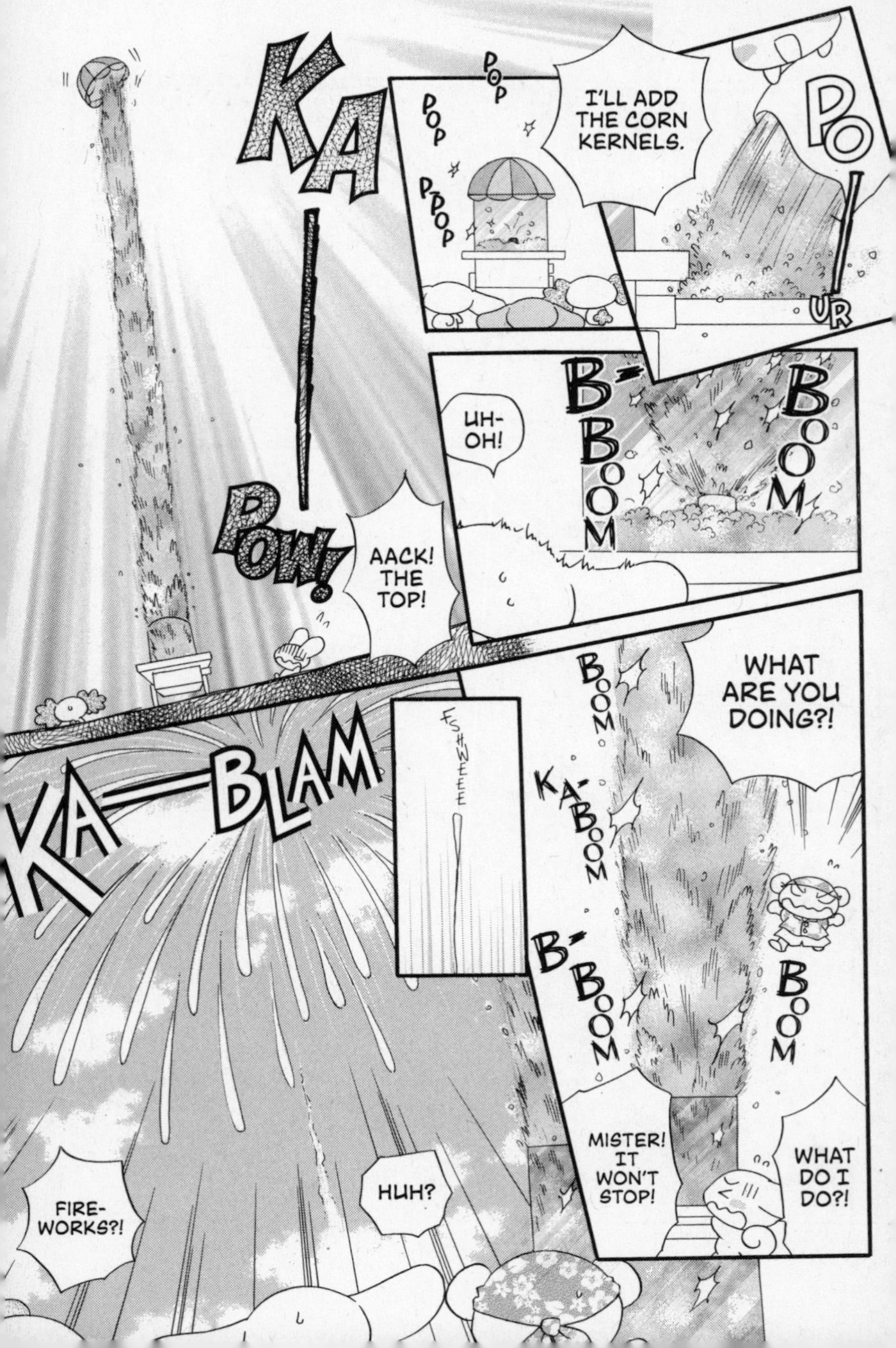
I'LL ADD THE CORN KERNELS.
PO-I-UR
POP
POP POP
P-POP POP
B-BOOM
BOOM
UH-OH!
KA-POW!
AACK! THE TOP!
WHAT ARE YOU DOING?!
BOOM
KA-BOOM
B-BOOM
BOOM
MISTER! IT WON'T STOP!
WHAT DO I DO?!
FSHWEEE
KA-BLAM
HUH?
FIRE-WORKS?!

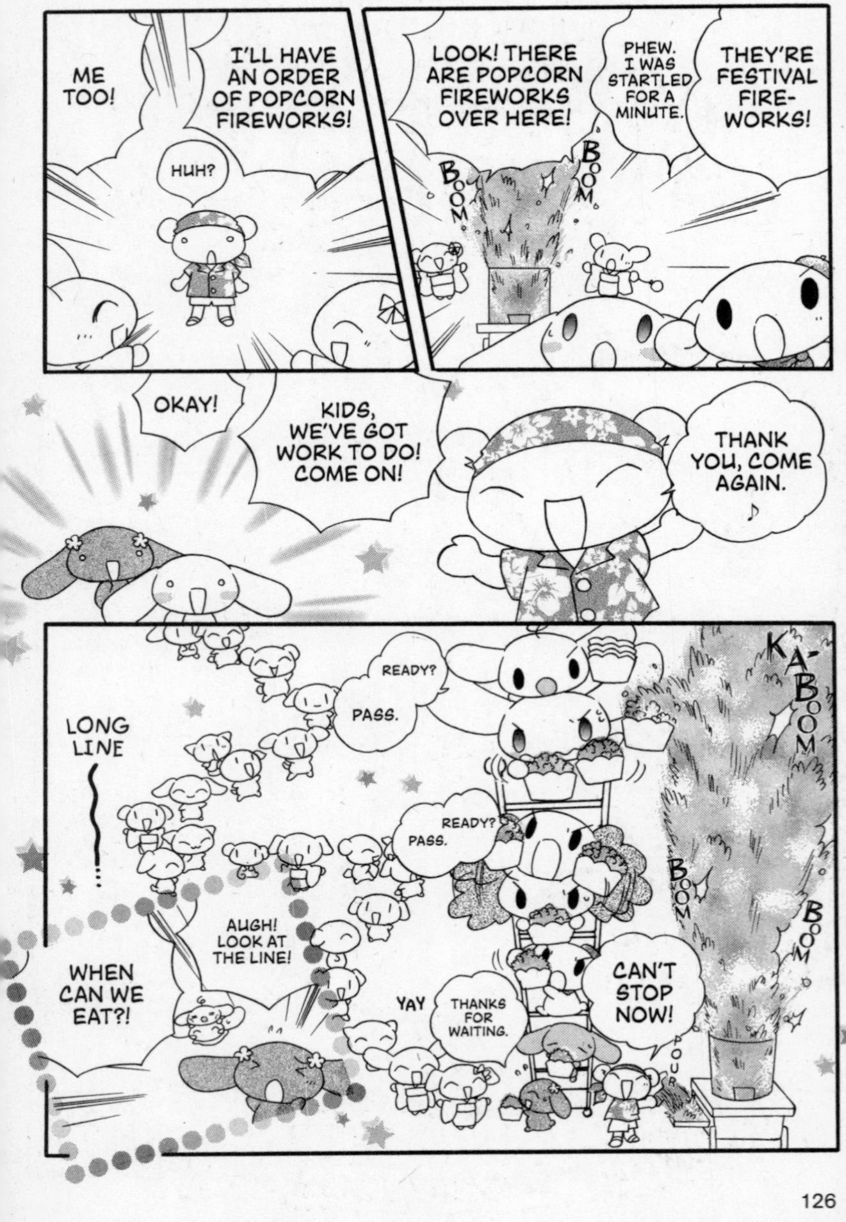
THEY'RE FESTIVAL FIRE-WORKS!
PHEW. I WAS STARTLED FOR A MINUTE.
LOOK! THERE ARE POPCORN FIREWORKS OVER HERE!
BOOM
BOOM
I'LL HAVE AN ORDER OF POPCORN FIREWORKS!
ME TOO!
HUH?
THANK YOU, COME AGAIN. ♪
KIDS, WE'VE GOT WORK TO DO! COME ON!
OKAY!
KA-BOOM
READY?
PASS.
READY?
PASS.
BOOM
BOOM
CAN'T STOP NOW!
POUR
THANKS FOR WAITING.
YAY
AUGH! LOOK AT THE LINE!
LONG LINE
WHEN CAN WE EAT?!

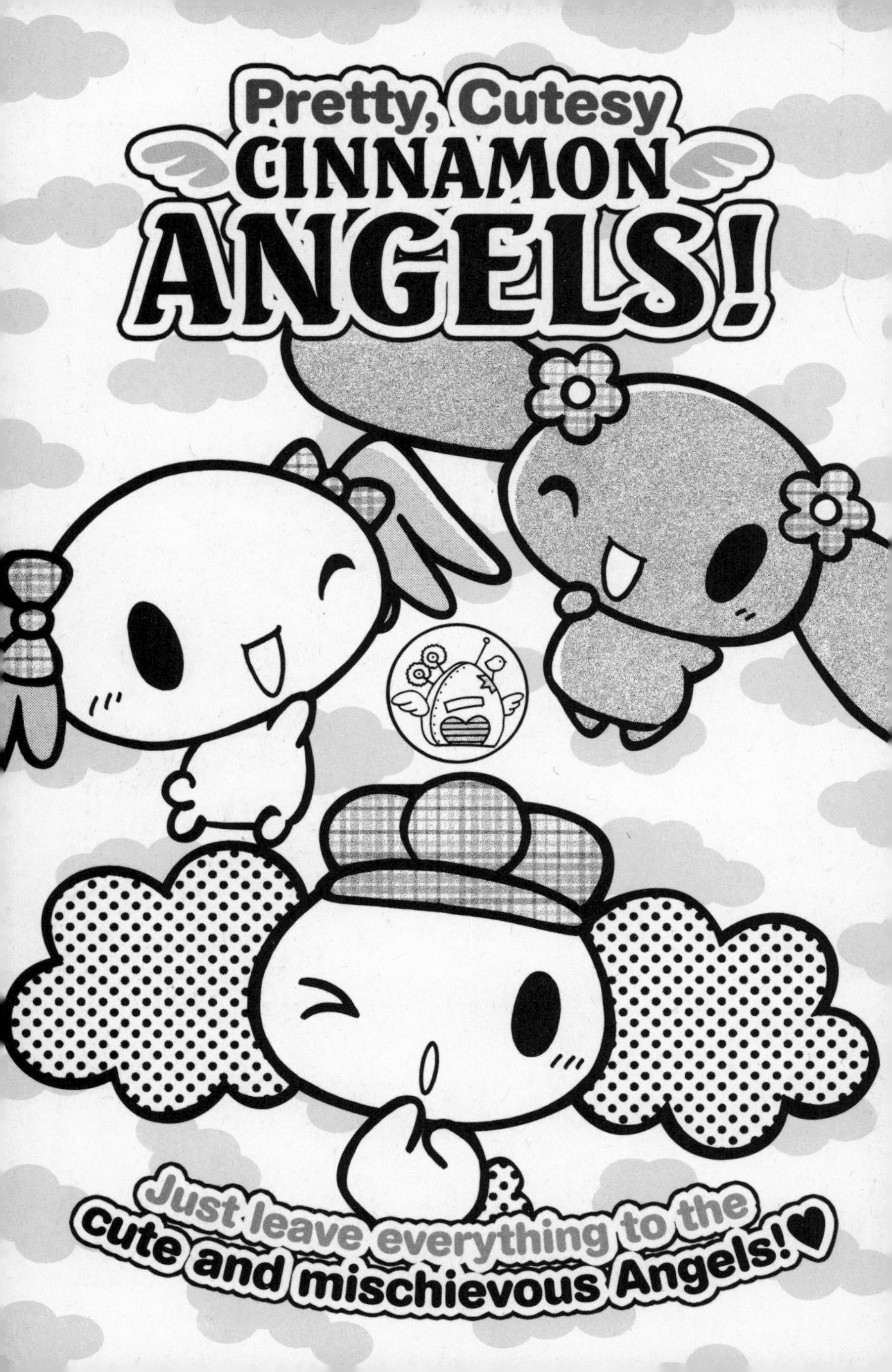
Pretty, Cutesy
CINNAMON
ANGELS!
Just leave everything to the
cute and mischievous Angels!♥

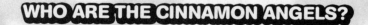

# WHO ARE THE CINNAMON ANGELS?

Three girls who love fashion make up this super-powerful girl unit! Their meeting spot is the Angel Lab, where they study beauty, fashion and boys! The three dream of becoming famous! They hope for a spectacular transformation one day to help them snag pop idols for boyfriends!

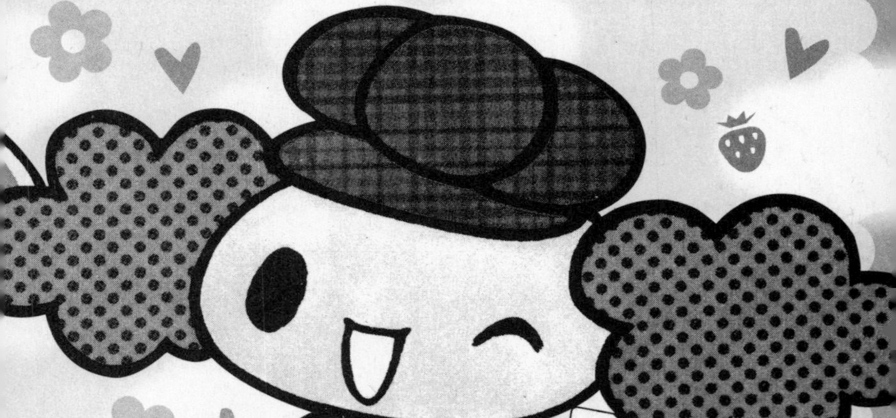

## CHIFFON

Energetic and inspiring to those around her. She keeps tabs on beauty and health. She believes that beauty comes from a healthy body, and can often be found exercising in her room.

## AZUKI

Ladylike but sometimes a little bit off. She's in charge of the Angels' manners and fortune-telling. She practices calligraphy and flower arrangement in hopes of becoming a true Japanese lady!

## Angel Lab

Dreamt up by Mocha, designed by Azuki, and built by Chiffon. The fashionable laboratory has rooms for each Angel, plus spaces for hanging out and doing research. The antenna on top catches breaking fashion news and senses when cute boys are around.

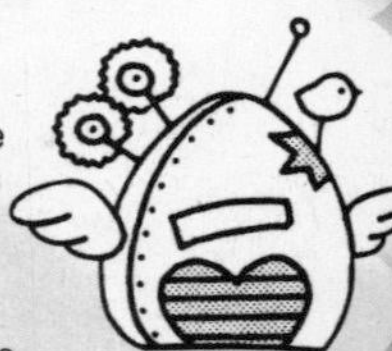

# Hello! We're the Cinnamon Angels

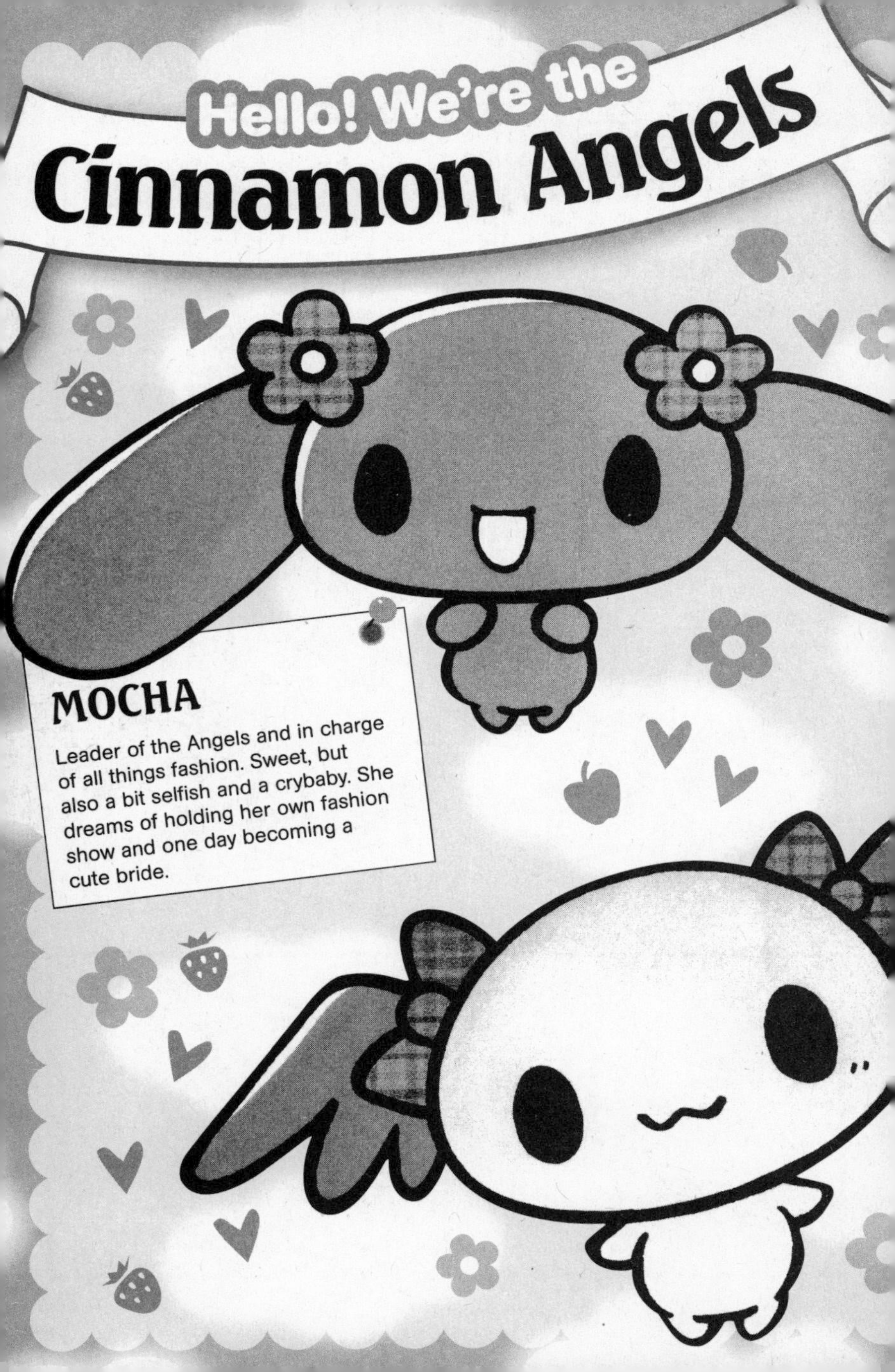

## MOCHA

Leader of the Angels and in charge of all things fashion. Sweet, but also a bit selfish and a crybaby. She dreams of holding her own fashion show and one day becoming a cute bride.

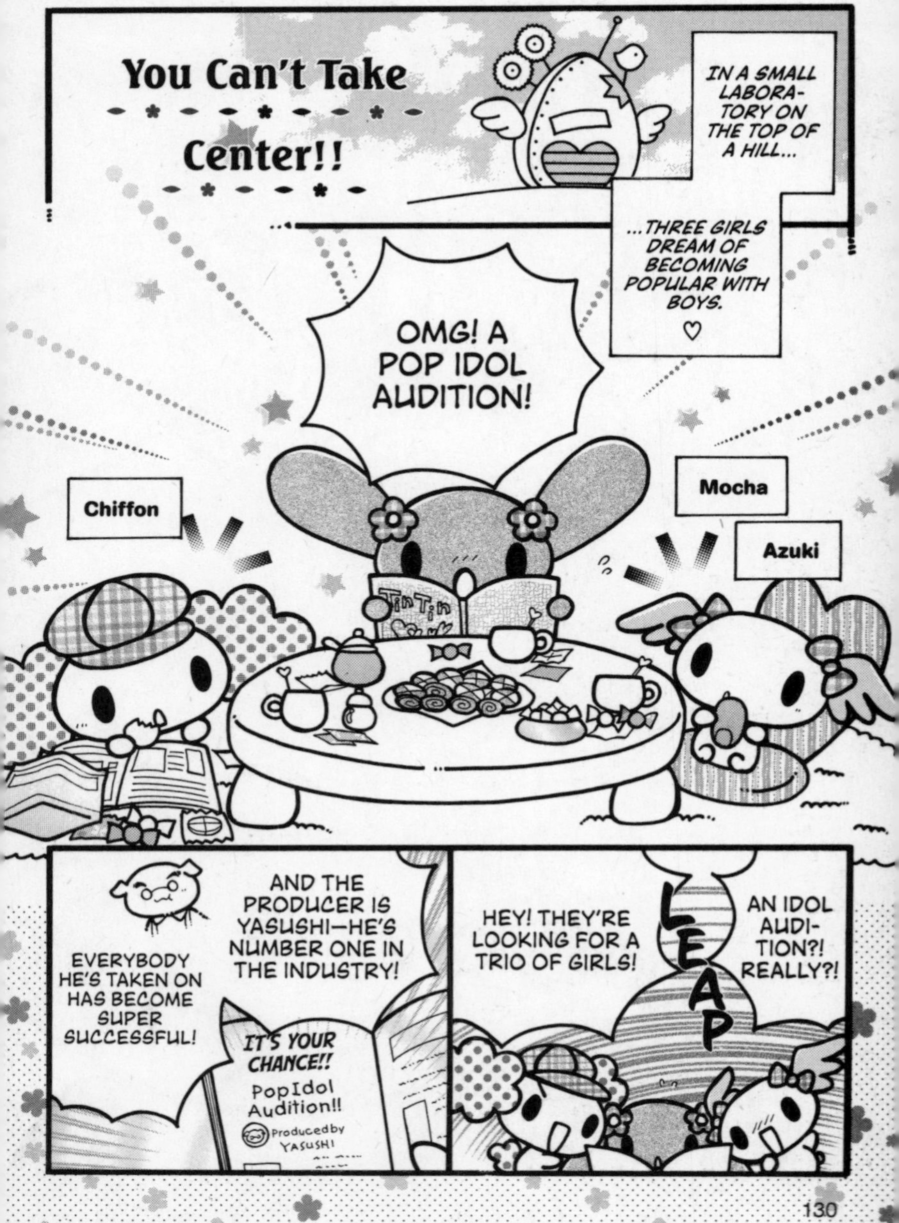
You Can't Take Center!!
IN A SMALL LABORATORY ON THE TOP OF A HILL...
...THREE GIRLS DREAM OF BECOMING POPULAR WITH BOYS. ♡
OMG! A POP IDOL AUDITION!
Mocha
Azuki
Chiffon
AN IDOL AUDITION?! REALLY?!
LEAP
HEY! THEY'RE LOOKING FOR A TRIO OF GIRLS!
AND THE PRODUCER IS YASUSHI—HE'S NUMBER ONE IN THE INDUSTRY!
EVERYBODY HE'S TAKEN ON HAS BECOME SUPER SUCCESSFUL!
IT'S YOUR CHANCE!!
PopIdol Audition!!
Produced by YASUSHI

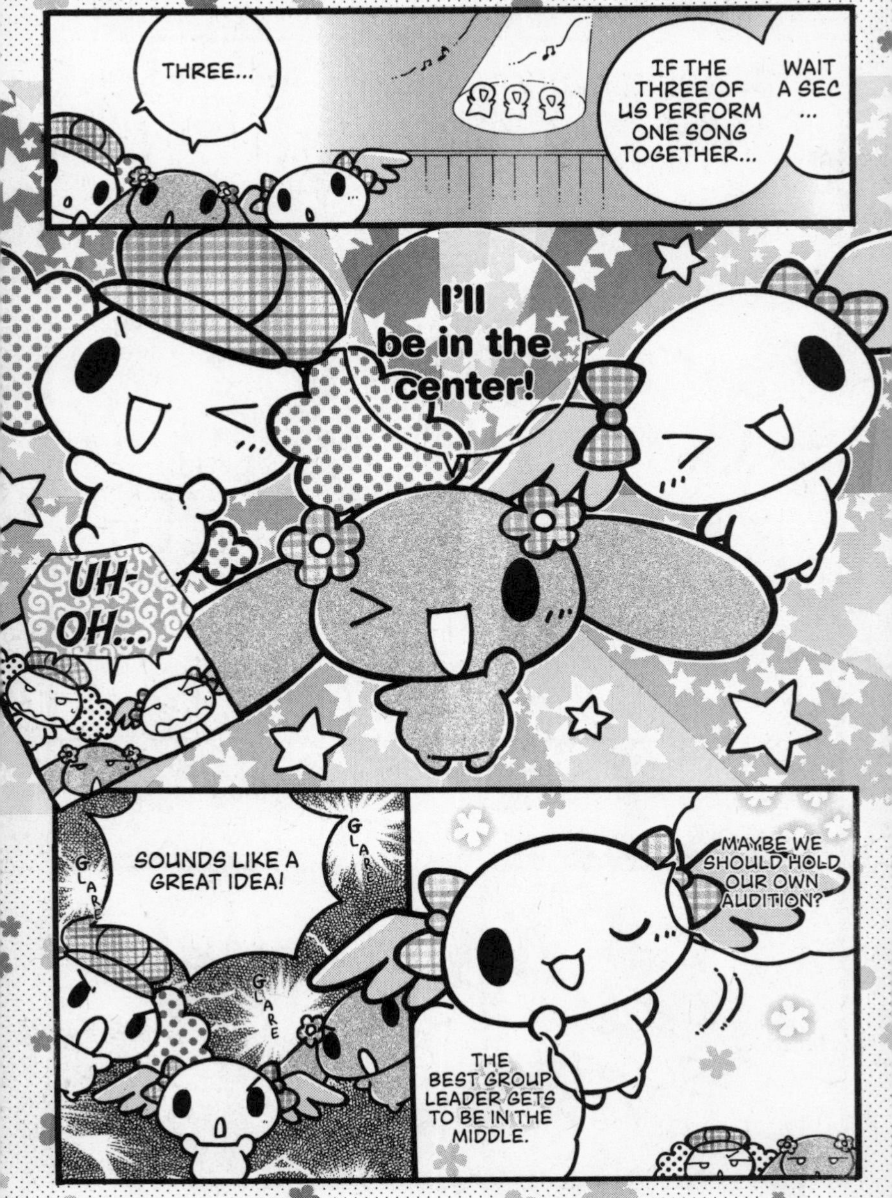
WAIT A SEC ...
IF THE THREE OF US PERFORM ONE SONG TOGETHER...
THREE...
I'll be in the center!
UH-OH...
MAYBE WE SHOULD HOLD OUR OWN AUDITION?
THE BEST GROUP LEADER GETS TO BE IN THE MIDDLE.
GLARE
SOUNDS LIKE A GREAT IDEA!
GLARE
GLARE

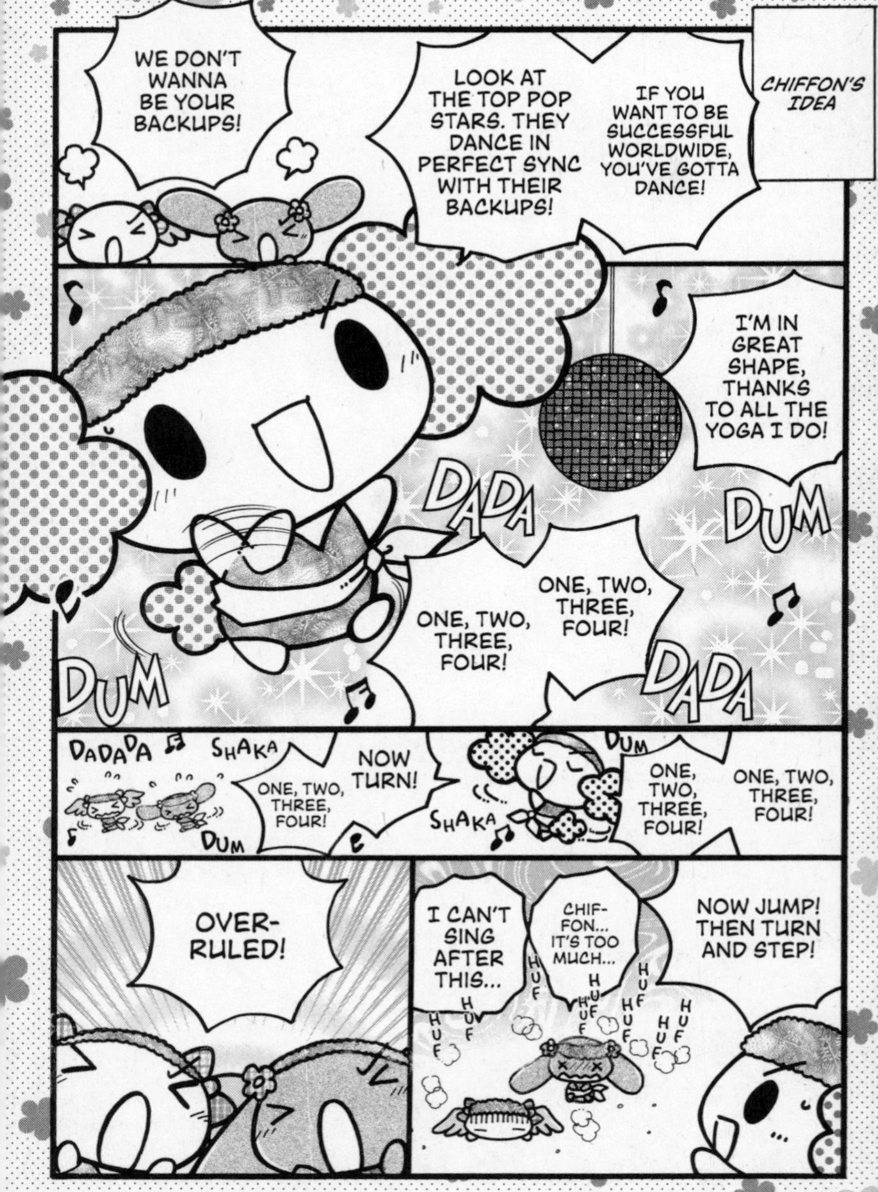
CHIFFON'S IDEA
IF YOU WANT TO BE SUCCESSFUL WORLDWIDE, YOU'VE GOTTA DANCE!
LOOK AT THE TOP POP STARS. THEY DANCE IN PERFECT SYNC WITH THEIR BACKUPS!
WE DON'T WANNA BE YOUR BACKUPS!
I'M IN GREAT SHAPE, THANKS TO ALL THE YOGA I DO!
DUM
DADA
ONE, TWO, THREE, FOUR!
ONE, TWO, THREE, FOUR!
DADA
DUM
ONE, TWO, THREE, FOUR!
ONE, TWO, THREE, FOUR!
DUM
SHAKA
NOW TURN!
ONE, TWO, THREE, FOUR!
SHAKA
DADADA
DUM
NOW JUMP! THEN TURN AND STEP!
CHIF-FON... IT'S TOO MUCH...
I CAN'T SING AFTER THIS...
HUF HUF HUF HUF HUF HUF HUF HUF HUF HUF
OVER-RULED!

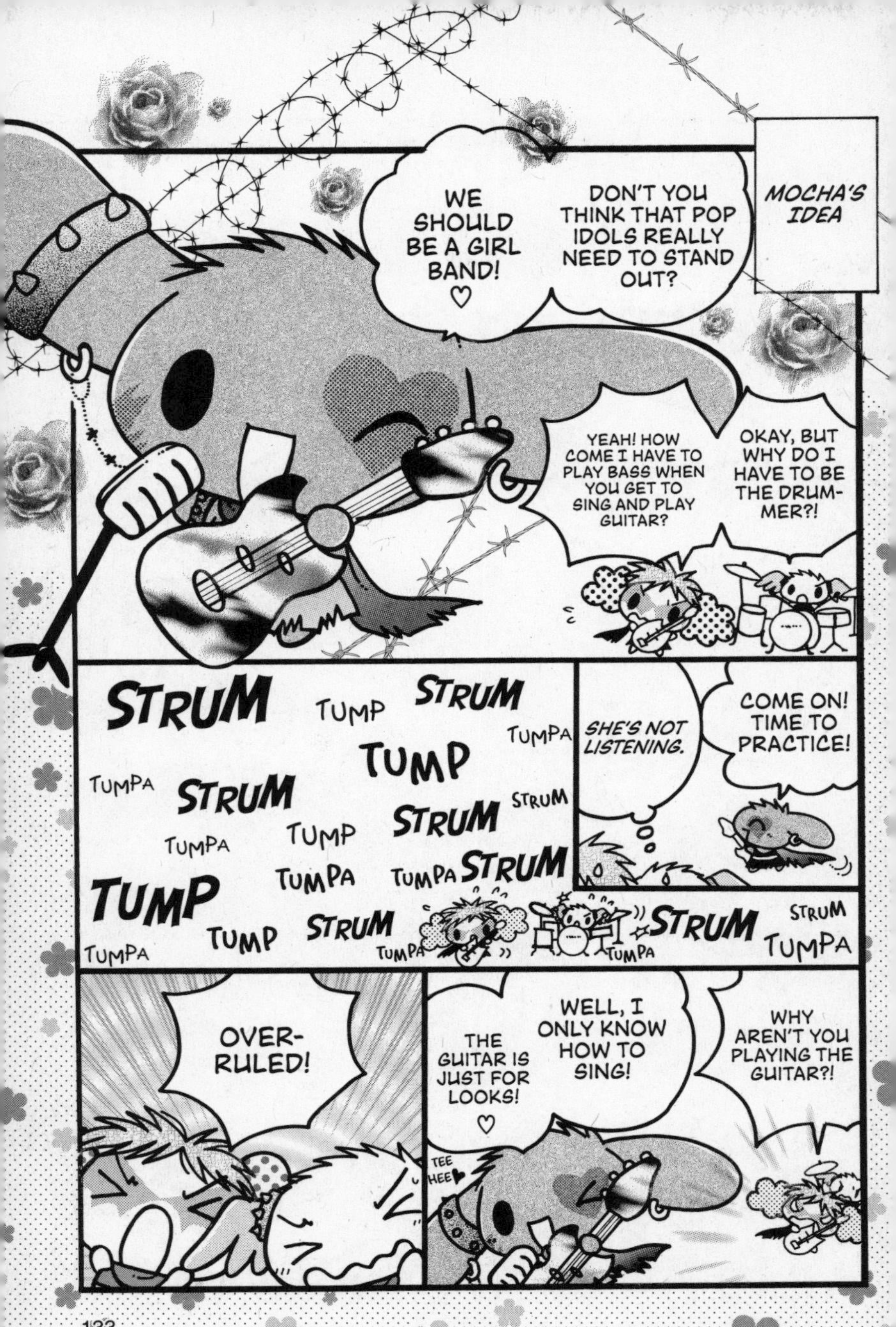
MOCHA'S IDEA
DON'T YOU THINK THAT POP IDOLS REALLY NEED TO STAND OUT?
WE SHOULD BE A GIRL BAND! ♡
OKAY, BUT WHY DO I HAVE TO BE THE DRUM-MER?!
YEAH! HOW COME I HAVE TO PLAY BASS WHEN YOU GET TO SING AND PLAY GUITAR?
COME ON! TIME TO PRACTICE!
SHE'S NOT LISTENING.
STRUM
TUMP
STRUM
TUMPA
TUMP
TUMPA
STRUM
STRUM
STRUM
TUMPA
TUMP
TUMPA
TUMPA
STRUM
TUMP
TUMP
STRUM
TUMPA
TUMPA
TUMPA
STRUM
STRUM
TUMPA
WHY AREN'T YOU PLAYING THE GUITAR?!
WELL, I ONLY KNOW HOW TO SING!
THE GUITAR IS JUST FOR LOOKS! ♡
TEE HEE♥
OVER-RULED!

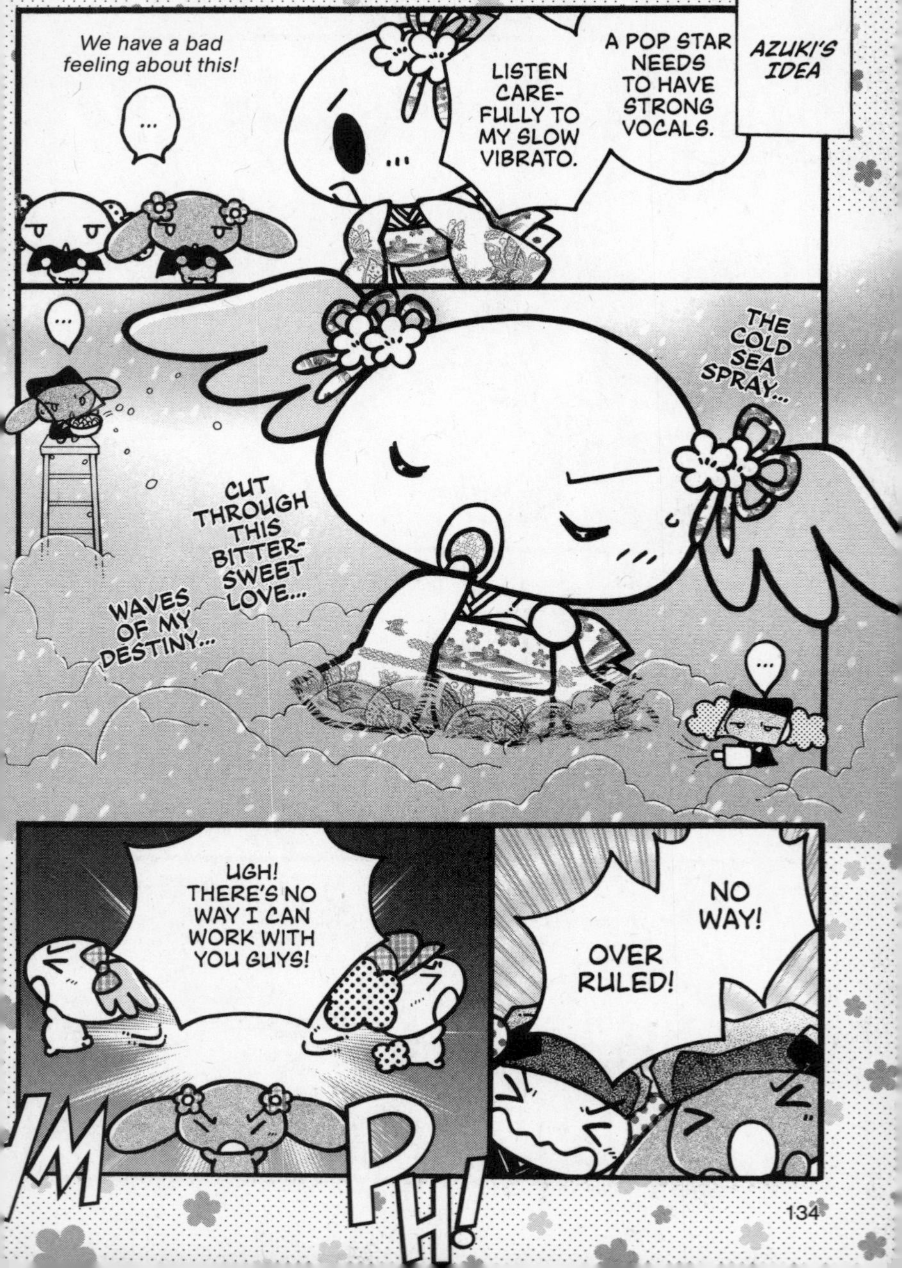
AZUKI'S IDEA
A POP STAR NEEDS TO HAVE STRONG VOCALS.
LISTEN CARE-FULLY TO MY SLOW VIBRATO.
We have a bad feeling about this!
...
THE COLD SEA SPRAY...
...
CUT THROUGH THIS BITTER-SWEET LOVE...
WAVES OF MY DESTINY...
...
NO WAY!
OVER RULED!
UGH! THERE'S NO WAY I CAN WORK WITH YOU GUYS!
MM
PH!

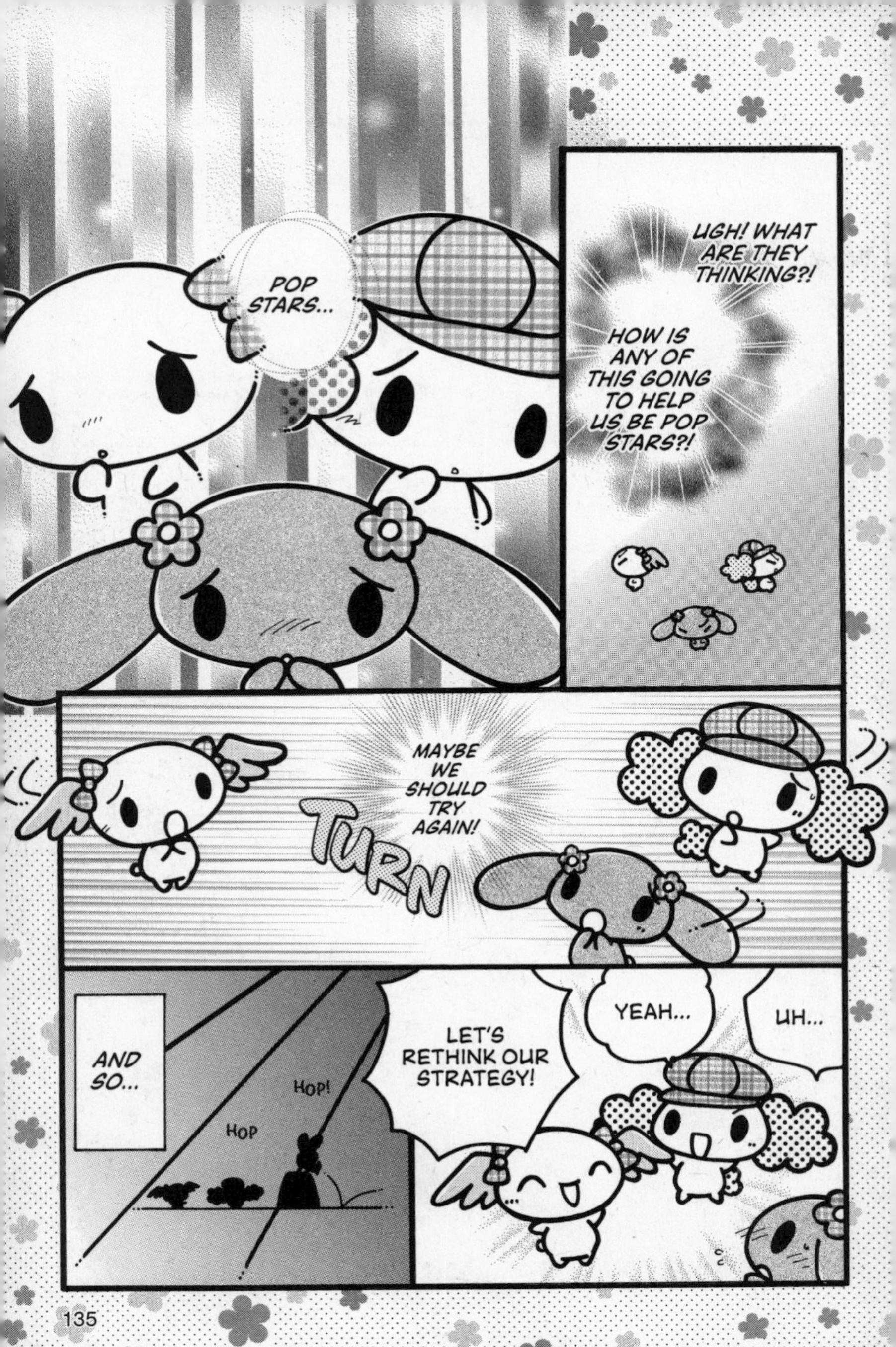
UGH! WHAT ARE THEY THINKING?!
HOW IS ANY OF THIS GOING TO HELP US BE POP STARS?!
POP STARS...
MAYBE WE SHOULD TRY AGAIN!
TURN
UH...
YEAH...
LET'S RETHINK OUR STRATEGY!
AND SO...
HOP!
HOP

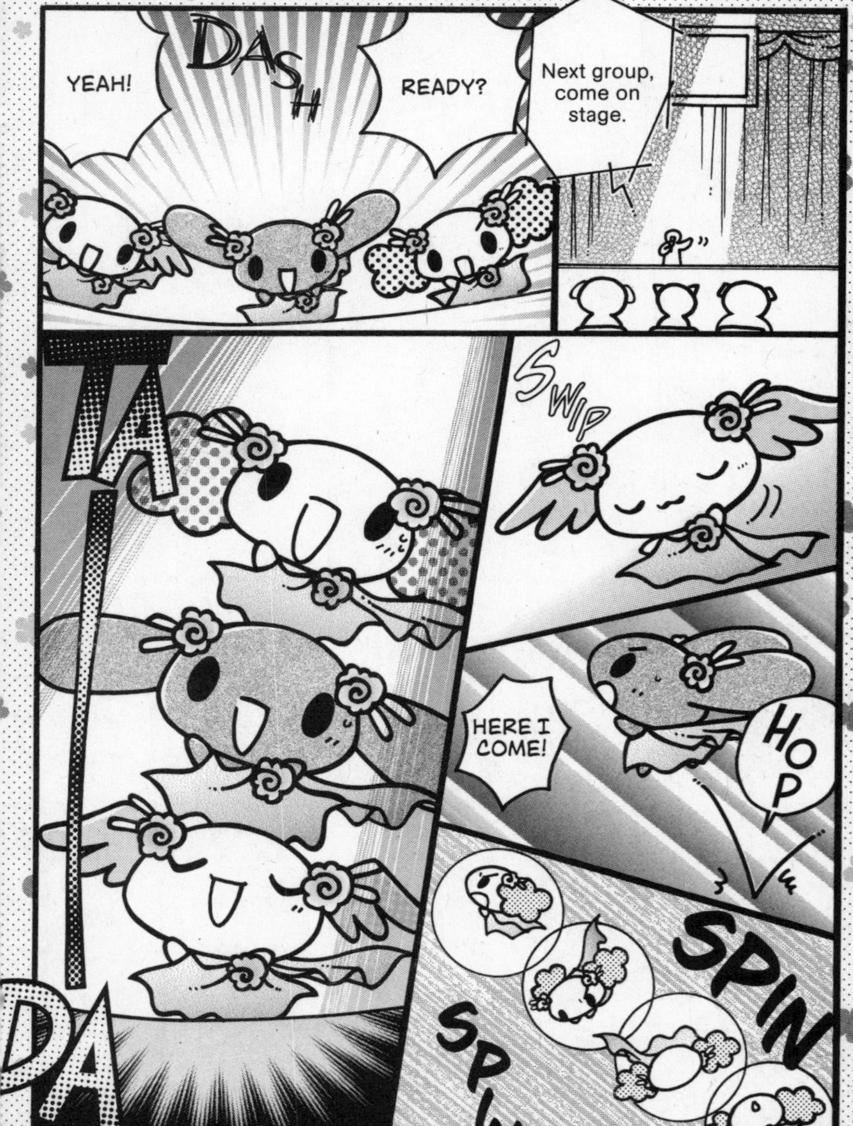
Next group, come on stage.
READY?
DASH
YEAH!
SWIP
HOP
HERE I COME!
SPIN
SPIN
TA
DA

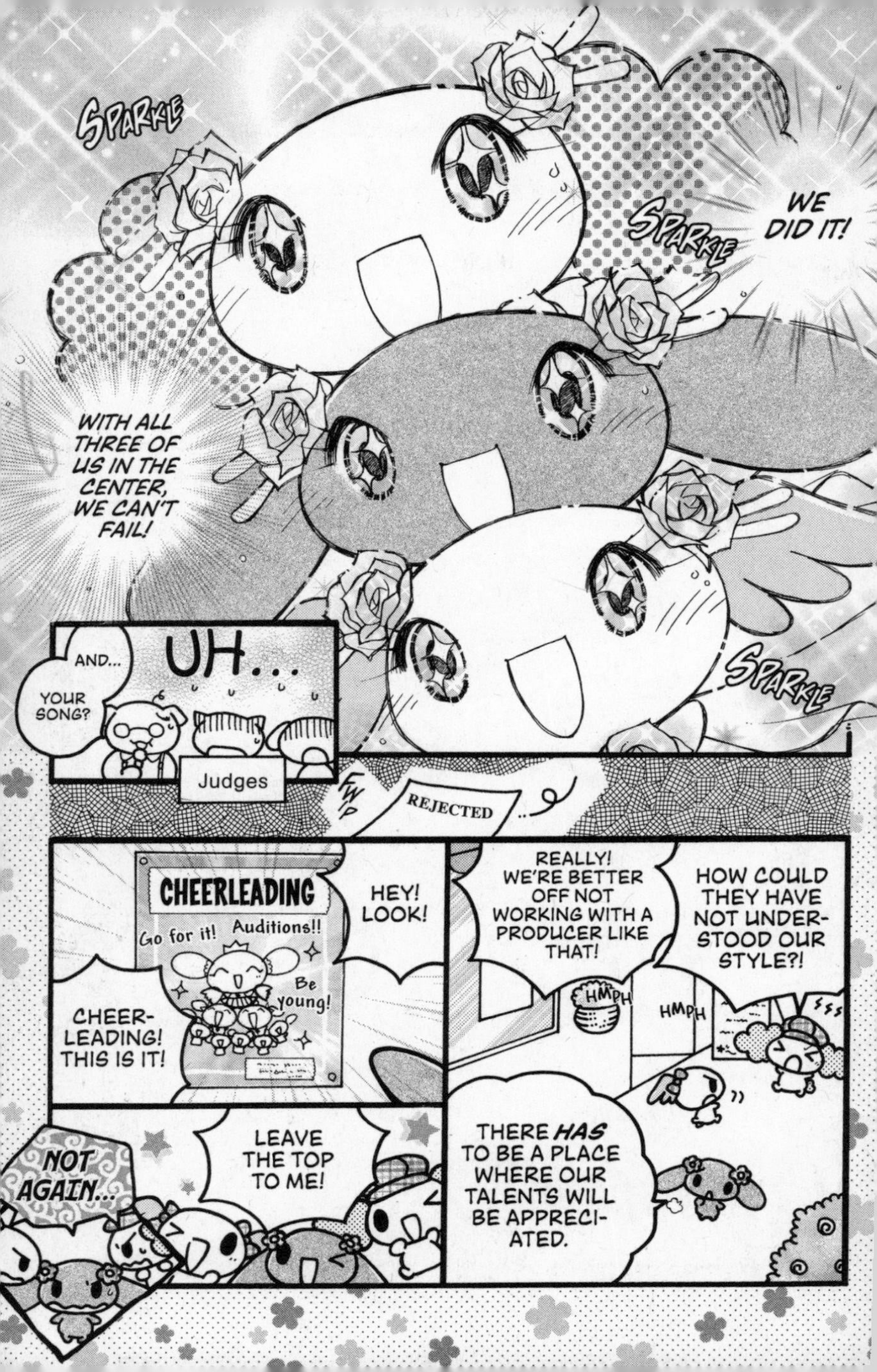
WE DID IT!
SPARKLE
SPARKLE
WITH ALL THREE OF US IN THE CENTER, WE CAN'T FAIL!
SPARKLE
UH...
AND... YOUR SONG?
Judges
FWIP
REJECTED
HOW COULD THEY HAVE NOT UNDER-STOOD OUR STYLE?!
REALLY! WE'RE BETTER OFF NOT WORKING WITH A PRODUCER LIKE THAT!
HMPH
HMPH
THERE *HAS* TO BE A PLACE WHERE OUR TALENTS WILL BE APPRECI-ATED.
HEY! LOOK!
CHEERLEADING
Go for it! Auditions!!
Be young!
CHEER-LEADING! THIS IS IT!
LEAVE THE TOP TO ME!
NOT AGAIN...

# Bikini Summer

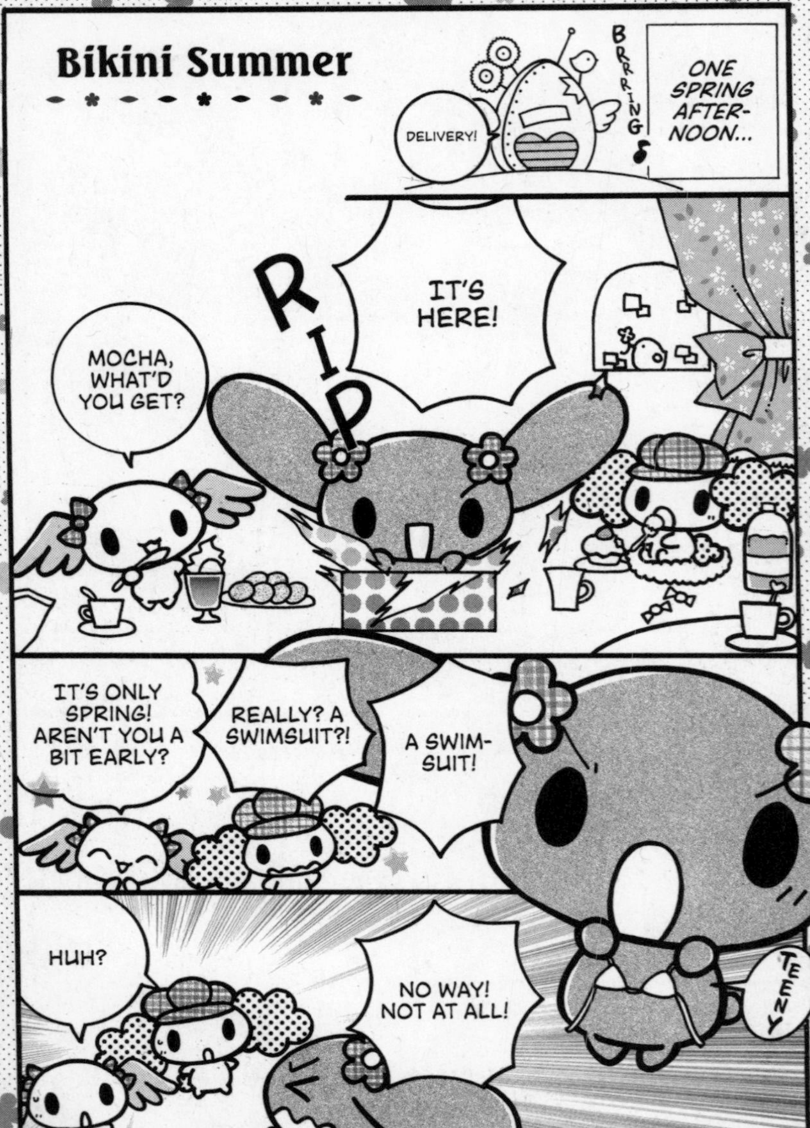
ONE SPRING AFTER-NOON...
BRRRING
DELIVERY!
IT'S HERE!
RIP
MOCHA, WHAT'D YOU GET?
A SWIM-SUIT!
REALLY? A SWIMSUIT?!
IT'S ONLY SPRING! AREN'T YOU A BIT EARLY?
TEENY
NO WAY! NOT AT ALL!
HUH?

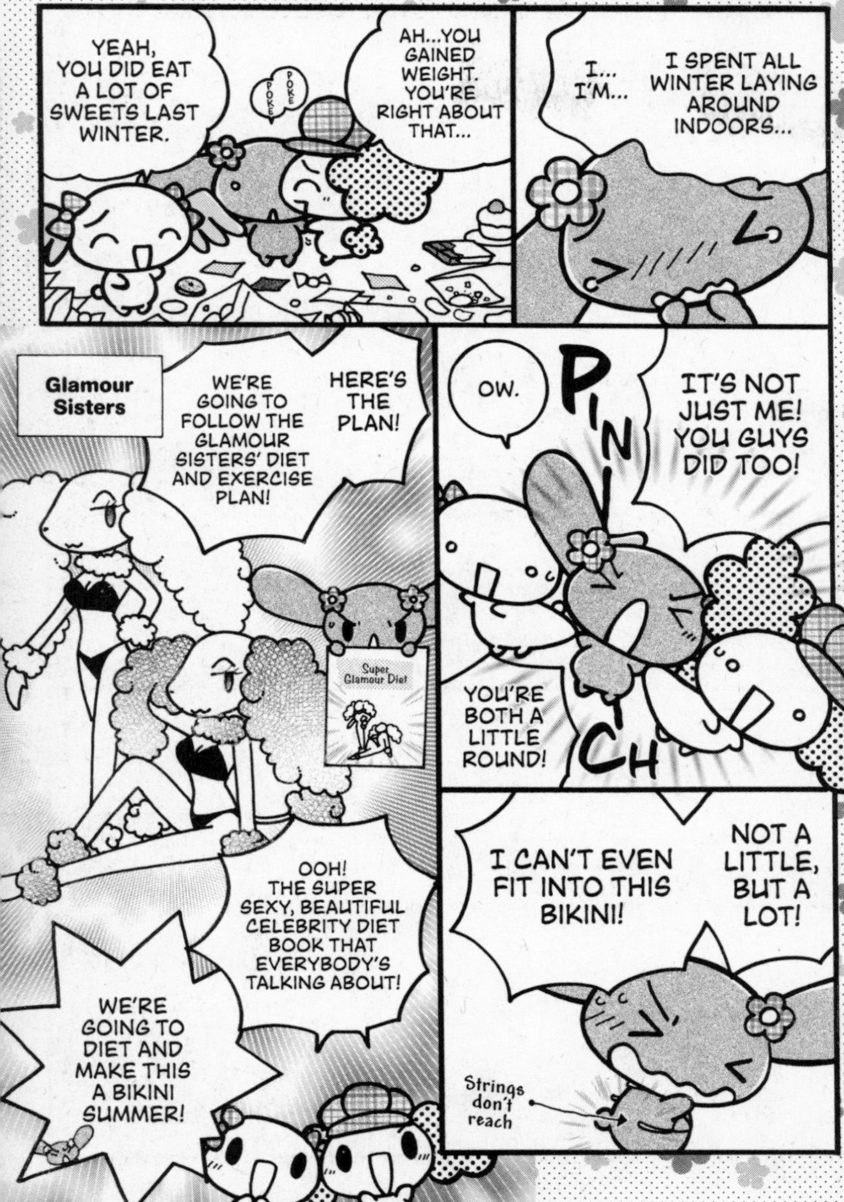
I... I'M...
I SPENT ALL WINTER LAYING AROUND INDOORS...
AH...YOU GAINED WEIGHT. YOU'RE RIGHT ABOUT THAT...
POKE
POKE
YEAH, YOU DID EAT A LOT OF SWEETS LAST WINTER.
IT'S NOT JUST ME! YOU GUYS DID TOO!
PINCH
OW.
YOU'RE BOTH A LITTLE ROUND!
NOT A LITTLE, BUT A LOT!
I CAN'T EVEN FIT INTO THIS BIKINI!
Strings don't reach
HERE'S THE PLAN!
WE'RE GOING TO FOLLOW THE GLAMOUR SISTERS' DIET AND EXERCISE PLAN!
Glamour Sisters
Super Glamour Diet
OOH! THE SUPER SEXY, BEAUTIFUL CELEBRITY DIET BOOK THAT EVERYBODY'S TALKING ABOUT!
WE'RE GOING TO DIET AND MAKE THIS A BIKINI SUMMER!

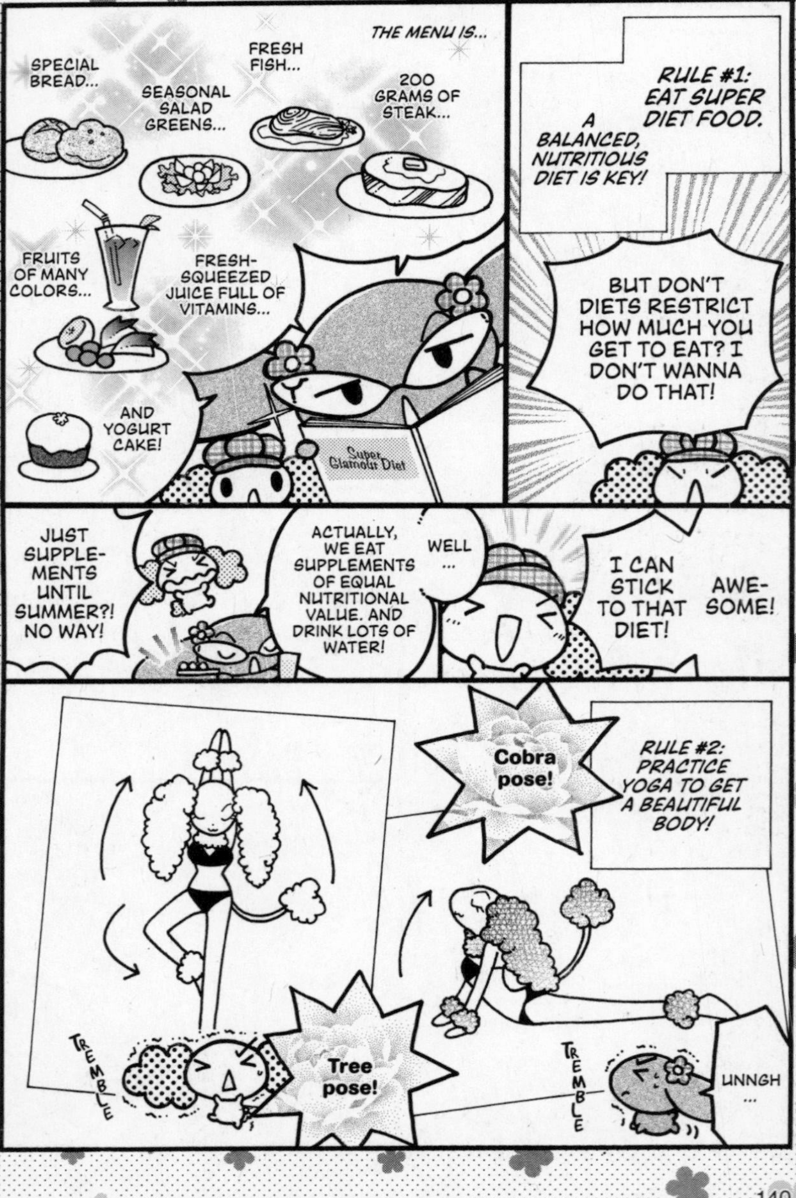
RULE #1: EAT SUPER DIET FOOD.
A BALANCED, NUTRITIOUS DIET IS KEY!
BUT DON'T DIETS RESTRICT HOW MUCH YOU GET TO EAT? I DON'T WANNA DO THAT!
THE MENU IS...
200 GRAMS OF STEAK...
FRESH FISH...
SEASONAL SALAD GREENS...
SPECIAL BREAD...
FRESH-SQUEEZED JUICE FULL OF VITAMINS...
FRUITS OF MANY COLORS...
AND YOGURT CAKE!
Super Glamour Diet
AWE-SOME!
I CAN STICK TO THAT DIET!
WELL...
ACTUALLY, WE EAT SUPPLEMENTS OF EQUAL NUTRITIONAL VALUE. AND DRINK LOTS OF WATER!
JUST SUPPLE-MENTS UNTIL SUMMER?! NO WAY!
RULE #2: PRACTICE YOGA TO GET A BEAUTIFUL BODY!
Cobra pose!
UNNGH...
TREMBLE
Tree pose!
TREMBLE

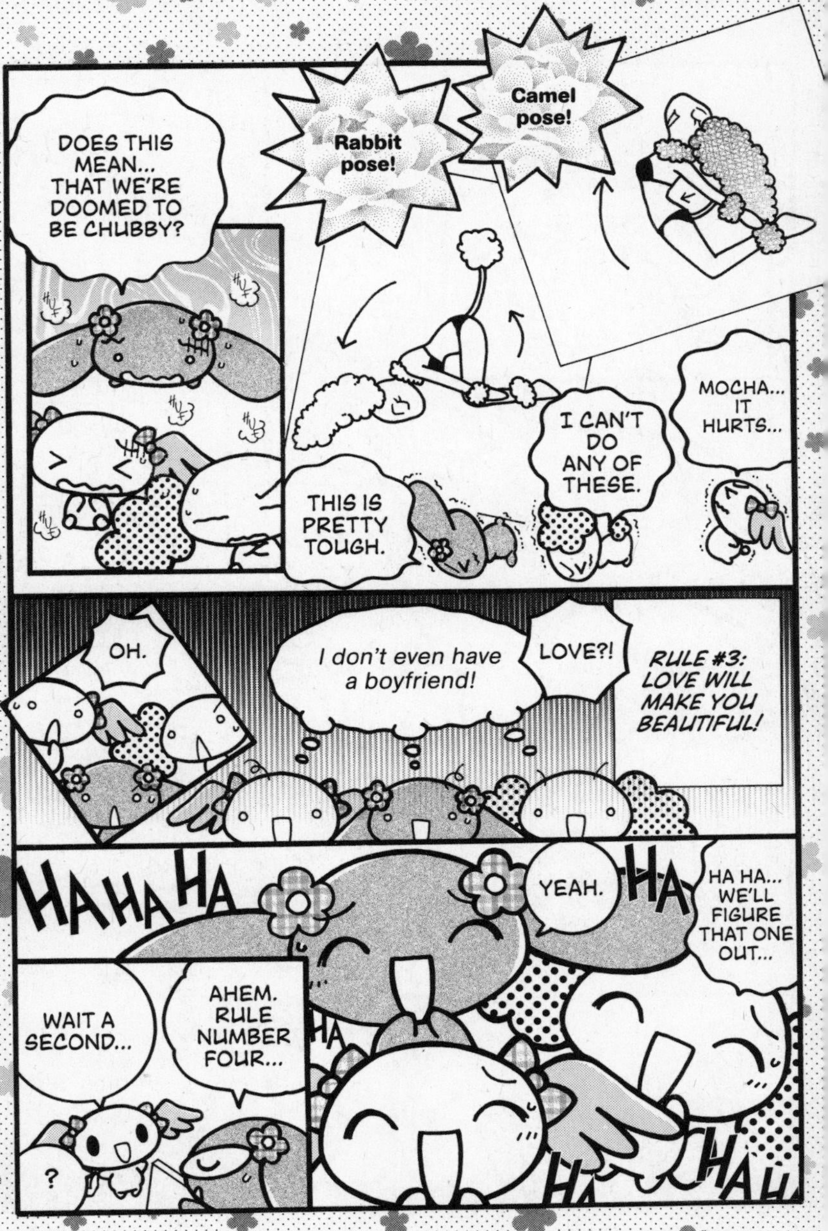
Camel pose!
Rabbit pose!
MOCHA... IT HURTS...
I CAN'T DO ANY OF THESE.
THIS IS PRETTY TOUGH.
DOES THIS MEAN... THAT WE'RE DOOMED TO BE CHUBBY?
RULE #3: LOVE WILL MAKE YOU BEAUTIFUL!
LOVE?!
I don't even have a boyfriend!
OH.
HA HA... WE'LL FIGURE THAT ONE OUT...
HA
YEAH.
HAHAHA HA
HA
HA
HA
AHEM. RULE NUMBER FOUR...
WAIT A SECOND...
?

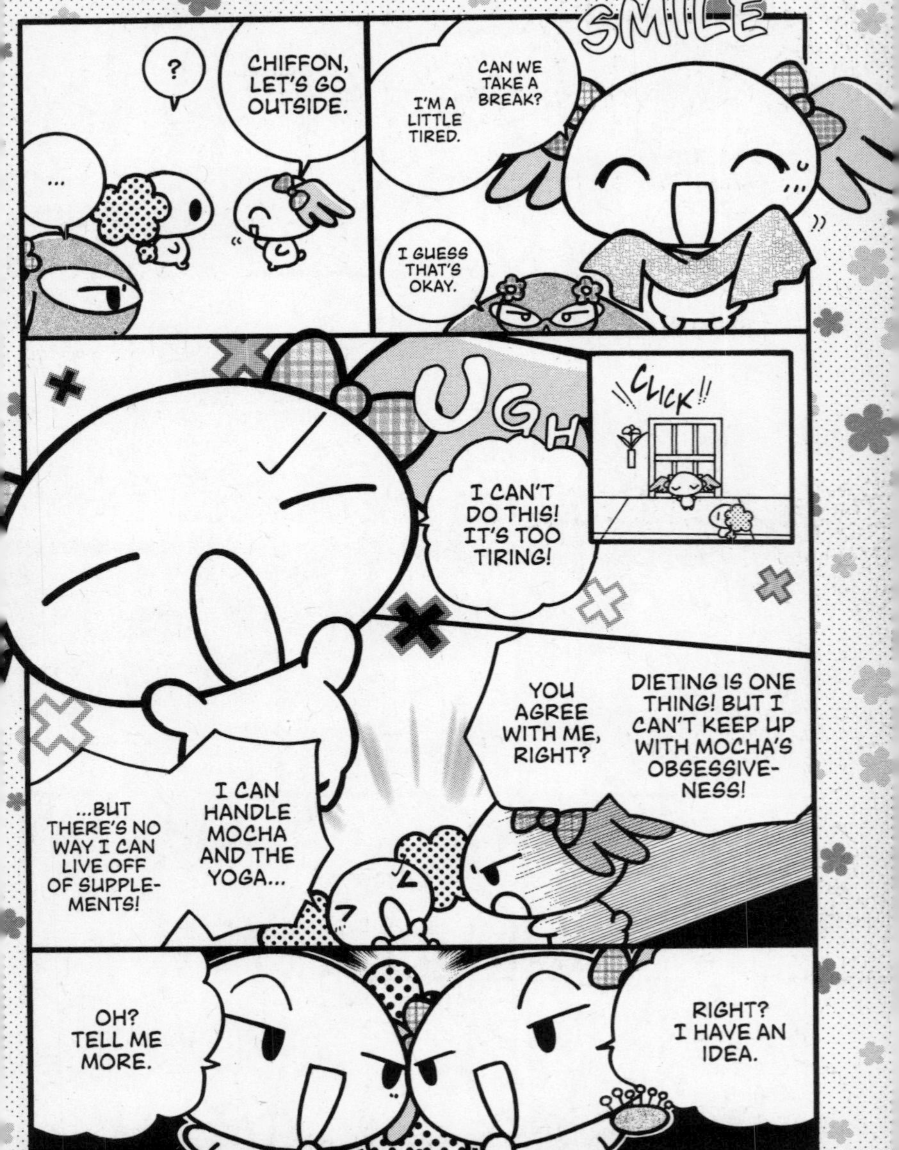
SMILE
CAN WE TAKE A BREAK?
I'M A LITTLE TIRED.
I GUESS THAT'S OKAY.
CHIFFON, LET'S GO OUTSIDE.
?
...
CLICK
UGH
I CAN'T DO THIS! IT'S TOO TIRING!
DIETING IS ONE THING! BUT I CAN'T KEEP UP WITH MOCHA'S OBSESSIVE-NESS!
YOU AGREE WITH ME, RIGHT?
I CAN HANDLE MOCHA AND THE YOGA...
...BUT THERE'S NO WAY I CAN LIVE OFF OF SUPPLE-MENTS!
RIGHT? I HAVE AN IDEA.
OH? TELL ME MORE.

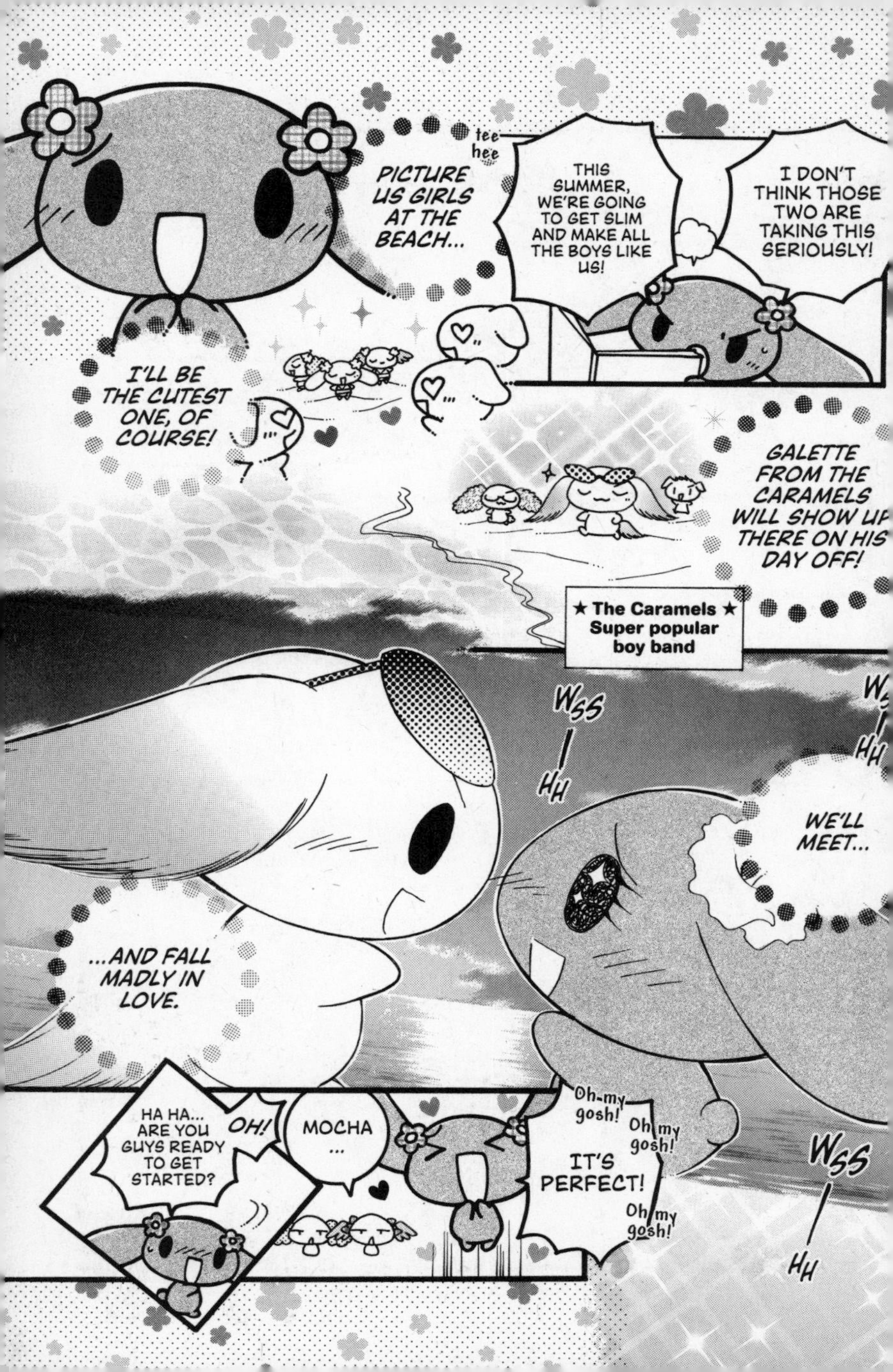
I DON'T THINK THOSE TWO ARE TAKING THIS SERIOUSLY!
THIS SUMMER, WE'RE GOING TO GET SLIM AND MAKE ALL THE BOYS LIKE US!
tee hee
PICTURE US GIRLS AT THE BEACH...
I'LL BE THE CUTEST ONE, OF COURSE!
GALETTE FROM THE CARAMELS WILL SHOW UP THERE ON HIS DAY OFF!
★ The Caramels ★ Super popular boy band
WSS-HH
WSS-HH
WE'LL MEET...
...AND FALL MADLY IN LOVE.
WSS-HH
Oh my gosh!
Oh my gosh!
Oh my gosh!
IT'S PERFECT!
MOCHA...
OH!
HA HA... ARE YOU GUYS READY TO GET STARTED?

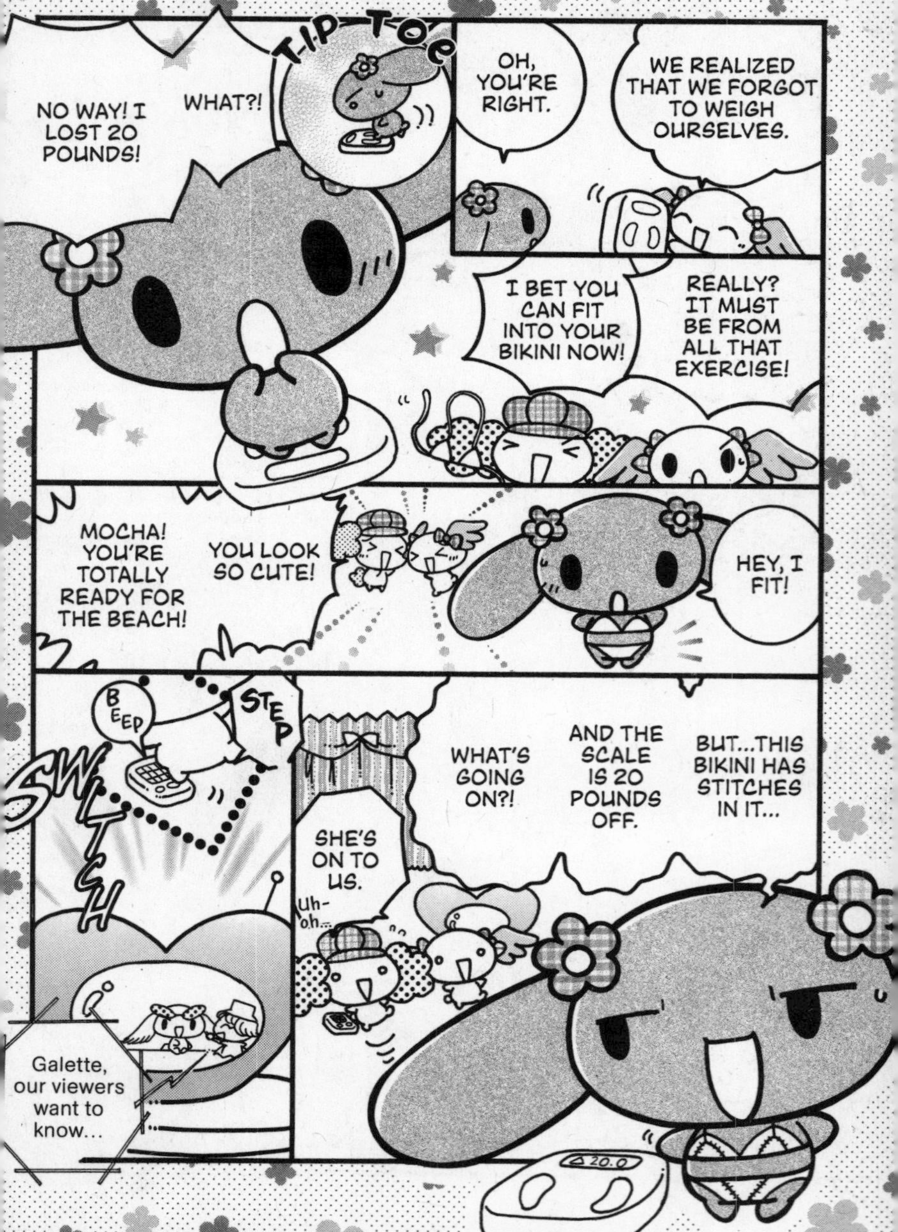
WE REALIZED THAT WE FORGOT TO WEIGH OURSELVES.
OH, YOU'RE RIGHT.
REALLY? IT MUST BE FROM ALL THAT EXERCISE!
I BET YOU CAN FIT INTO YOUR BIKINI NOW!
TIP TOE
WHAT?!
NO WAY! I LOST 20 POUNDS!
HEY, I FIT!
YOU LOOK SO CUTE!
MOCHA! YOU'RE TOTALLY READY FOR THE BEACH!
BUT...THIS BIKINI HAS STITCHES IN IT...
AND THE SCALE IS 20 POUNDS OFF.
WHAT'S GOING ON?!
SHE'S ON TO US.
Uh-oh...
20.0
STEP
BEEP
SWITCH
Galette, our viewers want to know...

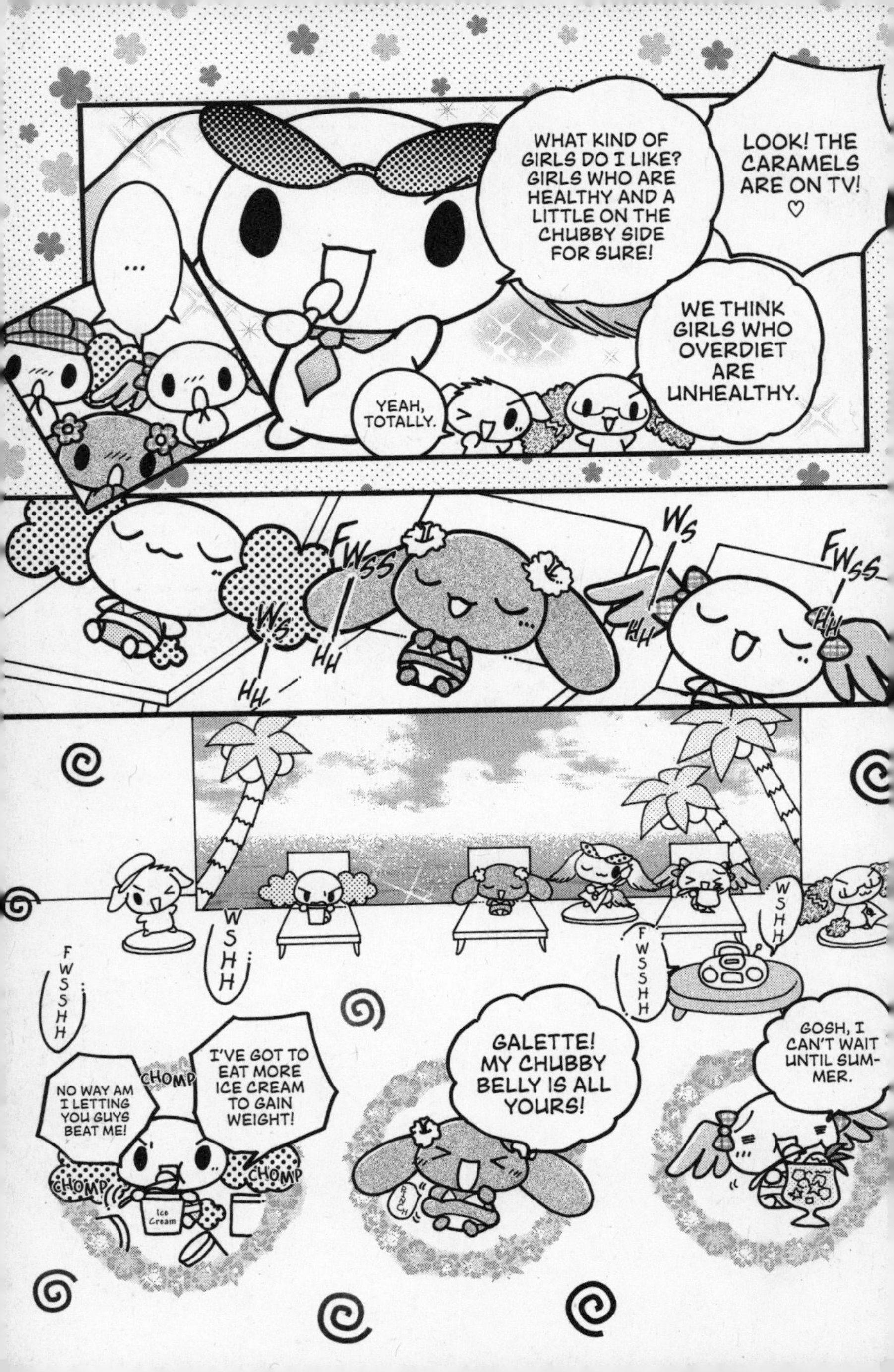

LOOK! THE CARAMELS ARE ON TV! ♡
WHAT KIND OF GIRLS DO I LIKE? GIRLS WHO ARE HEALTHY AND A LITTLE ON THE CHUBBY SIDE FOR SURE!
WE THINK GIRLS WHO OVERDIET ARE UNHEALTHY.
YEAH, TOTALLY.
...
FWSS
HH
WS
HH
FWSS
WS
HH
WS
HH
WSHH
FWSSHH
WSHH
FWSSHH
GOSH, I CAN'T WAIT UNTIL SUMMER.
GALETTE! MY CHUBBY BELLY IS ALL YOURS!
I'VE GOT TO EAT MORE ICE CREAM TO GAIN WEIGHT!
CHOMP
NO WAY AM I LETTING YOU GUYS BEAT ME!
CHOMP
CHOMP
Ice Cream

Fluffy, Fluffy ♥ Cinnamoroll

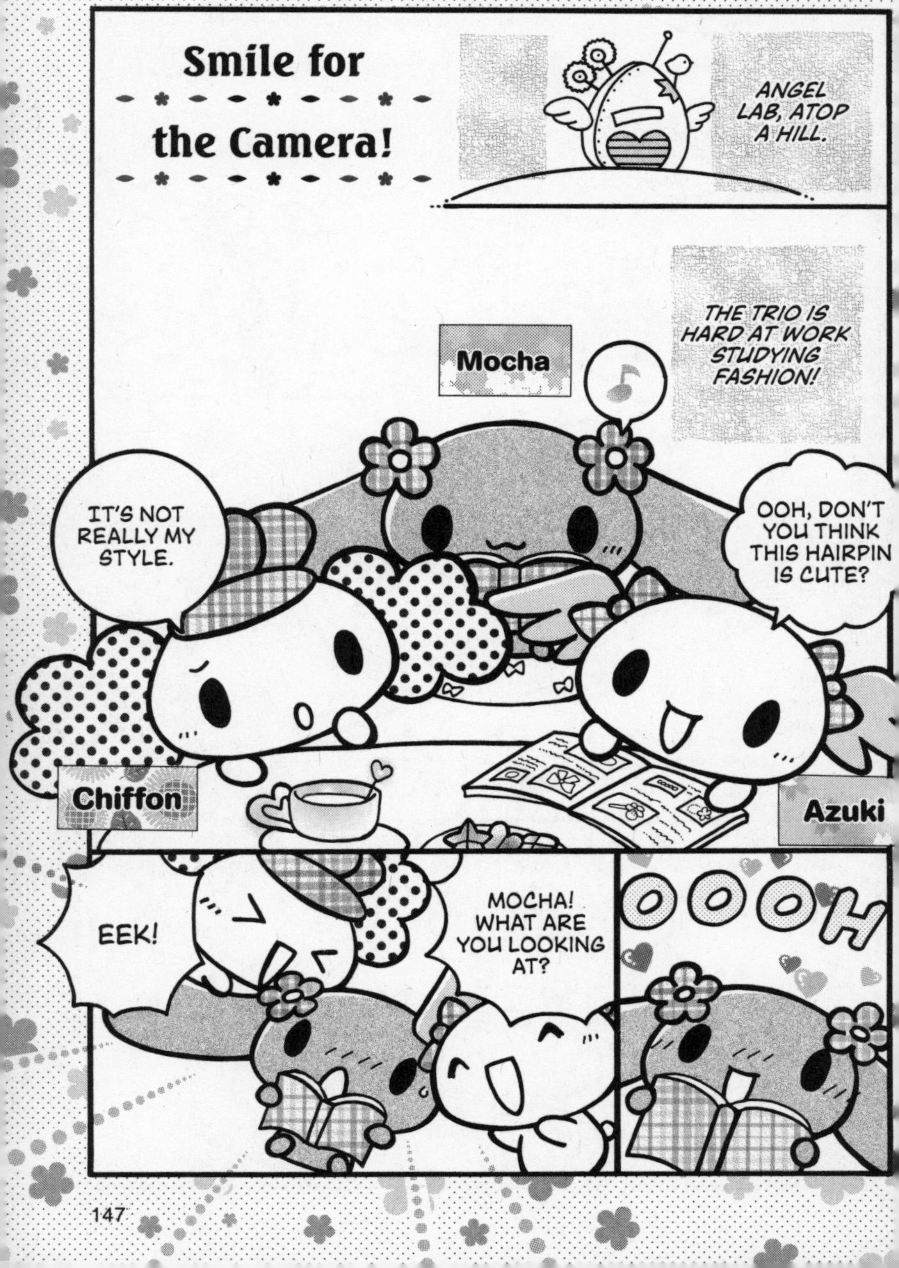
Smile for the Camera!
ANGEL LAB, ATOP A HILL.
THE TRIO IS HARD AT WORK STUDYING FASHION!
Mocha
OOH, DON'T YOU THINK THIS HAIRPIN IS CUTE?
IT'S NOT REALLY MY STYLE.
Azuki
Chiffon
OOOH
MOCHA! WHAT ARE YOU LOOKING AT?
EEK!

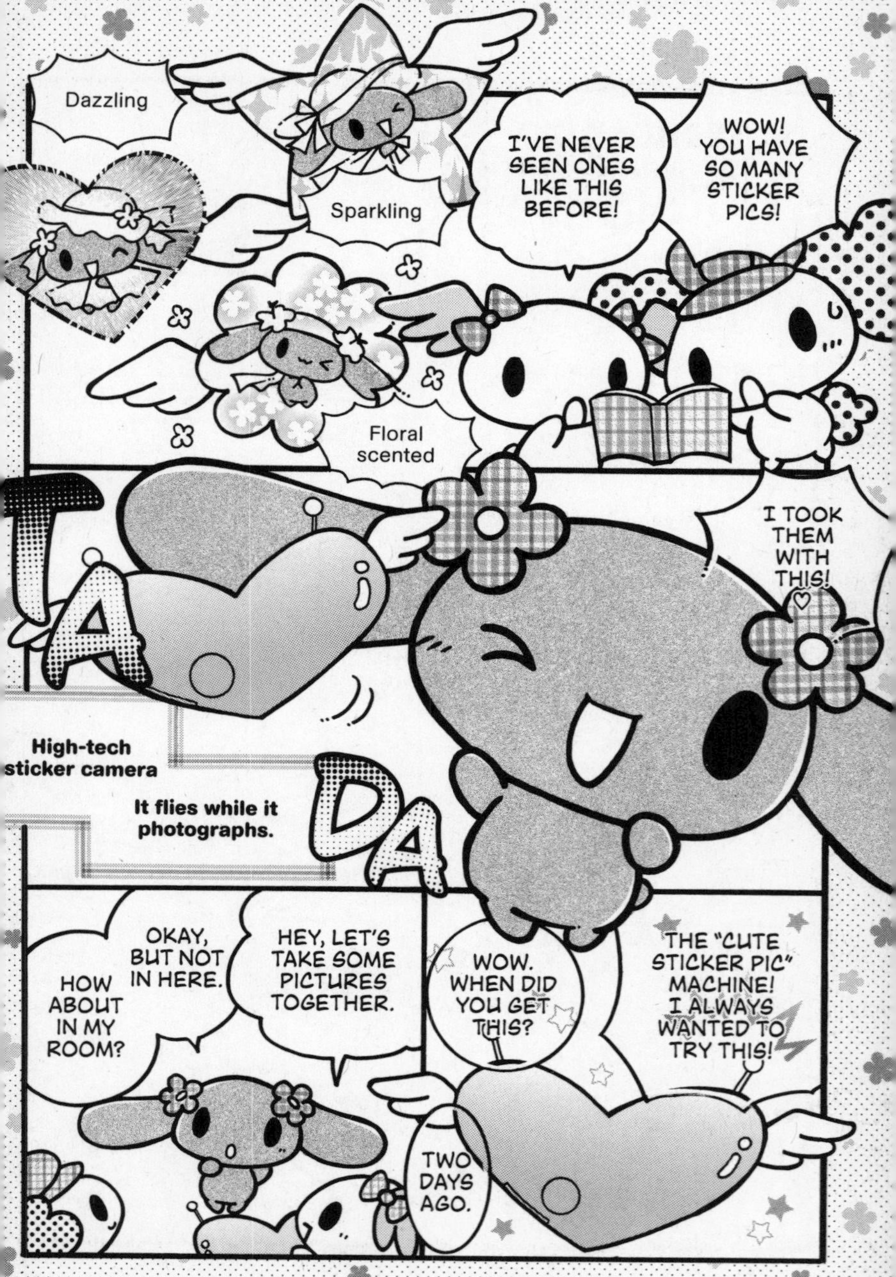
WOW! YOU HAVE SO MANY STICKER PICS!
I'VE NEVER SEEN ONES LIKE THIS BEFORE!
Dazzling
Sparkling
Floral scented
I TOOK THEM WITH THIS!
TA
DA
High-tech sticker camera
It flies while it photographs.
THE "CUTE STICKER PIC" MACHINE! I ALWAYS WANTED TO TRY THIS!
WOW. WHEN DID YOU GET THIS?
TWO DAYS AGO.
HEY, LET'S TAKE SOME PICTURES TOGETHER.
OKAY, BUT NOT IN HERE.
HOW ABOUT IN MY ROOM?

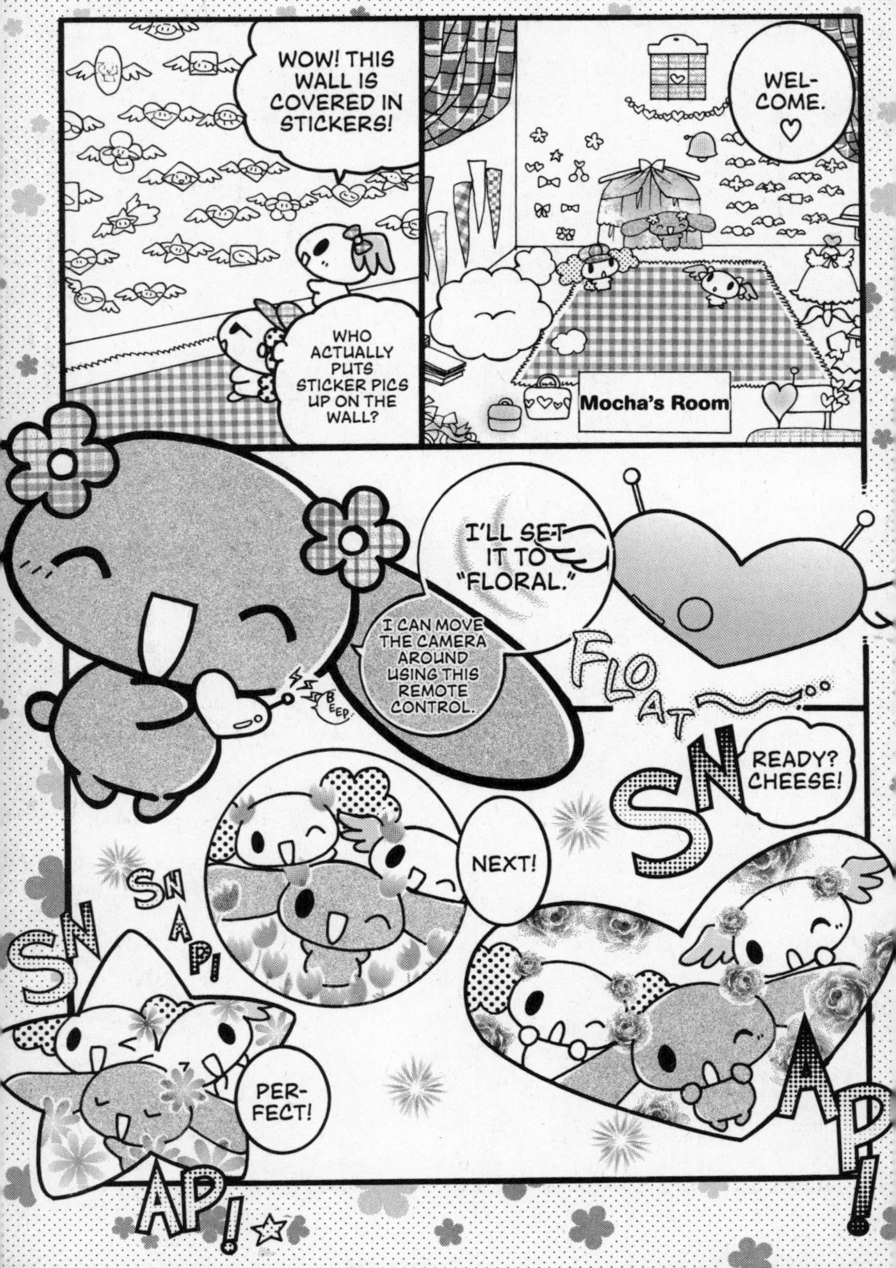
WEL-
COME. ♡
Mocha's Room
WOW! THIS WALL IS COVERED IN STICKERS!
WHO ACTUALLY PUTS STICKER PICS UP ON THE WALL?
I'LL SET IT TO "FLORAL."
I CAN MOVE THE CAMERA AROUND USING THIS REMOTE CONTROL.
BEEP
FLOAT
READY? CHEESE!
SNAP!
NEXT!
SNAP!
PERFECT!
SNAP! ☆

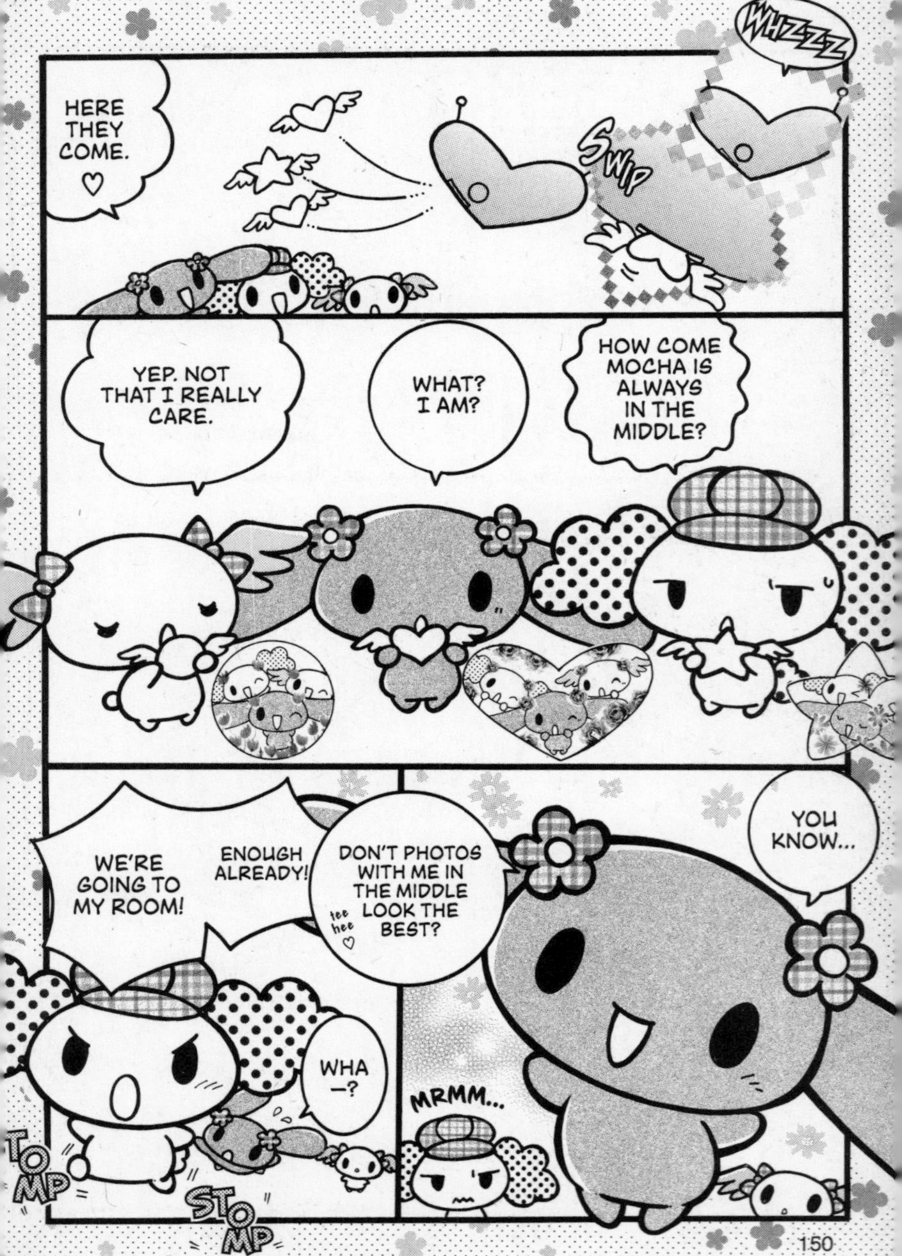
WHZZZZ
SWIP
HERE THEY COME. ♡
HOW COME MOCHA IS ALWAYS IN THE MIDDLE?
WHAT? I AM?
YEP. NOT THAT I REALLY CARE.
YOU KNOW...
DON'T PHOTOS WITH ME IN THE MIDDLE LOOK THE BEST?
tee hee ♡
MRMM...
ENOUGH ALREADY!
WE'RE GOING TO MY ROOM!
WHA—?
STOMP
STOMP

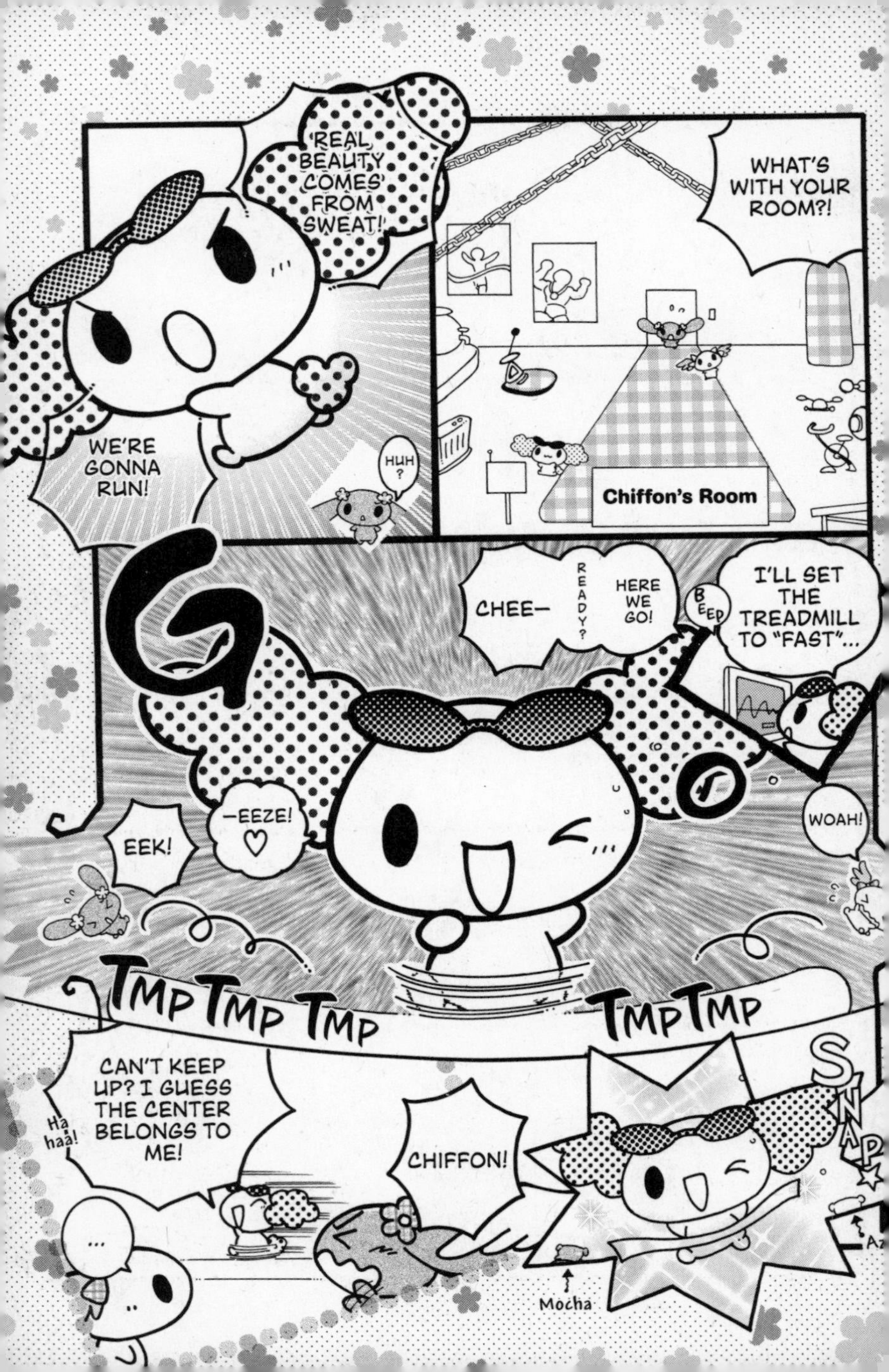
WHAT'S WITH YOUR ROOM?!
Chiffon's Room
REAL BEAUTY COMES FROM SWEAT!
WE'RE GONNA RUN!
HUH?
I'LL SET THE TREADMILL TO "FAST"...
BEEP
HERE WE GO!
READY?
CHEE—
G
—EEZE! ♡
WOAH!
EEK!
TMP TMP TMP TMP TMP
SNAP
CHIFFON!
Mocha
CAN'T KEEP UP? I GUESS THE CENTER BELONGS TO ME!
Ha haa!
...

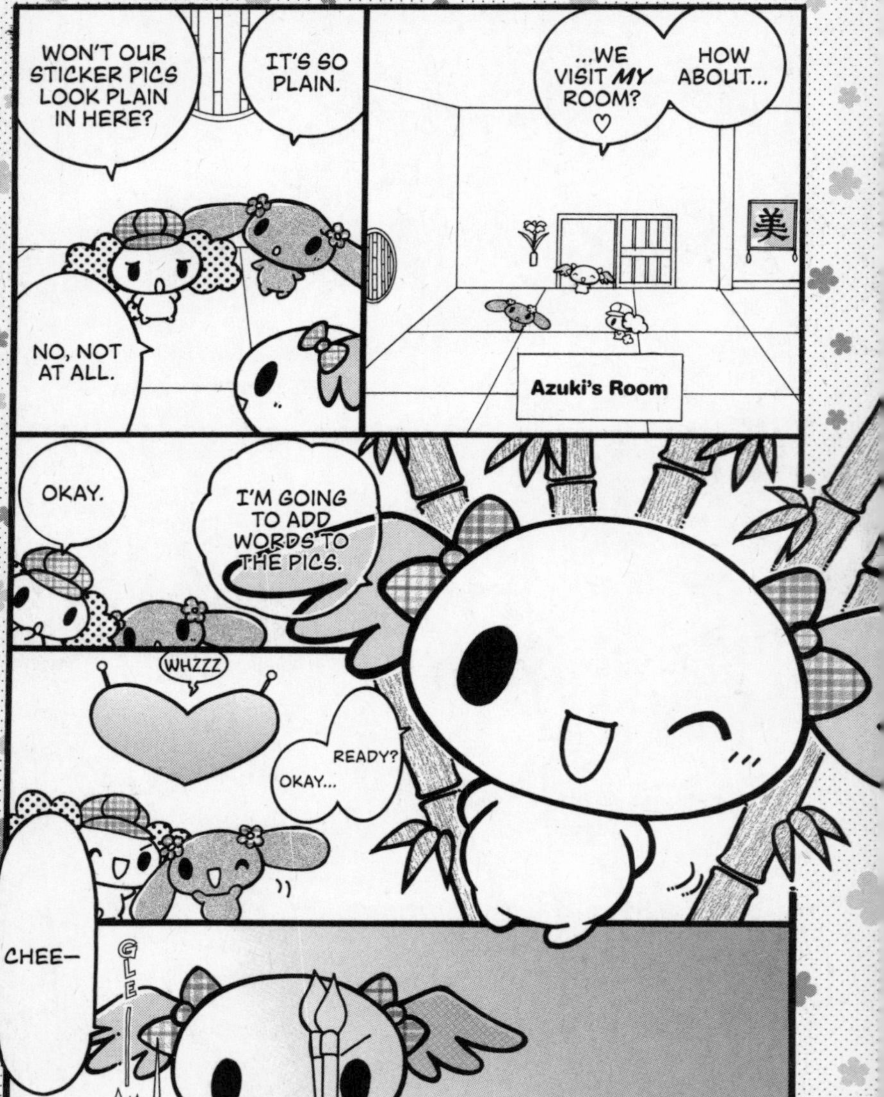
HOW ABOUT...
...WE VISIT MY ROOM? ♡
Azuki's Room
IT'S SO PLAIN.
WON'T OUR STICKER PICS LOOK PLAIN IN HERE?
NO, NOT AT ALL.
I'M GOING TO ADD WORDS TO THE PICS.
OKAY.
READY? OKAY...
WHZZZ
CHEE—
GLE—AM
INK

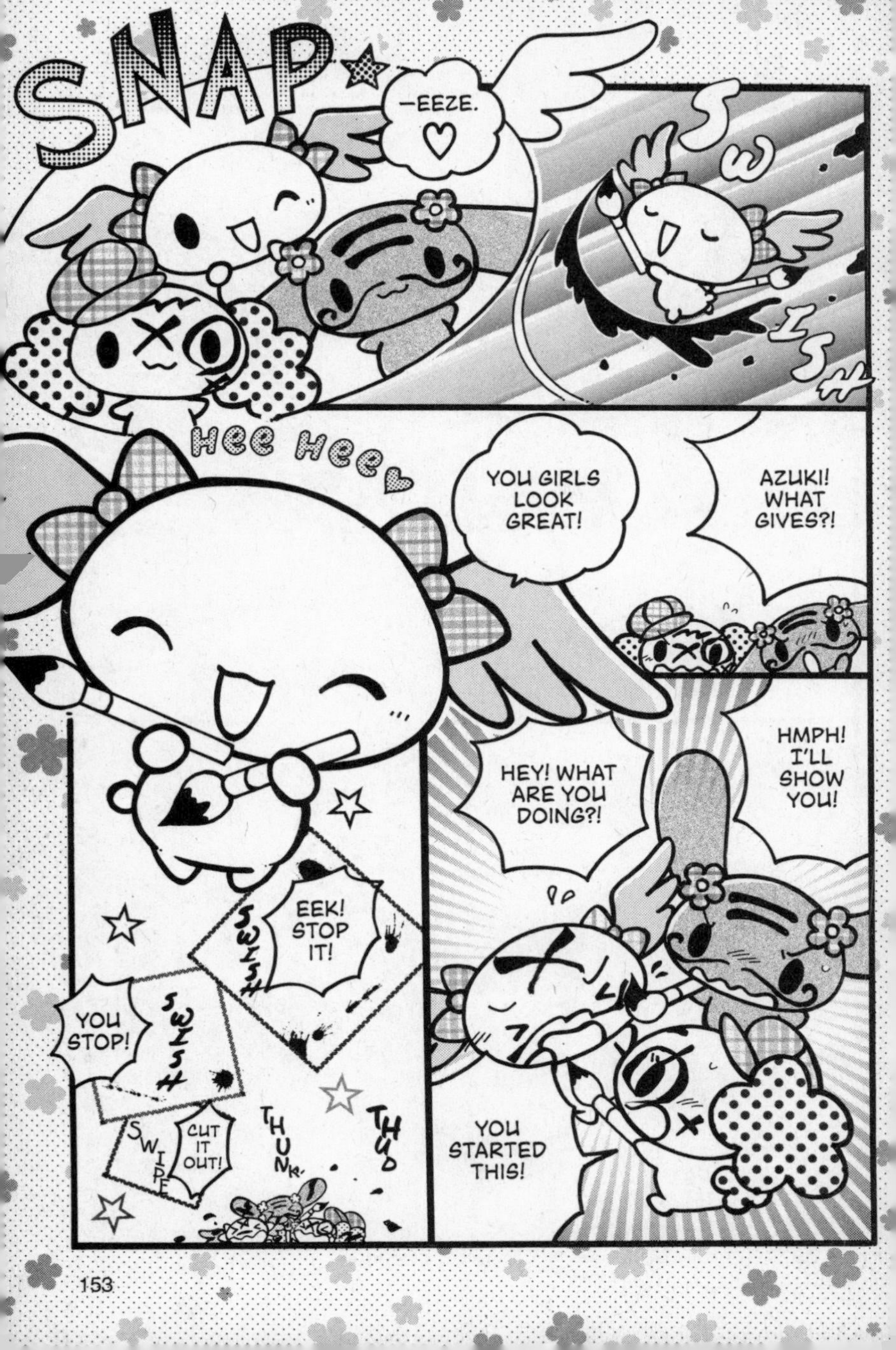
SWISH
SNAP
—EEZE.
AZUKI! WHAT GIVES?!
YOU GIRLS LOOK GREAT!
HEE HEE
HMPH! I'LL SHOW YOU!
HEY! WHAT ARE YOU DOING?!
YOU STARTED THIS!
EEK! STOP IT!
SWISH
YOU STOP!
SWISH
THUD
THUNK
CUT IT OUT!
SWIPE

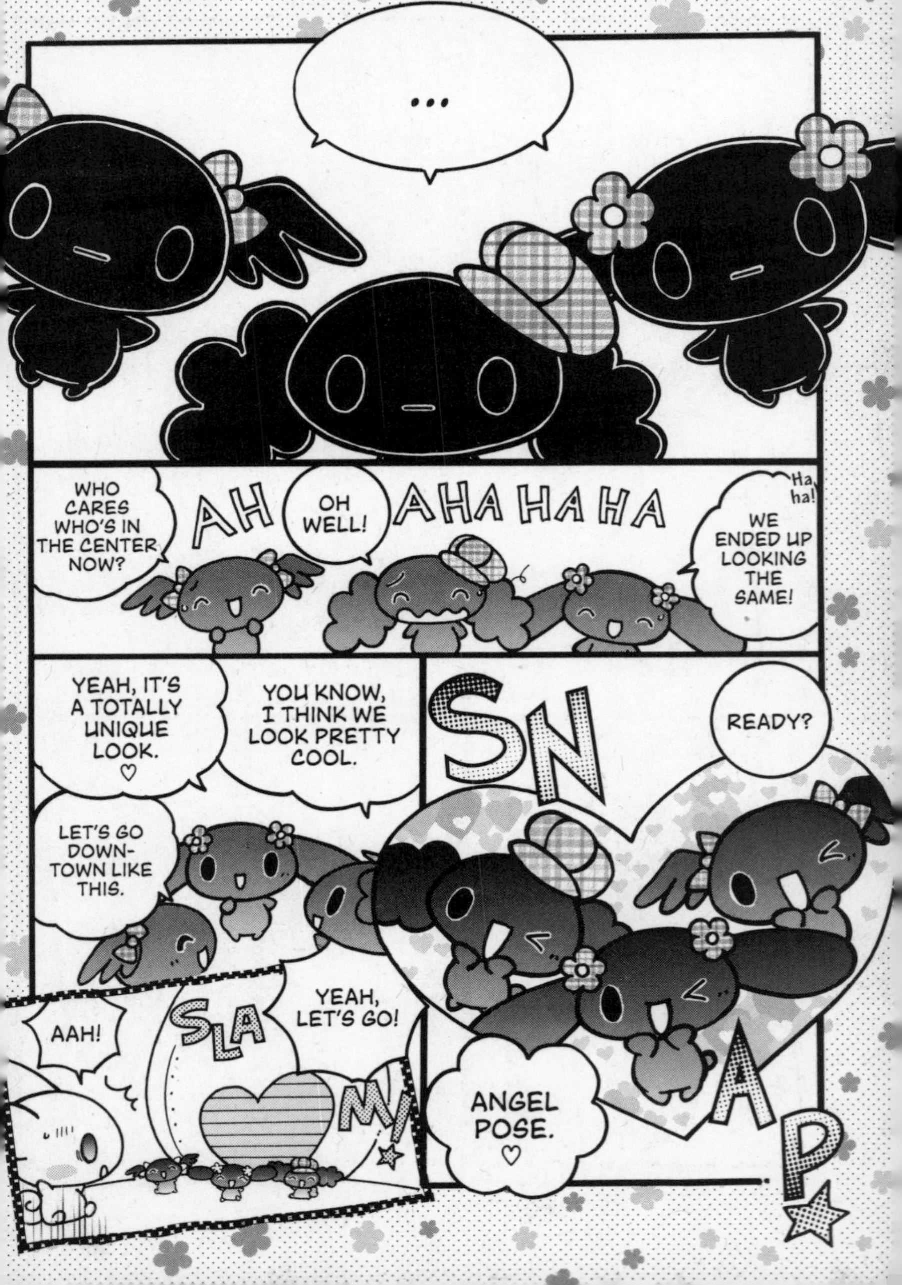
...
Ha ha!
WE ENDED UP LOOKING THE SAME!
AH AHAHAHAHA
OH WELL!
WHO CARES WHO'S IN THE CENTER NOW?
READY?
SNAP
ANGEL POSE. ♡
YOU KNOW, I THINK WE LOOK PRETTY COOL.
YEAH, IT'S A TOTALLY UNIQUE LOOK. ♡
LET'S GO DOWN-TOWN LIKE THIS.
YEAH, LET'S GO!
SLAM
AAH!

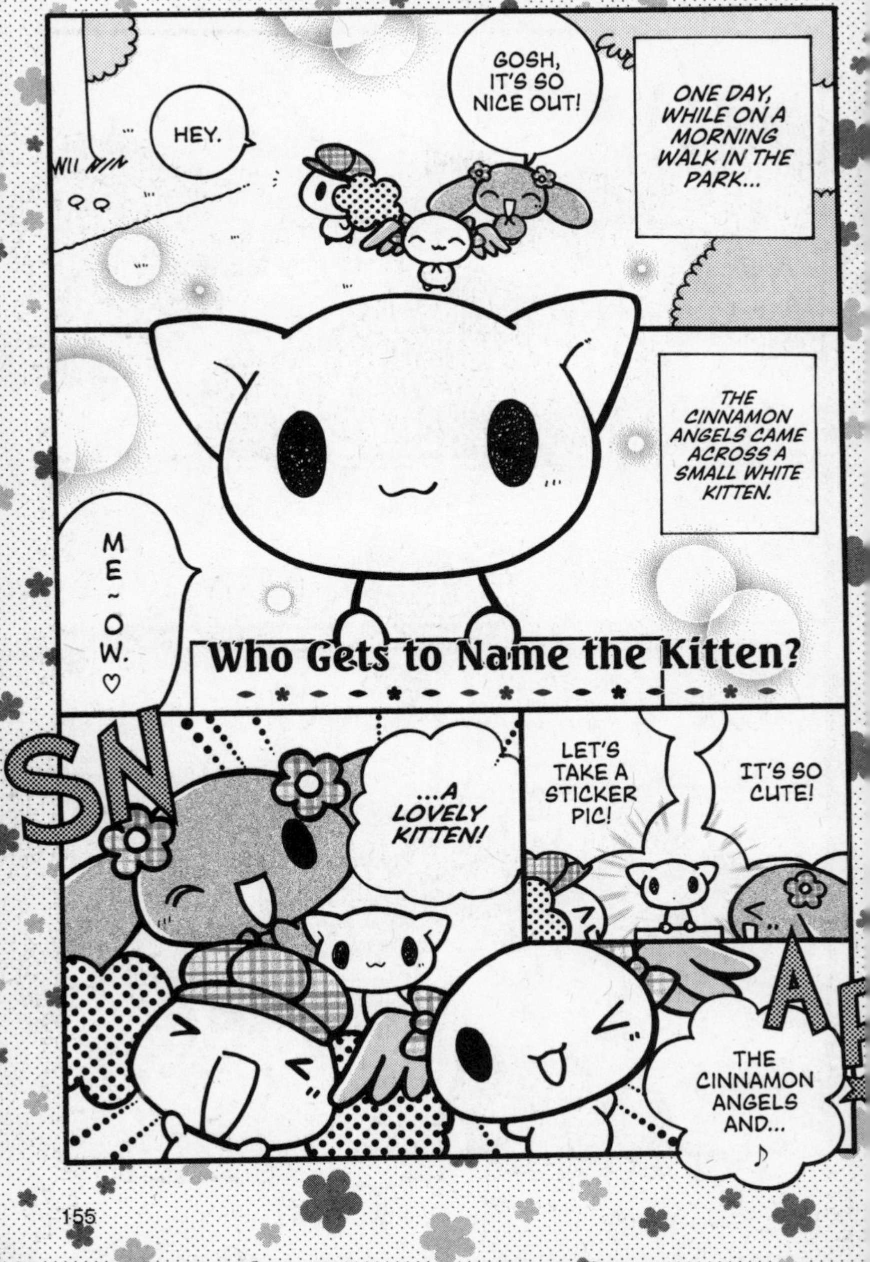

ONE DAY, WHILE ON A MORNING WALK IN THE PARK...
GOSH, IT'S SO NICE OUT!
HEY.
THE CINNAMON ANGELS CAME ACROSS A SMALL WHITE KITTEN.
Who Gets to Name the Kitten?
ME~OW. ♡
IT'S SO CUTE!
LET'S TAKE A STICKER PIC!
...A LOVELY KITTEN!
SN
AP
THE CINNAMON ANGELS AND... ♪

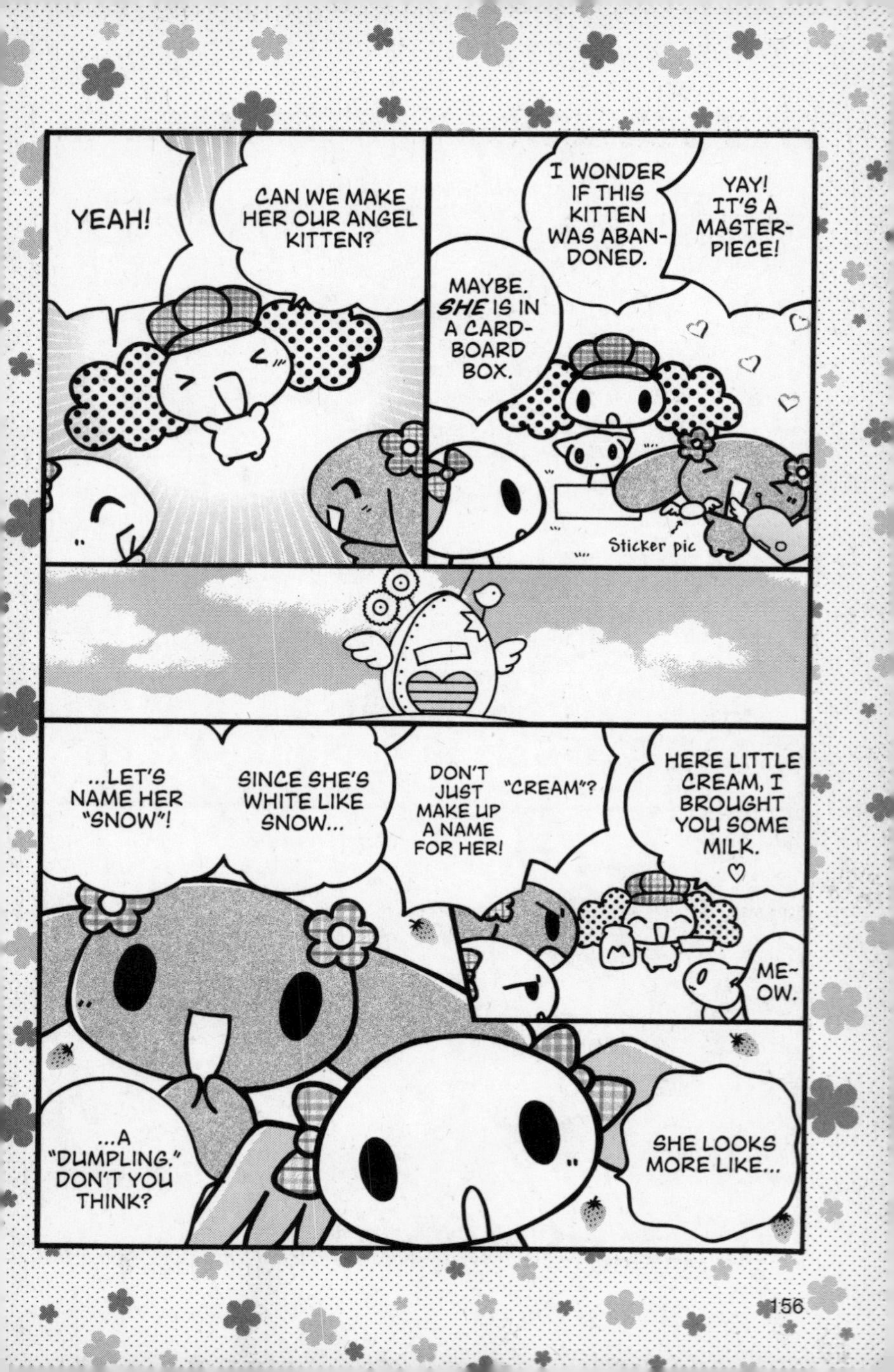
YAY! IT'S A MASTER-PIECE!
I WONDER IF THIS KITTEN WAS ABAN-DONED.
MAYBE. *SHE* IS IN A CARD-BOARD BOX.
Sticker pic
CAN WE MAKE HER OUR ANGEL KITTEN?
YEAH!
HERE LITTLE CREAM, I BROUGHT YOU SOME MILK. ♡
"CREAM"?
DON'T JUST MAKE UP A NAME FOR HER!
ME-OW.
SINCE SHE'S WHITE LIKE SNOW...
...LET'S NAME HER "SNOW"!
SHE LOOKS MORE LIKE...
...A "DUMPLING." DON'T YOU THINK?

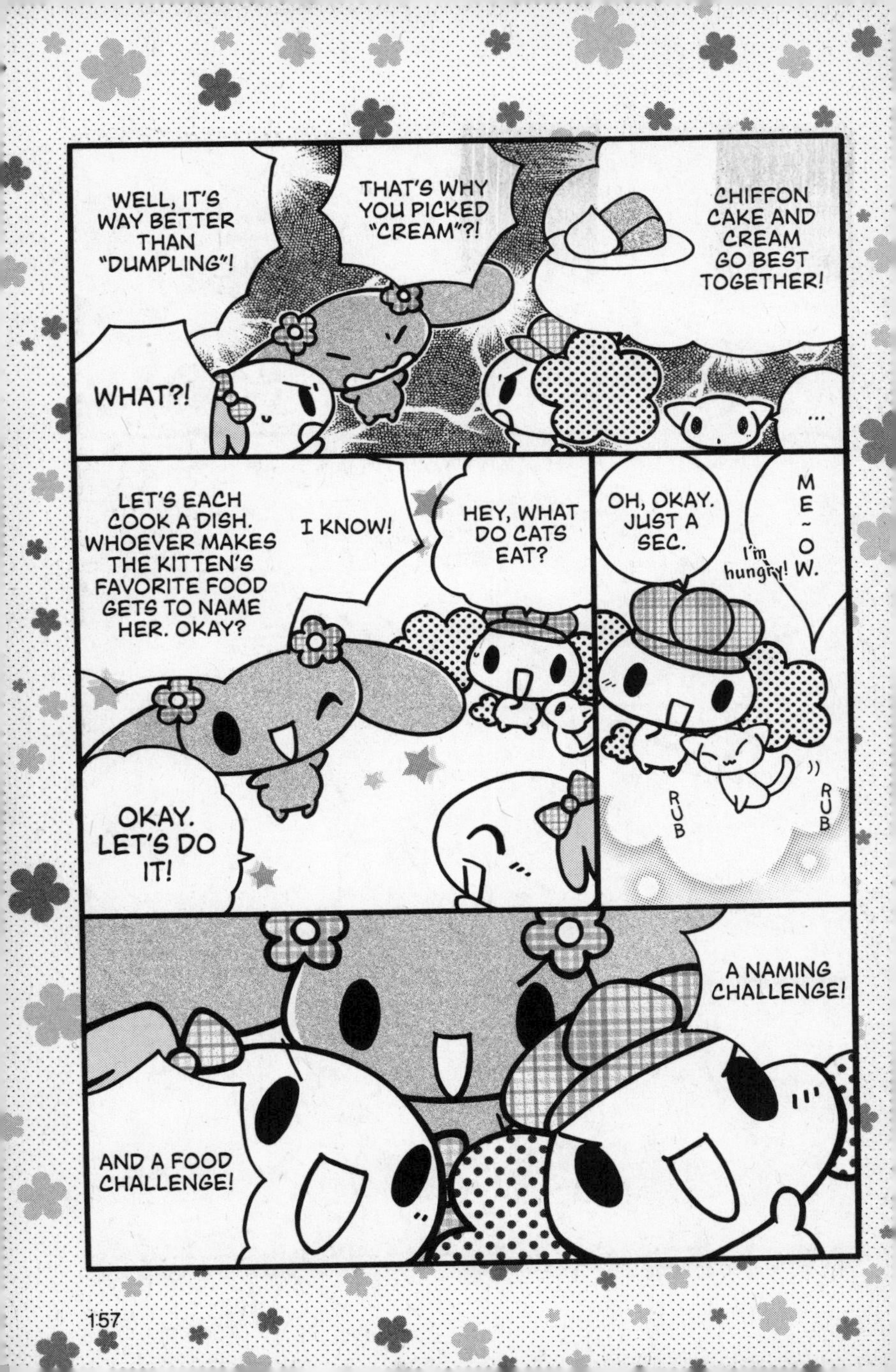
CHIFFON CAKE AND CREAM GO BEST TOGETHER!
THAT'S WHY YOU PICKED "CREAM"?!
WELL, IT'S WAY BETTER THAN "DUMPLING"!
...
WHAT?!
ME~OW.
I'm hungry!
OH, OKAY. JUST A SEC.
RUB
RUB
HEY, WHAT DO CATS EAT?
I KNOW!
LET'S EACH COOK A DISH. WHOEVER MAKES THE KITTEN'S FAVORITE FOOD GETS TO NAME HER. OKAY?
OKAY. LET'S DO IT!
A NAMING CHALLENGE!
AND A FOOD CHALLENGE!

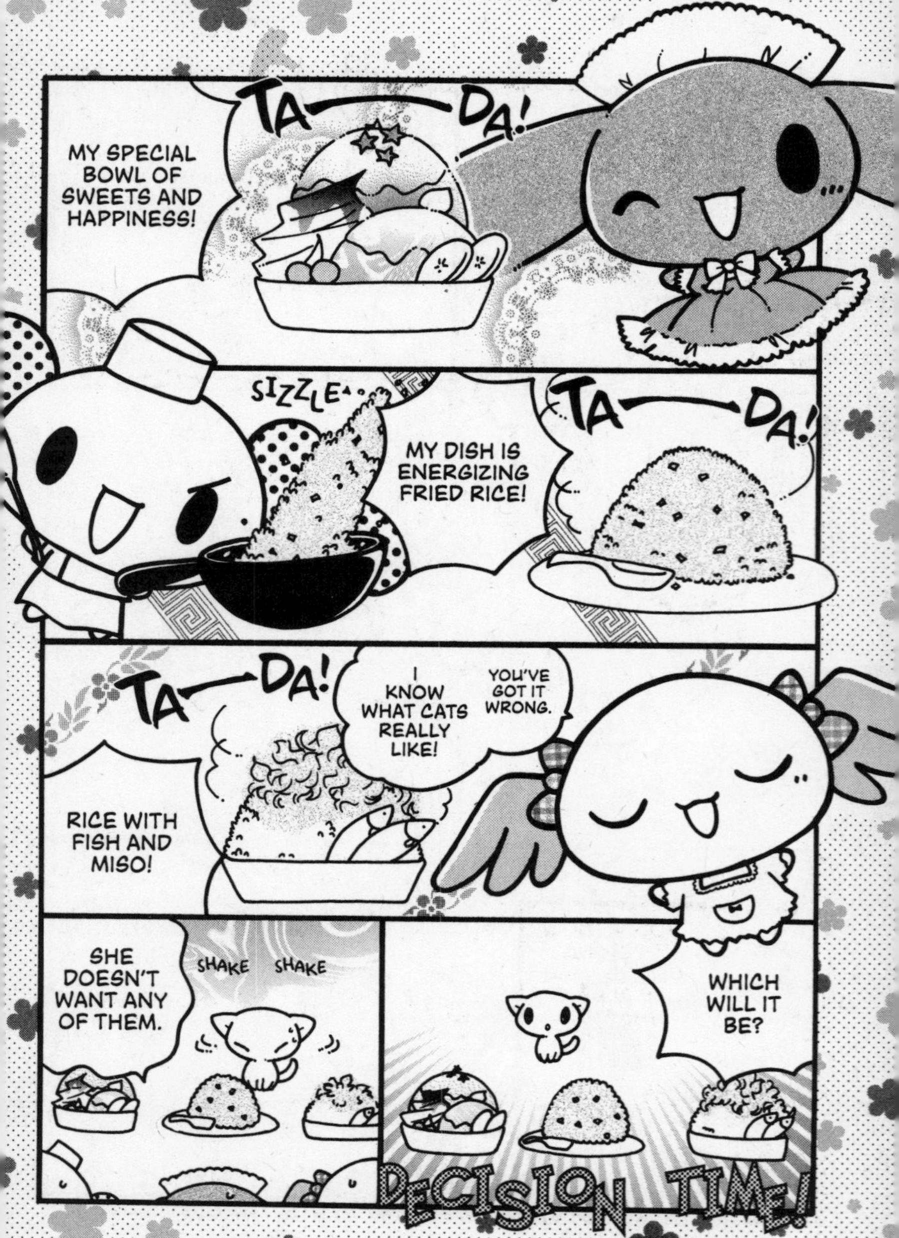
TA—DA!
MY SPECIAL BOWL OF SWEETS AND HAPPINESS!
TA—DA!
MY DISH IS ENERGIZING FRIED RICE!
SIZZLE
YOU'VE GOT IT WRONG.
I KNOW WHAT CATS REALLY LIKE!
TA—DA!
RICE WITH FISH AND MISO!
WHICH WILL IT BE?
DECISION TIME!
SHE DOESN'T WANT ANY OF THEM.
SHAKE SHAKE

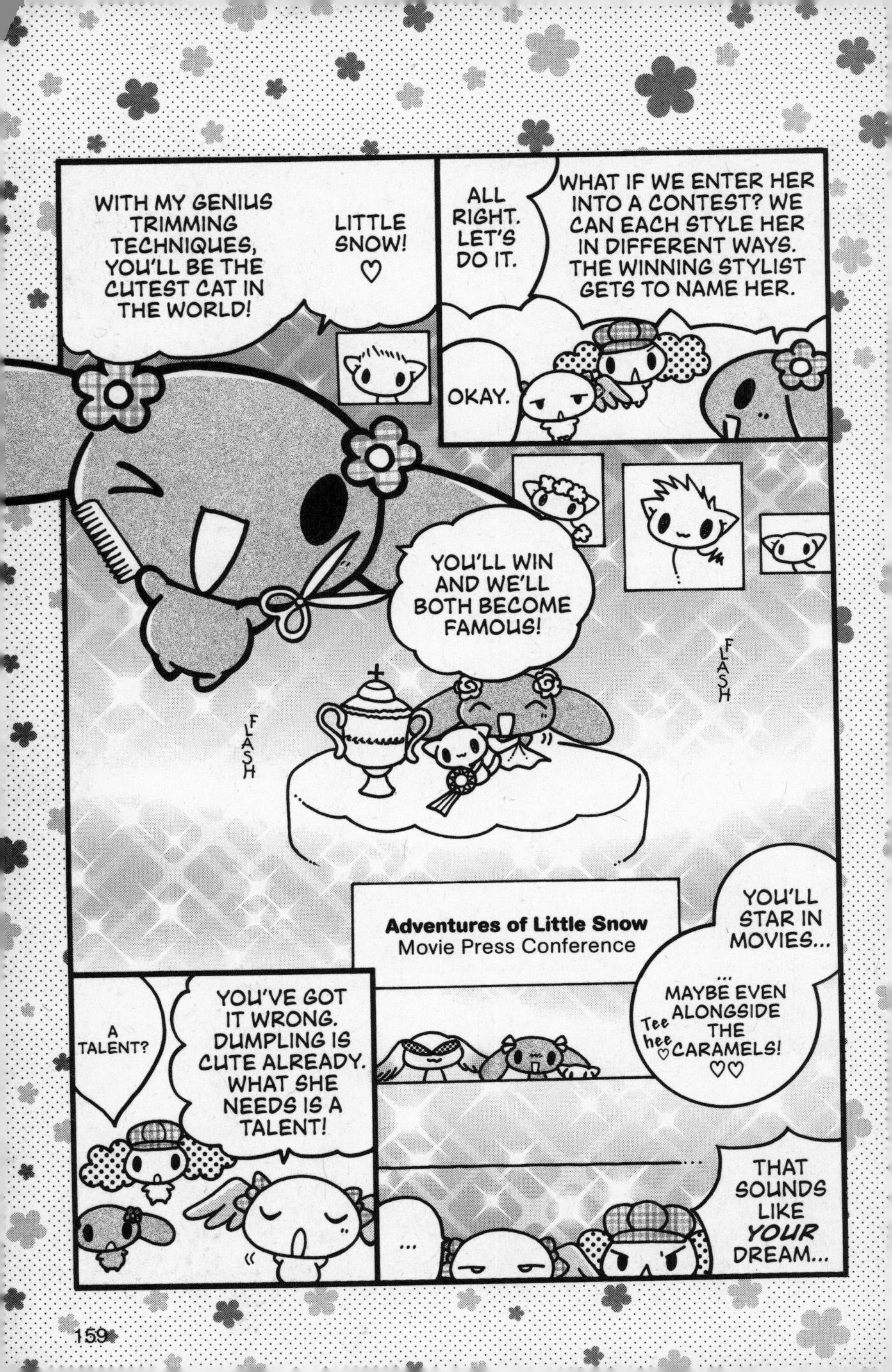
WHAT IF WE ENTER HER INTO A CONTEST? WE CAN EACH STYLE HER IN DIFFERENT WAYS. THE WINNING STYLIST GETS TO NAME HER.
ALL RIGHT. LET'S DO IT.
OKAY.
LITTLE SNOW! ♡
WITH MY GENIUS TRIMMING TECHNIQUES, YOU'LL BE THE CUTEST CAT IN THE WORLD!
FLASH
YOU'LL WIN AND WE'LL BOTH BECOME FAMOUS!
FLASH
YOU'LL STAR IN MOVIES...
...MAYBE EVEN ALONGSIDE THE CARAMELS! ♡♡
Tee hee ♡
Adventures of Little Snow
Movie Press Conference
THAT SOUNDS LIKE *YOUR* DREAM...
...
YOU'VE GOT IT WRONG. DUMPLING IS CUTE ALREADY. WHAT SHE NEEDS IS A TALENT!
A TALENT?

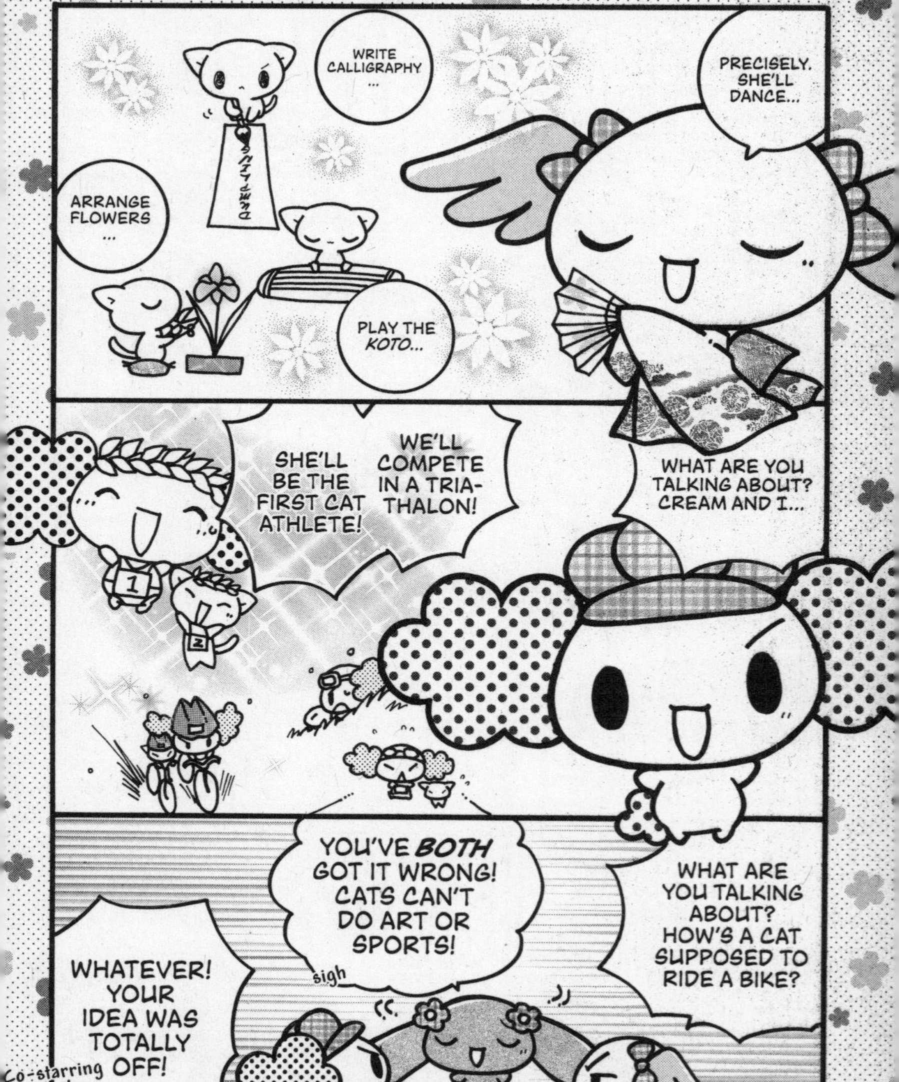
PRECISELY. SHE'LL DANCE...
WRITE CALLIGRAPHY ...
PLAY THE *KOTO*...
ARRANGE FLOWERS ...
WHAT ARE YOU TALKING ABOUT? CREAM AND I...
WE'LL COMPETE IN A TRIA-THALON!
SHE'LL BE THE FIRST CAT ATHLETE!
WHAT ARE YOU TALKING ABOUT? HOW'S A CAT SUPPOSED TO RIDE A BIKE?
YOU'VE *BOTH* GOT IT WRONG! CATS CAN'T DO ART OR SPORTS!
sigh
WHATEVER! YOUR IDEA WAS TOTALLY OFF!
Co-starring with the Caramels...

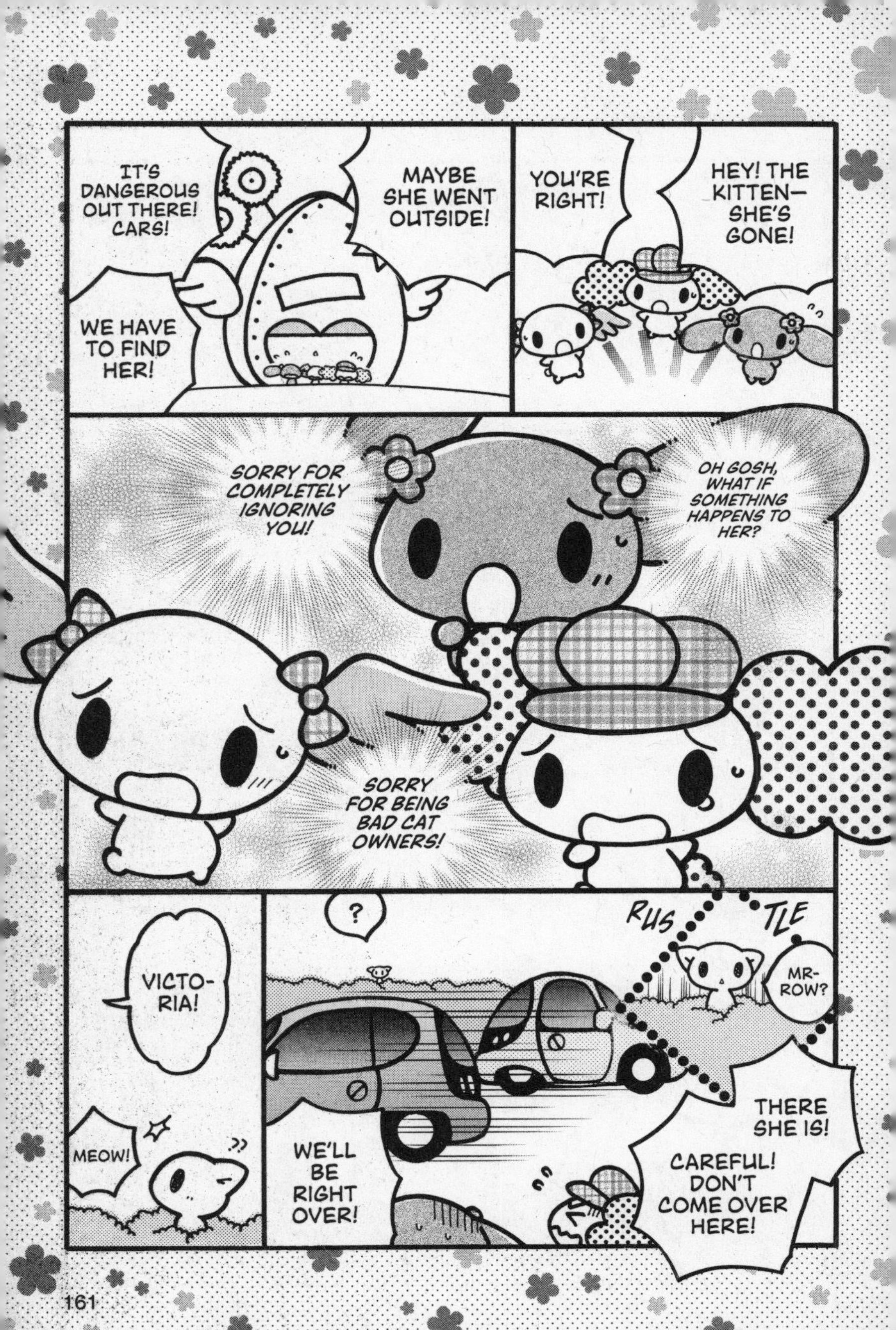
HEY! THE KITTEN—SHE'S GONE!
YOU'RE RIGHT!
MAYBE SHE WENT OUTSIDE!
IT'S DANGEROUS OUT THERE! CARS!
WE HAVE TO FIND HER!
OH GOSH, WHAT IF SOMETHING HAPPENS TO HER?
SORRY FOR COMPLETELY IGNORING YOU!
SORRY FOR BEING BAD CAT OWNERS!
RUS TLE
MR-ROW?
?
THERE SHE IS!
CAREFUL! DON'T COME OVER HERE!
WE'LL BE RIGHT OVER!
VICTO-RIA!
MEOW!

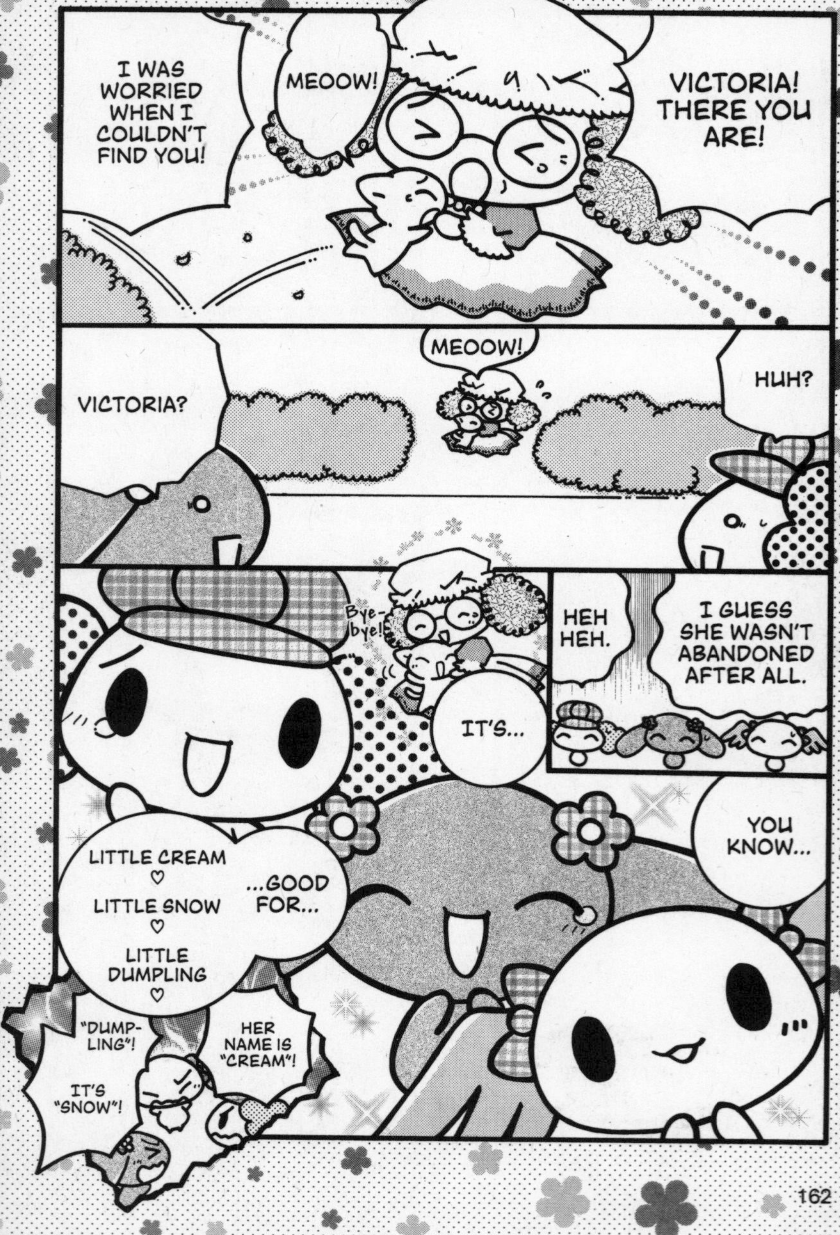
VICTORIA! THERE YOU ARE!
MEOOW!
I WAS WORRIED WHEN I COULDN'T FIND YOU!
HUH?
MEOOW!
VICTORIA?
I GUESS SHE WASN'T ABANDONED AFTER ALL.
HEH HEH.
Bye-bye!
IT'S...
YOU KNOW...
...GOOD FOR...
LITTLE CREAM ♡ LITTLE SNOW ♡ LITTLE DUMPLING ♡
HER NAME IS "CREAM"!
"DUMPLING"!
IT'S "SNOW"!

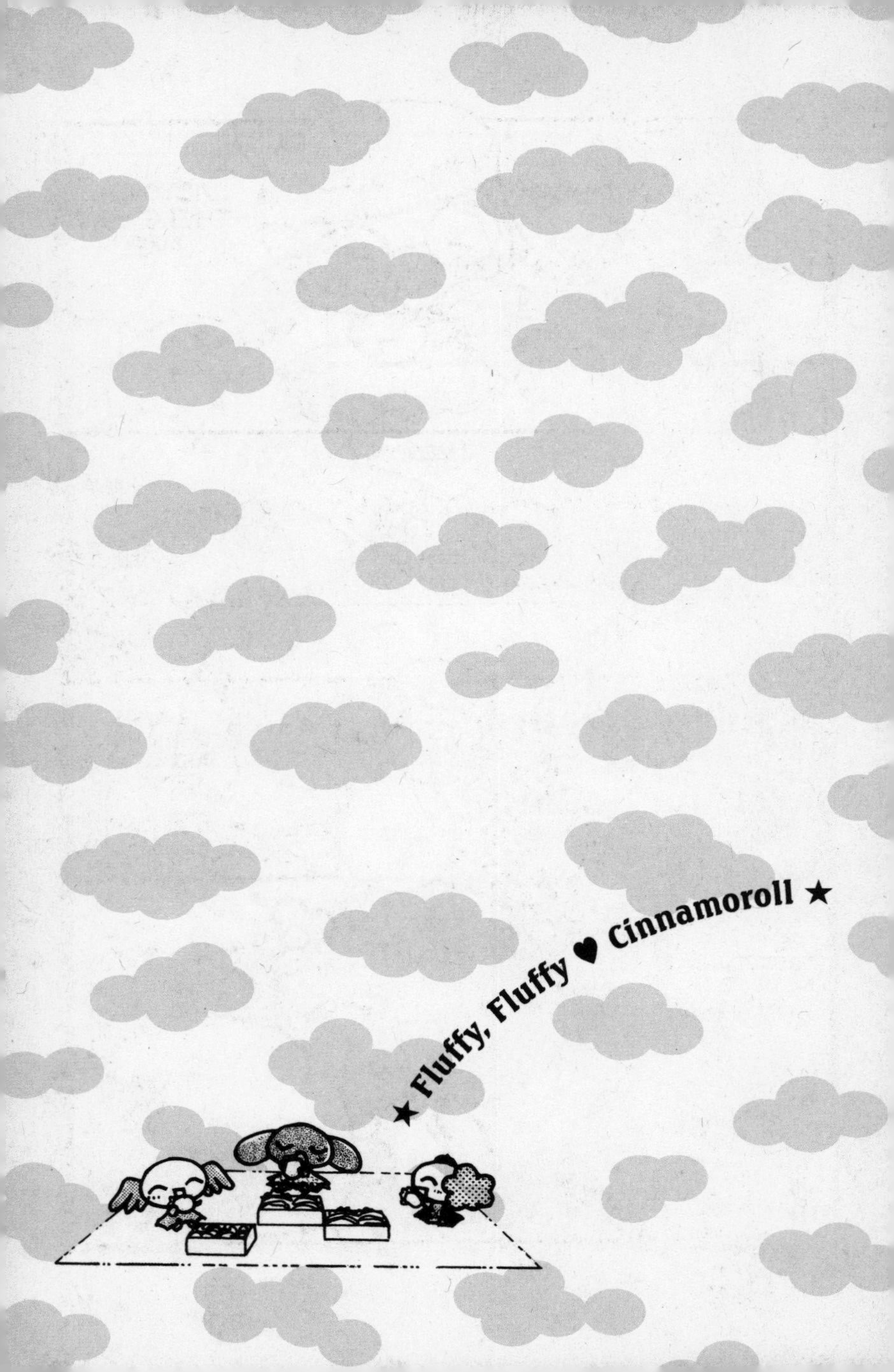
★ Fluffy, Fluffy ♥ Cinnamoroll ★

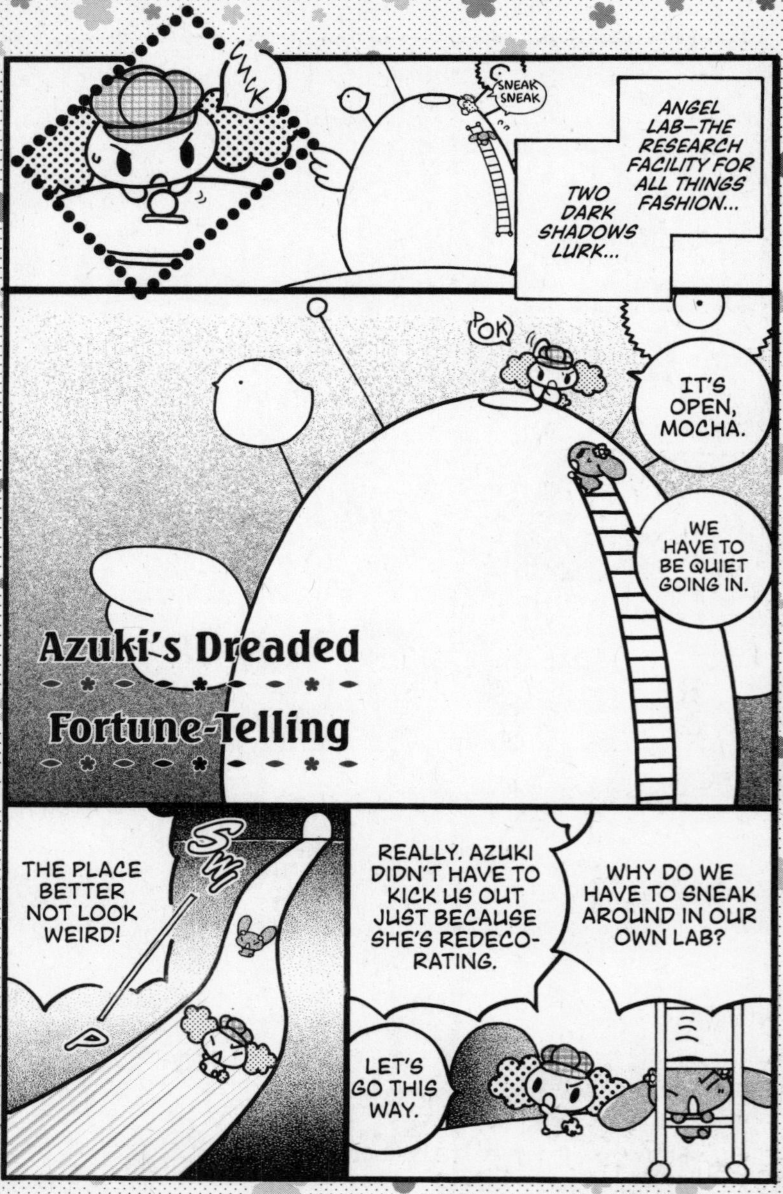
ANGEL LAB—THE RESEARCH FACILITY FOR ALL THINGS FASHION...
TWO DARK SHADOWS LURK...
SNEAK SNEAK
CLICK
POK
IT'S OPEN, MOCHA.
WE HAVE TO BE QUIET GOING IN.
Azuki's Dreaded Fortune-Telling
WHY DO WE HAVE TO SNEAK AROUND IN OUR OWN LAB?
REALLY. AZUKI DIDN'T HAVE TO KICK US OUT JUST BECAUSE SHE'S REDECO-RATING.
LET'S GO THIS WAY.
SWI
P
THE PLACE BETTER NOT LOOK WEIRD!

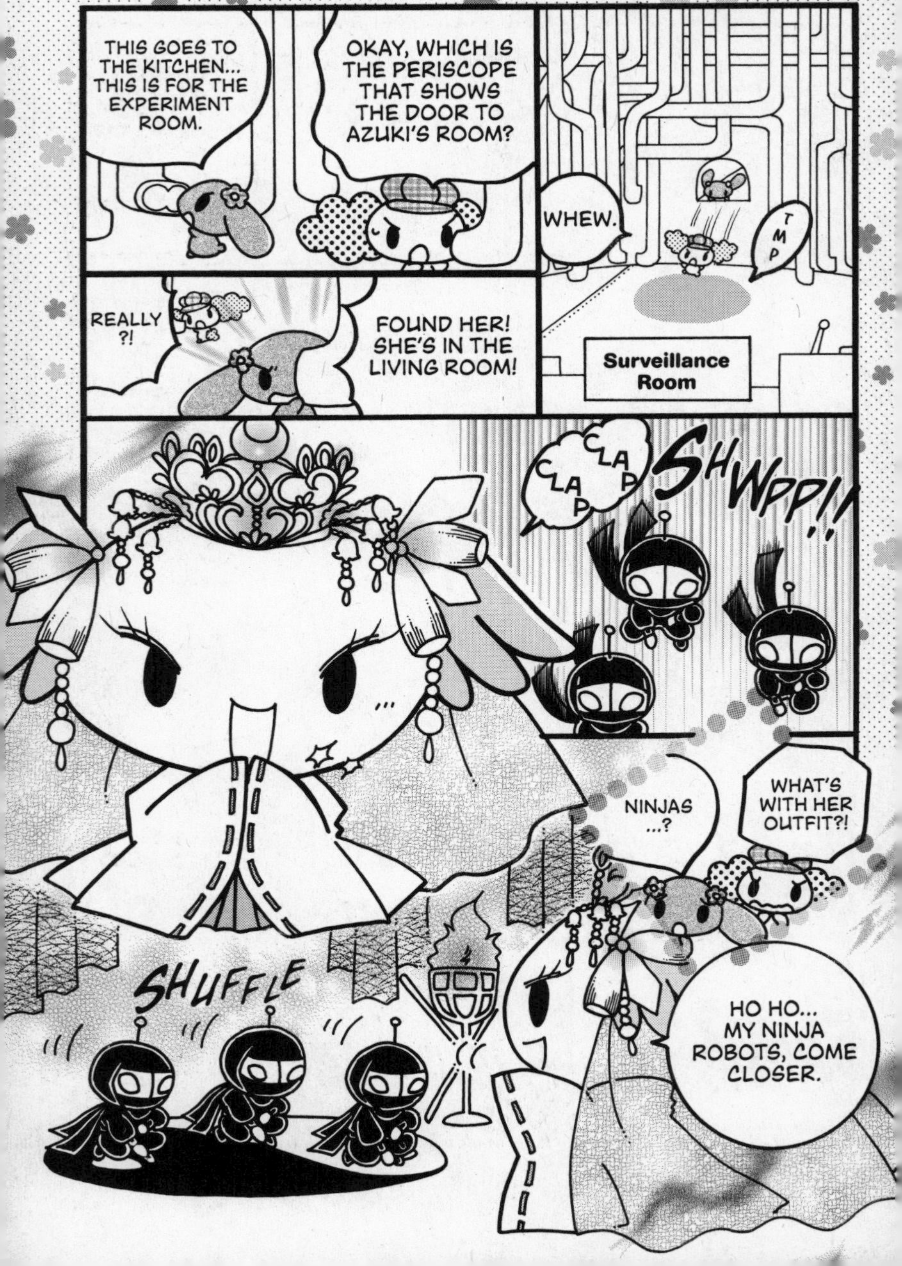
TMP
WHEW.
Surveillance Room
OKAY, WHICH IS THE PERISCOPE THAT SHOWS THE DOOR TO AZUKI'S ROOM?
THIS GOES TO THE KITCHEN... THIS IS FOR THE EXPERIMENT ROOM.
FOUND HER! SHE'S IN THE LIVING ROOM!
REALLY ?!
SHWPP!!
CLAP CLAP
WHAT'S WITH HER OUTFIT?!
NINJAS ...?
HO HO... MY NINJA ROBOTS, COME CLOSER.
SHUFFLE

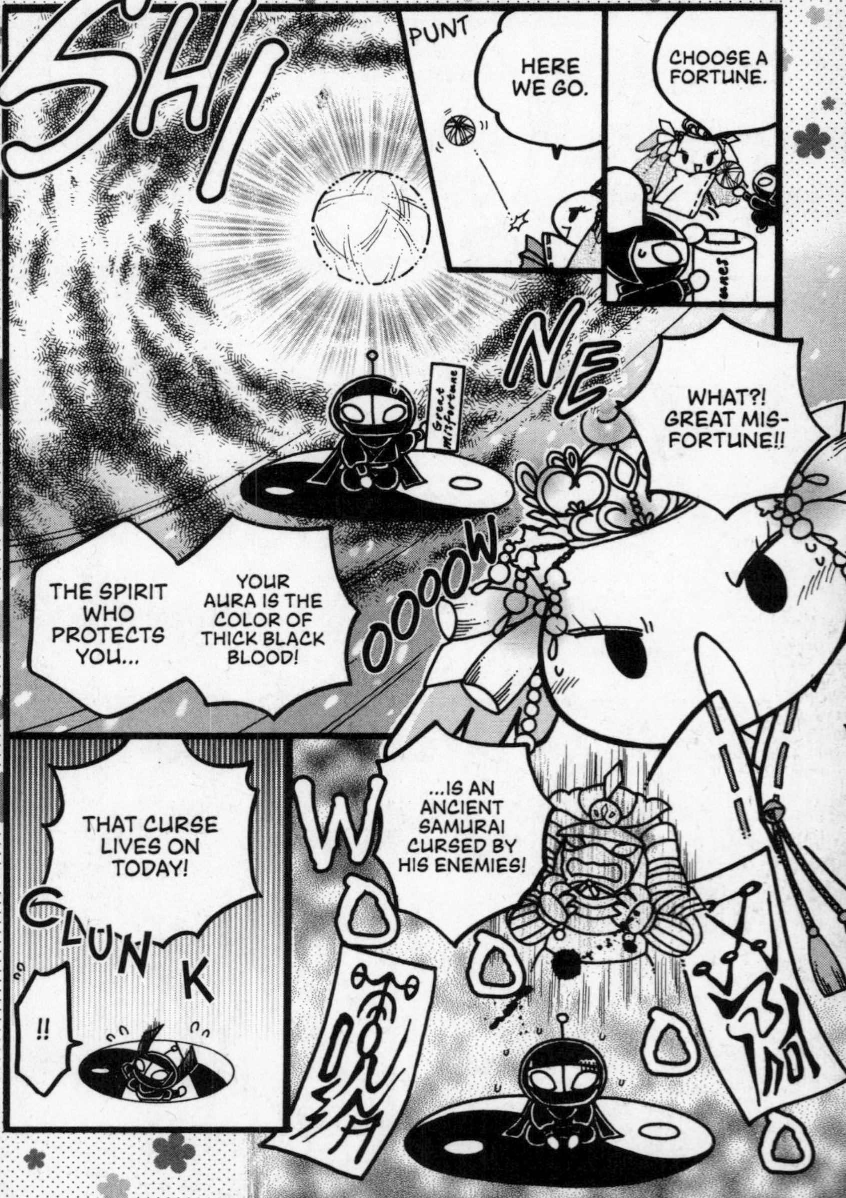
CHOOSE A FORTUNE.
PUNT
HERE WE GO.
SHI
NE
Great Misfortune
WHAT?! GREAT MIS-FORTUNE!!
OOOOOW
YOUR AURA IS THE COLOR OF THICK BLACK BLOOD!
THE SPIRIT WHO PROTECTS YOU...
...IS AN ANCIENT SAMURAI CURSED BY HIS ENEMIES!
WOOOOO
THAT CURSE LIVES ON TODAY!
CLUNK
!!

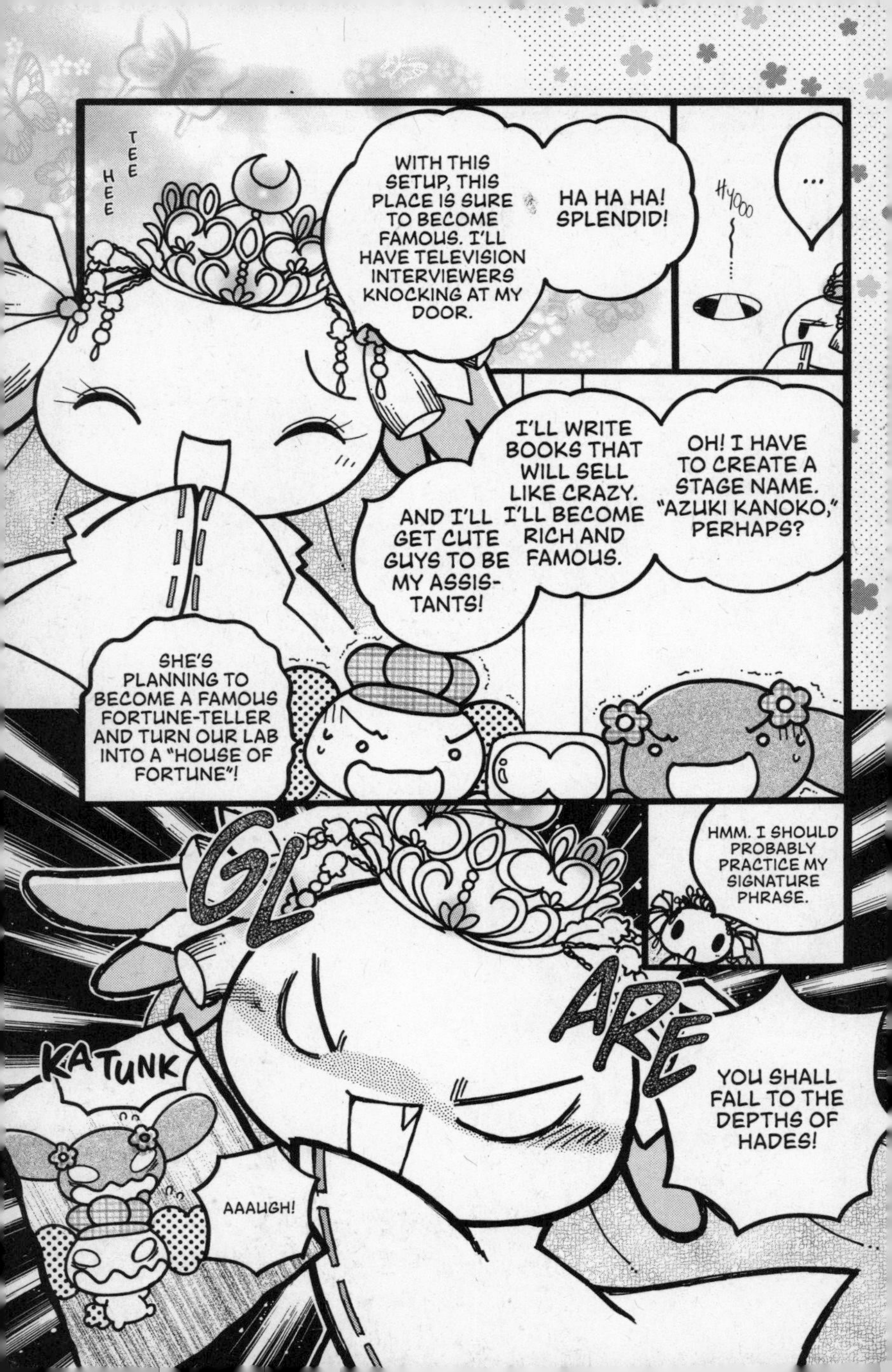
...
HYOOO
TEE HEE
WITH THIS SETUP, THIS PLACE IS SURE TO BECOME FAMOUS. I'LL HAVE TELEVISION INTERVIEWERS KNOCKING AT MY DOOR.
HA HA HA! SPLENDID!
OH! I HAVE TO CREATE A STAGE NAME. "AZUKI KANOKO," PERHAPS?
I'LL WRITE BOOKS THAT WILL SELL LIKE CRAZY. I'LL BECOME RICH AND FAMOUS.
AND I'LL GET CUTE GUYS TO BE MY ASSIS-TANTS!
SHE'S PLANNING TO BECOME A FAMOUS FORTUNE-TELLER AND TURN OUR LAB INTO A "HOUSE OF FORTUNE"!
HMM. I SHOULD PROBABLY PRACTICE MY SIGNATURE PHRASE.
GLARE
YOU SHALL FALL TO THE DEPTHS OF HADES!
KATUNK
AAAUGH!

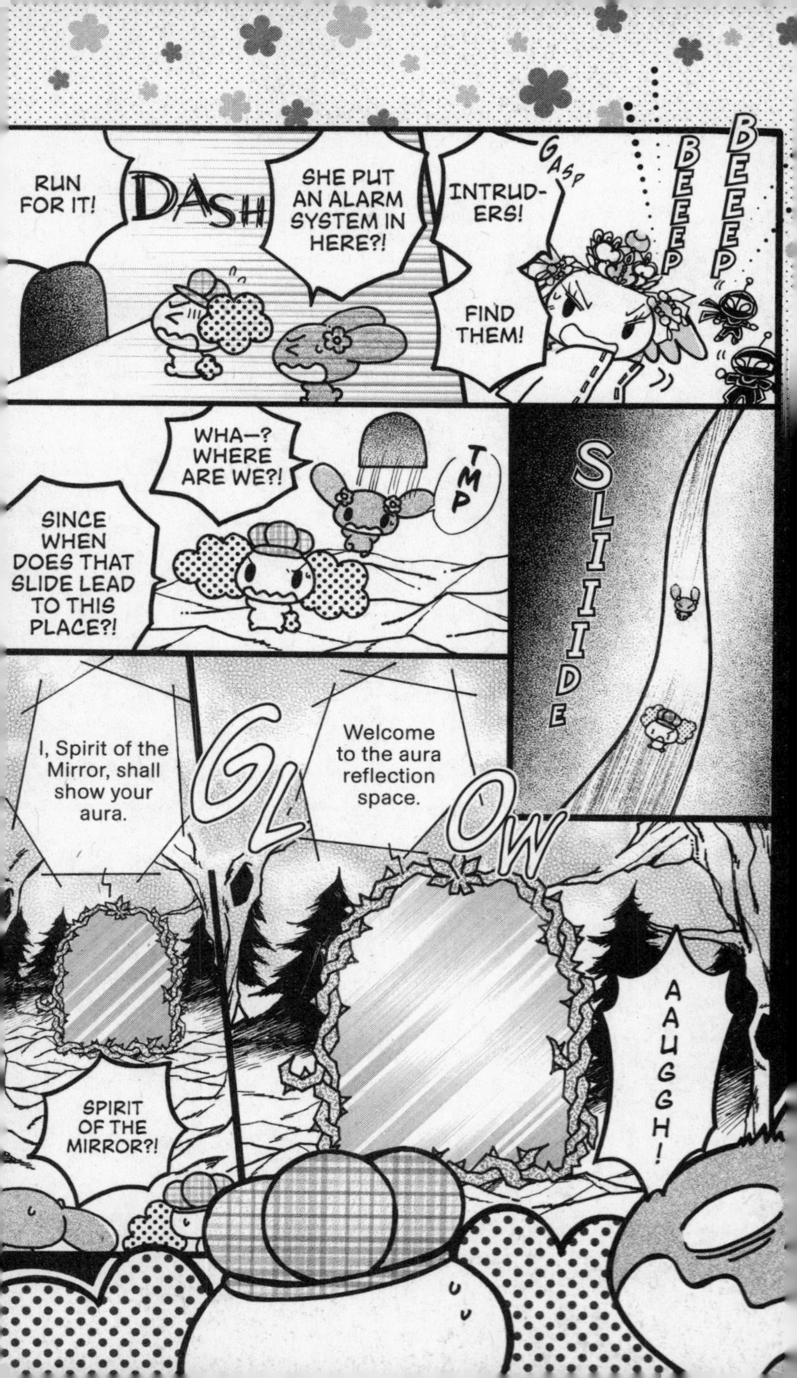
BEEEEP
BEEEEP
GASP
INTRUD-ERS!
FIND THEM!
SHE PUT AN ALARM SYSTEM IN HERE?!
DASH
RUN FOR IT!
SLIIIIDE
WHA—? WHERE ARE WE?!
TMP
SINCE WHEN DOES THAT SLIDE LEAD TO THIS PLACE?!
Welcome to the aura reflection space.
GLOW
AAUGGH!
I, Spirit of the Mirror, shall show your aura.
SPIRIT OF THE MIRROR?!

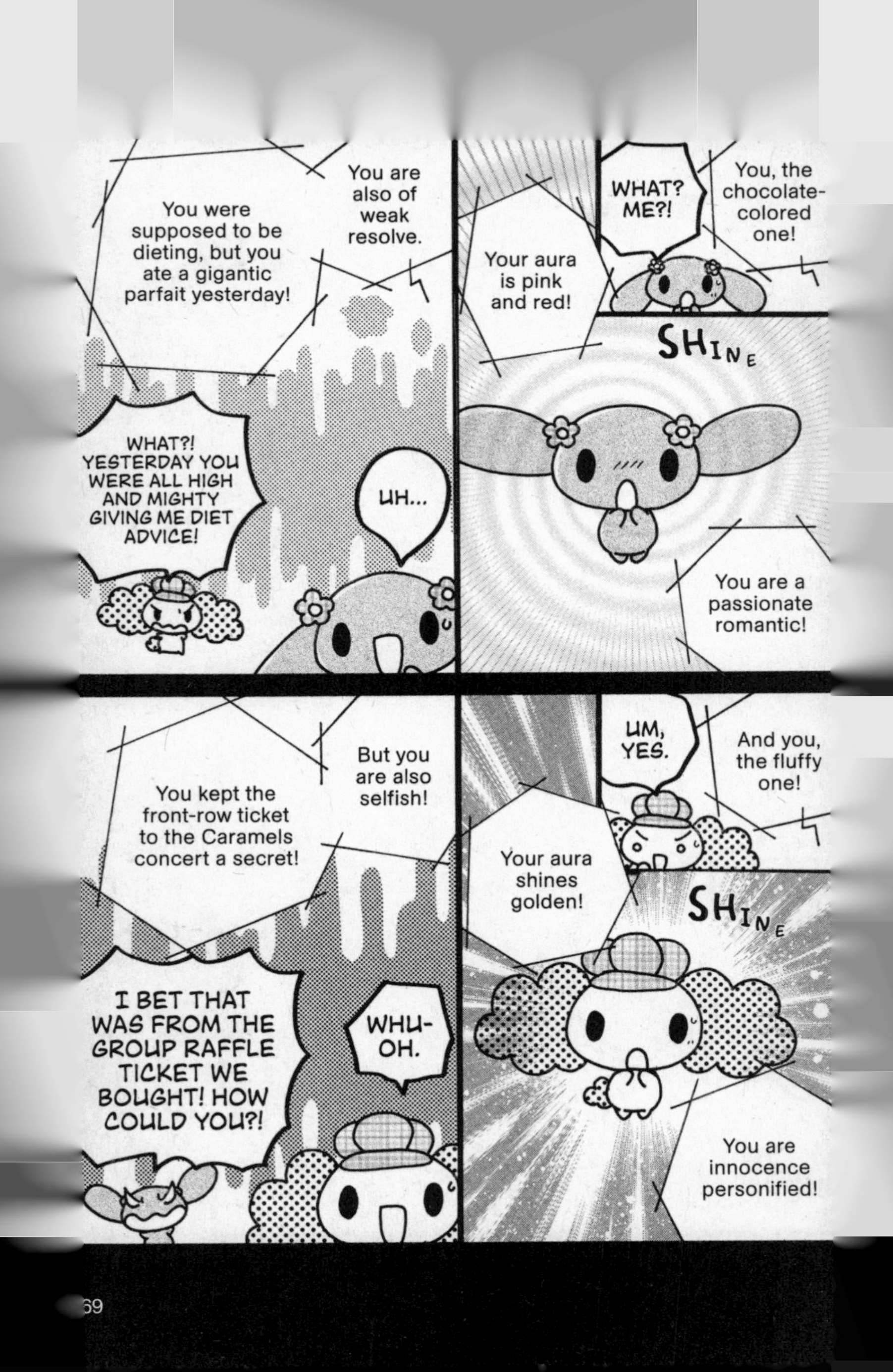
You, the chocolate-colored one!
WHAT? ME?!
Your aura is pink and red!
SHINE
You are a passionate romantic!
You are also of weak resolve.
You were supposed to be dieting, but you ate a gigantic parfait yesterday!
WHAT?! YESTERDAY YOU WERE ALL HIGH AND MIGHTY GIVING ME DIET ADVICE!
UH...
And you, the fluffy one!
UM, YES.
Your aura shines golden!
SHINE
You are innocence personified!
But you are also selfish!
You kept the front-row ticket to the Caramels concert a secret!
I BET THAT WAS FROM THE GROUP RAFFLE TICKET WE BOUGHT! HOW COULD YOU?!
WHU-OH.

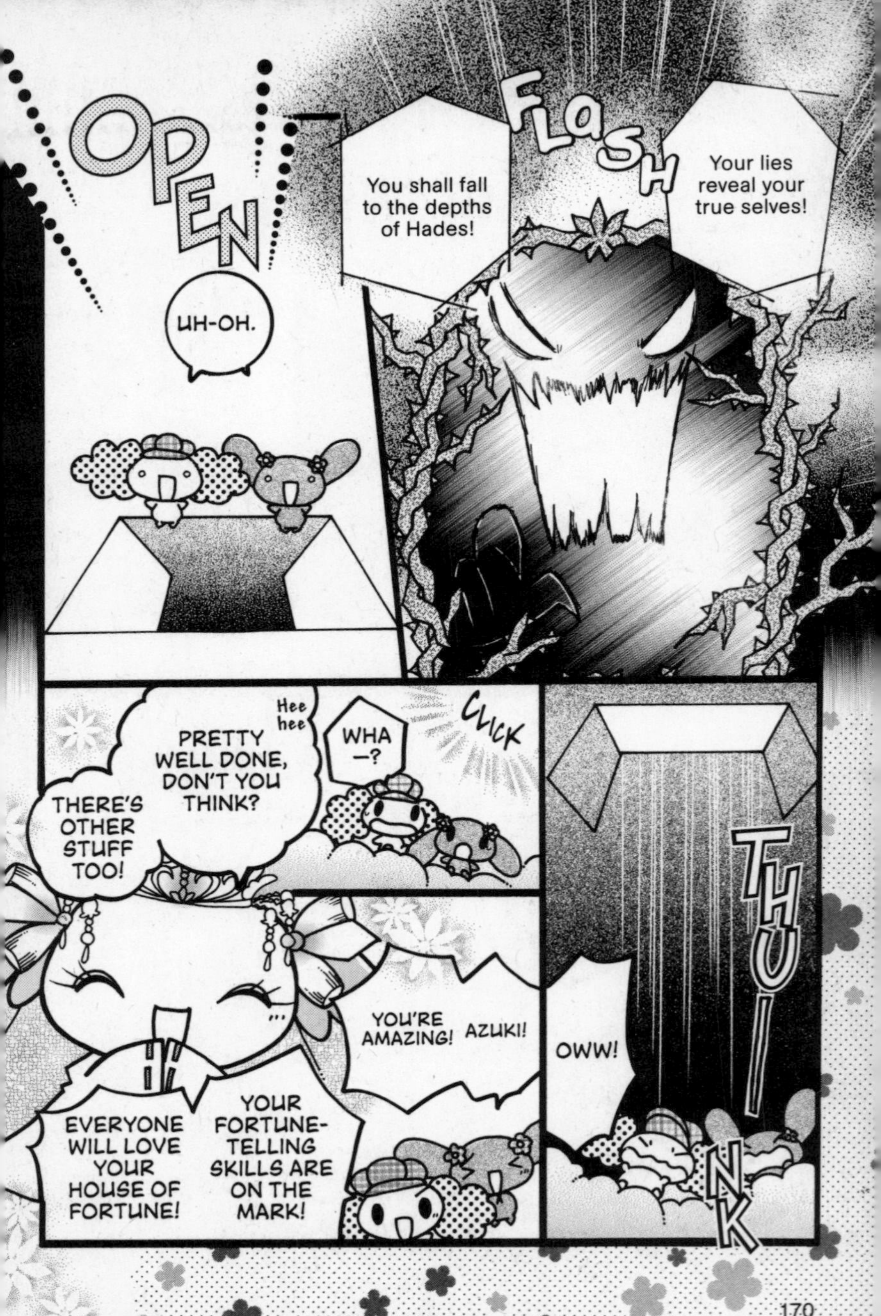

Your lies reveal your true selves!
FLASH
You shall fall to the depths of Hades!
OPEN
UH-OH.
THUNK
OWW!
CLICK
WHA —?
Hee hee
PRETTY WELL DONE, DON'T YOU THINK?
THERE'S OTHER STUFF TOO!
AZUKI!
YOU'RE AMAZING!
YOUR FORTUNE-TELLING SKILLS ARE ON THE MARK!
EVERYONE WILL LOVE YOUR HOUSE OF FORTUNE!

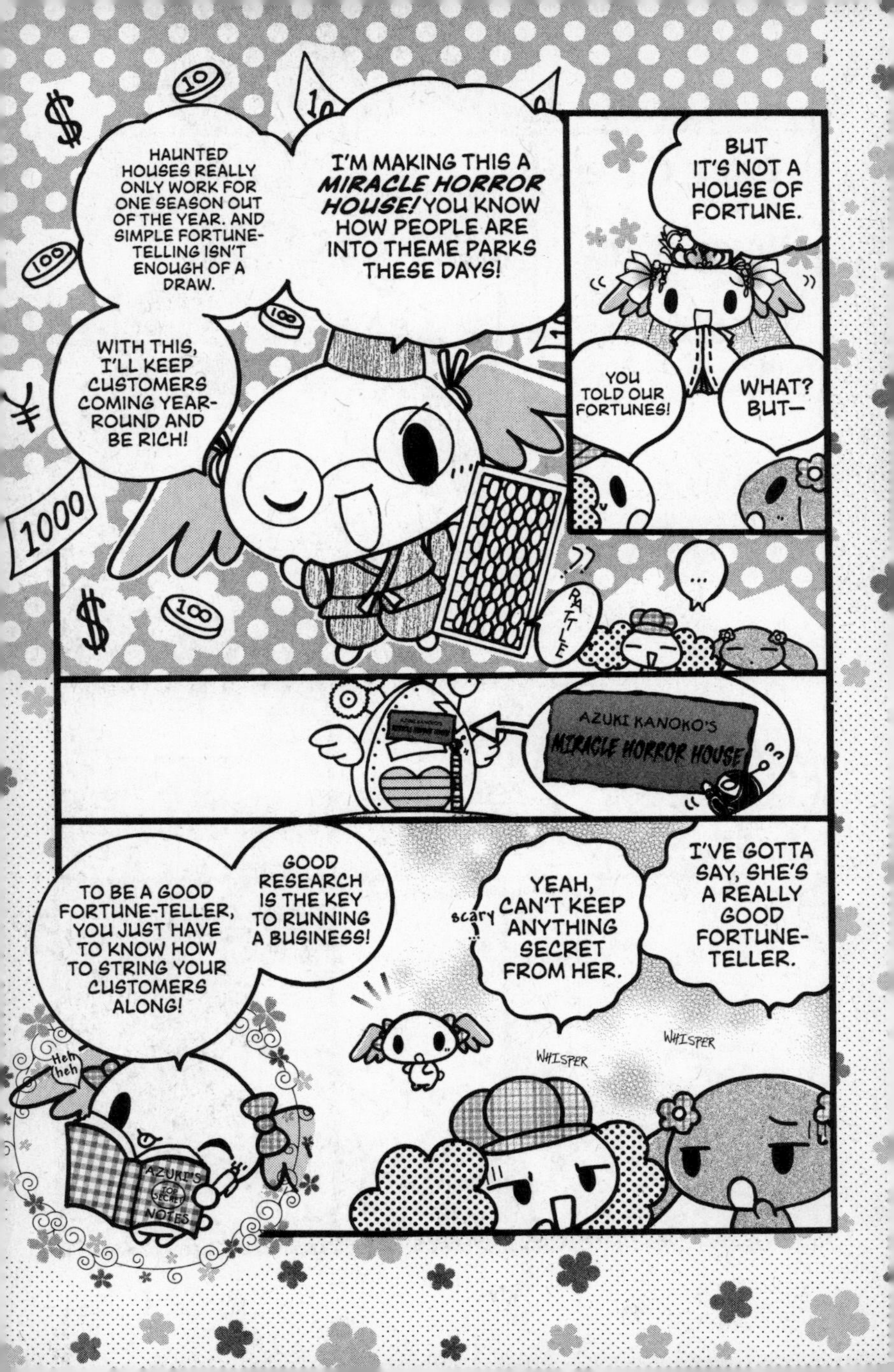
BUT IT'S NOT A HOUSE OF FORTUNE.
WHAT? BUT—
YOU TOLD OUR FORTUNES!
I'M MAKING THIS A *MIRACLE HORROR HOUSE!* YOU KNOW HOW PEOPLE ARE INTO THEME PARKS THESE DAYS!
HAUNTED HOUSES REALLY ONLY WORK FOR ONE SEASON OUT OF THE YEAR. AND SIMPLE FORTUNE-TELLING ISN'T ENOUGH OF A DRAW.
WITH THIS, I'LL KEEP CUSTOMERS COMING YEAR-ROUND AND BE RICH!
$
10
100
1000
RATTLE
...
AZUKI KANOKO'S
MIRACLE HORROR HOUSE
I'VE GOTTA SAY, SHE'S A REALLY GOOD FORTUNE-TELLER.
YEAH, CAN'T KEEP ANYTHING SECRET FROM HER.
scary
WHISPER
WHISPER
GOOD RESEARCH IS THE KEY TO RUNNING A BUSINESS!
TO BE A GOOD FORTUNE-TELLER, YOU JUST HAVE TO KNOW HOW TO STRING YOUR CUSTOMERS ALONG!
Heh heh
AZUKI'S TOP SECRET NOTES

# I See Cute Boys in the Forest!

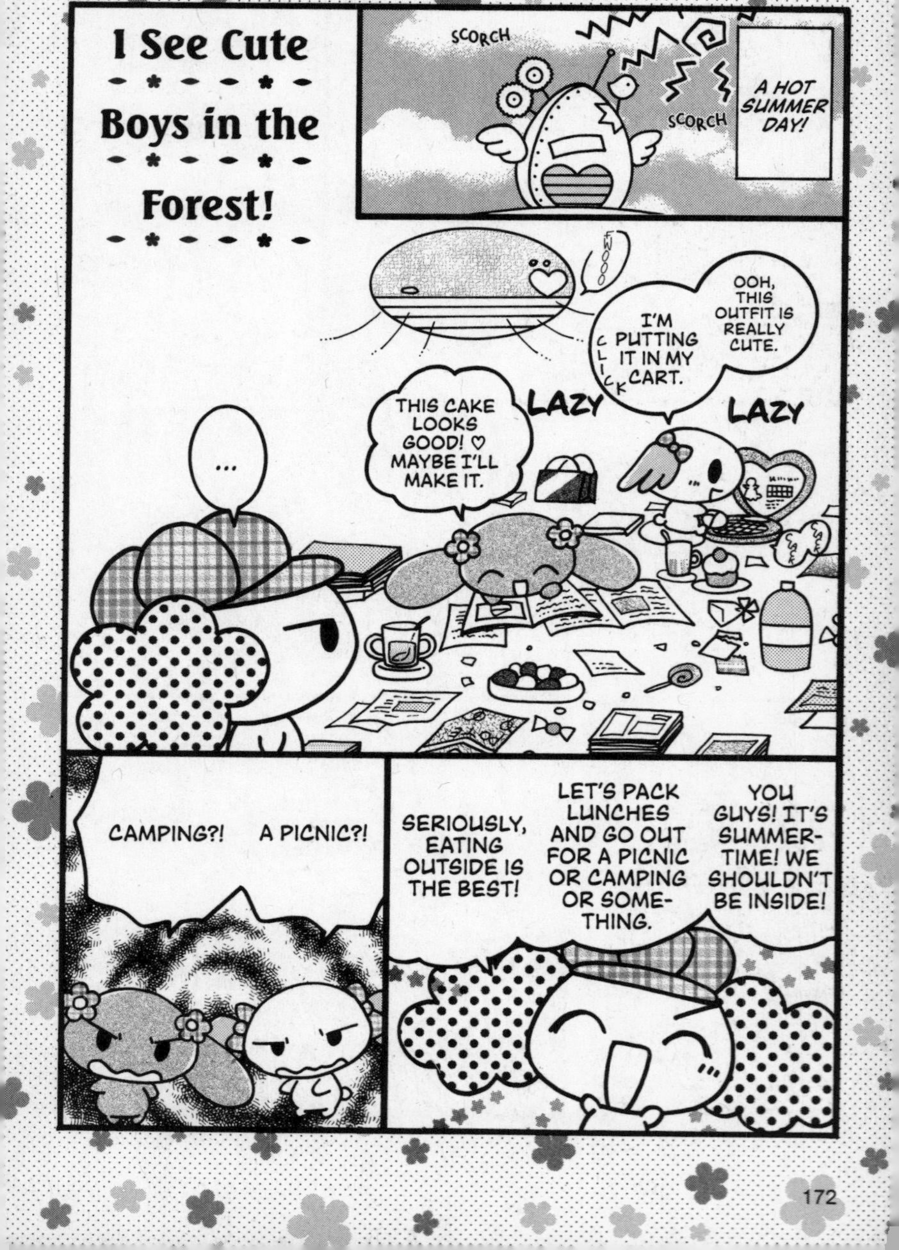
A HOT SUMMER DAY!
SCORCH
SCORCH
FWOOO
OOH, THIS OUTFIT IS REALLY CUTE.
I'M PUTTING IT IN MY CART.
CLICK
LAZY
THIS CAKE LOOKS GOOD! ♡ MAYBE I'LL MAKE IT.
LAZY
...
YOU GUYS! IT'S SUMMER-TIME! WE SHOULDN'T BE INSIDE!
LET'S PACK LUNCHES AND GO OUT FOR A PICNIC OR CAMPING OR SOME-THING.
SERIOUSLY, EATING OUTSIDE IS THE BEST!
A PICNIC?!
CAMPING?!

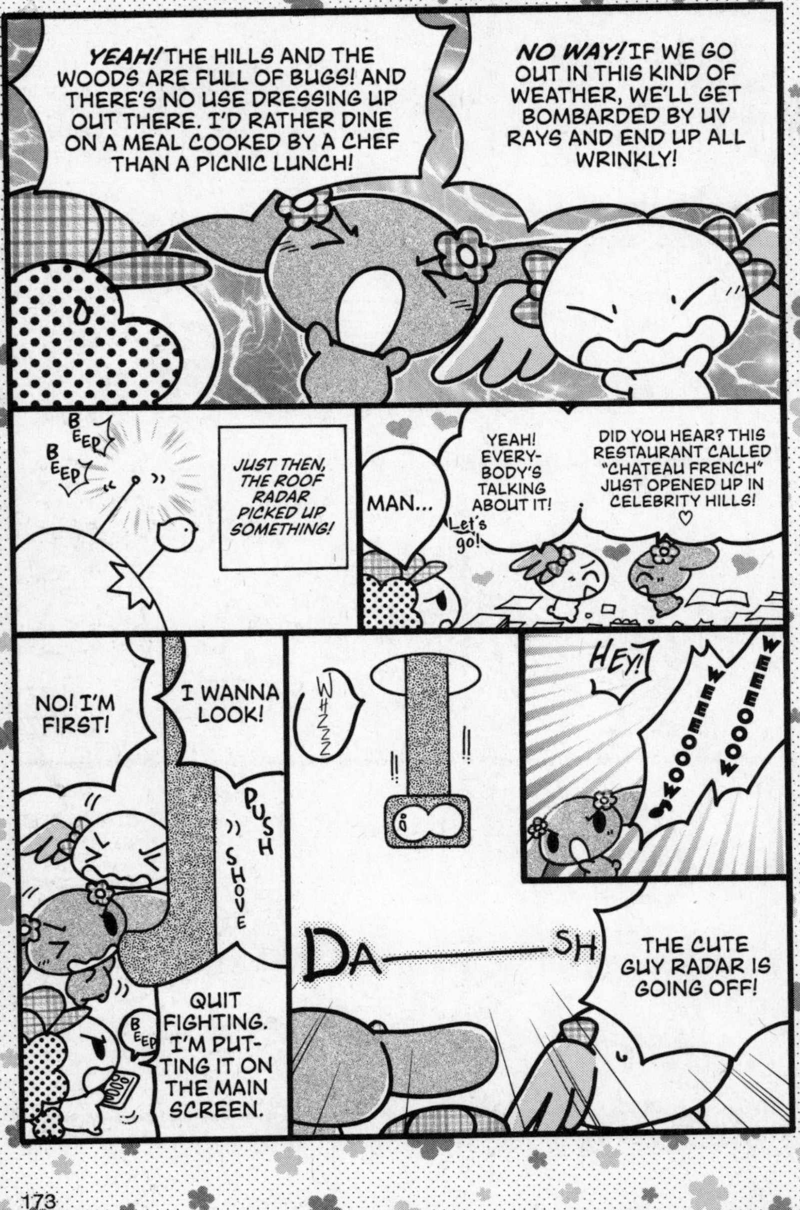

NO WAY! IF WE GO OUT IN THIS KIND OF WEATHER, WE'LL GET BOMBARDED BY UV RAYS AND END UP ALL WRINKLY!
YEAH! THE HILLS AND THE WOODS ARE FULL OF BUGS! AND THERE'S NO USE DRESSING UP OUT THERE. I'D RATHER DINE ON A MEAL COOKED BY A CHEF THAN A PICNIC LUNCH!
DID YOU HEAR? THIS RESTAURANT CALLED "CHATEAU FRENCH" JUST OPENED UP IN CELEBRITY HILLS! ♡
YEAH! EVERY-BODY'S TALKING ABOUT IT!
MAN...
Let's go!
JUST THEN, THE ROOF RADAR PICKED UP SOMETHING!
BEEP
BEEP
HEY!
WHIZZZ
THE CUTE GUY RADAR IS GOING OFF!
DA———SH
I WANNA LOOK!
NO! I'M FIRST!
PUSH
SHOVE
BEEP
QUIT FIGHTING. I'M PUT-TING IT ON THE MAIN SCREEN.

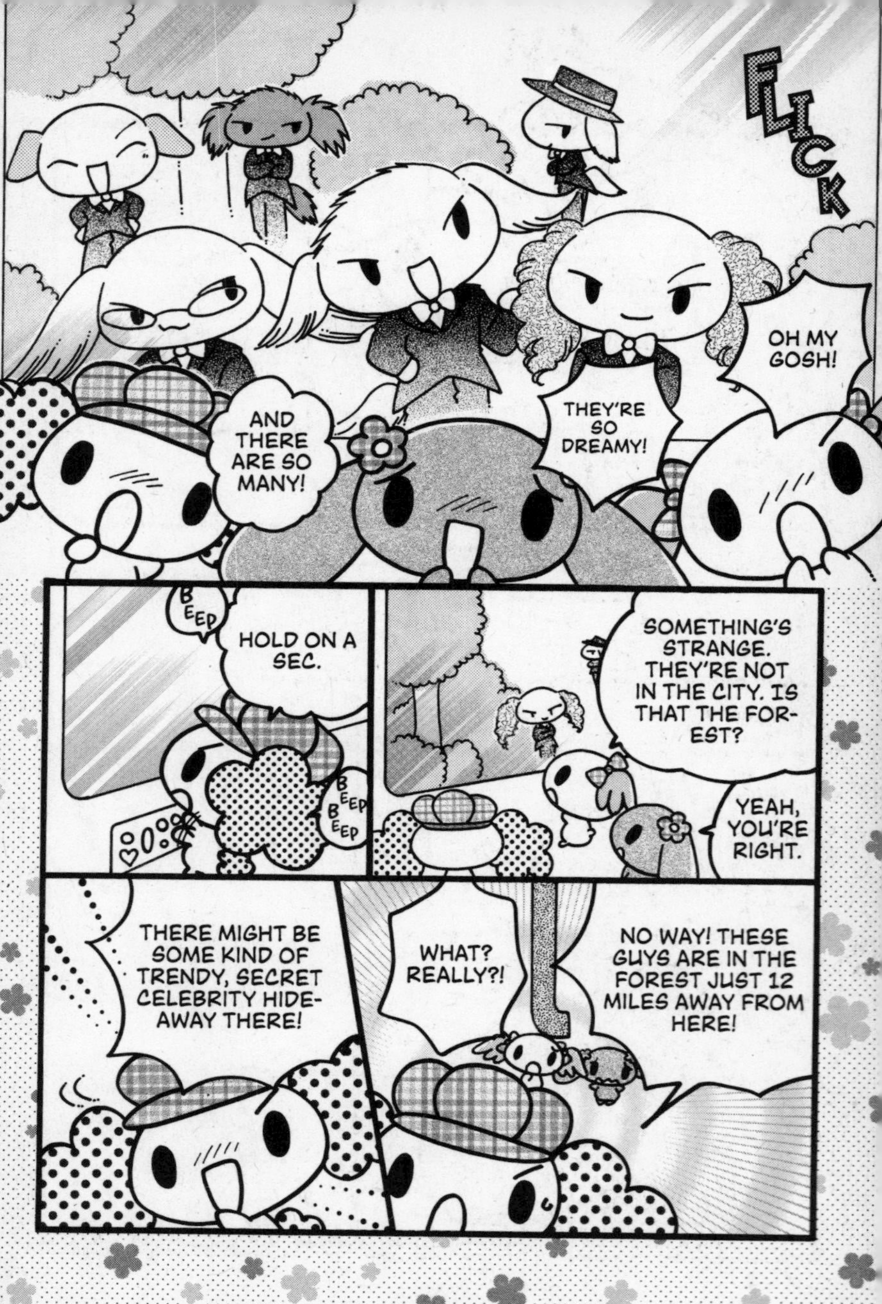
FLICK
OH MY GOSH!
THEY'RE SO DREAMY!
AND THERE ARE SO MANY!
SOMETHING'S STRANGE. THEY'RE NOT IN THE CITY. IS THAT THE FOREST?
YEAH, YOU'RE RIGHT.
BEEP
HOLD ON A SEC.
BEEP BEEP
NO WAY! THESE GUYS ARE IN THE FOREST JUST 12 MILES AWAY FROM HERE!
WHAT? REALLY?!
THERE MIGHT BE SOME KIND OF TRENDY, SECRET CELEBRITY HIDE-AWAY THERE!

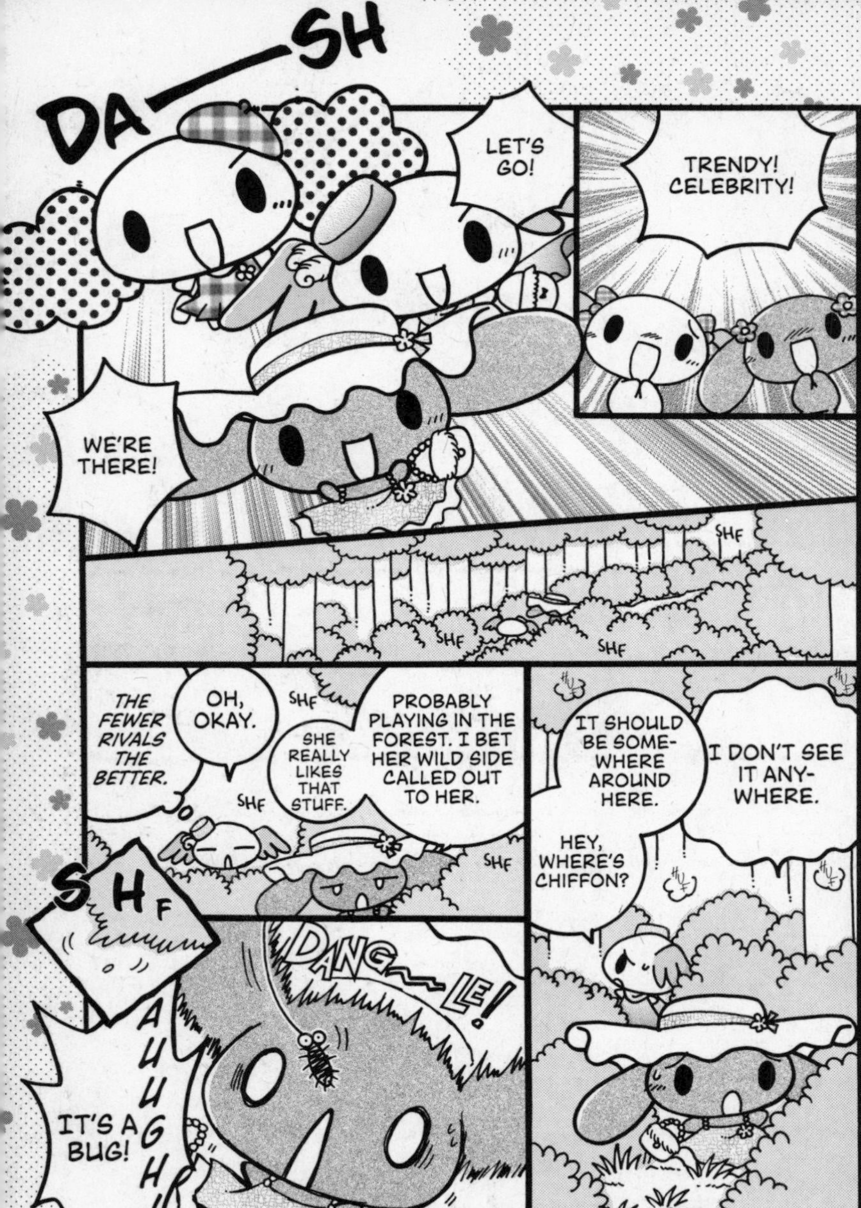
TRENDY! CELEBRITY!
DA—SH
LET'S GO!
WE'RE THERE!
SHF
SHF
SHF
I DON'T SEE IT ANY-WHERE.
IT SHOULD BE SOME-WHERE AROUND HERE.
HEY, WHERE'S CHIFFON?
PROBABLY PLAYING IN THE FOREST. I BET HER WILD SIDE CALLED OUT TO HER.
SHE REALLY LIKES THAT STUFF.
SHF
OH, OKAY.
THE FEWER RIVALS THE BETTER.
SHF
SHF
SHF
DANG—LE!
AUUGH!
IT'S A BUG!

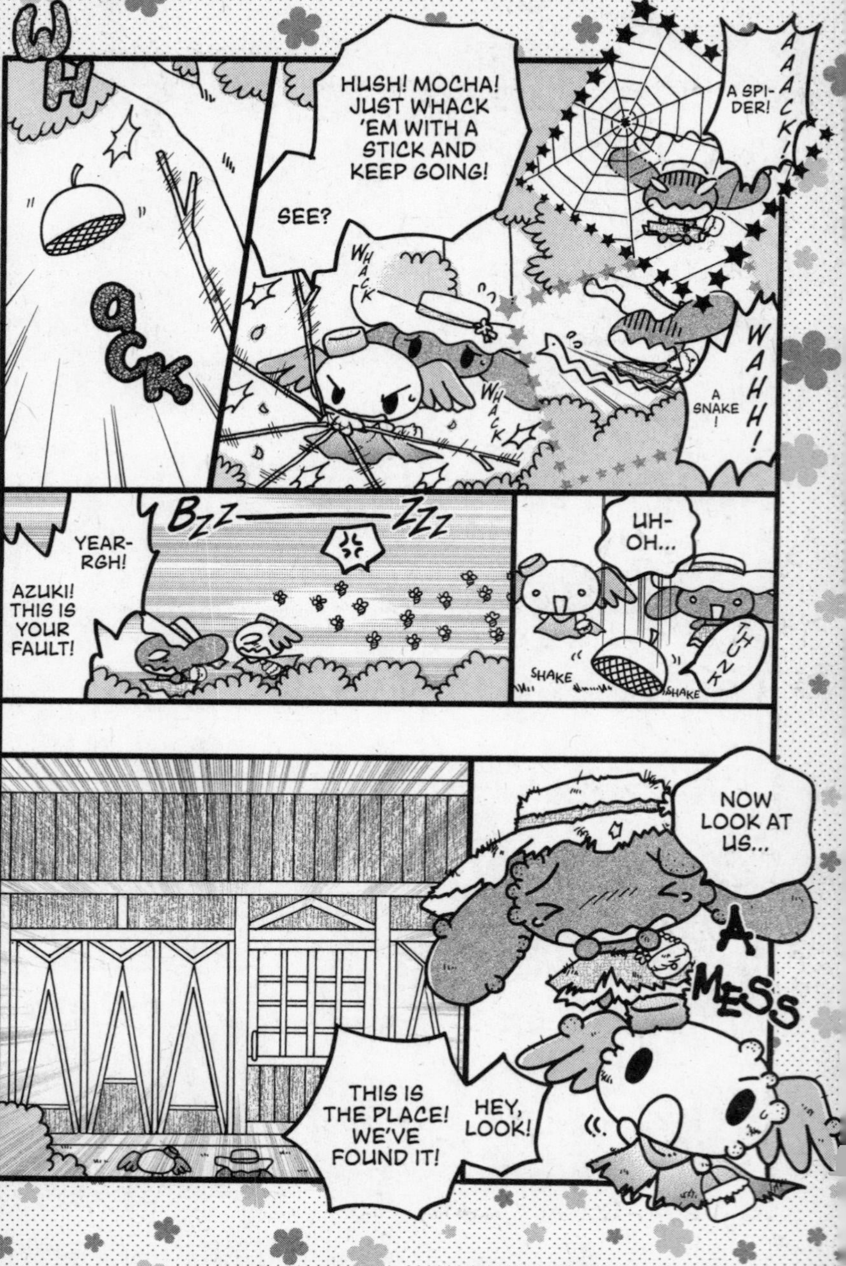
AAAACK!
A SPIDER!
WAHHH!
A SNAKE!
HUSH! MOCHA! JUST WHACK 'EM WITH A STICK AND KEEP GOING!
SEE?
WHACK
WHACK
WHACK
UH-OH...
THUNK
SHAKE
SHAKE
BZZZ——ZZZ
YEAR-RGH!
AZUKI! THIS IS YOUR FAULT!
NOW LOOK AT US...
A MESS
HEY, LOOK!
THIS IS THE PLACE! WE'VE FOUND IT!

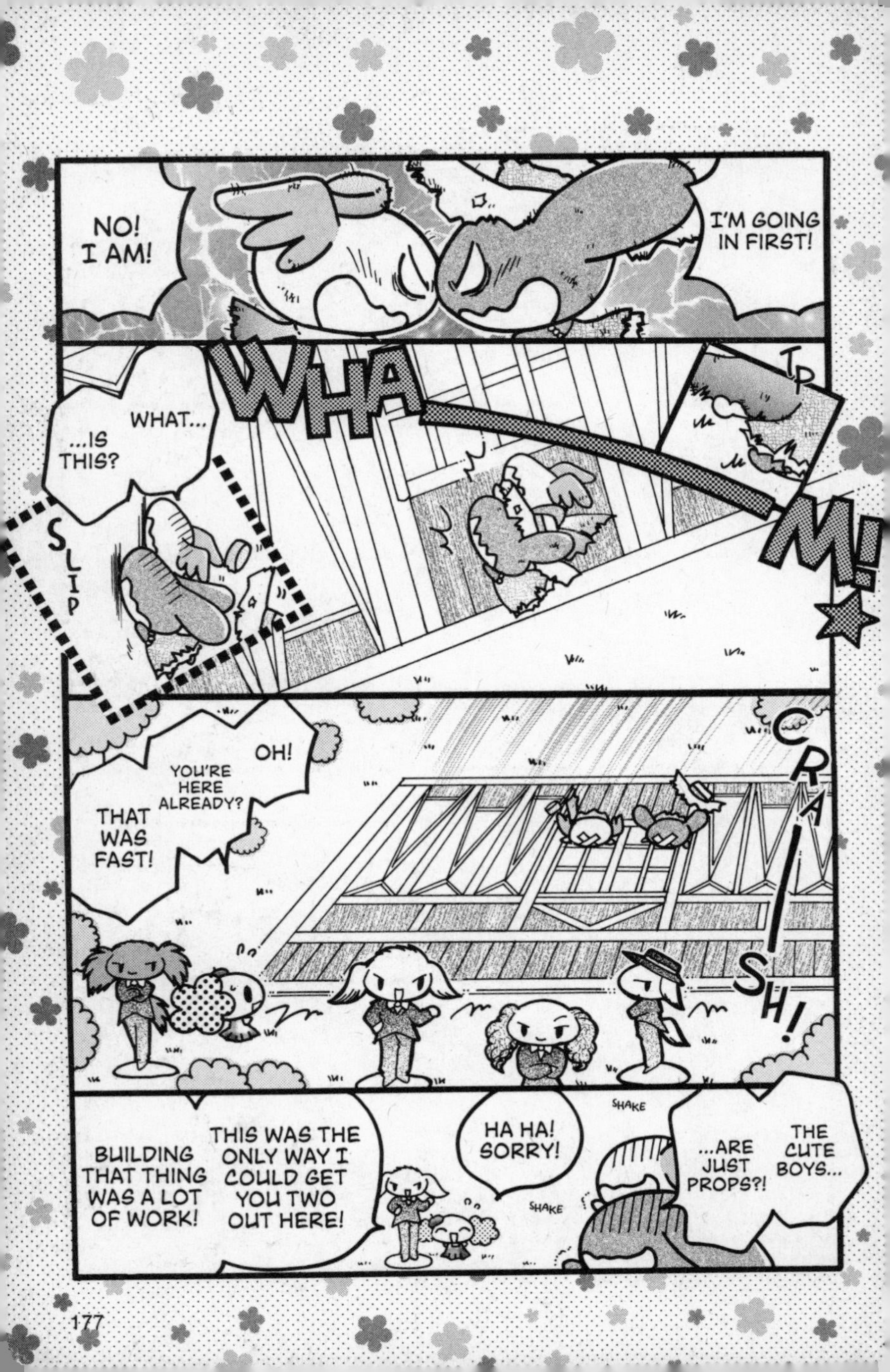
I'M GOING IN FIRST!
NO! I AM!
WHAM!
SLIP
WHAT... ...IS THIS?
CRASH!
OH! YOU'RE HERE ALREADY? THAT WAS FAST!
THE CUTE BOYS... ...ARE JUST PROPS?!
SHAKE
SHAKE
HA HA! SORRY!
THIS WAS THE ONLY WAY I COULD GET YOU TWO OUT HERE!
BUILDING THAT THING WAS A LOT OF WORK!

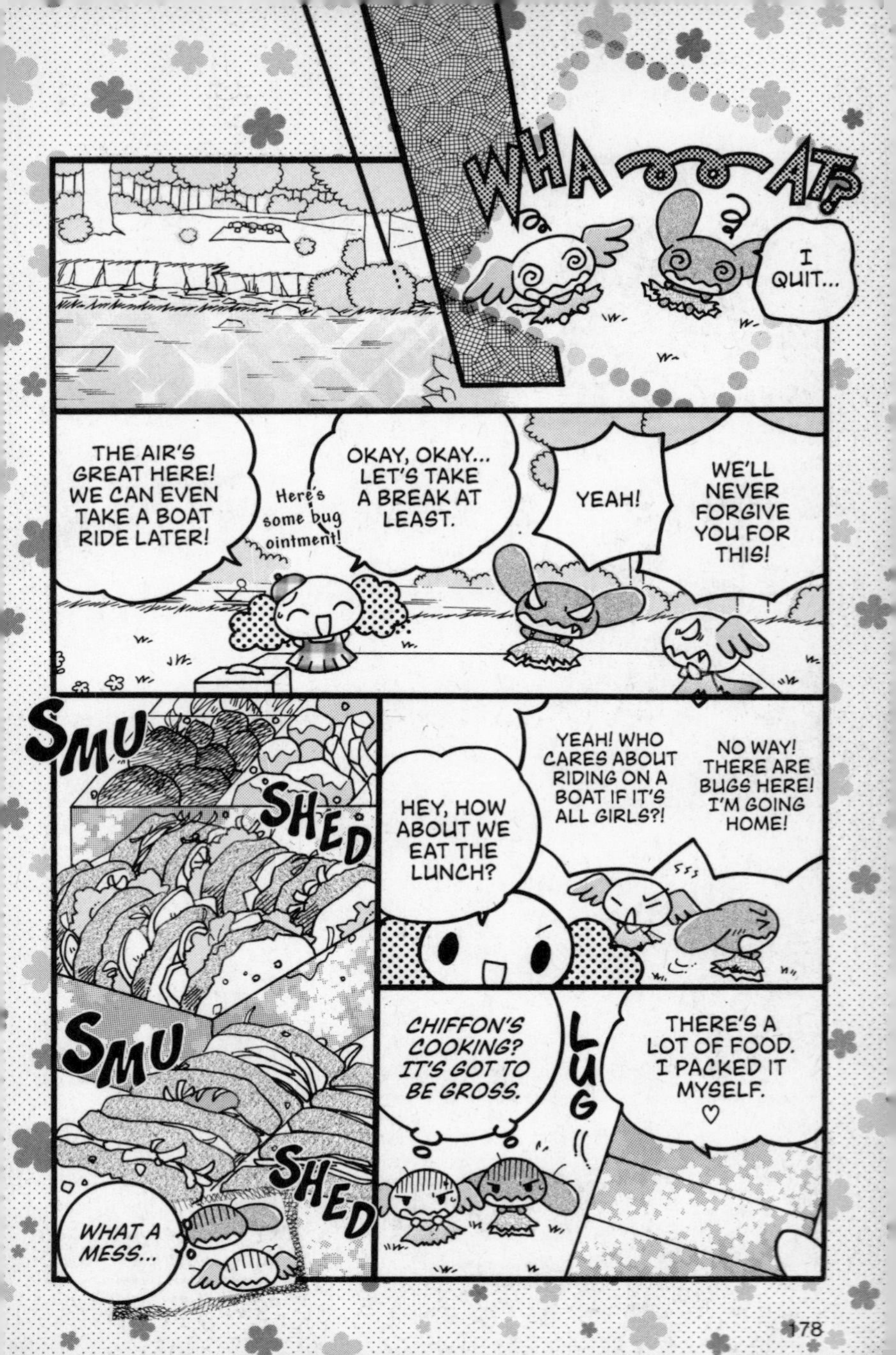

WHA~~~AT?
I QUIT...
WE'LL NEVER FORGIVE YOU FOR THIS!
YEAH!
OKAY, OKAY... LET'S TAKE A BREAK AT LEAST.
Here's some bug ointment!
THE AIR'S GREAT HERE! WE CAN EVEN TAKE A BOAT RIDE LATER!
NO WAY! THERE ARE BUGS HERE! I'M GOING HOME!
YEAH! WHO CARES ABOUT RIDING ON A BOAT IF IT'S ALL GIRLS?!
HEY, HOW ABOUT WE EAT THE LUNCH?
THERE'S A LOT OF FOOD. I PACKED IT MYSELF. ♡
LUG
CHIFFON'S COOKING? IT'S GOT TO BE GROSS.
SMUSHED
SMUSHED
WHAT A MESS...

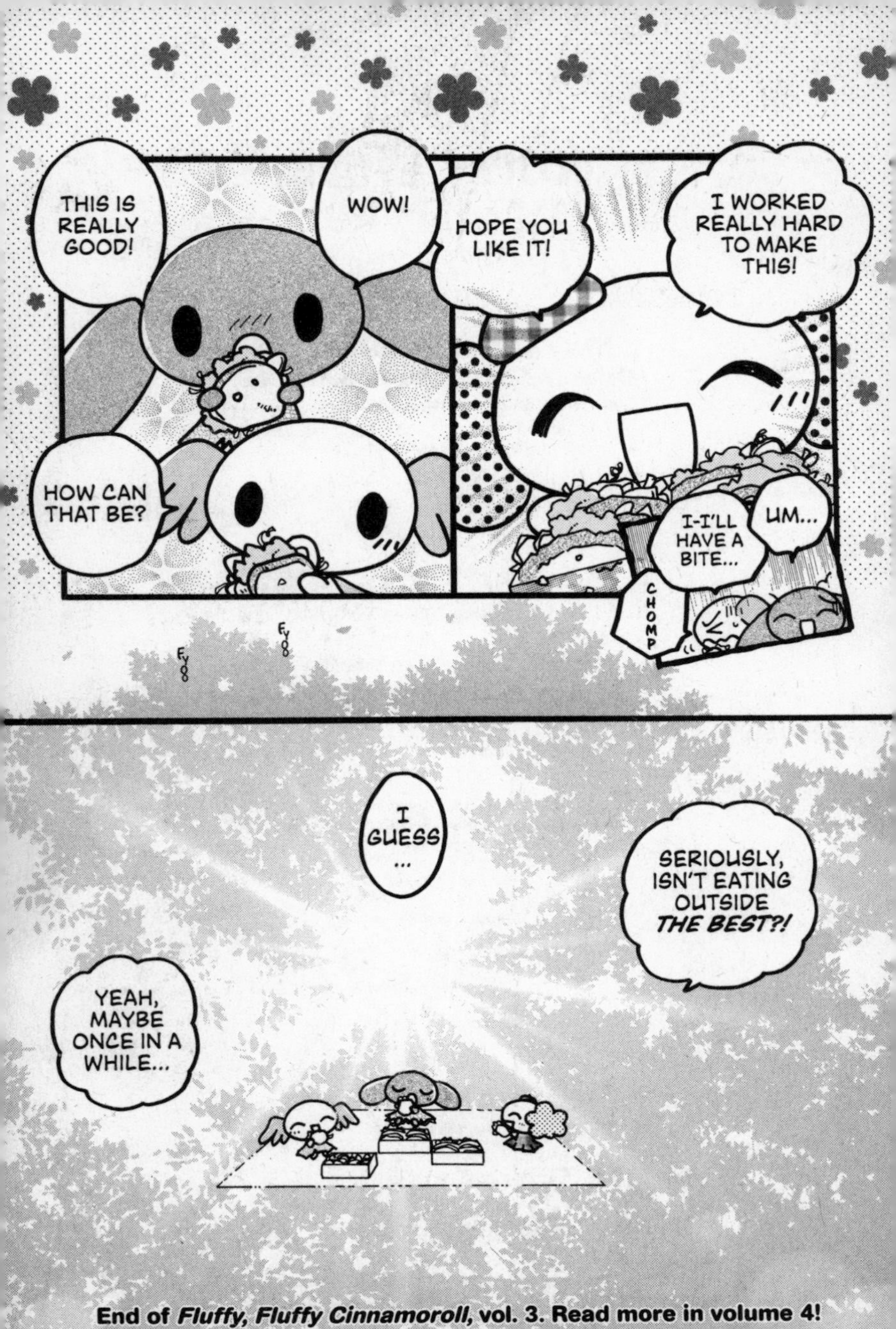
I WORKED REALLY HARD TO MAKE THIS!
HOPE YOU LIKE IT!
UM...
I-I'LL HAVE A BITE...
CHOMP
WOW!
THIS IS REALLY GOOD!
HOW CAN THAT BE?
SERIOUSLY, ISN'T EATING OUTSIDE *THE BEST?!*
I GUESS ...
YEAH, MAYBE ONCE IN A WHILE...

**End of *Fluffy, Fluffy Cinnamoroll*, vol. 3. Read more in volume 4!**

# FLUFFY, FLUFFY CINNAMOROLL

## Volume 3

VIZ Kids Edition

## Story & Art by Yumi Tsukirino
## Original Concept by Chisato Seki

© 2005 Yumi TSUKIRINO, Chisato SEKI/Shogakukan
© 2001, 2012 SANRIO CO., LTD.
All rights reserved.
Original Japanese edition "FUWA FUWA CINNAMON"
published by SHOGAKUKAN Inc.

| | |
|---|---|
| Translation | **Emi Louie-Nishikawa** |
| Touch-up & Lettering | **Erika Terriquez** |
| Design | **Fawn Lau** |
| Editor | **Carrie Shepherd,** |
| | **Hope Donovan** |

Printed in the U.S.A.

Published by VIZ Media, LLC
P.O. Box 77010
San Francisco, CA 94107

10 9 8 7 6 5 4 3 2 1
First printing, April 2012

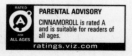

www.viz.com

www.vizkids.com